Set Free, Indeed

Set Free, Indeed

Finding Peace without Pills

A biblical prayer-based program to teach individuals how to pray effectively about their emotions and find genuine joy and peace without pills.

Dr. Jim Gardner

All Scriptural quotations are taken from the New American Standard Bible, except where noted otherwise. Scripture taken from the the New American Standard Bible, Copyright © 1960, 1962, 1963, 1968, 1971, 1972, 1973, 1975, 1977, 1995, by The Lockman Foundation. Used by permission.

All names have been changed to protect the privacy of the individuals.

Printed by CreateSpace, An Amazon.com Company

Copyright © 2016 Dr. Jim Gardner
All rights reserved.

ISBN: 1537184873
ISBN 13: 9781537184876

ACKNOWLEDGMENTS

Fifteen years ago I attend a training seminar conducted by Dr. Edward Smith. I had completed nine years of college and been a mental health professional for twenty-five years but had concluded that the counseling approaches I had learned and was using were inadequate. This seminar was revolutionary for me, both personally and professionally. For the last fifteen years since then, I have been using prayer ministry as my primary counseling approach and have been accumulating case histories. I am very grateful to Dr. Ed Smith for his teaching, which has been the foundation for my own prayer ministry approach and for the seminars that I teach. This book is an effort to put the content of my seminars in a written form so that it can be taught in church Sunday school classes and spread more easily.

This book has been a challenge and has required a great deal of persistence and sacrifice. Most of the sacrifice has been made by my wife who has patiently endured my long hours of absence. Not only has she endured my absence but she edited the book repeatedly to help eliminate my typos, misspellings, and punctuation errors, and to recommended better wording in numerous places. Any remaining errors in the text are my responsibility. She deserves a lot of credit for the completion of this book and has again shown herself to be a "suitable helper." I am thankful to God for her love and support. Without her help this book would not have been written.

I am also very grateful for the many individuals and friends who have encouraged me and supported me in the establishment of Set Free Prayer Ministry. Some of those are Judy Day, Nicole Mann, Josh Holmes, Nathan Tuck, Dave and Frances Williams, Vincent Scamardo, Michelle and Mark Miller, and John and Mary Ann Waller. Director of Missions of the Leflore County Baptist Association, Neil O'Donnell, has been a great source of support and encouragement, as well as Pastor Mark Cook. Along with these two pastors, Bruce Pipkin has served on the advisory board for this ministry and made some very helpful recommendations on the text of this book to help improve it.

Of course, I am most grateful to the "Wonderful Counselor" (Isaiah 9:6) who is my "Comforter" and "Friend" and who implores each of us, "come to Me, all who are weary and heavy-laden, and I will give you rest" (Matthew 11:28). It is my hope and prayer that many people will be blessed and drawn to Him for their comfort, rest, and salvation as a result of this book.

Jim Gardner, Ph.D.

TABLE OF CONTENTS

OVERVIEW

Welcome to "Set Free Prayer Ministry." I am excited about introducing you to the life-changing principles of this ministry which will teach you how to pray effectively about your emotions. In contrast to many Christian ministries, we believe that emotions are a gift and blessing from God and that He wants us to be filled with His love, joy, and peace. However, we cannot experience these feelings when our hearts are full of grief, anger, shame and fear. There is no doubt that the Scriptures teach that the Lord wants us to experience His peace and joy in our lives, which is the goal of this ministry.

Traditional counseling theories and techniques are not effective in resolving basic emotions such as grief, anger, shame, and fear, which are the underlying emotional issues behind most mental health problems. Most other Christian approaches, with a few exceptions, mimic the techniques of the secular theories and offer no more effective alternatives for resolving these basic emotions. Set Free Prayer Ministry was built upon the foundation of another Christian ministry, but has worked hard to simplify it so that it could be used readily by Christians and churches everywhere. It teaches individuals how to resolve their feelings of grief, anger, shame, and fear through prayer so that they can live victoriously.

This book, *Set Free Indeed: Finding Peace without Pills* is the basic textbook for this ministry, which provides the basic curriculum for the 24-week Set Free program, and the lessons presented at the weekly meetings. However, you cannot recover from your emotional struggles by just attending these meetings. The Scriptures say that we must be "doers of the Word, and not hearers only" (James 1:22). You must learn to personally apply these principles to your life, with the help of others who have already gone through this process. In order to facilitate your application of the basic prayer principles to your life, four workbooks are provided to assist you, and these correspond to the four sections of this book.

The first section, entitled "The First Step to Change" will address your need for hope for change when the world is telling you that there is no hope. The other five chapters of this section will help you focus on being completely honest, and identifying and releasing feelings of anger and resentment that have impaired your life emotionally and spiritually. This section will also explore any anger that you may have unconsciously toward God, and consider the many consequences of carrying anger too long. It will end with a critical life principle for maintaining emotional freedom once you have found it.

The second section of this book, "Giving God your Feelings," will address the other "fact-based" emotions of grief, sadness, and genuine guilt. Each of these negative emotions can be resolved in the same manner as anger but need to be addressed as distinctive emotions. Grief is a powerful emotion that is the number one cause of depression and other mental disorders, so it is critical for us to resolve feelings of grief and loss. Sadness is closely related but a distinctive emotion that needs to be resolved, also. Genuine guilt creates strong feelings that can destroy us, so it is vital that each person learn how to completely resolve these feelings and then learn to maintain a clear conscience.

The third section, entitled "Letting the Truth Set You Free," addresses the emotions of shame and other belief-based emotions such as fear, hurt, helplessness, hopelessness, and aloneness. Each of these emotions can be disabling and are difficult to resolve because they are usually rooted in early-life experiences. Using traditional techniques and cognitive approaches, including classroom instruction and preaching, is usually ineffective in changing these underlying feelings, but the Lord is able to change these feelings very quickly through prayer and the Holy Spirit. After helping participants apply these principles to their life, this workbook will also help them understand sinful habits and how the Lord can set them free from them and lead them to Christ-like living.

Finally, the fourth section, "Being a Disciple of Jesus," will help the participant learn how to maintain their freedom on a day-by-day basis and share it with others in an exciting personal ministry. It is part of God's plan to use you to share how He has set you free so that many others like you will find freedom as well. We want you to catch a vision for what God wants to do in your life and in the world as you learn to walk with Him in your newfound victory and freedom.

It is a very exciting decision for you to make to participate in this program. You may have tried other programs, but they can't compare with what the Lord can do in your life when you apply His principles of prayer and experience Him changing your life. May God bless you as you begin this biblical walk into His peace.

In His Peace,
Jim Gardner, Ph.D.

SECTION A:

The First Step to Change

1

IS RADICAL CHANGE POSSIBLE?

As I sit at my desk to begin writing this book, I have a stack of papers sitting in front of me. These papers are counseling notes from individuals I have seen in the last two weeks. Each one of them documents my conversation with someone who sought help for a personal struggle, and each person seen experienced some radical change for good in their life.

One was a seven-year-old boy whose mother brought him for counseling due to the loss of his grandfather a month earlier. He was a cute kid and I began by building rapport with him and trying to help him relax before talking about anything serious. I asked him how old he was, where he went to school, did he like his teachers, and if he was married. He laughed and we had fun talking for a few minutes, then I asked his mother why she brought him to me. She told me that his grandfather died a month earlier and she was concerned that he might have some feelings he needed to talk about.

I asked him if he missed his grandpa, and he nodded and began to pucker up, on the verge of crying. "It's ok to cry," I reassured him. "Do you know who Jesus is?" I asked. He nodded and I told him, "Did you know Jesus cried? One time he cried when one of his closest friends died. So, it's okay to cry when someone dies; it's normal." He nodded to indicate his understanding, then I asked him if he would like to get rid of his sadness about losing his grandpa if he could. He nodded again and I explained that there were two things he needed to do. First, he needed to be honest and talk about what he missed about his grandpa, and then he needed to say a prayer and ask God to take his sadness from him.

I asked him what he missed about his grandpa. He quickly responded and said he missed sitting on his lap, he missed his hugs, and playing "pretend" games with him. He also missed playing catch with him, watching TV with him (especially Garfield), going to McDonald's with him, playing hide-and-seek, and riding on the lawn mower with him. He was very cooperative and quickly identified fifteen things he missed about his grandpa. Then I led him in a prayer and he repeated each item after me, telling Jesus what he missed about his grandpa while bravely holding back his tears, and then he asked Jesus to take his grief and carry it for him. I asked him how he felt now; he said, "I feel kind of sad. I'm glad he's in a better place. I feel a little happy."

"What makes you feel sad?" I asked the boy. "He went away; he's not here, and seeing him in the hospital" he replied. I asked him if he would like to give those sad feelings to Jesus also, and he nodded, so I led him in another prayer and he gave his sad feelings to the Lord. I asked the Lord if there was anything he wanted this boy to know. "He's in a better place," he said. How does that make you feel?" I asked. "I feel happy about him. I just feel happy I got to do all that stuff with him."

He told me that he no longer felt sad; he was just happy that he got to spend time with his grandpa and that he is in a better place. His mother smiled and thanked me for praying with him and helping him, but no one felt happier than me, to see a sweet child like this be set free of such sadness and hear from Jesus like this boy did.

What a joy it is to see a child like this be set free from some sadness that could forever cause problems in his life! Unresolved grief in a child often turns to depression or anger, and can lead to alcohol or drug abuse as the child becomes a teenager, but this boy was able to release it and to learn that Jesus is able to take all his pain and sadness from him and to replace it with His peace, when we learn how to pray about our feelings. But it is not just children who need to learn to pray about their emotions; everyone experiences trials and difficulties in life that stir up bad feelings that can lead them to seek comfort and peace through drugs, alcohol, or pills.

Another page lying in front of me tells the story of a woman whose husband committed suicide four months earlier, after twenty-three years of marriage. She was full of justified anger, and understandable grief and shame when we started, but when she left she said she felt "very good" and had no more anger, grief or shame after one sixty-minute session. Another page tells about a woman who struggled with anger and grief and had a gambling compulsion, but after two months of prayer sessions she was set free from her gambling. A fourth case involved a Christian man who was very frustrated and angry at his wife, when we began talking. After about thirty minutes I asked him how he felt toward his wife, and all his anger was gone. He said that he felt "peace and love" and he loved his wife. I asked him what he thought about this change of feelings and he said it was "bizarre." He was so shocked at the sudden change in his feelings that he kept saying, "That's bizarre!" He even deliberately tried to stir up his anger again and he couldn't. A fifth case involved a woman who had a long history of drug abuse and who had been physically and sexually abused all her life. She was extremely depressed, especially about the loss of custody of her two children. After one session she said she felt "relaxed, calm, and peaceful," and she felt confident that "everything was going to be okay." She said, "my shoulders are not as heavy, my heart is no longer burdened, and my breathing is much better." Her depression level dropped from a rating of 10 to a rating of 5 after one hour of counseling.

I have five additional cases documented in front of me, involving individuals who were set free from grief, anger, shame, depression, and addictions. One of them was a woman who was going through a divorce after nineteen years of marriage because her husband was having an affair. She had initially been very depressed and was taking antidepressants that were not helping her, but after five sessions she was no longer depressed, and she felt so peaceful and calm that her husband's efforts to provoke her were completely ineffective. She began calmly taking care of her children and living life without her unfaithful husband, and she began sharing her newfound peace with her hairdresser and began helping her with her marriage. Her hairdresser even called her one day and offered to fix her hair again at a special discount so she could talk with her some more about her marriage!

These types of experiences have become so common and routine for me in my counseling practice that I cannot keep up with them. It makes me so excited that I want to share these stories with everyone, and teach others how to be set free from their grief, anger, shame, addictions, and depression, and how to help their friends and family members be set free, as well. People can be radically transformed through prayer and grow in their relationship with the Lord when they learn how to pray about their emotions.

Everybody's Messed Up

There are some people whose lives are relatively peaceful and happy but they still struggle with behaviors and emotions that they would like to change, such as bad habits and feelings of irritation. This book and the principles taught in it can set you free from bad habits and negative behaviors that have persistently followed you throughout your life. Even mature Christian men and women have areas of their lives, when they are honest, that they wish they could change. The primary reason why it is so difficult to change is because of underlying emotions that lead us to act in problematic ways or make us feel bad. As we learn how to recognize and release these emotions we will find freedom from undesired behaviors and experience greater peace and joy.

This book is written for all people who have emotional struggles, however great or small they may be. Those who struggle with addictions will find a powerful way to overcome their addictions by identifying the underlying negative emotions behind their addictions and getting healing for them. Those who struggle with depression will learn how to identify their losses and how to resolve other contributing factors to their depression so that they can overcome their depression. Those who struggle with anger issues, grief and loss issues, fears, and feelings of guilt and shame will learn how to overcome these issues. If you are going through a divorce or are still struggling with the effects of a divorce you can find freedom from all of the negative emotions that have resulted. If you have been traumatized by some form of physical or sexual abuse, you can find freedom from your trauma. All of us struggle with something that we would like to change, whether it is our weight, our anxiety, getting off of sleeping pills or psychiatric medications, or just being a more peaceful, gracious, loving person.

Some readers may be experiencing a simple problem such as grief over the loss of a close friend or family member, and may be tempted to skip ahead to the chapter in the book that talks about how to overcome grief. That's okay, but it is my hope and prayer that you will read the entire book, because you will learn how to pray about your emotions on a day-by-day basis, to prepare you to face many other emotional struggles that you will encounter in your life. In addition, you need to learn how to help your children, your spouse, your family members, your friends, and many people with whom you associate on a daily basis. Professional counselors do not generally know how to help you overcome these feelings of grief, anger, or shame so you will benefit from reading the entire book even if you do not need every chapter at this time in your life.

Finding Peace

The goal of this book and Set Free Prayer Ministry is to help people overcome emotional struggles that interfere with their life, and to develop an intimate relationship with the Lord that will enable them to experience genuine peace in their lives, which is described in the Bible as a "fruit of the Spirit." Recovery programs try to help individuals abstain from their addiction, usually because the addictive behavior is seen as the cause of most of their life difficulties. However, when addicts abstain from their addiction for a while they realize that they have a lot of emotional struggles that can make them miserable even though they are no longer engaging in their addictive behaviors. When they are set free from their grief, anger, and shame and experience peace, however, they are able to abstain from their addiction without having cravings for it.

A Christian man came to me for help after abstaining from his drinking for over a year. He told me that he thought that drinking was the cause of all of his problems, but he was so full of anger, and grief, and shame that he was depressed and miserable. It was very painful for him to talk about his emotions and his past because he had never done this before, but he began slowly talking about the significant losses in his life that he had never resolved, and one-by-one he was able to release them. Then we talked about the major sources of his anger, including his father who had been abusive to him, and one-by-one he was able to release his anger and felt more peaceful. We also discussed his feelings of guilt and shame from his past and he was able to release all of this. After several months of counseling sessions he began smiling a lot and his marriage improved, as well as his relationship with his children and co-workers. He was no longer having urges to drink or feeling miserable in his sobriety. He was experiencing peace and joy in his life and praying regularly about his emotions when he terminated counseling sessions.

The Lord says, "Let not your heart be troubled [agitated], nor let it be fearful" (John 14:1, KJV) and "My peace I give to you" (John 14:26). This is the Lord's desire for you and me, and the Scriptures tell us that love, joy, and peace are achievable because they are the "fruit of the Spirit" (Galatians 5:22), so it is very clear that the Lord is saying that each of us can experience His peace through a relationship with Him, without the use of drugs or medications.

My Story

My father was a very strong Christian whose life was radically transformed when he was saved a few years before I was born. He was so excited to learn about salvation by faith, apart from any works, that he passionately shared it with everyone possible during his lifetime. As I grew up he made a point of teaching us children about the Lord and our need for salvation, and I was saved at eight years of age. We faithfully attended a small church full of sincere believers who believed the Bible and sincerely tried to follow it.

During my teenage years I struggled with low self-esteem and some feelings of depression. I began to notice that other people in my church also had personal struggles. A young woman committed suicide after a year or two of marriage, there was a family that had some domestic violence, a young lady developed some serious mental issues and was hospitalized and medicated for her entire adult life. There were also individuals who struggled with addictions and marital problems. As I began to witness more and more emotional problems in our church members, I was amazed that the church leaders did not attempt to help them. They were godly men who studied the Bible seriously, but they had no idea how to help others with their emotional problems. This motivated me to pursue a career as a mental health counselor so that I could help people who struggled with emotional problems. I attended a Bible college to develop a firm biblical foundation before launching into the study of psychology in a secular college, where I knew I would encounter a lot of humanistic ideas and teaching.

I received a bachelor's degree in psychology and then went on to receive a master's degree in psychology, with an emphasis in behavior therapy. As I began to work as a mental health professional I felt the need for more training and entered a graduate program to receive a degree in counseling. After several more years of practice

I felt the need for more training and returned to graduate school to receive a Ph.D. in Counselor Education. After nine years of college and twenty-five years of practice I had not found anything that helped clients overcome feelings of grief, anger, or shame, and even the Christian counseling and "Biblical counseling" approaches I studied were ineffective in dealing with these issues. I came to realize that I could not significantly help people in my own strength or by using secular models, and that apart from God I could truly do nothing.

Then I attended a seminar that was led by a pastoral counselor, and I was amazed at the stories he told about clients he had seen who were set free from feelings of grief, anger, and shame in a very rapid way. He shared credible stories of people with depression, sexual abuse, and many other mental health problems, being set free through this simple prayer-based process. I left the seminar determined to learn how to use this prayer process to help people overcome their emotional problems. As I began using it I was even more amazed at how people were getting relief from their emotional problems through prayer and I was not giving advice or using the techniques I had learned in my psychological training. The more I used this new approach, the more excited I became about prayer and about the Lord. I had always believed that the answers to life's problems were in the Lord, but I had never seen the power of the Lord to set people free in such a dramatic manner.

Traditional Mental Health

I have been working in the mental health system for almost forty years now, and have tried hard to help people with emotional struggles. Most of my clients would say that I was helpful to them; I listened to them, encouraged them, gave them my best clinical and biblical advice, and used my professional training to help people with all types of problems. I enjoyed having Christians look up to me for advice because of my professional training, and having pastors refer their church members to me for help.

I originally began as a "biblical counselor," using techniques advocated by those who rejected traditional counseling approaches, but I found them to be limited and ineffective in dealing with many common problems such as anger, grief and depression. Then I began to use behavior therapy, cognitive therapy, and family therapy. I maintained my commitment to being a biblical counselor but changed my treatment model several times in my career in my search for something more effective, and I attended seminars and workshops regularly to learn how to be more effective. But after twenty-five years of working as a professional mental health counselor I was frustrated because there were so many people that I could not help with common problems like anger, grief, depression, and sexual abuse even when I prayed with them and used scriptures.

After I attended the seminar conducted by the pastor counselor I was very excited about it and eager to learn how to use it effectively. As I have used this prayer-based form of therapy I have found that it is effective in helping people with addictions, depression, anxiety disorders, posttraumatic stress disorder, anger problems and every type of disorder that I have had to deal with in my practice. I have also read outcome-research studies carefully on these disorders, and learned that no therapy techniques or psychiatric medications are effective with them. There are many sincere, caring, intelligent mental health professionals who are trying their best to help people with their emotional problems, but they are not able to help people overcome feelings of grief, anger, or shame, or any of the mental disorders based upon these underlying feelings, using traditional techniques, any better than I did.

Research has shown that there are no effective ways of helping people with normal grief, complicated grief, anger, or feelings of shame and guilt, and the specific research studies will be discussed in more detail in subsequent chapters in this book. Addictions are mostly based upon unresolved feelings of anger, grief, and shame. Depression is mostly caused by unresolved feelings of grief and shame, so when therapists do not know how to help clients overcome their anger and grief and shame, they are unable to help them with their depression or addictions. In fact, most mental health counselors simply refer their clients with depression or addictions to a psychiatrist for medications, which are also ineffective.

The Call for More Mental Health Treatment

In spite of the fact that mental health professionals are ineffective in helping people overcome addictions, depression, and anger, whenever there is another mass killing in our nation, most of the news media and political leaders begin calling for more mental health services. The truth is that most of the shootings and mass killings are committed by individuals who are already being treated by the mental health system and taking psychiatric medications that cause them to become violent (Breggin, 2015). Our mental health system is ineffective and has no real solution to the anger, rage, and violence in our society.

Dr. Peter Breggin, a Harvard-trained psychiatrist and researcher, has written extensively about the dangers of psychiatric drugs and their ability to cause aggression and violence. After 26-year-old Chris Harper Mercer shot and killed ten students on a college campus in Oregon, Dr. Breggin wrote the following comments: "Once again we have a shooter who has been through the 'mental health' system and has probably been taking drugs" (Breggin, 2015). In his article, Dr. Breggin compared Mercer to Eric Harris (one of the Columbine shooters) who was taking the antidepressant Luvox for a year before he became violent, and to James Holmes (the Aurora theater shooter) who became increasingly violent while taking the antidepressant Zoloft. He wrote, "We now have strong scientific evidence that SSRI antidepressants do indeed cause violence," which is why violence is listed as a potential side-effect for these medications. Breggin goes on to write, "We are once again reminded of one conclusion that comes out of nearly every act of mass violence: Going through the mental health system often makes people feel more humiliated and angry, and commonly leads to psychiatric drugs which do more harm than good, causing or inflaming the aggression. Calls for more investment in the current mental health system are distracting and will increase the likelihood of more violent deaths" (Breggin, 2015).

Dr. Daniel Amen, a triple-board-certified psychiatrist and popular writer, echoed similar sentiments about psychiatric medications and the public calls for more mental health treatment. At "The Gathering on Mental Health and the Church" at Saddleback Church on October 8, 2015, Dr. Amen affirmed in a workshop what Dr. Breggin said, stating that antidepressants are ineffective and have FDA black-box warnings about their dangerousness. In contrast to Dr. Breggin, however, he said that he was not opposed to medications but to the indiscriminate use of medications, and he affirmed what Dr. Breggin said about the use of psychiatric medications to deal with violence in our society. He said, "We do not need more mental health treatments like we currently have to deal with violence." In other words, psychiatric medications are not a solution to the problems with violence in our society, but are a part of the problem.

I have learned from my twenty-five years of failure as a mental health professional that the techniques used by mental health therapists for dealing with the emotions of grief, anger, and shame that underlie most mental health problems do not work well. But I have found that the simple prayer-based techniques I am using now work extremely well. When individuals go to a counselor, whether it is a secular counselor or a Christian counselor, they believe that they are going to an expert who has studied psychology and knows techniques that will help them with their problems. They would be very disillusioned to learn that many of the counselors are freshly out of school where they learned a dozen major theories of counseling, and then were told to pick one that they liked. The new counselor is very confused when he or she graduates from their counseling program, but is assigned clients whose lives and futures depend upon their skills.

It is my hope that through Set Free Prayer Ministry many Christians will learn how to help others overcome their emotional problems through prayer and through a relationship with Jesus. I have seen many people complete this training and become very competent in helping others find healing, even dealing with complicated cases that most professional counselors dread to face. I pray that the Lord will raise up, through this ministry, an army of prayer ministers who can share the good news of how Jesus can set us free, so that He gets the credit, and so that people will begin turning to the churches for help with their emotional problems rather than to the broken mental health system of our world.

The Gospel of Mark chapter 5 tells the story of a time when Jesus was walking with a multitude of people surrounding him, and a woman came up behind Him and touched his garment in order to be healed. She had had a blood hemorrhage for twelve years, and Mark 5:26 says she "had endured much at the hands of many physicians, and had spent all that she had and was not helped at all, but rather had grown worse." When she touched His garment He felt some power leaving His body and He turned and asked, "Who touched my garments?" His disciples said, "You see the crowds pressing in on You and You say, 'Who touched Me?'" He looked through the crowd and found the woman who came to Him and she confessed that she had touched Him, and she told Him the whole story and how she felt in her body that she was immediately healed of her affliction.

This story exactly parallels the situation we currently find in our mental health system. There are many people who have turned to the mental health system over the past several decades and been through therapy after therapy and medication after medication, and whose lives are far worse now than ever before. Many people are addicted to, or dependent upon, psychiatric medications that are ineffective and which have serious, even disabling, side effects. The Lord has a far better way; one touch of the Savior set this woman free from her physical condition, and He has given us a better way to set people free from their emotional problems and to give them peace through prayer, without pills.

Hopelessness

I heard a man speak at a mental health conference who told how he had worked as a policeman for twenty years in a large police department in New York. He said that he became extremely depressed and suicidal and had to be ordered by his commanding officer to surrender to the police so that he could be hospitalized. During his hospitalization he was placed on several medications, and several days later was being released when he told the nurse who was wheeling him to his car in a wheelchair how he planned to kill himself when he reached home. The nurse turned him around and readmitted him. He was placed on more medications and given a series of electroconvulsive shock treatments and then was eventually released under heavy medications.

This man stated that he left the police department and began working as a part-time consultant to the police, instructing officers in how to handle mentally ill individuals. He changed his career and became a pastor while continuing to take his medications faithfully each day. Approximately ten years later he had a relapse and was hospitalized again and given more shock treatments; each time these treatments caused more brain damage and mental deficits. He ended his speech by saying, "I have suicidal thoughts every day and take six medications every day, which I will have to take the rest of my life, because I have a brain disorder."

I appreciated the honesty and courage of this gentleman to share his struggles with depression, but I was not encouraged. It left me with a feeling of hopelessness, which was accentuated by the fact that this man was a pastor who was essentially saying to us and to his church congregation, "this is as good as it gets."

I also know a pastor who was an alcoholic before he was saved. He loves the Lord and loves to share the gospel with others and to share how he was delivered from his drinking when he got saved.

But he also admits to his congregation that he still struggles with the urge to drink and has said, "I feel like drinking every Sunday night after preaching." I think it is wonderful for pastors to be candid about their own struggles to avoid giving a false impression of perfection, but such statements as this lead believers to think that they have to live with such urges to drink and that this is "as good as it gets." In contrast, I have seen many addicts overcome their alcohol and drug abuse who also stop having urges to use when they released their underlying feelings of grief, anger, and shame. This is a much more hopeful message to convey to those struggling with addictions than the message of recovery groups who say "Once an alcoholic, always an alcoholic."

The secular world is very ineffective in helping people with addictions and depression, and yet they are quick to impose their beliefs on the rest of the world. The Bible has a much more positive message than the world and offers hope to those struggling emotionally. Jesus promised to give us His peace which is something the secular world cannot provide (John 14:27).

The Challenge of the Church

The Church needs to step up to the challenge of helping those suffering from depression, addiction, and other emotional struggles, because the answers are found in the Word of God and prayer. Complicating this challenge are the efforts of some conservative, evangelical pastors who are attempting to persuade churches across America to embrace the mental health system in their churches. Rick Warren, pastor of Saddleback Church and author of numerous best-selling books has had a great impact on the Christian community. He established Celebrate Recovery in his church with John Baker, which has spread across the country and around the world with almost 20,000 Celebrate Recovery programs today. In 2014 Rick Warren and his wife tragically lost their 27-year-old son when he committed suicide. Warren withdrew from the pulpit for four months, then came back with a new energy and determination to help the church address mental health problems, calling depression a "brain disorder." He and his wife tried their best for 27 years to help their son, providing him the best doctors, counselors, and psychiatrists available, but they all failed. Pastor Warren organized the first "Gathering on Mental Health and the Church" in 2014 and held a second one in 2015.

This second conference began with an address by a psychiatrist who set the tone for the entire conference by declaring that there has been a revolution in brain science and we now know that mental disorders are all "brain disorders" that can be effectively treated using psychiatric medications. However, at the same conference Dr. Thomas Insel, director of the National Institute of Mental Health, admitted that the psychiatric and mental health communities cannot necessarily help those with depression. Another presenter at the conference, Dr. Daniel Amen, quoted Dr. Insel as saying, "Current medications help few people to get better and very few people to get well."

None of the psychiatrists and mental health professionals who authoritatively declare that all of our emotional issues are brain disorders have probably ever seen a single depressed person get well, but I see this on a routine basis. The word "hope" was displayed in large white letters on the stage of Saddleback Church throughout the conference, but convincing people that they have a brain disorder and need to be on medications the rest of their lives does not give hope. It leads to resignation or despair and may lead to the acceptance of the person's emotional condition as permanent, but that is not true hope. This hopeless philosophy is now being spread throughout the 20,000 Celebrate Recovery programs around the country.

Finding Hope

In the midst of this dark and gloomy worldview the scriptures shine the light of hope into our hearts. Romans 15:13 says, "Now may the God of hope fill you with all joy and peace in believing, so that you will abound in hope by the power of the Holy Spirit." We have a God of hope who desires for us to be full of His joy and peace, and to "abound in hope." Individuals who are full of depression and believe that they will always be depressed do not "abound in hope." Depression is by definition a feeling of hopelessness and the Lord does not want any of us to live in hopelessness.

The Scriptures say that we can experience His peace and joy in all circumstances (2 Thessalonians 3:16), and that gives us true hope. Genuine hope comes from learning that the Lord can set you free from your emotional pain and suffering, and that you are not destined to live in depression or to take dangerous medications the rest of your life in order to endure life. When you look at the Bible it clearly states that we can have genuine peace in our lives. Jesus said, "Peace I leave with you; My peace I give to you" (John 14:27). In John 14:1 He said, "Let not your heart be troubled. Believe in God; believe also in Me." In Matthew 11:28 He said, "Come unto Me, all who are weary and heavy-laden and I will give you rest." Then in Galatians 5:22 the apostle Paul wrote under the inspiration of the Holy Spirit, "The fruit of the Spirit is love, joy, peace..." These three "fruits" are the natural outcome of the Holy Spirit working in our lives, which means that they are realistically achievable and should be normative in the life of Christians.

There is a great deal of hopelessness in the world around us, but the Church ought to be holding up a beacon of light and hope to the world. They cannot do this as long as they believe, as the world does, that all our emotional struggles are simply brain disorders and chemical imbalances. Thankfully the Lord has told us in His Word that we can "abound in hope by the power of the Holy Spirit" (Romans 15:13) and that we can have peace in our hearts in all circumstances.

Honesty

One of the essential components of Set Free Prayer Ministry is the encouragement to believers to be honest about their feelings with themselves, with God, and with others. This does not happen in most churches, but rather most Christians in our churches keep their personal struggles to themselves and pretend to be happy and well. James 5:16 says, "Confess your faults to one another and pray for one another, that you may be healed." The early New Testament church was "devoted to prayer," and I believe that part of that devotion was a commitment to be honest with one another, speaking the truth in love (Ephesians 4:15), and rejoicing with those who rejoice and weeping with those who weep (Romans 12:15).

In order for individuals to benefit from this book and from this ministry they must begin by being honest about their feelings, and truly confess their "faults to one another" (James 5:16) by honestly acknowledging their struggles. This is something that does not happen in most churches. Many people have suppressed their feelings for so long that they cannot even recognize when they are feeling bad. They may be angry, sad, or depressed, but just smile and deny that they have negative feelings. In order for this to change, participants must be able to be honest about their feelings without fear of judgment or gossip. For this reason all Set Free meetings and Set Free prayer groups begin with a public declaration of confidentiality. Those who cannot make such a declaration are encouraged to leave so that others can share their struggles and receive healing for their emotions.

In order to change we must also identify what we need help in changing. It is important to have some specific goals that you want to accomplish, so take a few minutes before proceeding to the next chapter, to identify some goals you want to target for yourself. Think about what New Year's Resolution you would like to make next year. Perhaps you want to lose weight, to be a better parent, to exercise more regularly, to control your anger better, to love your wife more, or to quit drinking or using drugs. Whatever you would like to change about yourself, identify it and write it down.

When we are honest with one another we will admit that there are areas of our lives that need improvement. Even the healthiest, most mature Christians have areas of their lives that they would like to improve because we all fall short of God's standards. It may be helpful to examine the nine "fruits of the Spirit" identified in Galatians 5:22-23, "love, joy, peace, patience, kindness, goodness, faithfulness, gentleness, self-control; against such things there is no law." These "fruits" are the evidences and results of the Holy Spirit working in our lives, and if we are lacking in some of them we can include these as personal goals to target during participation in this program. The Holy Spirit, prayer, fellowship, and the Bible are all part of God's plan for changing us and making us more like Him in these nine specific areas.

It is significant that the first three fruits mentioned in Galatians 5:22 are primarily emotions. The implication of this is that emotions are very important to God and these three emotions are foundational to the other six fruits, which are character qualities. We need to have love, joy, and peace before we can develop the six character qualities of patience, kindness, goodness, faithfulness, gentleness, and self-control. Peace appears to be foundational to love and joy, because when we are stirred up and not experiencing peace it is very difficult to be loving and to have joy. Set Free Prayer Ministry focuses upon helping individuals find peace so that they can develop love and joy, and then the subsequent six character qualities will develop in their lives. In the next chapter we will begin with a discussion of the greatest hindrance to peace and teach you how to overcome it to begin this journey of being set free to serve Jesus.

2

OVERCOMING ANGER AND DISAPPOINTMENT

After learning how the Lord can set people free through prayer, I began using this new-found prayer process every opportunity I had in my church and with individual cases referred to me. Then my wife and I moved to Nashville, Tennessee to be closer to our children and I opened up a private practice where I began to use this prayer ministry with individuals and couples. I also began working for several group homes for boys, and it was there that I had many opportunities to gain valuable experience using this ministry.

At one of the group homes I was asked to provide counseling for a young man who was 17 years old. He was one of the more mature young men in this facility and he tried to follow the rules of the home and cooperate with the staff. When I first met with him I asked him what he wanted help with, and he said, "My anger." I asked him to give me an example of a recent time when he got angry and he said, "Just this last weekend I got angry." I asked him what happened and he said, "One of the other boys said something to me that made me mad, so I got in his face and was ready to jump on him and the staff rushed in and separated us. I was so mad that I couldn't calm down for half an hour. Then it happened again the next day; another boy said something that made me mad and I got in his face and was ready to hit him when the staff came rushing in and separated us again. It took me thirty minutes, again, to calm down. Then I started getting angry at the staff who were intervening; I've been angry at everyone all week!"

"So, you want to get rid of this anger?" I asked. He nodded and said, "Yes, I'm tired of it; it gets me in trouble all the time." "Well, let me ask you this," I said. "When is the first time that you can remember getting really mad like this?" Without a moment's hesitation he said, "When I was eight years old." "What happened when you were eight?" I asked him.

"My parents were divorced and all us kids lived with our mom, and sometimes she would take me and my little brother over to Dad's house and we would hang out with him and play, then she would come get us and take us home. When I was eight years old, one day my mother took us to our dad's house and dropped us off and said, 'I'm going to the store down the street on the corner to get some cigarettes then I will come back to pick you up.' So, she took off and my brother and I began to play. We played for quite a while, then stopped to look up for Mom to see if she was on her way, but we couldn't see her so we kept on playing. Then it started to get dark and sometime that evening I realized that my mother was not coming back. That was the last time that I ever saw her." He continued, "When that happened I was so angry that I stayed angry for two solid years! I didn't care about anything; I didn't care about school and began skipping it, I began getting into a lot of fights, and I began drinking and using drugs because I was so mad!"

"Well, I don't blame you for being angry," I responded. " I would be angry too if my mother did that to me. That's just normal to be angry about something like that; you have a right to be angry. But that was nine years ago; do you want to stay angry or would you like to get rid of that?" I asked. "No, I'm tired of getting angry and getting in trouble all the time," he said. "I'd like to get rid of it."

"I can show you how to do that. There are basically two things you have to do," I told him. "The first thing you have to do is just be honest about why you are angry at your mother."

"Well, she was a pretty good mother until this happened," he said, "but it makes me angry that she lied to me, she abandoned me, and she hasn't called me even once in the last nine years."

"Okay, that's a short list but it's an honest list," I said. "Now the second step is, would you be willing to say a simple prayer and just tell God why you are angry at her, then ask Him to take your anger from you?" He paused for a moment then said, "I'm not a religious person, but I believe in God and prayer and I'm willing to give it a try."

I led him in a prayer in which he told the Lord what he resented about his mother. He prayed, "Lord, when I think about my mother it makes me mad. It makes me mad that she lied to me, it makes me mad that she abandoned me, and it makes me mad that she hasn't called me once in the last nine years." Then he said, "Lord, all of this makes me angry, but I'm tired of being angry so right now I choose to give all this to You, and I ask You to please take it from me and carry it for me. I give it to you now, in Jesus' name. Amen."

When he was finished with the prayer I said to him, "Okay, now think about your mother and tell me how you feel." He thought for a few moments and said, "I feel a lot better; I feel like a load was lifted from me." "Okay, that's good," I said. "Now, think about your mother and that day that she lied to you and abandoned you." He sat there for a short while and then said, "I don't feel angry. I just feel calm about her." Then he said, "You know, I haven't seen my mother for nine years; I'd like to see her again."

It shocked me when he said this because I wasn't expecting to hear that so quickly, but I said to him, "Well, you're going home to your father's house this weekend, aren't you? Why don't you talk to him and see if he could arrange for you to see your mother?" He agreed to do that and went home for the weekend. When he told his father that he'd like to see his mother again, it shocked his father because he knew how angry this boy was at his mother, and the father was still angry at her for divorcing him.

It was fascinating to see this young man when he came back to the Boy's Home; he was more calm and his explosive temper was gone. He had normal anger that lasted for a few minutes but he no longer wanted to kill someone or destroy something when he became angry. I was amazed because I had never seen this before when I taught Anger Management classes, but I realized that the reason why it worked was because we had gone to the source of his anger, his mother, and he had released it.

Steps for Overcoming Anger

This young man was very fortunate to have only one major source of anger, his mother. If he had other major sources of anger he would have needed to go through the same process with each of them to release all his anger. Some people have a dozen or more sources of anger and they need to repeat these same steps for each person on their anger list until they all have been resolved.

Notice the two simple steps taken by this young man to release his anger toward his mother, and the one additional step that I have added:

> **Step One:** Be completely honest about your feelings of anger by making a detailed list of what you resent about the person.
>
> **Step Two:** Tell the Lord why you are angry about the person and ask Him to take your anger from you and carry it for you.
>
> **Step Three**: Make a list of other persons toward whom you have some anger, and repeat these steps for each one of them.

The biblical basis for these steps is found in Ephesians 4:26-27:

"Be angry and yet do not sin; do not let sun go down on your anger, and do not give the devil an opportunity."

There are four significant points to be noticed in this passage. First, the apostle Paul says to "be angry." That means it is okay to be angry at times, just as the Lord Jesus was righteously angry at times. When you experience injustices or hear about or witness an injustice it should make you angry. That is not a sin; it is simply a normal response to a wrong that occurs.

Second, Paul tells us "do not sin" when we are angry. James 1: 20 says, "the anger of man does not achieve the righteousness of God," and that's why Paul warns us not to sin when we are angry. When we are angry we are very prone to say and do things that we regret later, so we have to be very careful not to sin while we are angry.

Third, Paul says, "do not let the sun go down on your anger." This means that we should literally release our anger by the end of each day; whatever evil or wrong occurs in the day should be released before the day ends. That may seem too literal an interpretation to some people, especially when a serious wrong has occurred, but the truth is that none of us can afford to hold onto our anger any longer.

A remarkable example of this occurred on June 17, 2015 in Charleston, South Carolina when Dylan Roof, a young white man, sat through a Bible study at the Emmanuel African Methodist Episcopal Church and then left and returned with weapons and killed nine innocent black Christians, in an attempt to start a racial war. He was caught, and at a hearing the next day some of the surviving family members of the victims appeared in court to address the court and Mr. Roof. They told him that they forgave him for what he did and they were praying for him to repent and to come to know Jesus.

These Christians at this church were simply following the example of the Lord Jesus and following this command given by Paul in this passage to "not let the sun go down on your anger." It is humanly impossible for us to do this in our own strength, but if we are willing to make a list of the reasons for our anger and then ask the Lord to take them and carry them for us, He will do so and set us free from our anger.

Victor's Story

A man named "Victor" came to a Set Free meeting one night with a fishing buddy of his. He was a Christian and he sat quietly through the meeting, listening as we talked about the basic prayer principles of the ministry and sharing stories of how the Lord had set many people free from their anger and grief. It was a small group of about ten people, and when I asked if anyone wanted to pray about anything a young man sitting next to me volunteered. He said that he had a lot of anger toward his father that he would like to release.

I asked him what his father had done or said that made him angry and he began telling us how abusive his father had been to him and how full of anger he was at him. I wrote down each reason he gave for his anger until he could think of no more, then I asked him if he would like to get rid of this anger. He said that he would like to so I led him in a prayer and he gave his anger to the Lord and asked Him to carry it for him. Immediately, his facial expression changed and he said that he was no longer angry at his father but said he felt sorry for him and loved him.

After the meeting "Victor" came to me and shook my hand and thanked me for the meeting and left. Three days later he called me and asked if he could meet with me. Later that day we met and he told me that he had been a Christian for forty years and had had a problem with his anger all his life. This anger led to many problems in his life, including three failed marriages. He tried everything possible to release this anger, he read the Bible, memorized it, prayed for deliverance, went to several Christian counselors, and spoke to pastor after pastor but no one could help him with his anger. But when he witnessed the young man release his anger with me the previous week, he went home and spent the entire weekend on his knees giving his anger to the Lord about each source of anger he had. He smiled and told me that he felt a tremendous burden lifted from him and he felt no more anger. He had just lost his third marriage after going to a Christian counselor for almost a year, but he felt that he received far more help from witnessing one prayer session at the Set Free meeting, than he had received from a year of counseling with his Christian counselor.

Victor continues to participate in Set Free Prayer Ministry and is a mentor now, who prays with men with drug and alcohol problems. He continues to testify that his anger was resolved that weekend by going through the three steps given in this chapter and praying about each person who had harmed him in his life.

The Right to Be Angry

Some readers probably noticed that when I was talking with the young man about his anger toward his mother I told him that he had a right to be angry, and some may question this statement. In the past I would have confronted him gently with his anger and encouraged him to forgive his mother. I probably would have quoted some scripture such as Luke 6:27-28 that says, "Love your enemies, do good to those who hate you, bless those who curse you, and pray for those who mistreat you." Sometimes this worked and the individual would repent for their anger and say that they wanted to forgive the person who had hurt them. But many times this approach led the person to become defensive and say they could never forgive them.

The apostle Paul says, "Be angry, and yet do not sin," and I have learned to say something similar. I usually say, "I don't blame you for being angry; I would be, too, if my mother did that to me. That's okay. But do you want to stay angry?" Usually when I express myself in this way people will feel understood and not condemned and say they are tired of being angry and would like to release it.

People who are abused have a right to be angry, and telling them they need to forgive before communicating your acceptance and understanding, makes them feel misunderstood and judged and can lead them to dig in their heels. It is important that we provide a biblically balanced perspective to them and let them know that it's okay to talk about their anger and it's okay to be angry, but to lovingly let them know the dangers and consequences if they choose to hold onto their anger for long.

Matt's Story

A man and his wife came to me after being court-ordered to go to counseling after this man brutally abused his wife in a drunken rage. After he sobered up and realized how badly he had hurt her he begged her to not leave him and promised that he would never drink again if she would not leave. She stayed with him, and surprisingly he kept his promise and quit drinking after twenty-five years of drinking, but she still became very fearful of him when he became angry during arguments.

I gathered background information on him to identify the sources of his anger, grief, and shame and I made a prayer plan that listed all of the major traumas and losses in his life. We prayed about the loss of a former wife who had died and he was able to release his grief over this painful loss. We prayed about abuse that he had experienced from his father, his mother, and his grandfather and he was able to release his anger toward them. We discussed other people who had wronged him previously and other significant losses that he had experienced, and one-by-one he released his anger and grief toward each of them.

After releasing all of the major sources of his anger, he and his wife were getting along well and they began coming to sessions holding hands and cuddling like newly-weds. After this man had been sober for eight months I asked his wife how he was doing. She smiled and said, "He's a sweetheart." She said that she was no longer afraid of him and she could not remember the last time he got angry at her.

This man was a hard worker and very skilled in his trade, but his business never prospered due to his anger and his drinking. After he released his anger and stayed sober his business began to prosper and his clients commented about how well he was doing. He proudly wore a Set Free hat and shared with them how the Lord had set him free from his drinking and his anger.

The Impact of Anger

This program begins with anger because it has such a broad, pervasive impact on people. It is obvious that our society and world are full of anger and hatred, which is reflected in the growing frequency of mass murders in our country and the terroristic acts occurring around the world.

Every time another act of mass violence occurs in our country there are immediate cries from the media and the politicians for gun control and more mental health treatment. The truth is, as stated in the previous chapter, that most individuals who commit acts of mass murder are already involved in the mental health system which is ineffective and are taking psychiatric medications that are known to cause more aggression and violence in many individuals.

Anger touches the lives of almost everyone, both in Christian homes and in the homes of non-Christians. Anger is not a "mental disorder," but it sometimes leads to a diagnosis of oppositional-defiant disorder, conduct disorder, attention-deficit hyperactivity disorder, bipolar disorder, posttraumatic stress disorder, or intermittent explosive disorder. Alcoholics Anonymous states in their "Big Book" that "Resentment is the 'number one offender' for alcoholics" (Alcoholics Anonymous, 1976, p. 64) so it is believed to be a major contributor to alcoholism and drug addictions.

In addition anger leads to adolescent rebellion, family problems, smoking, antisocial behavior, vocational problems, and marital problems. Matt's story illustrates how anger was a significant cause of his drinking and led to serious marital and vocational problems for him, as well.

Most church-attending people would deny that they have anger problems, but churches are full of people with anger, which leads to much bickering and quarreling among church members. Many people who attend church and are highly regarded by their church are actually full of anger, and they are very critical of their family members at home, or even emotionally abusive, while maintaining the appearance of godliness at church. Anger significantly impacts the lives of most people in some way.

In addition, anger has a profoundly negative impact upon the spiritual lives of people. Individuals who are full of anger often have belief-based emotions like fear, shame, and hopelessness, and these feelings cannot be resolved until the anger is first eliminated. Many people, including strong, mature Christians and pastors, deal with anger toward God that prevents them from being able to enjoy God's peace in their lives. When they pray they are unable to receive wisdom from God due to their anger toward Him (See James 1:5).

Anger Management

Anger management classes have become very popular and widespread across the country and in other countries, and have been widely publicized by a movie about anger management and a television series about anger management. Courts all around the country order individuals to attend anger management and domestic violence classes when they are involved in cases of domestic violence or assaults.

Many celebrity actors and sports figures have been court-ordered to take anger management classes after committing acts of violence. In 2002 Ron Artest, a professional basketball player with the Indiana Pacers, was ordered to go to anger management classes after assaulting his girlfriend. Then in 2004 he was at the center of a big brawl during an NBA game when a fan threw ice on him and he charged into the stands and engaged in a fist fight with a spectator on national television. He has been repeatedly involved in anger management since his childhood.

In 2010, after undergoing extensive psychotherapy for his anger, he changed his name to "Meta World Peace." In 2013 he was playing for the Los Angeles Lakers and once again demonstrated his anger during a game with the Oklahoma Thunder. After dunking the ball he began leaping around beating his chest and in the process he elbowed a Thunder player and knocked him out, and gave him a concussion. If it had been a mere accident he should have stopped to assist the injured player and express concern, but he never stopped to help him. He has received the best anger management treatment that money can buy, but it has not helped Mr. World Peace.

I used to teach anger management classes and quickly learned that they were ineffective. It was very unpleasant to have a group of young men in the anger management class who were angry about being in the class and who were resistant to anything said in class. Teaching them to count backwards from 100 to 1, or do some deep breathing and positive self-talk, did very little to help any of them.

One of the top researchers in the area of anger management, psychologist Ray DiGiuseppe, said: "Anger management classes, I think, are a Band-Aid; they allow people to feel they've done something, but they haven't had any kind of real treatment" (Carey, 2014). He conducted a 2003 review of 92 anger-management treatments, including more than 1800 people, and concluded that the classes can reduce feelings of anger somewhat in people who are motivated to change their behavior. But in a review of 22 studies of state programs, a team of psychologists in Texas and New York reported that the courses had little positive effect (Carey, 2014). The research has shown very little evidence of any reduction in anger levels of those who complete anger management, and no evidence that it reduces recidivism rates among inmates who complete anger management classes in prison programs.

I serve as a volunteer in the local county jail where I go once a week to talk with inmates in jail about how to be set free from anger, grief, shame, and addictions. Many times I ask the inmates how many of them have completed anger management and find that about 80% have. When I then ask them how many of them were helped by the anger management classes, no one raises their hand. Occasionally I find an individual, maybe one in a hundred, who tells me that it was somewhat helpful to them, but it is common knowledge among inmates that it is ineffective.

David's Story

I was speaking one day to a group of about ten inmates in the jail about anger and how to get rid of it, and I asked how many of them had been to anger management classes. Eight of them raised their hands. When I asked how many of them felt it helped them no one raised his hand, but one young man said, "I know that I have an anger problem but the problem is that I don't believe in God."

"That's okay," I replied. "Have you been to anger management classes?" I asked. He said that he had been through anger management classes four times and he was only 19 years old. I asked him if it helped him and he said it did not. Then I said to him, "Let me ask you this. If I could show you how to get rid of your anger through prayer would you consider that maybe there is a God?" He smiled and shrugged his shoulders slightly and I decided not to press the point any further at that time.

A few days later I was back in the jail and as I was leaving I noticed someone in a holding cell by the admission center who was waving his arms and trying to get my attention. It was this same young man who had been moved to this cell due to medical issues. I went to his cell and asked the guards to open it so I could speak with him. When his door was opened I asked him if he wanted to try to get rid of his anger, and he said he did.

I asked him who he was angry at and he said he was angry at his grandfather. I asked him why he was angry at his grandfather. He told me that his grandfather was abusive to him and mean; one time he recalled his grandfather holding him down while his brother beat him up. He identified seven reasons for his anger which I wrote on a pad of paper. I said to him, "Being honest about your anger is the first step to releasing your anger and you've done that. The second step is to sincerely say a prayer and ask God to take your anger from you. Are you willing to do that?" He said that he was.

I led "David" in a prayer and he repeated after me as I read off his list of resentments and asked the Lord to take his anger from him and carry it for him. When he finished his prayer I asked the Lord to take his anger and carry it for him and replace it with His peace. Then I instructed David to think about his grandfather and tell me how he felt. He stood there quietly, thinking, but saying nothing. I asked him again how he felt and he said, "I don't feel anything."

"Think about those seven things you resented about your grandfather and tell me how it makes you feel," I said. He stood quietly thinking and said nothing so I repeated myself. "How do you feel as you think about your grandfather?" Once again he said he felt nothing.

"Do you mean to tell me that five minutes ago you hated your grandfather but you feel nothing now?" He nodded his head. "So, where did your anger go?" I asked. He pointed up with his finger. "Do you think that there might be a God?" I asked. He nodded again and I left.

The next day I returned with another man who ministered in the jail and we got "David" out of his cell and sat across a table from him. "How is your anger today?" I asked him. He said, "I don't feel any anger." "Well, what do you think about that?" I asked. "I think it's amazing," he replied.

"Well, let me ask you this, 'David.' If you could be 100% sure that you're going to heaven when you die would you like to?" He said that he would, so I invited my friend to share the salvation message with him and in a few minutes he bowed his head, confessed his sins, and asked Jesus to come into his life.

An Evangelistic Tool

Set Free Prayer Ministry is a wonderful evangelistic tool that is especially effective in reaching people who are resistant to traditional gospel presentations. We have seen many people converted as a result of seeing the power of God set them free from some anger or grief.

Initially, this puzzled me and made me question the reality of the ministry because I had always believed that God would never hear the prayer of an unbeliever. Isaiah 59:2 says, "Your sins have hidden His face from you, so that He does not hear." But as I considered this further I came to realize that Jesus healed many people who did not have faith in him. In John 5:5-14 Jesus healed a man who was lame, and then he slipped away in the crowd. When the Jewish leaders questioned him and asked him who had healed him he did not know who it was. Then Jesus later saw him in the Temple and the man then knew it was Jesus who healed him. Since he did not know who had healed him, his healing was obviously not based upon his faith in Jesus.

In Luke 17:12-19 ten lepers met Jesus on the road and begged Him to heal them of their leprosy. He told them to go show themselves to the priests, and as they were on their way they suddenly noticed that their leprosy was gone. They all ran to their homes to see their families except one man, who was a Samaritan. He returned to Jesus first to thank Him for what He had done for him and to worship Him. It would appear that the nine other lepers lacked faith in Jesus and simply ran home to resume their lives. Yet they were all healed anyway.

In the Sermon on the Mount in Matthew 5:45 Jesus said "He causes His sun to rise on the evil and the good, and sends rain on the righteous and the unrighteous." He explicitly tells us in this passage that God does kind things to ungrateful and evil men. It should not surprise us, therefore, that He will answer the prayers of unbelievers when they sincerely cry out to Him to carry their anger and grief. After all, He said to the multitudes, "Come to Me, all who are weary and heavy-laden, and I will give you rest" (Matthew 11:28). He invited the masses, not just his disciples and followers, to come to Him for rest.

Families of Murder Victims

I was invited to speak, one Sunday morning, at two churches in Arkansas about grief and anger. At the first church I spoke about grief and how to be set free of grief feelings through prayer, then I hurried down the highway to the second church and spoke about how to be set free from anger. Some people followed me to the second church to hear both messages, and after having lunch with the pastor I returned to the first church where I promised that I would pray with people who requested prayer.

When we returned to the first church after lunch there were two women waiting for prayer. Both of them had grown children who had been murdered. We made a list of the reasons for their anger and grief and gave their emotions to the Lord, as the pastor observed. Both of these women were able to release their anger and grief and to leave the session feeling peace in their hearts and smiling. One of them was an inpatient client at a Christian psychiatric facility who had been repeatedly hospitalized for a year after her son had been murdered, but even this woman was set free from her grief and anger during a brief prayer session.

The pastor who observed me told me afterwards, "It's one thing to hear you tell stories about being set fee, but it's a whole different thing to actually witness it!" The next day he texted me and told me that he had prayed with first woman's sister the next day who was also grieving and angry over the murder of her nephew. The pastor used the same prayer process with this woman and was able to lead her to peace after observing only two prayer sessions.

Anger and Marital Problems

Unresolved anger is a major source of marital problems. All couples get angry at times, but angry overreactions lead to an escalation of conflicts between couples. Overreactions are caused by unresolved past experiences that are triggered off by a present conflict. This is the reason why the Bible says, "Do not let the sun go down on your anger, and do not give the devil an opportunity"

(Ephesians 4:26-27). When we have unresolved anger from our past it spills over into our present relationships whether we are aware of it or not.

Once the two spouses resolve their own past issues, they are able to get along and communicate well without any coaching or being taught communication skills or how to "fight fair." Even normal couples who get along relatively well can benefit from making up a "resentment list" of things they resent about their partner, or things they resented about their parents or previous partners, and giving them to God. Some spouses are guilty of just chronic "negativity" which is caused by unresolved feelings of anger from the past, and when they specifically identify their resentments and give them to the Lord, they are set free from this chronic negativity.

I saw a couple several times to help the husband deal with an addiction problem and with some marital problems. They had been married for twenty-two years and while he was in the hospital they had an argument and the wife filed for divorce. He had told me in my last session with him that he did not have an anger problem, but that his wife did. When she came for our appointment he texted her from the hospital and told her that he was being released and he said he would see her at home after the appointment with me. She texted back and told him that he couldn't come home because she had filed for divorce. He texted back and said that he had not received the divorce papers so he would be home waiting for her when she arrived.

This woman admitted to me that she was the one with the violent temper; she told me that there were times that she became so angry and violent that she tore doors off their house and became physically aggressive. We talked about the source of her anger and she said that she had been angry since childhood at her sister and mother, so we made a list of the reasons for her anger toward her sister and mother, then prayed about her anger toward them and gave it to the Lord. When we were finished praying she said that she felt peaceful and was no longer angry at them. She left the session peaceful but a little apprehensive about what would happen between her and her husband when she got home.

Thirteen days later they returned for another counseling session and she said they just had the best thirteen days of their entire marriage. They were getting along well, they weren't fighting, and their teenage son was amazed at how well they were doing. He commented that he had never seen his father laugh before due to all the tension between them at home. This couple continued to do well long after they stopped coming for counseling. Their marriage was saved by the wife resolving her anger, which she had harbored for over thirty years toward her mother and sister.

Helping Angry People

Sometimes people ask about angry people they know who have been angry all their life, and wonder if this prayer ministry works with them. I explained that there is no such a thing as an "angry person" or someone whose anger is part of their personality. Anger is something that is learned or developed through life experiences, not something that is inherited.

Anger is rooted in past abuse, trauma, or losses, so when you find someone who has been angry a long time, they need help in identifying the historical reasons for their anger. Once again, this is very biblical and is not a throw-back to Sigmund Freud. The Scriptures told us to "not let the sun go down on your anger, and do not give the devil an opportunity" (Ephesians 4:26-27) 1,900 years before Freud was born.

When I meet "angry people" I ask them when was the first time that they can remember being really angry. If they say, "I have always been this way," I ask them when is the first time they can remember being very angry. As they explore this they usually remember some of the first people toward whom they were angry.

Once we identify an early memory, I then ask the person if they would like to get rid of their anger if that were possible. If they say they would and say they are willing to pray, then I help them make a list of the reasons for their anger and ask the Lord to take their anger from them. Once they give their anger to the Lord this "angry person" suddenly loses his or her anger and is transformed into a more calm person, because the reasons for their anger are resolved.

Dealing with Disappointment and Frustration

Many people will say they are not angry; they are just "frustrated" with someone or "disappointed" in them. If they prefer to use the words "frustration" or "disappointment" I will use them, but these are simply mild forms of anger. When a pastor of a church falls into immorality or is found guilty of some legal misconduct which disqualifies him from the ministry, it is very disappointing, but it is a form of anger and can be released in the same way as anger.

Other individuals prefer to say they are "upset" about someone, or "frustrated" with them, or just "irritated" with them. All of these are forms of anger and can be resolved in the same way as anger. At times people will say they are not angry at an individual but they "hate" them or are "disgusted" with them. These are more extreme forms of anger but they, too, can be resolved through simple, sincere prayer to the Lord, asking Him to take their anger and carry it for them.

Many people have difficulty admitting that they are angry at people from their past. Some people say they do not blame anyone but themselves for their behavioral and emotional problems, and they cannot talk about those who have wronged them without feeling like they are blame-shifting and not taking responsibility for their life. Others struggle with being honest about their feelings toward their parents because they feel they are dishonoring their parents by talking about them. It would, indeed, be dishonoring to their parents to talk about them with others simply to vent their anger toward them, but if they are seeking to release their anger by talking about it and letting it go, then that is not dishonoring to their parents.

It is wonderful to watch individuals go through this simple process and find freedom from anger that has held them in bondage for many years. And it pleases the Lord and opens up our communication channels with Him when we do so. Once we release our anger, we forgive our offenders from our heart, and are able to forgive, as the apostle Paul instructed us to do in Ephesians 4:32 when he said, "Be kind to one another, tender-hearted, forgiving each other, just as God in Christ also has forgiven you."

Hindrances to Release of Anger

Sometimes when people make a list of the reasons for their anger at someone and pray about them and give them to God, they still say they feel angry afterwards. There are two major reasons for this: First, they may have missed some important details or memories. Second, they may have prior sources of anger that need to be discussed first and resolved.

Most of the time when the anger is not completely resolved after praying about it, this simply means that they missed something, in which case they should make another list of why they are still angry. The person may repeat some of the same items that were on the first list, but they may need to give more details about the reasons for their anger. This is especially true when the individual has been severely abused and there are certain aspects of their abuse that were especially traumatic to them. They should be assisted in making a second list of the reasons for their anger, focusing upon more details, and giving them to the Lord.

When an individual prays several times about their anger list and sincerely gives it to the Lord but anger is still present, it is probably due to previous sources of anger that need to be addressed first. When there are strong feelings of anger from an earlier source, this can spill over into later anger sources and lead the person to overreact repeatedly. When this is suspected, you should ask the individual when was the first time he can remember feeling such intense feelings of anger. Once an earlier memory is identified, he should then be assisted in making a list of the reasons for his anger and led in a prayer to give it to the Lord and ask Him to take it from him.

There is always a reason when the prayer does not work, but once these two hindrances are removed, the person will find that their anger has gone away. I have also found a few cases of individuals who did not want to release their anger so they did not sincerely ask the Lord to take it, or they suppressed their feelings and refused to feel any anger while they were praying. This, of course, prevents them from having any success in releasing their anger. The Lord wants to set people free and will release them if they will sincerely and honestly present the specific reasons for their anger to Him and ask Him to take it from them and carry it for them. This is God's promise.

> *"Come to Me, all who are weary and heavy-laden, and I will give you rest" (Matthew 11:28)*

3

BEING COMPLETELY HONEST: MAKING A PRAYER PLAN

A man came to a Set Free meeting one time who had been told about the ministry by his pastor. This was his first visit and he listened quietly and attentively as we talked about how to be set free from grief and anger. After several group members shared their stories about being set free, I asked him if he had any questions.

He stated that he came to the meeting because he had a problem with anger and he was looking for help. He said that he was a Christian and taught a Sunday school class. He had a good job, a good wife, and three wonderful children but he had angry outbursts and he was afraid that he was going to permanently damage them with his anger. He said he had prayed about his anger and could not figure out why he got so angry. His father was a violent alcoholic who was abusive to him as he grew up, but he had changed and this man had already forgiven him and he stated that they were good friends now.

When people have anger problems like this man there are always underlying reasons for it based upon their past, and I was skeptical about his claim that he had completely forgiven his father, so I asked a few questions to try to understand the source of his anger. I asked him what his father used to be like and some of the things he did when he was angry and abusive. He said, "Well, one time when I was a teenager my dad put a loaded gun in my mouth and threatened to pull the trigger because he thought that I had had sex with my girlfriend."

"How did that make you feel?" I asked. He suddenly began to shake and cry as the memories returned to him. He talked about some other bad memories he had of his father, and how he had been so abusive and intimidating. As a young man he hated his father, but when he grew up his father changed and apologized for his past behavior. He thought that he had already forgiven him, but it was clear that he still had a lot of unresolved anger toward his father that needed to be released.

I made a list of the reasons for his anger and then led him in a prayer, and he told the Lord how angry he was at his father for his abuse. He asked the Lord to take his anger and carry it for him. After the prayer I asked him how he felt now about his father while thinking about things he had done to him. He said he loved him and felt peaceful and calm. He was able to think about his father's abuse and violence without feeling tearful or upset. He smiled and said that his anger was completely gone.

Forgiveness from the Heart

This man had forgiven his father the best way he knew how, but it didn't get to the core of his anger. In order to get to the core we have to be completely honest about what we are forgiving. In Matthew 18:35 Jesus said, "So shall My heavenly Father do to each of you who does not forgive from his heart." Forgiveness from the heart is more than telling a person, "I forgive you." It refers to a genuine forgiveness at the core of your being, regardless of whether it is verbally expressed or not. "Genuine forgiveness" is not superficial forgiveness but a deep forgiveness based upon reality. This is the reason why it is important to be very specific and detailed about our anger before we can release it. It is important to write a detailed list of the major reasons for our anger before we give them to the

Lord. Then, when we tell the Lord to carry our anger for us, He is able to take all our anger and carry it for us.

After praying with someone about their anger, I always ask the person afterwards how they feel "now" as they think about the person they want to forgive. If they still have some anger I ask for the specific reasons in order to identify what we missed or what we need to release more specifically. Once they release all their anger, they will feel peace and have no anger toward the person about whom they had prayed.

Self-Deception

1 John 1:8 says, "If we say that we have no sin, we are deceiving ourselves and the truth is not in us." Many people are self-deceptive and deny having anger toward people in their past. They may not have any open hostility toward them and they may get along well with them now and enjoy spending time with them, but there may still be some underlying feelings of anger that continue to affect them.

A man came to a Set Free Sunday School class who had a long history of drug abuse and criminal offenses. But he was drug-free and had begun attending church and seeking to follow the Lord. He said that he needed to learn how to control his anger better because he still got upset easily and got into fights and confrontations occasionally.

I asked him how old he was when he first remembered being angry and getting into fights. He said, "Oh, I remember handcuffing a boy when I was five years old and beating him up." I asked what had happened before age five that made him angry and he said that he had a brother that died before that, but he quickly became emotional and said he didn't want to talk about it. He said that his anger had nothing to do with that. I asked how he got along with his mother and he said "she was mean as a snake but I don't resent her for that because it made me who I am today."

I made several other attempts to help this man talk about painful events in his childhood and he was resistant to it, always insisting that his anger had nothing to do with his childhood and that he had forgiven his parents and those who had abused him as a child. He would pray about present-day events and feelings of resentment he had toward people who wronged him, but he was rarely willing to pray about those in his childhood who had offended and wounded him. He was unable to be completely honest about his anger so that he could release it all.

Finding a Mentor

Most people who are seeking help have already exhausted all their resources and solutions for change. They are seeking help because they have been unable to change on their own. Therefore, when they come to a Set Free meeting they are looking for help and for new insights. As you attend Set Free Prayer Meetings you will hear stories about individuals who have found freedom through the Set Free principles, and this may encourage you to study the Set Free literature and to return to learn more about the program. The prayer principles taught are powerful and effective, and in some cases individuals will be able to apply what they hear to themselves and find relief from the feelings or behaviors that trouble them.

In other cases, the individual will receive some relief but continue to struggle with other issues. For example, an individual may get some relief from a specific loss, but still struggle with depression because there are more underlying emotional issues contributing to the depression. Or an individual may get rid of some anger but still have outbursts of anger, which means there are more underlying sources of anger that need to be addressed.

In the weekly general meetings, you will learn the basic principles of the ministry, hear encouraging stories of victory, and have the opportunity to be honest with a small prayer group of same-sex individuals, but it may not be adequate for you to deal with the daily, overwhelming impulses you have. In such cases, it is recommended that you join a Study Group of individuals with a group leader who has already experienced some significant victory and prayed with others for healing. This Study Group leader can be a mentor to you and help you identify the underlying emotional issues that interfere with your life, and teach you how to be set free from these emotions.

These Study Groups meet on a different day of the week, in a home or church, and study workbooks that help guide the group members through the steps and apply the principles to them directly. If you join such a group you will develop a bond and trust with those in your group as you all pray together for healing in your life. Even if you are capable of praying on your own for healing, it is recommended that you go through the Study Group curriculum and experience so that you will experience what it is like to be in a Study Group. This will prepare you to start a group in your own church, or to lead a group effectively in the Set Free program.

Listing all Known Sources of Anger

In order to overcome an anger problem it is necessary to identify any unresolved sources of anger from the past. When I begin counseling someone, I generally like to get a thorough history on the person to understand events in their past that continue to affect them, but sometimes there is not time for that. At such times it can be helpful to simply ask the individual to make a list of every significant person from their past who hurt them. If the person is very honest they can make this list and then take one person at a time from the list, make a list of the reasons for their anger toward each person, then pray and release all their anger toward them. If they do this thoroughly for each person they can be set free from their anger.

A woman came for counseling who admitted that she had an anger problem. The first time I saw her I asked her what brought her to the clinic and she said, "My husband says I'm crazy." "Why does he think you are crazy?" I asked.

"Because we got into an argument recently and he grabbed my arm. I told him to take his hands off me or I would beat his head in with a ball bat and call the police and tell them I did it in self-defense." She admitted that she had an anger problem which she had had from her childhood and she wanted help with it. She said she was angry at her husband because he quit his job nine months earlier and she learned that while she was at work to support the family, he was watching pornography and playing video games all day. She had a right to be angry, but her threats to beat his head with a ball bat were an obvious over-reaction.

We discussed the sources of her anger and she admitted that she was very angry at her father, mother, and grandmother since childhood. Her father was an abusive alcoholic who abused her mother in front of her and her siblings. He also had multiple affairs but then accused her mother of having affairs, so she was very angry at her father. At times her father threatened to leave her mother, who then begged for him to not leave, and this made this woman angry at her mother. She was angry at her paternal grandmother for being so mean and violent. As a child she remembered her grandmother becoming extremely angry, screaming and cussing at her for spilling some water.

We made a list of the reasons for her anger toward each of these individuals, and then one-by-one we prayed about each of them and she asked the Lord to take her anger and carry it for her. When we were done she was calm and smiling and said she felt a lot better. The following week she was still smiling and she said that her husband said he could already tell a difference in her. She was less angry and intense after releasing her anger toward these three individuals.

However, we were just getting started because there was more anger from her past. I conducted a social history on her in order to identify other events in her past that may have contributed to her anger, then I listed them in two columns. In the first column I listed the sources of her anger and in the second column I listed her sources of grief. This process provides a much more thorough way of identifying the critical prayer issues for an individual and I like to call this their "Prayer Plan." The following was the prayer plan for this woman.

Anger Issues

1. Mother: critical and unloving
2. Father: an abusive alcoholic who had affairs
3. Aunts: mean and judgmental
4. Paternal Grandmother: mean and violent
5. Stepfather: mean
6. School Bullies: teased and bullied her
7. Dad's Ex-girlfriend: broke up their family
8. Husband: quit job, watched porn, played video games

Grief Issues

1. Age 9: maternal grandfather died
2. Age 10: great grandmother died
3. Age 18: best friend died from car accident
4. Age 20: favorite aunt died
5. Age 27: favorite uncle died

This woman denied any history of sexual abuse or any other sources of guilt or shame, so her prayer plan had only two columns, listing the sources of her anger and her grief. With individuals who have been sexually abused or who report having strong feelings of guilt and shame from past events I make a third column for shame on the prayer plan for the sources of their feelings of shame. We prayed about her anger toward her father, mother, and maternal grandmother during the first session, which helped her greatly. In our second session we prayed about her anger toward two aunts and this relieved her of more anger.

The following week she had a few bad days where she was very emotional for no apparent reason, which she believed was due to her medications, and she prayed on her own about other people on her list. She said she made a list of the reasons for her anger toward the school bullies, her husband, her stepfather, two more aunts, and her father's ex-girlfriend. As she prayed she cried about these people, but then after her prayers she felt calm and peaceful. She said that she felt good after that, and had no depression or anger.

This is one of the wonderful things about making a prayer list; it enables people to pray on their own about other significant issues from their past, without the assistance of the counselor or prayer minister. This is the best case scenario, for clients to learn to pray independently about their emotions and to learn how to have an intimate relationship with the Lord.

Losses sometimes contribute to feelings of anger so we prayed about the loss of her best friend at age 18, who died tragically from a car accident. His death was very traumatic for this young woman. She made a list of 17 things she missed about him and gave it to the Lord and felt peace about the loss, except for some sadness. She then gave her sadness to the Lord, also, and when I prayed and asked the Lord if there was anything that He wanted her to know she said, "I'll take care of it; he's okay; He's not hurting anymore."

These words of truth and comfort brought complete peace to her heart and relieved her of all the pain and sadness connected to this significant loss. We then prayed about the loss of her great grandmother, her maternal grandfather, her favorite aunt, and her favorite uncle. Once she resolved all of these losses she was calm and peaceful and was no longer so angry at her husband. She was able to deal with her husband in a much more rational and helpful way without all the anger she had previously.

Making a Prayer Plan

There are many reasons for making a prayer plan for individuals when beginning to minister to them, or for ourselves as we seek emotional healing in our lives. One reason is to understand the origin and root of our problems. Those who struggle with addictions, depression, and other emotional issues are confused about their behaviors and their emotions and have no idea how to stop them.

Just telling people it is sin and to stop it does not help, because the underlying feelings continue to keep them upset, and when people are constantly upset they are very vulnerable to sinning in order to feel better.

Another benefit of making a prayer plan is that it makes it more clear what the specific underlying grief, anger, and shame issues are that caused the problems, so that individuals better understand their own behavior. Those with addictions gain a clearer understanding of how their addiction began, and those with depression understand more clearly what events triggered off their depression.

A third reason for making a prayer plan is that it enables us to be more honest with ourselves about our feelings. Some people have difficulty being honest because they have never talked about their feelings with anyone. Some have been trained from their childhood to suppress their feelings and never talk openly about them, such as when they are told as children, "if you cry I will give you something to cry about." Others have been raised in religious homes where they were taught that expressing their feelings was disrespectful or dishonoring to their parents, so they learned to suppress and deny them. In order to be set free, it is essential that the individuals be completely honest with themselves and with God about their feelings.

Finally, a prayer plan is very helpful to the individual in understanding the origin of their problems, giving them hope of change. By identifying the specific issues about which they need to pray, they realize that there are a finite number of events that have affected them, so it is not so overwhelming to them.

Components of the History

When beginning to pray with someone about their emotional issues it is helpful to ask, "When did you start using drugs or drinking?" If their problem is with depression, anger, or some other emotional issue, ask when they first began to have problems with their depression or anger. Once they begin to identify a starting point, it is then helpful to try to understand how that problem began by asking them how they felt at that time. I generally ask permission to ask some personal questions about their background, so that I can better understand them. Most people will readily grant you permission to ask personal questions when they understand that you are trying to help them.

The following categories of information will provide a fairly comprehensive history of information to enable you to understand the individual or yourself. As you inquire into each of these areas, try to identify anything that could be a source of feelings of grief, anger, or shame.

- Parental Influences: Mother and Father figures
- Sibling Influences: anyone raised with client …
- School/Peer Influences: Grade School, Middle, HS…
- Marriages and Romantic Relationships…
- Symptoms of Problems: arrests, addictions…
- Traumas: physical, verbal, sexual…
- Losses: These are often overlooked and should include other losses in addition to deaths, such as divorce.

While this may seem like a difficult process to learn, it is not, and after doing it several times you will find that it is simple to remember by just discussing the person's life from birth to adulthood without trying to memorize the list. We will briefly examine each of these areas to consider why they are so important to explore.

Parental Influences

Our parents have a profound influence on our lives so it is important to be honest about the nature of our relationship with them.

A good starting place is to identify who raised you, or helped raise you, as you were growing up. It may be very simple if your biological parents raised you from birth to adulthood, but it can become very complicated when step parents, adoptive parents, grandparents, foster parents, and others have helped raise you.

Identify who helped raise you and state how they got along with each other. Answer the questions, "did they argue often, did they ever become violent, did they ever separate, or did they ever divorce?" It is also important to learn how the individual got along with each of these caretakers; were they close to them or did they ever resent them? If there were step-parents, grandparents, or foster parents who helped raise them, how did they get along with each of them? Each of these questions can expose some significant sources of anger, grief, or shame.

Sibling Influences

Our sibling position and relationships can also have a profound impact on us. It can be important to identify each sibling or person who was raised with the individual, and identify how they got along with them. Never assume that they got along well unless they clearly state this, and even then it is important to ask questions to verify this.

I was interviewing a man in a treatment program who stated that he and his brother are good friends and they get along great. Just to be sure there was no hidden problem between them I asked, "Did you two ever have any problems getting along?" He replied, "Oh, yeah. He used to beat me up every day when I was younger, before I was 13 years old."

"What ended that?" I inquired. "Well," he replied, "One day I hit him in the head with a ball bat and knocked him out. When he came back into consciousness I stood over him and shook the bat at him and said, 'if you ever touch me again I'm going to kill you!' That was the last time he ever bothered me. We've been good friends ever since."

When inquiring about sibling relationships it is helpful to ask the individual if they always got along well, or if he/she ever had any resentments toward any of his/her siblings. This line of questioning is much more likely to produce some helpful information about their emotional history than a simple question like, "How did you get along with your siblings?"

School and Peer Influences

Many problems begin to manifest themselves at school as the individual grows up, so it is helpful to ask about each school level and how they did in school. First, ask how they did in grade school, did they make good grades, were they ever held back, were they in special education classes, did they get in trouble for misbehaving, and did they have plenty of friends? Children who get into a lot of trouble in school usually have problems at home that make them misbehave, so this can open the door to insights into their family life.

Next, ask about their experience in middle school, if they made good grades, had any behavior problems, and had plenty of friends. It is often around age 12 or 13 when young people with anger problems become rebellious and begin smoking, experimenting with drugs and alcohol, and getting involved in romantic relationships.

Finally, ask about their experience in high school, whether they graduated from high school or not, if they still made good grades, behaved well, and had plenty of friends. It is also helpful to find out if they had any other traumas in high school or previously, to see if there was any form of sexual abuse that they experienced.

Relationship Problems

During middle school, and especially high school, many young people become involved in relationships that end painfully, and years later there are still underlying feelings of hurt, anger, and grief from these break-ups. It is helpful to ask if they had any serious boyfriends or girlfriends to see if there were any heartbreaks that led to feelings of grief or anger.

In addition, for adults it is important to find out how many times the individual has been married or involved in a long-term relationship, then to ask what type of problems led to their divorces or break-ups. When there are unresolved losses and sources of anger it often leads to later relationship problems with their spouse, so it is important to identify these relationships and help the individual talk about their feelings and pray about them to resolve them.

Symptoms of Problems

Drug or Alcohol Abuse: While gathering background information from the individual it is also helpful to inquire about other signs of adjustment or emotional problems, such as alcohol and drug abuse. I like to ask if the person experimented with drugs or alcohol as a teenager, and if so, ask if they ever drank or used drugs on a regular basis. It is helpful to learn if they ever got drunk or high on a regular basis, and if they ever went through any form of drug or alcohol treatment.

Legal Problems: It is also helpful to inquire about legal problems. Ask if they have ever been arrested and if so, how many times and for what types of offenses. Exploring these legal issues provides much helpful information regarding the individual's emotional issues. Someone who has been arrested repeatedly for assaults or domestic violence clearly had anger issues prior to those arrests. Individuals who have DUIs or public intoxication charges clearly had a problem with substance abuse, regardless of how much they may minimize it and deny it.

Mental Health Problems: Then it is helpful to find out if the person ever saw a mental health counselor, took psychiatric medications, or was committed to a psychiatric facility. If so, ask when this happened, what was the reason for the counseling, medication or admission. All of these questions help you understand their history and the personal, emotional issues.

Significant Losses

Losses are a significant factor in the development of mental health issues so it is especially important to ask the individual how many significant losses they had and to list them in chronological order. Even when these events have a strong impact on the individual it takes some effort for most people to name these losses, because they have suppressed them and tried to forget them.

Sometimes it helps to specifically ask them if they lost any grandparents, relatives, or close friends. Ask them if they had any serious relationship losses that affected them. For each loss identified, ask if they were close to the individual and ask how it affected them when the person died or left them.

Some losses have no impact upon them while others led to feelings of depression, drug abuse, and even suicidal ideation. Many people will not mention losses unless asked specifically so it is important to specifically probe into their losses to understand them. Losses of relationships, parents through divorce, and friends through moving, can have as much impact as losses through death.

Nola's Story

A woman named "Nola" called for help, requesting counseling for an addiction. She admitted that she had a problem and her husband and family were urging her to go to a Christian counselor for help or to be admitted into a treatment program. Almost all of her family members were taking psychiatric drugs of some kind so they were urging her to go to a psychiatrist to get on some medications. She and her husband came together and agreed to see me for free in exchange for allowing me to videotape her sessions. She was seen for four therapy session over a three-month period with her husband present at each of these sessions. This series of video sessions is very unique and is helpful for learning how to do this prayer ministry.

"Nola" and her husband had been married for over fifteen years and they had three children. She and her husband both worked full-time and they attended church and took their children to church. She stated that she got saved at age 14 and was deeply involved in her youth group at church as a young person. She and her husband got married when she was 22 years old. Neither one of them used drugs or drank, but when she was 36 years old she broke her leg and was placed on pain medications, to which she became addicted. When her doctor ended her pain medications she began drinking to numb her feelings, and she began neglecting her children while drinking, and it was this that led her to seek counseling. Her family intervened and her brother took care of her children for a while to avoid any involvement with the Social Services for her state, and urged her to get treatment for her addiction.

During the first session with "Nola," I conducted a standard social history to learn about her background and to understand how a Christian woman like this could become addicted to alcohol at such an age without any prior history of alcohol or substance abuse. This interview took about an hour, and then we spent another fifteen to twenty minutes praying about the loss of her father-in-law that was very traumatic to her. She left the first session feeling better, having resolved some significant grief issues.

The following are significant life events that she disclosed during this first session as I conducted the Social History:

- Age 4: Her biological father died
- Age 5: Her mother married a violent alcoholic
- Age 8: Her half-sister and paternal grandparents died in a car wreck
- Age 14: She was molested by her stepdad
- Age 14: She got saved and "forgave" her stepfather, then "blocked out" this memory
- Age 20: She was date-raped
- Age 22: Her maternal grandmother died
- Age 27: Her father-in-law died
- Age 34: She and her husband lost their business
- Age 36: She broke her leg and got addicted to pain killers

Nola's Prayer Plan:

After gathering this information from "Nola" I made three lists of prayer issues that needed to be addressed. I explained to her how she could be set free from her feelings of grief, anger, and shame, and that her addiction would stop, including her urges to drink or use pain pills. She and her husband were very open to trying this as a last resort before seeking inpatient treatment which her family was strongly recommending. The following three lists include the items that were placed on her "Prayer Plan" and I asked her which of these was the most difficult for her at that time.

<u>Grief and Loss Issues</u>

1. Age 4: Dad died
2. Age 8: Sister died
3. Age 8: Paternal grandparents died
4. Age 22: Maternal grandmother died
5. Age 27: Father-in-law died

<u>Anger Issues</u>

1. Biological Father
2. Biological Mother
3. Stepfather
4. Peer Abuse
5. Man who date-raped her

<u>Shame Issues</u>

1. Age 14: Sexual Trauma
2. Age 20: Sexual Trauma

She stated that the loss of her father-in-law at age 27 was most difficult for her due to her closeness to him. We made a list of everything that she missed about him, then we prayed and she gave her grief and sadness to the Lord and asked Him to take it from her and carry it for her. She left feeling better and hopeful that this prayer ministry could help her with her addiction. She also agreed to try to pray on her own about some of these issues on her prayer plan.

When "Nola" returned for her second session she indicated that she was doing well and was able to think about, and talk about, her father-in-law without any deep grief or sadness. She stated that she had prayed on her own about the losses of her maternal grandmother, her father, and her sister and she felt like these losses were resolved. We discussed her sexual abuse at age 14 and again at age 20 and she prayed about her feelings of anger and shame and was able to completely resolve these feelings during this session.

When "Nola" came to her third session two weeks later she admitted that she had had difficulty the previous week when she was alone at the house and she drank some hand sanitizer in her desperation for relief from her negative feelings. We explored the feelings of aloneness that she felt and prayed about these feelings that were rooted in a childhood experience, and she was set free from these feelings. We also prayed about her anger toward her biological mother, and several people she had not included on her original prayer plan. She left this session feeling peaceful and calm.

Three weeks later, "Nola" and her husband were seen again for the fourth session. She said that she was doing very well and she proudly announced that she had taken herself off three psychiatric medications and was still doing well. She had been cautioned about stopping these medications so quickly because there are often withdrawal symptoms and because it can be dangerous to abruptly stop taking these medications, but she fortunately had no adverse side effects from withdrawing from them. We prayed about her anger toward her father, and her school peers who had teased and bullied her, and we dealt with some more feelings of shame that she identified.

At the end of this session she was feeling very good, she had had no more cravings or urges for alcohol or pain killers for three weeks, and her husband was asked what he thought about her progress. He said, "I feel extremely good about how she is doing! It's amazing! It has helped me." Subsequent to this last session she gave several follow-up phone interviews and said that she was much closer to her sisters and she was talking to her mother every day. Her family agreed that she was doing very well in spite of her stopping her medications and their insistence that she needed to be on these psychiatric medications.

"Nola" remained sober for the next eighteen months and affirmed that she was still doing great. She reported that it had improved her marriage and stated, "Our relationship is 100% better!" Her son noticed a significant improvement in her moods and remarked to her one day, "That's the first time I've seen you laugh in a long time." What a marvelous thing it is to witness such a transformation in the life of someone like "Nola" who had a serious addiction and was set free after four sessions through prayer. Those who wish to observe these four prayer sessions can purchase a copy of them on the Set Free Prayer Ministry website.

It Will Make Sense

When you conduct an interview with an individual in order to create a prayer plan for them, it will help you understand the reasons for their depression, substance abuse, and anger. If their emotional struggles or behavior problems still do not make sense when you are finished, it means that you missed something and it would be appropriate to ask questions to see if there were any losses, traumas, or other events that occurred prior to the onset of their emotional struggles or behavioral problems that would help you make sense of, and understand, the reasons for their problems.

I saw a young man who admitted that he had been compulsively abusing marijuana since age 13. When I interviewed him about his family relationships and background to understand his drug abuse he stated that he got along well with his mother and stepfather, and he got along well with his brothers. He also denied any history of traumas or sources of anger as a child. I was puzzled because there was no good reason for him to abuse drugs given these facts, so I said to him, "I have found that there are always underlying emotional reasons when someone begins abusing drugs. Can you think of anything that happened to you before age 13 that would help me understand why you felt so bad that you began abusing marijuana?" He immediately replied, "Maybe it was the fact that I was raped every night from age 7 to 10."

I was shocked, but not surprised, and asked him, "By whom?" "I don't know," he said. "It was dark and I never knew who it was." "Well, that would explain it," I said. I knew that there had to be something missing from his story because it made no sense. When you hear the full story of a person's life, the traumas they have experienced and the relationships they had, you will understand the emotional problems they were experiencing that led them to develop their specific behavioral or emotional problems. It will make sense because there are always underlying emotional factors that lead individuals to drink excessively, abuse drugs, or engage in some other problematic behavior or experience emotional problems.

Honesty and Thoroughness

The reason why it is so important to make a prayer plan for yourself, or to enlist the assistance of a mentor in making one, is that there are usually multiple factors that contribute to our behavioral or emotional struggles. Praying about one incident in our life may help, but usually there are other issues that will continue to interfere with our life until they are systematically and thoroughly explored and resolved.

Many people have partially forgiven people who have offended them, and they have suppressed their feelings for so long that they cannot identify their unresolved feelings. It requires the help of an outsider, at times, to identify these sources of their feelings that are still unresolved so that they can pray about them for healing.

Sharing your life story with someone can be a very liberating experience, but it can also be a very frightening experience, since most people have never told anyone about their past struggles. The Bible makes it clear that this should be the norm in churches because it teaches us to "confess your faults to one another and pray for one another so that ye may be healed" (James 5:16 KJV). We are also instructed in Romans 12:15 to "rejoice with those who rejoice and weep with those who weep," so this type of personal disclosure is important to enable us to break free of our emotional bondage.

However, it is not just the honesty and disclosure that will liberate you. There are programs like Alcoholics Anonymous who provide the opportunity for complete honesty under conditions of anonymity, but this does not bring freedom by itself. In addition to honest disclosure, individuals also need instruction in how to release their anger, grief, fear, and shame, or these feelings will continue to affect them and lead them to drink or engage in other destructive behaviors.

The good news is that at your Set Free Prayer Ministry group you can find a place where you can be honest about your past, and where you can learn principles for releasing your negative emotions, because, "if the Son makes you free, you will be free indeed" (John 8:36). It is by the power of God, through sincere, specific prayer that you can find this freedom, and it is these specific prayer principles that you will learn as you continue your involvement with your Set Free Prayer Ministry, your Study Group, and your mentor.

4

RELEASING ANGER TOWARD GOD

The book of Job in the Bible is the story of a righteous man in the Old Testament who served God with all his heart, but he was a wealthy man whom God had blessed with many material blessings. One day Satan approached God to request permission to test Job, alleging that he was faithful to God only because of all his worldly comforts. He challenged God to allow him to afflict Job with financial problems and the loss of his children, and Satan asserted that Job would certainly turn from God and curse Him.

God gave Satan permission to afflict Job and in one day he lost all his children and many of his servants and cattle, but Job did not curse God or sin. In Job 1:21 he said,

> *"Naked I came from my mother's womb,*
> *And naked I shall return there.*
> *The LORD gave and the LORD has taken away.*
> *Blessed be the name of the LORD."*

Then Satan requested permission to inflict Job with medical problems, and God gave him permission as long as he did not take Job's life. So he struck Job with boils all over his body so he was in much pain, and his wife told him to "Curse God and die" (Job 2:9). But

Job did not; he remained faithful to God and blessed Him still, and did not curse God or sin with his lips. Then he had three friends who heard about his plight and when they came to comfort him and saw the great pain he was in, they sat with him quietly for a week and said nothing.

After seven days Job spoke to them and cursed the day of his birth. His friends began to rebuke him and falsely accused him of doing something to bring these curses on himself and his family, until he finally became angry at them and at God. Finally, after much complaining God spoke to him and challenged his arrogance in accusing Him of injustice. Job repented of his anger toward God and God restored to him his health, wealth, and his family. God also justified Job over his friends who had falsely accused him and blamed him for his infirmities.

This story in the Bible makes it clear that even righteous, god-fearing people become angry at God at times. Satan uses the same strategies with us that he used with Job. First, he uses the loss of our children or loved ones to accuse God of being unloving. Then he uses financial losses and tragedies to make us angry at God. Third, he uses medical problems and physical pain to lead us to turn against God. But when we give God our anger and ask Him to take it from us, He takes it, gives us new insights, and forgives us for our arrogance and short-sightedness. Everyone is capable of becoming angry at God when bad things happen, and we can learn a great deal from Job's example.

Jane's Story

A woman came to a Set Free meeting with her husband several weeks and seemed to enjoy it but did not talk about any personal issues. I asked her if she had any questions and she said that she had "lots of issues" to pray about. I asked which issue was the most prominent one in her life and her husband nudged her and said "Anger at God." She smiled and agreed but said she was embarrassed to admit that because "you're not supposed to be angry at God," she said.

I asked this woman why she was angry at God and she told me that He doesn't answer her prayers. She said she had cancer twice and almost died, and now she has heart problems and her husband has had serious back problems and surgery. She was also angry because of their financial problems and how they had struggled financially and had to do without many things that most people had. Her family sued her five times for an inheritance she had been given and it cost her a lot of money to hire lawyers to defend her in court. She had become bitter and angry, lost many friends, and felt abandoned by God because she had prayed many times for Him to take her anger and carry her burdens for her, but He never helped her and she felt her burden was too heavy for her to bear. She complained that God never answered her prayer and she never heard an audible answer.

As I listened I wrote out fifteen things that she resented about God and she said she would like to get rid of this anger, so I led her in a prayer and she told God the reasons for her anger, then she asked Him to take her anger and carry it for her. I then prayed and asked the Lord what He wanted this woman to know. She began crying and said, "Come to Me now; I am here. Bring your burdens to Me and leave them. You are My child. Nothing is too heavy for Me to carry. Let go and believe I will be with you."

These thoughts were very clear thoughts that she believed were from the Lord. I also believed that these thoughts came to her from the Holy Spirit, because they were consistent with the Word of God. I asked her if it felt true that she was His child, and she said it did. I asked her how she felt now and she said, "I feel a white light is surrounding me; I feel love. I no longer feel angry at God." She looked relieved, and she took a deep breath and said, "I have had a tightness in my chest all week, and now I can breathe again. Now I can be who I really am, by His help."

This woman was encouraged to begin giving her anger to the Lord one-by-one, using this same process with each person toward whom she was angry. She agreed to do this and left with a smile on her face and peace in her heart. She had never heard from the

Lord previously, but after she released her anger toward God she received a clear message from the Lord.

Steps for Releasing Anger toward God

Anger toward other people is usually justified; there is nothing wrong with it, and it is normal to feel angry when someone harms us or our loved ones. Most anger is justifiable and truth-based, and all we need to do to release it is to express it to the Lord and ask Him to take it from us. He is always ready to take our emotional burdens from us and carry them for us. All we have to do is be honest with Him and give it to Him.

With anger toward God it is never justifiable; it is lie-based because it is lies we believe that lead us to feel that God has wronged us. However, when dealing with anger toward God the process is the same as for dealing with other anger.

> **Step One**: *Be completely honest with God and tell Him why you are angry at Him.*

> **Step Two:** *Ask God to take your anger from you and carry it for you.*

After releasing your anger toward God, it is very helpful to ask Him what He wants you to know and then to listen quietly. As you listen quietly you will be amazed to see that He will often speak words of truth into your heart to take away your anger, in the same way that He did with Job and with the woman above.

In the book of Genesis we are told that a day came when Cain and Abel both brought an offering to the Lord. Abel brought a lamb to present to the Lord, and Cain brought his best produce to present to the Lord, and the Lord had regard for Abel's offering but not for Cain's. Perhaps the reason why the Lord accepted Abel's offering was because it was a blood sacrifice for his sins that represented the need of accepting the perfect sacrifice for forgiveness of sins. Cain's offering, on the other hand, represented a works-based offering for his sins and the Lord did not accept it because salvation is not based upon works, but upon faith in the blood sacrifice of the lamb of God (Romans 3:28).

Cain became angry and the LORD said to Cain, "Why are you angry? And why has your countenance fallen? If you do well, will not *your countenance* be lifted up? And if you do not do well, sin is crouching at the door; and its desire is for you, but you must master it" (Genesis 4:6-7). The Lord gave Cain the opportunity to bring a blood sacrifice to Him but he refused and remained angry. The following verse tells us the consequence of this anger, "And it came about when they were in the field, that Cain rose up against Abel his brother and killed him" (Genesis 4:8). Cain's anger at God led to anger toward his brother, and this led him to commit murder.

The lesson to be learned from this story is not that we should never be angry at God. The Lord know that we are "but dust" and He is patient with us and can deal with our anger toward Him, but we cannot afford to hold onto our anger for long. If we do hold onto our anger for long it can lead to total rebellion against God and engaging in sinful activities, including violent outbursts and anger.

Jerry's Story

A man was referred to me who had lost his son a year earlier and was still grieving heavily. He told me that his son was 21 years old and was healthy; he had no known health problems. He was a big boy and he lived with his father and worked faithfully every day. One evening he went to bed at about 10:00 pm and thirty minutes later he suddenly died in his sleep of a brain aneurism. It was devastating to this father because this was his only son.

I asked him what he missed about his son the most and he began sharing memories of him. He said that he missed spending time with him in the evenings, seeing him stretched out on the couch, watching TV with him, sitting on the porch talking, and discussing guns with him. His son was a gun enthusiast and he also enjoyed digging up Indian artifacts. He missed his son's easy-going personality and hearing his voice.

After identifying the things he missed about his son I explained that there were two steps to releasing his grief; the first step was to be honest about what he missed about his son, and the second step is to pray and ask God to take the grief from him. We had already completed the first step so the next step was to pray and ask the Lord to take his grief from him. He told me that he had a problem with this because he had not been talking to God since this loss occurred. He was angry at God and could not talk to Him.

I asked him if he would like to get rid of that anger and he said he would, so I asked him what made him angry at God. He told me that it made him angry that his son was a good boy and never got into trouble, but he sees other young men who are in trouble all the time who live. It didn't seem right to him that God would take his son's life while letting these trouble-makers live. It also made him angry that his son was the only one who could carry on the family name for him. He made a list of everything that he could think of that made him angry at God. Then I asked him if he would like to get rid of this anger and he said he would.

I led this man in a prayer in which he told the Lord the reasons for his anger, then asked the Lord to take it from him. Afterwards, I asked the Lord if there was anything that he wanted this man to know. He said, "God has His reasons; we don't always understand it but He has his reasons. I'll be okay." I asked him how he felt "now" and he said he felt peaceful, and he was no longer angry at God.

Then I asked him if he would like to get rid of the grief over his son, and he said he would. I led him in another prayer and he gave his grief and sadness to the Lord and asked Him to carry it for him. Afterwards, he said that he no longer felt anger or grief. He said he just felt peaceful and calm. His anger had prevented him from talking to God, but once he gave his anger to the Lord he was able to pray and release his grief over the loss of his son, and move on with his life.

Christian Woman Gets Angry at God

A Christian woman was referred to me for help with her depression. She had five tragic losses in her childhood, including the loss of her brother and her best friend around age 11 that led her to begin drinking and to become an alcoholic by age 16. She quit drinking at age 19 and began going to church, and as an adult she became a strong Christian woman whom everyone turned to for help.

However, the death of her mother ten years earlier led her to become depressed, and the following year she lost her father and six close relatives of hers, which deepened her depression. Then six months earlier her favorite aunt died and she cried a lot and quit eating, which led her to lose 50 pounds. She also lost custody of a foster child she had raised for three and a half years and lost two other friends.

I explained how she could get rid of her grief through prayer and asked her if she would like to do that. She told me that she couldn't pray because she was so angry at God for taking all her closest friends from her. She said she was afraid to make new friends for fear of losing them, she felt that God did not accept her, and she was angry at Him because she had prayed repeatedly for Him to take away her anxieties and He didn't do it. She was also angry at Him for allowing bad things to happen to innocent children, and because He allowed her to be hurt as a child. I asked her if she would like to get rid of her anger at God by telling Him why she was angry and asking Him to take her anger from her. She said she would like to do that.

I led this woman in a prayer and she gave all her anger to Him, then I asked the Lord if there was anything that He wanted her to know. After a moment of quiet contemplation she said, "He loves me!" In spite of her complaints to God and telling Him how angry she was at Him, He told her that He loved her. I asked the Lord if there was anything else He wanted her to know. She said, "He has protected me from other harm; I don't have control over what happens to others. Stay in prayer." With these thoughts from the Lord she said she felt better but still felt some anger because He brings so many needy people into her life, He lets her worry about her financial needs and then provides for her needs. She wanted Him to provide for her needs in advance before sending the needy people to her.

I led her in another prayer and she gave these resentments to the Lord, then I asked the Lord, again, what He wanted her to know. She said, "Stay in prayer; keep praying." She said that she knew God had not left her and that He was there with her. She relaxed and told me that she was no longer angry at God; she was at peace.

It amazes me how patient God is with us. We become angry at Him and He patiently listens to our complaints and then tells us He loves us, and gives us His peace. Psalms 103:13-14 says, "Just as a father has compassion on his children, So the LORD has compassion on those who fear Him. For He Himself knows that we are but dust."

False Prophecy Leads to Anger toward God

I saw a woman who became angry at God because at age 16 she lost three of the people in her life who were closest to her. She grew up with loving parents and grandparents who took her to church and provided her a stable home, but when she was 16 years old one of her grandparents died suddenly and then another one died slowly. Several preachers and "so-called prophets" prayed for her paternal grandfather and told her that the Lord had told them that he was going to be healed. She prayed earnestly for him but he died anyway. This made her very angry at the Lord, and then she began spending a lot of time with her uncle and he died very suddenly without any warning, which intensified her anger at God.

Her anger led her to begin associating with the wrong crowd and experimenting with drugs. She married a man who was not a godly man and he became abusive to her, which led her to engage in other behaviors that led her to feel guilty and shameful. When I initially spoke with her she was very tearful and anxious and was not ready to do any praying, but the next time I saw her she had been through another crisis and said, "I'm ready to do whatever I need to do." I asked her to tell me why she was angry at God and she told me how the preachers and "prophets" misled her to believe God would heal her grandfather, how she prayed for him in vain and believed her prayers would be answered, and how her uncle then died after she became really close to him and it seemed to her that God was deliberately taking away from her everyone with whom she was close.

When I first began using this prayer ministry I struggled with helping people with anger toward God, because anger at God is not rational or justified. What I learned is that we can still lead people to identify the reasons for their anger and ask Him to take the anger from them. So, this is what I did. I led her in a prayer to be honest with the Lord about her anger and to then ask Him to take it from her. In her prayer she said, "Lord, I'm tired of carrying all this hate and so I choose now to give it to you and ask you to take it from me. In Jesus' name."

I prayed and asked the Lord if there was anything that He wanted her to know and she said, "I don't feel angry; I just feel shameful because He has done so much good for me; I have two wonderful kids and a good family." I led her to confess her anger at God and another sin she felt guilt about and to ask His forgiveness, then I asked the Lord what He wanted her to know. "He's already forgiven me for that" she said. She told me that she no longer felt any anger at God or any feelings of shame or guilt.

With her anger at God out of the way I asked her if she would like to get rid of some of her grief and she said she would. We made a list of fifteen things she missed about her grandfather, who was a preacher, and she gave this grief to the Lord and asked Him to carry it for her. I prayed again and asked the Lord if there was anything He wanted her to know and she said, "We'll get to see each other again someday." I asked her how she felt and she said, "My chest isn't so heavy. I still miss him but it's not painful. I feel happy!" she said with a big smile.

Many people are angry at God because of losses or difficult circumstances that He allows them to experience, and this leads them to withdraw from Him, quit going to church, and to get involved in sinful behaviors in order to feel better. But the Lord is able to take away their anger toward Him when they are willing to give it to Him. This young woman was willing because she saw how harmful her anger was to her and her children, and she was desperate for help. Even good, sincere believers (and preachers) become angry at God, but the solution is simple; be honest with God about your anger toward Him and give it to Him, and He will carry it for you and replace it with His peace.

Anger toward God: An Important Clinical Issue

Anger toward God is not something that only Christian counselors encounter or that is found only in dealing with religious people. It is found in clinical settings everywhere and must be dealt with by counselors of all sorts. It is only the Christian counselor, however, who can deal with it openly, if they know how to help the individual release anger toward God.

I worked at a state prison for several years, then left that job for another opportunity. When I returned to that prison job my former boss was gone and a new clinical supervisor interviewed me and hired me to return to my former position. On my first day back at work my new boss told me that one of the prison staff had told him that I was "overly Christian," and he said that I would not be allowed to talk with any inmates about spiritual things. I reasoned with him, but he was firm in his decision and insisted that I must not talk with inmates about God or anything spiritual.

If I had been told this before being hired I would probably have declined the job, but now that I was hired and had no other source of income, I reluctantly consented to this rule. I performed my job duties and steered clear of any spiritual or religious topics for a period of time and built my relationship with this new boss. Then one day I was talking with an inmate who was discussing his background and he told me that when he was a child his father died and he became very angry at God, and his anger became a driving force in his life that led to rebellion, drug abuse, and criminal behavior. I wondered how I was going to help this young man with his emotional issues without discussing God.

I spoke with my supervisor and explained the situation and asked him how he wanted me to deal with this inmate. He had developed confidence in my integrity and professionalism by this point and agreed that this issue needed to be discussed. He agreed that it was impossible to avoid talking with this man about these spiritual issues and he gave me permission to talk with the inmate about his anger toward God. From that point on I was given full freedom to exercise my own discretion in talking about spiritual matters with inmates. Clearly, anger toward God was a significant issue that needed to be addressed.

Anger toward God is an issue that many people experience and it must be addressed, but if the counselor is an unbeliever he or she will not have any way to help the client with this issue. Even if the counselor is a Christian, he will not be able to effectively help the client with this issue unless he knows how to overcome anger toward God. At that time, I did not know how to help this young man overcome his anger toward God, so we talked about it and I reasoned with him but I did not know how to advise him to resolve it.

Inmate gets Angry at God

I had the privilege of leading a young man to the Lord in the local jail one time. He was a young man. but he had been in prison for over ten years, and when I asked him if he was 100% sure that he was going to heaven he admitted that he was not, and he was interested in knowing how. I shared the "Overcoming Doubts" booklet with him and he prayed and received the Lord into his life.

After his new birth he looked much happier and assured me that he was certain that he was going to heaven when he died. One day I asked him about his tattoos and he pointed out one tattoo of a person's name. He told me that this was a 2 year-old child he knew very well who died after he had prayed fervently for her healing. When his prayers failed and the child died, he became very angry at God. Although he was saved now and happy to be a Christian he admitted, when I inquired, that he still felt some anger at God about the death of this child. I asked him if he would like to get rid of it if he could, and he said he would.

We sat down at a table in the cell house and I asked him why he was angry at God. He told me, "Because He allowed Erin to die." I asked for other reasons for his anger and he told me he was angry because he has been in prison for ten years, God could have guided him and kept him from this type of life; He didn't ask to be born and God let him be born and go through such painful things. He also said that it seems that God is playing games with us and showing Satan what He can do.

Although anger is generally truth-based, anger at God is not. So I led him in a prayer to tell God why he was angry, then I prayed and asked the Lord to take this man's anger from him and I asked the Lord if there was anything He wanted this man to know. He said, "He loves me. I am picturing Him (the Lord) in white and He is saying, 'I love you, my son.'" I asked him how that made him feel and he said that he felt calm and peaceful. He said that he felt no more anger at God. Weeks later I continued to see him and he was always smiling and happy to see me. He said he had no anger at God and he continued to read his Bible and pray.

Consequences of Anger toward God

When people are angry at God it can be very damaging to them emotionally and spiritually. I have prayed with several pastors who were angry at God but continued to preach each week, but they were set free in the same way. Just be honest, tell the Lord why you are angry, and give your anger to him. Don't try to talk people out of their anger toward God or justify His actions. Just pray and ask Him what He wants them to know, then tell them to listen to the still, small voice of God bring truth and comfort to their heart. God can handle our anger toward Him, and He will take it from us if we will just be honest with Him and give it to Him. When He sets you free from your anger, you will be free indeed, even when you are angry at Him!

When people become angry at God it leads to many different kinds of problems. Anger at God leads people to avoid praying, reading their Bible, and going to church. It can also lead to open involvement in sin as a way of showing rebellion to God or even denying the existence of God. But one of the most subtle effects of anger toward God is the inability to hear the "still small voice of God" when praying for truth or comfort.

James 1:5 says, "But if any of you lacks wisdom, let him ask of God, who gives to all generously and without reproach, and it will be given to him." "Wisdom" is defined by W.E. Vine in the *Expository Dictionary of New Testament Words* as "insight into the true nature of things." This is very helpful because it accurately reflects how the Holy Spirit speaks to us and comforts us in times of need. He provides us "insight into the true nature of things" when we ask for wisdom from Him. But when people are angry at Him they rarely receive such "insight," comfort or truth from Him.

A young father was putting his 8 year-old daughter to bed one evening and after praying with her and kissing her he started to leave. She asked him to leave a light on; she said she was afraid of the monsters in the closet. He asked her if she would like for him to pray for her, and she said she would, so he prayed and asked the Lord what He wanted her to know about the monsters in the closet. She had prayed with her father before and had heard from Him but this time she said, "Daddy, God is not talking to me."

Knowing that this is usually caused by anger, he asked his daughter if she was angry at someone. She looked down and nodded her head. "Who are you angry at?" he asked. "Mommy," she said.

"Why are you angry at Mommy?" her father asked. "Because she won't let me invite my best friend to my birthday party" (because they had other plans already) the daughter said. "Well did you know that anger is like ear plugs to God?" he said to her. "When you are angry you can't hear from Him. Would you like to get rid of your anger?" She nodded and said that she would so her father led her in a prayer and she told the Lord why she was angry at her mother, and then she asked Him to take her anger from her.

Her father then prayed again, "Lord is there anything you want Melissa to know now?" "He said there are no monsters, and if there were He is stronger than them." She smiled, told her father "good night," then rolled over to go to sleep.

It's the same for adults. When we are angry toward God we are generally unable to hear his voice of comfort and truth in times of need. Anger at God creates a barrier between us and the Lord which interferes with close communion with Him. When this happens we must talk with Him about our anger and ask Him to take it from us. When we do this, we have close intimacy with Him again and are able to hear God's "still, small voice" again and receive His comfort.

Female Inmate Angry at God

I was in the local jail speaking with some female inmates about how to get rid of anger. One of them came up afterwards and asked for prayer. She said that she was angry at two former husbands and at God. She was very tearful and said that it was hard to admit that she was angry at God but she wanted to be honest and wanted help in getting rid of it.

I asked her why she was angry at God and she burst into tears and began sobbing so heavily that I could barely understand her. She said that her mother abandoned her, she was adopted by her grandmother who died when she was 12 years old, her first husband physically abused her, her second husband died from cancer, and her third husband emotionally abused her and took her children from her. She was angry at her former husbands but also was angry at God for allowing these tragic things to happen to her.

I asked this woman if she would like to get rid of her anger and she said that she would, so I led her in a prayer and she told the Lord why she was angry at Him. Even as she prayed she sobbed so heavily that I could barely understand her, but then she told the Lord that she was tired of carrying these feelings and she asked the Lord to carry them for her. She suddenly quit crying and wiped away the tears. She became calm and said that she was no longer angry at God. We then prayed about her anger toward her two former husbands and when we were finished she just smiled and said that she felt lighter. Her burden of anger was lifted from her and she was set free.

It's amazing how many people, including Christians, have anger toward God that they carry and they don't know how to release it. I have prayed with several pastors who were angry at God and didn't know how to release it, but once they did, they were set free. Anger is one of the primary, underlying causes of mental health problems and the Lord has given us a simple, effective way to remove our anger. First, be completely honest with the Lord about your anger by making a thorough list of the reasons for your anger toward Him or someone else. Second, say a simple prayer in which you tell the Lord why you are angry at Him or an individual, then ask Him to take your anger and carry it for you.

It's also amazing that the world has no way to eliminate anger. Anger management is ineffective and mental health professionals do not know how to help you with your anger, but the Lord is able to set you free when you take these two simple steps. He truly is able and willing to carry all our emotional burdens for us when we are willing to give them to Him in prayer.

5

THE CONSEQUENCES OF ANGER

The day I began writing this chapter I met with a woman who had received a lot of healing previously. She indicated that she was doing well but she was concerned about her two daughters who were living with her. Both of them were very angry and treated her disrespectfully at times, due to their anger. She stated that her older daughter had been to prison and was so full of anger that she was fearful that she would get into a confrontation with their neighbors and become violent with them. She said, "She's angry at the world; I don't know why but every little thing sets her off." She agreed that there were things in her daughter's past that made her angry and she had invited her to our Set Free meeting so she could get help with her anger.

The Influence of the Past

Some Christian teachers believe that it is wrong to encourage people to talk about their past, and that counselors should not discuss the past with clients but just focus on future behavior. Some even assert that examining our past is a humanistic practice taught by Sigmund Freud and secular therapists in an effort to excuse people for their behavior. But the Bible makes it clear that the past does affect us. Consider the words of the apostle Paul in Ephesians 4:26-27 where he said, "Do not let the sun go down on your anger, and do not give the devil an opportunity." What he is saying here is that when we hold onto our anger overnight, it gives the devil the opportunity to do harmful things to us. In other words, unresolved anger from one day can lead to sin the next day, so we cannot afford to hold onto our anger even for one day.

When he said this he was making it clear that there are consequences to holding onto our anger from the past, even from the recent past. The past does influence us, according to this passage in the Bible, and this passage was written 1900 years before Freud. Freud did have a lot of strange ideas and we should be careful about accepting his worldview, but he was right on this one point, that the past has a strong influence on our future. If holding onto our anger for one day can give the devil an opportunity in our lives, imagine the impact of holding onto our anger for years. The consequences of holding onto anger for years must be magnified a hundred-fold from that of holding onto it for one day.

The impact of anger on individuals and on our society can be seen in the rising amount of violence in our society and in the world today. Mass killings occur more and more frequently, and every time there is another mass killing the media and the politicians immediately begin calling for more gun control and more mental health treatment. Neither of these measures, however, will be effective in curbing the violence because it is rooted in the anger of individuals. Only a supernatural release of anger in individuals will do anything to reduce the violence in our society. Set Free Prayer Ministry can have a profound impact on the world as we use it to teach people how they can be set free from anger, because anger is at the root of marital problems, parenting problems, violence, substance abuse, church disunity, and violence in our world.

Anger Leads to Marital Problems

The number one problem in marriages that leads to divorce is unresolved anger from the past of the two spouses.

Many couples who struggle in their marriages could resolve their differences if they would simply release their anger toward one another and toward all those in their past who have wronged them. Once they release their anger they are able to get along and communicate well with one another.

A man who has been involved in this ministry for several years called me a few days before I began this chapter. He was excited to tell me that he and his wife had met and prayed with a woman from their church who was separated from her husband and on the verge of divorce. She shared her frustrations about her marriage as this man and his wife listened and made a list of the reasons for her anger toward her husband. They asked her if she would like to get rid of her anger and she said she would, so they led her in a prayer and she gave it to the Lord.

They also recognized that this woman had some feelings of sadness from her past and they prayed for her and asked the Lord to take her to the source of her feelings of sadness. She remembered a childhood memory and began crying and said, "Why would I remember some silly incident like this in my life?" She recalled a time as a child when some of her peers made fun of her about her clothing and she was deeply hurt and felt that she was not good enough. This couple prayed for her again and asked the Lord what He wanted her to know about that belief. She began to cry and said, "It doesn't matter what they think. God loves me." Her tears were tears of joy and relief. The Lord told her that he loved her and she was overwhelmed with joy and peace. When they inquired about her salvation she stated that she had been doubtful previously but that she was now confident of her salvation because she had gotten saved at age 10 and hearing the Lord's voice gave her reassurance of her salvation.

Something very similar happened when this ministry friend prayed with this woman's husband a week earlier. All of his anger and frustration with his wife had been lifted and he left feeling much more loving and peaceful than he had been before. This couple received emotional healing and was able to get back together and to save their marriage because these prayer ministers, with no professional counseling or psychological training, were able to share with them how to be set free from anger and other emotions that were destroying their marriage.

Another young man who has learned this ministry told me a similar story. He had a friend contact him whose wife left him and was determined to divorce him after 23 years of marriage. He was very distraught and requested some prayer ministry to deal with his emotions. During the prayer session he identified the reasons for his anger toward his wife and then prayed and gave his anger to the Lord. This had such a profound impact on his friend that he began speaking openly with his wife and confessing his failures and she agreed to pray with the young man about her emotional issues, too.

This woman also made a list of the reasons for her anger and released them, and her heart attitude changed profoundly toward her husband. They reunited and on their 24th wedding anniversary had a second honeymoon to celebrate their new relationship. Their marriage was saved through the prayer ministry of a young man who has no training in marital counseling or psychology, but who knows how to help others resolve their negative emotions.

Anger Leads to Harsh Parenting

A man came for counseling who had been sober for a year. He was tormented from things in his past and he got angry easily at his son, so his son was afraid of him. We prayed over a period of weeks about his anger toward his abusive father, and others who had harmed him or mistreated him as a child. Then we prayed about some unresolved grief and shame that he had from other events in his life. After several months of prayer sessions he began to feel good and began coming to our sessions smiling.

He confessed that his anger had led him to respond in anger toward his son to the point that his son avoided him and was afraid of him. After releasing his anger and grief from his past he began to soften his attitude toward his son and spending time with him. Eventually, he reported that they were spending time together and his son was more open to him. His anger had led him to overreact to his son and led him to be too harsh with him in his discipline.

Another Christian man came for counseling for his anger after he slapped his teenage daughter so hard that it left a hand imprint on her face. The state department of social services intervened and ordered him to get counseling for his anger in order to maintain custody of her. He was very open and unashamed of his Christian beliefs and wore a ball cap that prominently displayed the name of Jesus. When I met his daughter I found her to be a sweet, Christian girl but she wanted to live with her mother who was not a Christian and who lived an immoral lifestyle. However, this girl felt more loved by her mother than by her Christian father who took her to church.

When I asked this man about his anger and where it came from he said he didn't know, but he thought it was genetic because his father and his grandfather both had problems with their anger. He told me that he was very close to his pastor who confided in him that he used to have an anger problem and he began taking medications in order to reduce his anger. The pastor recommended that he should talk to a counselor about taking medications, and see if it would help him, because the pastor said that taking medications helped him. I explained the dangers of psychiatric medications and how they often lead to anger and violence rather than reduce them.

I shared with him how to release his anger through prayer and we began praying about events in his past that had led to his anger. The more we prayed, the more he began to calm down and release his anger, until he finally felt calm and said that his anger was under control. He was able to release his anger without the use of any dangerous psychiatric medications. Medications cannot take away anger about past events, though they can sometimes suppress them or numb them, but there are many adverse side-effects from them, including a risk of increased anger and even violence from many types of medications, including antidepressants, ADHD medications, and anti-anxiety medications.

Anger Leads to Violence

When I go into the local county jail to minister to inmates I have the opportunity to meet many men with anger problems who have committed violence. These men are often very open with the volunteers who are willing to talk with them and pray with them about their problems. I have also worked in a number of state prisons and personally counseled many men and women who have committed terrible acts of violence. I have found that these individuals consistently have strong feelings of anger from past events that occurred prior to committing acts of violence, unless their violence was induced by psychiatric medications.

In his book, *Medication Madness,* Dr. Peter Breggin documents numerous cases of individuals he has investigated who had no violent history but became violent as a result of the psychiatric medications they were taking. He points out that there is a proper diagnosis for such cases, which is "medication-induced mood disorder." This is a diagnosis that is accepted by the medical establishment and included in the diagnostic manual of psychiatric disorders, but is rarely recognized by doctors, psychiatrists, or mental-health professionals.

I saw a young teenage boy who was brought to me for therapy because he was aggressive and made threatening statements toward his stepmother. When I first met him he admitted that he was very angry at her because of the way that she treated him, ridiculed him, and punished him so severely. He admitted that he had violent thoughts toward her and had thoughts of stabbing her. I asked this young man if he would like to get rid of his anger if he could, and he said that he would. So, I shared with him that he needed to be honest about his anger and give it to God in a prayer.

We made a list of everything that his boy could remember that he resented about his stepmother, then he prayed and gave his anger to the Lord. Afterwards, he told me that his anger was gone and he felt calm when thinking about her. This young man had the potential for acting out violently toward his stepmother or toward others but fortunately was able to release his anger before it ever got to that point.

Anger Leads to Alcohol and Drug Abuse

In Chapter 2 I told the story about a man who was an alcoholic and who had a terrible anger problem. He brutally beat his wife in a drunken rage and when he sobered up and realized what he had done he was very remorseful and begged his wife to not leave him. He promised that if she would stay with him he would never drink again. Interestingly, he kept his promise and quit drinking but he still had such an explosive temper that he frightened his wife when he became angry. Given sufficient time he would probably have resumed his drinking again.

This man had good reason to be angry because he had been seriously abused by his father while growing up, and by his grandfather, also. We made a list of the reasons for his anger and he prayed and released his anger toward his father and grandfather. He also had a lot of anger toward several people in his past who had wronged him, so we made a list of the reasons for anger toward each of them and he was able to release his anger. After each prayer session he was able to think about these people and feel no more anger toward them.

This man's anger was so completely resolved that his wife lost her fear of him and they became affectionate again. They held hands during sessions and she said that she couldn't remember the last time they had a serious fight. He not only abstained from his drinking but he had no urges to drink anymore, and he was happy and developed a good relationship with his wife after he released all his anger.

Anger in our Society and World

Our world is full of anger and hatred and has been from the beginning of time. Even in the early pages of the Bible it can be seen that anger and hatred have been rampant in the world. As discussed in the previous chapter, Adam and Eve's oldest son, Cain, became angry at God and jealous of his brother when God accepted Abel's sacrifice but not his, and he arose and killed his brother, Abel. Genesis 4:5-8 says,

> *Cain became very angry and his countenance fell. The LORD said to Cain, "Why are you angry? And why has your countenance fallen? If you do well, will not your countenance be lifted up? And if you do not do well, sin is crouching at the door; and its desire is for you, but you must master it." And it came about in the field, that Cain rose up against Abel his brother and killed him.*

This was the beginning of violence in this world and it has continued ever since, wherever there is anger that is not resolved. Genesis 6:13 says, "God said to Noah, 'The end of all flesh has come before Me; for the earth is filled with violence because of them; and behold, I am about to destroy them with the earth.'" The Lord regretted that he had made man because the earth was "filled with violence," and this led Him to bring the flood upon the earth to destroy mankind and start over with Noah and his family.

But even after Noah, once the world was repopulated, violence became rampant all across the world, as it is today, except where there was the restraining influence of Christianity. Where genuine Christianity has prospered throughout the world it has brought a healing influence on societies and brought much peace and harmony into the world. The United States has been very strongly influenced by this Christian influence because it was founded upon biblical principles and upon Christianity.

As our country deviates further and further from its Christian foundation it becomes more and more violent. After World War II there was a strong Christian foundation, but soon situation ethics emerged and the moral foundation of our society began to erode.

Divorces became common and marriage became optional as more and more couples began to cohabit outside of marriage. The courts ruled against prayers in schools, then made abortions legal, and more and more families began to fall apart, and single-parent families became more common.

This rejection of biblical standards and Christian morality has had an impact on the children who have grown up without the support of two parents. They have grown up with anger in their hearts and have turned to drugs to calm their anger and feelings of abandonment. Crime has increased, violence has increased, and drug abuse has become epidemic in our society, and all of this is due to the underlying feelings of anger in our society. The leaders in our society tell us that we need more mental health treatment, but they do not know how to reduce the anger in individuals or in our society. The psychiatrists and mental health professionals in our country do not know how to deal with their own anger, let alone how to help others resolve their anger.

It shouldn't surprise us to see this natural progression in our society as we have turned from God. The church should be holding up the standard for our society and teaching it how to release anger and forgive, but most churches are just as full of anger as society, and divorce and marital problems are just as common in churches as in the rest of society. It is the goal of this ministry to see the church step up to the challenge and begin demonstrating and teaching the society how to release anger by giving it to the Lord in prayer.

The Solution to Violence

Imagine what would happen if you were to release all your anger from your past and then on a daily basis, and you began sharing with your family members how to do this. Imagine the impact it would have on your spouse, children, and family. Imagine what would happen if you shared this with your church and your entire church began to teach and practice this principle and released their anger. The impact on the church would be profound and obvious to everyone as marriages were healed and the church began to demonstrate joy and excitement about the Lord. It would totally revolutionize your church. And imagine what would happen if all the churches in your city began to do the same and they all began releasing their anger and reaching out to the community around them and teaching them how to release anger. This would have a profound and dramatic impact on our cities, our counties, our states, and our country.

The dream and prayer of Set Free Prayer Ministry is that churches all across the country will embrace, teach, and practice this simple principle of releasing their anger and giving it to God. It could come to the point, eventually, that everyone would know that those who struggle with anger problems need to go to church, not to anger management classes or to the mental health professionals, to learn how to release their anger.

God will be glorified as the church becomes a living witness to the world of the Lord Jesus, who set the example for us by praying for those who were crucifying Him, "Father, forgive them for they know not what they are doing?" (Luke 23:34). The Lord instructed us to forgive "seventy times seven" times (Matthew 18:22) and He also taught us, "Everyone who is angry with his brother shall be guilty before the court" (Matthew 5:22). When teaching His disciples how to pray He even said, "If you do not forgive others, then your Father will not forgive your transgressions" (Matthew 6:15). As we learn to give our anger to the Lord He will carry it for us so that we can truly forgive those who trespass against us. As the church carries on this mission of forgiveness the world will turn back to the Lord for help.

In the next chapter we will talk about a pledge that needs to be made by each person to release their anger and never allow it to return. This is the first step, the starting point for change. Each participant in this program must begin with this in their "recovery" or life change program. Without releasing our anger we will never be able to overcome our other emotional bonds and struggles.

6

MAKING THE FIRST PLEDGE: "DO NOT LET THE SUN GO DOWN ON YOUR ANGER"

The theme of these first six chapters has been to "not let the sun go down on your anger, and do not give the devil an opportunity" (Ephesians 4:26-27). We have discussed the impact of anger, the steps for overcoming anger, and the importance of being completely honest about our anger. The reader may wonder why so much time is being devoted in this book to the topic of anger, and the reason is that anger is the number one hindrance to happiness and spiritual health and is the first step to healing.

I am continually amazed at the numbers of people that I see in my practice who harbor feelings of anger that lead to marital problems, drug and alcohol abuse, violence, and relationship problems. Most of these people would probably tell you that they are not angry because they don't feel angry most of the time and they don't go around assaulting others. But the truth is that many people are full of anger that has never been resolved and which is simply being suppressed, and when some minor event occurs it triggers off their anger and comes out explosively.

I saw a young couple and the woman was a very nice, intelligent young woman who held a respectable position in her employment. She did not appear to be angry; she certainly did not appear to be full of rage. However, her husband complained that she would not listen to him when he tried to share his feelings because she was fearful that she would explode if she did. She said that there were several times in her life when she exploded in anger and she never wanted that to happen again, so when she felt upset she just walked away from the situation and refused to talk about it. This left him feeling very lonely and lacking in intimacy with her, and as a result he had become involved in several affairs. His wife was not responsible for his affairs, but when there is no emotional intimacy between a couple, it makes them both prone to having affairs.

Sherry's Story

Another young woman admitted to me that she had an alcohol abuse problem but she thought she had it under control until she got drunk on Christmas Eve and was thrown in jail for public intoxication for three days. She told me that she felt cheerful and happy most of the time, but every now and then she had an urge to drink and then she drank excessively. When she talked about her background she shared that her mother died when she was 5 years old, her father died when she was 13 years old, her stepmother and stepfather were abusive to her, her grandparents were very strict with her, she was bullied in school, and she had two boyfriends who physically abused her. It was no wonder that she was very angry as a teenager and began drinking excessively. When she was 22 years old her father-in-law committed suicide, which traumatized her, and her husband divorced her two years later. She had ten significant sources of her anger, and five significant losses that made her angry and depressed.

I asked this woman if she would like to get rid of her grief and anger and she said she would. While she was in jail a volunteer prayed with her and told her that she could not overcome her drinking on her own, but that she needed to give it to the Lord. She prayed and asked God to set her free and she "felt at peace" and came to realize that God was taking care of her. When I shared with her that she could get rid of her grief the same way, she was very receptive. She talked about her father and identified 23 things she missed about him, and then gave these feelings to the Lord and asked Him to take them and carry them for her. Immediately, her grief was lifted from her, but she had some anger toward her grandparents that she had to release. When she gave her anger to the Lord she felt her anger lifted from her, also. When I asked her how she felt toward her grandparents she said she had no more anger toward them and she said that she felt like calling them. This woman was on the road to recovery, and as she followed her prayer plan and prayed about all ten of her anger sources and all five of her significant losses, I knew that her urges to drink would stop.

Once addicted people release their grief, anger, and shame, their urges to engage in the addictive activities stop because they feel peaceful and no longer desire their addiction to feel better. In order to experience this kind of freedom, the individual must be completely honest about their feelings and their past, and pray through each of their resentments.

Two Critical Aspects

There are two distinct aspects to the biblical command to not let the sun go down on your anger. The first aspect is to deal with all our past resentments, even those that we believe are resolved and which we have not considered for a long time. Most people who have anger problems believe they have already resolved their past resentments and forgiven those who offended or wronged them. But the truth is that when people overreact negatively to an event in their life, it is always due to some unresolved event in their past. This is the reason why it is important to create a prayer plan, with help from someone else, to identify possible sources of anger from your past that might need to be reexamined and resolved.

Most couples that struggle in their relationship have issues from former relationships that continue to intrude into their current relationship. Until they recognize this and systematically and thoroughly resolve these past events, they will continue to overreact to their partner and have serious conflicts with them. The prayer minister must learn to look deeper when their prayer client continues to show anger after praying through their other sources of anger.

The second aspect of this biblical command is to release all your anger and resentments toward your current partner and in your present life. Even when you have resolved all past issues and forgiven all those in your past who have wronged you, new resentments can accumulate very quickly and lead to new feelings of anger. We cannot afford to allow these feelings to remain for long, not even for a single night. It is important to learn to live by this principle, day by day.

The Impact of the Pledge

One of the most important steps you can take to help you make positive changes in your life is to make a pledge to follow Ephesians 4:26-27, "Be angry, and yet do not sin. Do not let the sun go down on your anger, and do not give the devil an opportunity." This is not an unreasonable or impossible pledge to make; it is very achievable because it simply requires us to cry out to the Lord and ask Him to take our anger and carry it for us. It does not require us to have the supernatural strength to forgive, it simply requires us to sincerely ask the Lord to take our anger and carry it for us.

Imagine the impact of this principle on marriages. You may have a relatively happy marriage, but any marriage will be improved when both spouses release unresolved anger from their past and from their marriage. Many Christian marriages appear good on the surface but are full of conflict and are on a shaky foundation. The true state of many marriages is often hidden from sight until the couple separates or divorces, and then everyone is shocked to learn about it.

Imagine the impact of young couples who commit themselves to live by this principle in their marriage. Imagine what would happen if every new couple made this pledge as part of their marriage vows, and learned how to resolve all past anger, prior to their wedding. If these couples then entered into their marriage with a clean slate and without the weight of resentments and hurts from their past, they could focus on dealing with daily issues and releasing their anger and irritations on a day-by-day basis. Such a practice would virtually eliminate divorces in the Church and provide a powerful testimony to the world of a Christian home.

Imagine what would happen as young couples had children and demonstrated to them how to release their anger day-by-day. The mother-and-dad team would not get into arguments or serious quarrels in front of the children, they would remain together and avoid damaging the children by divorce, and the children would grow up in a loving, stable home. This provides the optimal environment for children to grow up happy, secure, and well-adjusted.

Imagine the impact it would have upon your church if every member made this pledge to not let the sun go down upon their anger. Church members would get along with each other, they would work together in harmony, and avoid ugly church splits that leave negative feelings and are a poor example to the world. Churches without anger would focus upon sharing the gospel and sharing their joy with their community. Based upon my experience in counseling Christians from all types of churches, I have come to believe that the major reason why Christians do not share the gospel with others is because they struggle so much in their own lives that they are not excited about the Lord or about Christianity. Pastors cannot get their members to share the gospel until they first experience peace and joy in their lives. A church without anger would be a loving church and would fulfill the words of Jesus who said, "By this all men will know that you are my disciples, if you have love for one another" (John 13:35).

Imagine the impact it would have if every church in your town took up this challenge to spread this truth in their church. Churches all across the city would be full of joy and peace, and the unsaved would know that if they had a problem with anger they need to go to church to get rid of it. Politicians and the media would quit calling for more mental health providers and begin to instruct people to go to church for help. Rather than sending people with anger to doctors to give them medications, or sending them to mental health providers, they would know there is a much more effective and inexpensive way to deal with anger and violence. Eventually, the jails and prisons would begin to empty as men and woman gave their hearts to the Lord and gave all their anger to the Lord, as well.

Imagine the impact it would have if inmates in the local jail were all to release their anger and make this pledge. Those who are incarcerated for acts of violence would be taught that they need to come to salvation and receive forgiveness of their sins, and they would immediately learn how to release all their anger from the past. They would not only be saved from their sins, but be set free from their past and their anger that led them into sin, so that they can live fruitful lives for the Lord.

Imagine the impact it would have upon your county, state, and the country if this movement spread across the country. Lives would be changed, families would be strong, churches would thrive, and the entire country would be transformed.

In His Steps

Charles M. Sheldon wrote a classic Christian novel in 1896 called, "In His Steps" that broke all sales records for years and whose circulation was said to have been surpassed only by that of the Bible and Pilgrim's Progress. In this fictional account, Mr. Sheldon described the transformation that occurred in a small town when members of a church pledged themselves to live for one year and not do anything without first asking the question, "What would Jesus do?" and then doing what they believed Jesus would do.

The story is fascinating, as it follows the lives of a church member who was the editor of the local newspaper, a businessman, a store owner, a musician, the pastor, a college professor, a doctor and many other significant citizens in the town who began to consciously live their lives as they believed Jesus would. It revolutionized their personal lives, their church, and their entire city as they began to walk in the steps of Jesus and to live as they believed He would.

As fascinating as this story is, it would be a profoundly difficult thing to try to understand what Jesus would do in each situation you faced, and to actually do it. It would be wonderful to see a church live in this way, but it would truly take great strength and commitment to make such changes.

The pledge being encouraged in this chapter is much less difficult than that found in this story, but it would nonetheless have a very profound impact on the lives of individuals, families, churches, and communities. It is a pledge that would give you peace in your heart and would not demand any great sacrifices. It would lead you to simply obey the command of the Lord in what is called "The Lord's Prayer" to "forgive us our debts, as we also have forgiven our debtors" (Matthew 6:12).

A Basic Discipleship Issue

Many sincere Christians struggle with their emotions and it leads them into spiritual defeat, damaged testimonies, a lack of boldness in talking about the Lord, and moral failure. Every believer needs to learn, at an early stage in their spiritual life, how to give their feelings to the Lord and how to pray for truth about belief-based emotions. If they do not receive this training they will struggle in their walk and fall by the wayside.

A perfect illustration of this can be found in the "parable of the sower" found in Matthew 13:3-8. Jesus said that a sower went out to sow seeds, and while he was on his way some seeds fell along the roadside and were eaten by the birds. Other seeds fell in rocky soil that grew up quickly but then withered away. Some seeds also fell among the thorns and grew but were choked out by the thorns. Finally, some seeds fell in good soil and grew up and produced a crop one hundred times as great.

In verses 18-23 Jesus explained to His disciples that the seed was the word of God, and those that fell beside the road were those who heard God's word but the devil came and took it from their hearts so they did "not believe and be saved " (Luke 8:12). The roadside soil represents the unsaved. He explained that the rocky soil represents those who hear and receive the word but have no firm root. They believe for a while, "but when affliction or persecution arises because of the word, immediately he falls away" (Matthew 13:21). These are believers who fall away due to afflictions or persecution. The thorny ground represents those who have heard the word of God and believe but they are choked with worries, riches, and pleasures (Luke 8:14), and bear no fruit in their lives. Finally, the good soil represents believers who hear the word and remain firm in their faith and bear much fruit, "some a hundredfold, some sixty, and some thirty" (Matthew 13:23).

As you read carefully these words of the Lord, it is clear that the roadside soil represents individuals who never received the Word of God and never believed. The rocky and thorny soils represent individuals who believed in the Word but were not fruitful. The trials and tribulations they experienced led them to fall away and be unfruitful. These are believers who were saved but were never set free, and their spiritual lives were choked out by trials, tribulations, and worries, which led them to pursue pleasures.

The Lord says that the seeds that fall in the good soil are those who hear the Word, hold it fast, and bear much fruit. These are believers who are not overcome by the trials and struggles of life and they produce much fruit. The fruit they demonstrate is probably both the "fruit of the Spirit" described by Paul in Galatians 5:22-23, and the fruit of souls led to the Lord. This is what the Lord desires for each believer, but our spiritual lives will be quenched and we will be unfruitful in our lives if we do not learn how to deal with trials, tribulations and worries as young believers. It is a critical and basic discipleship issue for each of us to learn to cast our cares upon Him and to replace our internal lies with His peace.

Jesus modeled good discipleship for us with His twelve disciples, with whom He lived for three years to equip them for their task of spreading the gospel and starting the Christian church. He taught them day by day, He demonstrated His power and divine nature through miracles, and He taught them how to deal with opposition and with their enemies. In John 14-17 Jesus spent time with His disciples in the last hours before His crucifixion, and He spoke about the coming of the "Comforter" who would comfort, strengthen, and guide them. He also taught them to pray, to love one another, to prepare for persecution, and to love their enemies. All of these issues are a critical part of discipleship, to equip new believers to know how to endure hardships and to be fruitful.

In John 14:27, Jesus taught them that they can have peace. He said, "Peace I leave with you; My peace I give to you; not as the world gives do I give to you. Let not your heart be troubled, nor let it be fearful." Then in John 15:11 he said, "These things I have spoken to you, that My joy may be in you, and that your joy may be made full." He was preparing His disciples for the persecution and trials they would endure by teaching them how they can have joy and peace, in spite of difficult circumstances. He also taught them the importance of prayer and abiding in Him and in the Holy Spirit so they can have peace and joy. Acts 9:31 says, "the church throughout all Judea and Galilee and Samaria enjoyed peace, being built up; and going on in the fear of the Lord and in the comfort of the Holy Spirit, it continued to increase."

The early church enjoyed peace because they knew how to enjoy the "comfort of the Holy Spirit." Believers today are no different; we must learn how to experience the "comfort of the Holy Spirit" also. Those who do not learn how to cast their cares upon the Lord and to receive comfort and truth from the Holy Spirit will be overwhelmed with life and will be unfruitful in their lives. Believers who learn how to enjoy the "comfort of the Holy Spirit" will enjoy peace and joy and be bold in witnessing for the Lord. They will produce much fruit in their lives, some a hundred-fold, some sixty, and some thirty.

Making the Pledge

The most important step that you can take to begin a new life free of emotional bondage is to make the pledge to "not let the sun go down on your anger." Releasing some anger will help you, but it will quickly re-accumulate if you do not make the pledge to release it every day. Those who make this pledge in this ministry are provided a wrist-band to wear as a reminder of their pledge, and as a witness to others of their pledge.

Apart from salvation this may be the most important commitment you will ever make. It will enable you to have a good marriage, experience joy and peace in your life, and hear from the Lord when you need comfort. Those who harbor anger in their heart "grieve the Holy Spirit" (Ephesians 4:29-31) and "give the devil an opportunity" (Ephesians 4:27) in countless ways. Your life cannot be productive and fruitful if you harbor anger and resentment in your heart.

If you are ready to make this pledge, do not do it flippantly, because it will not work. Realize that you must immediately identify all unresolved anger from your past and systematically and thoroughly release it all to the Lord. Then commit yourself to releasing all anger and resentment you are holding toward people in your current life, and release it immediately, committing yourself to doing this every evening before the day is done.

If you do not do this, you will be unfruitful; if you do it you can be fruitful and enjoy "love, joy, and peace" in your life, as you continue with the other pledges you will learn about in this book. As you learn to make these commitments and to "pray without ceasing" (1 Thessalonians 5:17) the "peace of God, which surpasses all comprehension, shall guard your hearts and your minds in Christ Jesus" (Philippians 4:7). What an awesome promise and an awesome goal to pursue in your life. "May the Lord of peace Himself continually grant you peace in every circumstance (2 Thessalonians 3:16).

SECTION B:

Giving God Your Feelings

7

OVERCOMING GRIEF: "BLESSED ARE THOSE WHO MOURN"

When I first learned this prayer ministry at a conference, it was taught with a strong emphasis on belief-based emotions like shame, fear, helplessness, and hopelessness. The fact-based emotions, like grief, anger, sadness, and disappointment were given little attention. They were treated as peripheral issues that were insignificant, and in the eight-hour seminar that I initially attended, only fifteen minutes were devoted to their discussion.

Shortly after my initial exposure to this prayer ministry I was asked by my pastor to talk with a young man in the church who had lost a close relative. I reviewed my notes from the conference to remind myself of how to help people dealing with grief and I was very confused. The notebook presented seven steps for dealing with grief and I could not remember them so I visited with the young man, with much anxiety about how to help him. As he shared with me his feelings about his loss, the best I could do was tell him to pray about his feelings and give them to the Lord. I know I wasn't very helpful.

After that frustrating start I reviewed the videos of the conference repeatedly and it was still very confusing. I simply could not remember seven steps to use in addressing feelings of grief.

Eventually, I concluded that there were only two essential steps: 1) Be completely honest about what you miss about the deceased person, and, 2) Pray and ask the Lord to take your grief and carry it for you. I determined that I would use these two steps the next time I encountered a person struggling with grief. However, I still focused mainly on belief-based emotions as I had been taught, and steered away from grief, anger, sadness, and disappointment.

Rick's Story

My wife and I moved to Tennessee and I began working for a group home for boys, where young men were sent who were getting in trouble with the legal authorities due to fighting, drug usage, skipping school, and running away. Shortly after I began to work at this group home a young man came to the facility. The staff were informed in advance that this young man, named "Rick", had lost his best friend three weeks earlier. I reviewed my notes on grief and the two simple steps for dealing with grief in preparation for his arrival. When he arrived at the group home I met with him to assess his emotional state and to try to help him.

I asked "Rick" what had happened to his best friend. He told me that his best friend was his cousin, and he had gone to his drug dealer to get some more marijuana. The drug dealer was strung out on some drugs and was delusional, and thought the cousin had come to rob him. He shot and killed "Rick's" cousin just a few minutes after he had been with him. "Rick" was very traumatized by this sudden, tragic loss of his best friend. I asked him how he was doing and he said, "Not very well. I think about him all the time, and it hurts so bad it feels like there is a knot in my chest." I asked him if he could get rid of his emotional pain would he like to do so. He said, "Yes, I would do anything to get rid of this." I said, "Well, I can show you how to do that."

I shared with "Rick" that after twenty-five years of failure in helping people with grief, I had learned a simple way to help people overcome it. I told him that there were two simple steps: first, he had to be completely honest about his grief and make a list of what he missed about his cousin, and second, he needed to pray and ask the Lord to take his grief and carry it for him. I asked him if he would be willing to try that. He said, "Well, I'm not a religious person, but I believe in God and prayer. I'm willing to try anything."

I asked him what he missed most about his cousin. He said, "I miss hanging out with him, I miss talking with him, I miss his sense of humor, and I miss hunting and fishing with him." I asked him what else he missed about his cousin and as he continued talking I wrote down everything he said. In a short while I had an entire page full of things he missed about his cousin. I said to him, "That's a good list and that's what it means to be honest about your grief. Now, the second step is to say a prayer and ask the Lord to take your grief and carry it for you. Would you let me lead you in a prayer and just repeat after me and tell the Lord what you miss about your cousin?" He said he would, so I began leading him in a prayer.

I went through his entire list as I led him in this prayer and told the Lord everything that he missed about his cousin. Then I led him to pray, "Lord, I miss all these things about my cousin, but I am tired of carrying this grief, so right now I choose to give it to you, and I ask you to take it and carry it for me. I pray this in Jesus' name. Amen."

When we finished praying I asked Richard to think about his cousin and tell me how he felt. He sat there for a short while thinking, then he said, "You know, I felt like a load was lifted from me while we were praying. I feel a lot better."

"Good," I said. "Now, think about all these things you just told me that you missed about your cousin and try to stir up those feelings again." He sat there thinking for a minute, then looked at me and said, "I don't feel anything. It's gone." "Good," I said, again. "Let's see how that works for you." I released him to go to his dorm.

The next morning I saw him outdoors mowing grass and I approached him, and he turned off his lawn mower. I asked him how he was doing. He said, "You know what? I slept for the first time in three weeks. And that knot that I had in my chest yesterday is gone. I don't feel it anymore."

"That's great!" I said. "Now, have you been thinking about your cousin this morning as you have been mowing grass?" "Yes," he said. "But I have only been thinking about the good times we had," he said with a smile.

I checked on him each week when I had my counseling session with him, and those strong feelings of sadness and grief never came back or occurred again for the next five months while he remained at this group home. He was able to think about his cousin and talk about him without any grief or sadness.

I believed that prayer would work, but I had never tried to use the two simple steps that I had developed from the original seven-step process I had learned. And this was the first time in my twenty-five years of practice as a professional counselor that I had ever seen anyone get rid of their grief.

This young man was not even a Christian at the time, although he believed in God and was receptive to prayer. Eventually, he received Jesus as his Savior and was saved, largely because his experience convinced him that God was real and God cared for him.

The Steps and Tests for Genuine Healing

There were just two simple steps that I used to help Rick experience healing of his grief:

> **Step One:** Be completely honest about your feelings of loss by making a detailed list of what you miss about the lost person.
>
> **Step Two:** Tell the Lord what you miss about the person, and ask Him to take your grief from you and carry it for you.

These two steps are so simple and easy to remember that anyone can remember them. The gospel is very simple, but is usually shared using some version of the "Four Spiritual Laws" which has four steps to remember, and every believer should be able to share this with others. But these two steps for finding emotional healing of grief are even simpler. I couldn't remember the seven steps that I was taught, but I had no difficulty remembering these two steps.

There were a number of significant outcomes from this counseling session with Rick. First, there was an immediate termination of his emotional pain when thinking about his cousin. This happened immediately after we prayed, so there was no question that it occurred as a result of the prayer. Second, he was unable to stir up the pain when he thought about his cousin and tried to stir it up. I have consistently found this to be the case when clients have thoroughly identified and released their grief. Third, he was able to sleep well after releasing his grief, so there was physical confirmation that it had been released. Fourth, he had long-term relief and resolution. It did not come back during the five months that I had contact with Richard.

Richard had 100% release from his grief and that is the goal of emotional healing prayer, 100% relief. He did not just feel "better" or "improved" but he felt no more grief or sadness after the prayer session. The best test of healing is when the individual can think about and talk about the deceased person and not feel any deep sadness or emotional pain. There is no need for a paper and pencil measure of the person's grief when there is no more grief at all. Researchers design written instruments to measure grief, but none of them asks the person to talk about the deceased person and try to stir it up to try to feel the grief again. That is simply unheard of and beyond any psychological instrument. There is no healing of grief like this using standard psychological approaches.

A Miracle from God

I was amazed at the power of God in setting this young man free from his grief, and I believed that I had just seen a miracle take place. Some people would hesitate to call this a miracle, especially if they had never tried to help people overcome feelings of grief. But I had tried for twenty-five years and had never seen this happen before, and I knew that it was very difficult to help people overcome feelings of grief.

Later, I did some research to find out what the grief counseling researchers were saying about grief counseling outcomes. I discovered a document written in 2003 by twenty-three of the top researchers in the field of grief counseling (Genevro, Marshall, & Miller, 2003). The article was entitled, "Report on Bereavement and Grief Research," and the researchers unanimously came to the following conclusion:

> For participants experiencing uncomplicated bereavement [normal grief], there was essentially no measurable positive effect on any variable and nearly one in two clients suffered as a result of treatment.

What this statement means, in simple terms, is that after approximately forty years of research into finding effective ways to help the bereaved, there was no evidence that anything done by grief counselors actually helped reduce the feelings of grief experienced by individuals, or decreased the amount of time it took for the grieving to recover from their loss. This statement also says that about half of those who participated in grief counseling even felt worse after their participation. This shocking conclusion stirred up some researchers in the field to challenge these findings, but others began to classify grief counseling as a technique that may actually do harm to clients.

In 2005 a "break-through" treatment approach was reported on the effectiveness of a new technique called "Complicated Grief Therapy." This new therapy focused on helping individuals with "complicated grief" and involved sixteen weeks of therapy involving repeated recall of painful memories each day for sixteen weeks.

One fourth of the participants dropped out of the study due to its painfulness and length, but about half of the remaining 75% reported feeling "much better" after 16 weeks of treatment, for a total of 37% of the original study participants (Shear, Frank, Houck & Reynolds, 2005). In contrast, with this prayer ministry I see most clients with complicated and normal grief being released completely from their pain after a single session.

In 2009 the results of another study were reported in a scientific journal. This study was conducted by two of the top researchers in the field of grief counseling, Robert Neimeyer and Joseph Currier, who conducted a meta-analysis of 61 outcome studies, making it the most comprehensive summary of research to that date. Their conclusion was, "Consistent with the majority of smaller-scale reviews, our test of overall effectiveness failed to yield an overly encouraging picture of grief therapies" (Neimeyer & Currier, 2009, p. 365).

These studies affirmed my belief that this prayer process was, indeed, a miracle. Each time I witness one of these miracles it excites me and makes me more amazed at the power of God. This is the way it was in the early New Testament church after the day of Pentecost. Acts 2:43 says, "Everyone kept feeling a sense of awe; and many wonders and signs were taking place through the apostles." They were witnessing physical miracles frequently, as well as radical transformations in the lives of believers who lost their fears and boldly began proclaiming Jesus in public. The apostle Paul was radically transformed after his conversion, and quit persecuting Christians and began speaking boldly about Jesus as the Messiah.

Although we do not witness as many physical miracles in the Church today as the New Testament Church did, we can witness emotional and spiritual miracles today as people are set free from emotional bondage through prayer. The reason why we can reliably witness these emotional miracles is because the Lord promised that we can have joy and peace as we go to Him in prayer and learn to cast all our cares upon Him (1 Peter 5:7) and allow the Holy Spirit to comfort us "in all our afflictions" (2 Cor. 1:4). We are told that the "fruit of the Spirit" is "love, joy, peace, patience" (Galatians 5:22), meaning that it is the Spirit that supernaturally gives us His peace as we learn to pray effectively about our emotions. Jesus even invited us, "Come unto Me, all who are weary and heavy-laden, and I will give you rest" (Matthew 11:28), so peace and rest are promised to those who will turn to Him for it. It is a promise, so as we step out in faith and give Him our burdens and listen to the Holy Spirit He replaces our emotional pain with His peace.

One of the reasons why the Church is so weak and declining today is that there is very little evidence in the lives of believers of God's supernatural power in their lives. Many people have gone to church for decades and continue to struggle with disabling emotions in their lives. When their children observe this, they become disillusioned and turn away from the Church and from the Lord. This ministry may help people to see that the Lord is powerful, and make churches relevant to their emotional needs so that they turn back to Him.

Grief is Normal

Individuals who suffer a loss typically experience feelings of deep sadness, intense longings, sleep difficulties, moodiness, depression, and may feel like they are going crazy. However, these are normal reactions to a significant loss, and grief is not considered a psychological disorder. But grief can lead to depression, behavior problems, substance abuse, marital problems, and a host of other difficulties. Such feelings will typically last up to twelve months, but when they last more than twelve months, the mental health profession considers it to be abnormal and calls it "Persistent Complex Bereavement Disorder" (DSM-5, APA, 2013, p. 789).

The psychiatric world changes their definitions frequently and periodically issues a new set of standards and definitions about what is normal and abnormal. But the Bible makes it clear that grieving is normal and can last for a long time. Abraham was the father of the nation of Israel and is described as a man of great faith that we should emulate (Heb. 11:8-12) but he grieved deeply over the loss of his wife who died at age 127, and the Scriptures tell us that "Abraham went in to mourn for Sarah and to weep for her" (Genesis 23:2). When Jacob died his son, Joseph, and "the Egyptians wept for him seventy days" (Genesis 50:3). And the Egyptians and Pharaoh were so devastated and heart-broken when all the firstborn sons in Egypt were struck dead during the ten plagues that Pharaoh finally allowed the Israelites to leave the country (Exodus 12:30-31). Many such biblical examples demonstrate that grief is normal.

But the greatest proof that grief is normal is the example of Jesus. In the shortest verse in the Bible we are told that "Jesus wept" (John 11:35). This short verse is one of the most profound scriptures because it shows us that Jesus, the Son of God, experienced sadness and grief when he saw how deeply saddened Mary and Martha were at the death of their brother Lazarus. Some people question this and believe that Jesus wept because of the unbelief of the people, but the immediate context gives no hint of this, and those who were witnesses of this event said, "See how he loved him" (John 11:36).

Jesus also apparently felt grief when John the Baptist died, because the scriptures say that when He heard that John had been executed He went off to a "secluded place by Himself" to pray (Matthew 14:13). He wanted to be alone for a while and apparently felt some sadness or grief over the news about John. The first and most obvious interpretation of these passages is that Jesus actually experienced feelings of grief and sadness at times. This plain and simple interpretation is consistent with other scriptures such as Hebrews 5:7 that says, "He offered up both prayers and supplications with loud crying and tears." The Lord Jesus experienced human emotions and demonstrated that they are normal.

Not only does this demonstrate that grief is normal, but it also demonstrates that grief is a fact-based emotion and not based upon distorted thinking or misinterpretations. Many secular therapists believe that all negative emotions are based upon distorted thinking, but Jesus was the Son of God and had no distorted thinking, yet He felt sadness and grief at times. If we assume that grieving people need help in identifying and eliminating their distorted thinking, we will only offend them and will be of no help to them. When we understand that grief is a normal, fact-based emotion, we can empathize with the bereaved and then teach them how to give their grief to the Lord.

The Impact of Grief

Grief can be deeply painful and can have a profound impact upon us. When King David's son died, he wept inconsolably and could not be comforted. In 2 Samuel 19:4 we read that, "The king covered his face and cried out with a loud voice, 'O my son Absalom, O Absalom, my son, my son!'" He was so distraught over the loss of his son that the commander of his army, Joab, had to confront him and urge him to go speak to the people who had fought for him and saved his life. He was overcome with grief at the loss of his son Absalom who had tried to kill him and take over his kingdom.

Grief is not a mental disorder but can lead to depression, substance abuse, violence, gambling, and marital and relationship problems that lead individuals to go to mental health professionals for help. In a study known as the "Virginia Twin Study" it was found that 87% of all depression results from some type of loss (Kendler, Myers & Zisook, 2008). A pastor was referred to me who had severe depression. The depression was triggered by the loss of his wife who committed suicide while he was preaching one Sunday morning, and he had a son who had previously committed suicide, also. He had tried numerous medications that did not help and was then hospitalized and given electroconvulsive shock treatments. When he was released from the hospital I began to see him for therapy, and his depression was still present although his memories were impaired. After several weeks of praying about his grief, anger, sadness, and shame his depression was completely resolved and he discontinued therapy.

When I first began using this prayer-based approach I worked for several group homes for boys and conducted a thorough social history on each of the boys that I counseled. I was surprised to discover that about 70% of them had significant losses prior to their onset of behavioral problems. Several years later I worked at an inpatient treatment unit for male substance abusers and for six months I interviewed each client who entered the program. I conducted a thorough social history on each of them to identify what types of childhood traumas each of them had experienced, and I found that more of them experienced significant losses prior to the onset of their substance abuse than any other traumatic events. Sixty-nine percent of them indicated that they had a significant loss prior to their abuse of alcohol or drugs.

A woman was referred to me by a friend who had known her a long time. This woman had had a drinking problem for twenty-five years, since her husband had left her for another woman. When I met her, she acknowledged that she began drinking after her divorce, and she had gone to AA for years and had completed an inpatient treatment program, but she continued to struggle with her drinking. I asked her if she would like to get rid of her grief and she said she would. I shared with her that she could get rid of her grief by making a list of everything that she missed about her ex-husband and asking God to take it from her. We made up a list of the things she missed about her former husband, and then she prayed and asked the Lord to take her grief and carry it for her. Immediately she said that she felt better.

When I saw this woman the following week I asked her how she felt and she said that she no longer missed him or longed for him, but now she felt angry toward him. She identified the reasons for her anger and prayed again and asked the Lord to take her anger from her. Her anger left her immediately, and she said that she felt peaceful and calm. The following week she saw her ex-husband and felt completely calm. She had no more anger or grief over him, and she has remained sober since that day. Most alcoholics have multiple sources of anger and grief, but her divorce was the primary source of her grief and anger. Once she resolved her feelings about her divorce and her ex-husband she no longer had an urge to drink.

Grief also has a significant impact on marriage. A young couple came for marital counseling and were on the verge of divorce after being married for only six months. They indicated that they got along well initially in their marriage, but two months after they were married the husband's mother died. He became depressed and sad and began fighting with his wife. I asked him if he would like to get rid of his grief over the loss of his mother and he said he would, so we made a list of the things he missed about her and gave his grief to the Lord to carry. Once his grief was gone he became happy again, and they began to get along well again.

Finally, grief can lead to rage and violence. I met a young man in jail who was very angry and was always starting fights and trying to bully other inmates and control them. I tried to speak with him but he was uninterested in spiritual matters. When he was released from jail he applied for admission into a substance abuse treatment program, but he was rejected because of his violent history. They referred him to an outpatient counselor, and one day he came walking into my office. He was shocked to see me again, but we began talking and I asked him when he began using drugs. He told me that he had started at age 14. I asked him if anything significant happened just prior to his using drugs, and he told me that his grandmother who had raised him had died. He became so angry that he started using drugs and fighting.

I asked him if he would like to get rid of his grief and he said he would, so I explained to him that he could get rid of it by identifying what he missed about his grandmother and then asking the Lord to take it from him. We made a list of the things he missed about her and I led him in a prayer and he gave his grief to the Lord. When we finished praying I asked him how he felt, and he said that he felt calm and peaceful. His grief and anger were both gone, and he was amazed. He was not saved at the time but later got saved and began praying on his own about ten more significant losses he had had as a teenager. He was able to resolve these feelings and he began serving the Lord and ministering to others once he was released.

Types of Losses

There are many different types of losses, and they all feel bad and can lead to depression. Relationship losses lead to a lot of depression and anger and can sometimes be more painful than a death. Young people who lose a romantic relationship frequently become very depressed and suicidal due to their breakup. Adults who go through a divorce can struggle deeply with the loss of their marriage and their dream of raising children in an intact home and growing old together.

Loss of health can be very traumatic, when it is sudden or debilitating. Young adults who experience significant health problems and lose their ability to work can feel worthless and depressed about this loss. Even gradual loss of health through aging can be difficult and lead to some depression. Older adults often become increasingly upset as they lose their ability to remember things, their ability to hear well, and their ability to do things they enjoyed.

Loss of a job is difficult and can lead to feelings of worthlessness, fear, and depression. I saw a woman who came for counseling due to the sudden onset of some serious depression. She could not identify any losses or events that caused her depression, but as we talked she stated that her depression began about a year before, which was when she partially retired from her full-time work with her husband in their family business. As we talked she came to realize that she missed working all day with her husband, talking, joking, and feeling useful. We made a list of everything she missed about her job, and asked the Lord to take her grief and carry it for her. Her grief lifted immediately, and she said she felt good and was no longer depressed.

Even the loss of a dream can lead to significant depression. Any type of loss feels bad and can lead to sadness and depression, whether it is a death, a relationship, a friendship, a job, a home, or a dream. And each of these losses can be resolved through the same simple process of identifying the specific components of the loss and then praying and giving them to the Lord.

Connected Emotions

After praying with someone about their grief it is always useful to ask them how they feel, now, while thinking about the deceased person. If they feel peaceful and calm and do not have any grief, then they have probably released all of their grief. If they say they still miss the person, it means that they missed something, so you should help them make another list and repeat the process, until it is all gone and they have 100% peace.

If the person still feels bad but appears to have released all of their grief, then there may be other, connected emotions that need to be addressed. A woman in a Sunday school class asked for prayer about a close friend who died a few weeks earlier while she was holding her hand. It was very traumatic for her because her friend was unsure of her salvation and was very fearful as she passed away. I asked her what the main emotion was that she felt while thinking about her friend; she said it was grief. We made a list of things she missed about her and prayed and gave it to God. After the prayer, I asked her how she felt, and she burst into tears and said she still felt badly.

I asked her what thoughts were connected to her feelings. She said, "Her children are going to grow up without their mother, she will not see her children grow up, and her husband has to raise them by himself." These were feelings of sadness, because they were not things that she missed about her friend, but they were genuinely sad things about the death of her friend. We made a list of the reasons for her sadness and prayed, asking God to take her sadness from her, just as we had done for her grief. After praying, this woman suddenly quit crying and said she felt peaceful and calm. Her sadness was gone.

A week later this woman told us that she had been able to think about her friend who died without feeling sadness or grief. She felt like her grief and sadness had been completely resolved. About a year later she told us that she had participated in a memorial gathering in memory of her deceased friend. She was asked to sing a song at the gathering and she did so without any overwhelming feelings of sadness and without breaking down in the middle of the song. She was completely released from her grief and sadness over this loss.

If there are still some negative feelings after resolving grief, there may be some connected emotions. The three most common emotions are sadness, anger, and shame. Sometimes individuals are angry at God for letting the person die, at the deceased for things he did or said, or at care-takers who could have prevented the person from dying. When feelings of anger are identified they should be addressed, as described in Chapters Two through Six, by identifying the reasons for their anger and then giving them to God.

In addition, there may be feelings of shame connected to their grief, and these should be addressed. Shame can be identified by the thoughts expressed by the individual such as, "It's my fault, I should have done more, I should have been a better friend, I should have known something was wrong." When these types of thoughts exist the person needs prayer about their feelings of shame, but this will be addressed in detail in Chapter Twelve.

Complicated Grief

Grief can be extremely painful and can even be disabling. However, it is regarded as normal by mental health professionals unless there are intense and persistent longings for the deceased person that occur daily for over twelve months. Once the intense grief continues beyond this arbitrary point it is considered to be "complicated grief" or "prolonged grief."

Research suggests that about 15% of those who experience a loss will develop Complicated Grief/Prolonged Grief with intense and persistent longings for the deceased, intrusive and troubling thoughts regarding the death, a sense of inner emptiness and hopelessness about the future, trouble accepting the reality of the loss, and daily struggles for more than twelve months.

An elderly man was referred to me by a physician because he was so distraught about the death of his 36-year-old daughter six months earlier that he could not talk with the doctor about his medical issues. When he came to my office, he could barely talk, but I asked him what had happened to his daughter. He told me that she had died from an illness, and he told me how painful it had been for him to watch her die. I shared with him that he could get rid of his grief by making a list of what he missed about her, and then giving it to God in prayer. He told me that he was a Sunday School leader in his church, and he was willing to do this.

We made a list of everything that he missed about his daughter, and then I led him in a prayer and asked the Lord to take his sorrow and grief from him and carry it for him. Afterwards, he quit crying, and he said he felt peaceful and calm. We talked about his daughter and about how the Lord does not want us to be stuck in our grief, then he returned to the doctor to have his medical appointment. He had no more difficulty with his grief once he gave it to the Lord.

The Woman who Hated Christmas

Once a week I used to travel to work at a mental health clinic in another town. I occasionally passed a woman in the hallways who I did not know, but we always smiled and greeted each other. Several weeks after Thanksgiving I passed her in the hallway and I asked her how her Thanksgiving went. She said, "It was great! We had our whole family over and had a good meal and a good time." Then she said, "But I'm not looking forward to Christmas."

"Really?" I replied. "Why don't you like Christmas?" She told me that she disliked Christmas because her mother had died on Christmas 16 years earlier and it made her sad when she thought about her mother on Christmas. I gave her my condolences and told her, "I know it can take a long time to get over a loss, but I have learned a way to get over it. If you're interested, let me know and I will share it with you sometime." She said that she would like to do that.

The following week when I went to that clinic she saw me and told me that she was ready to talk about her mother. We met in my office and she explained that she was born and raised in Thailand and she was very close to her mother who was very loving and was her best friend. They talked all the time, about everything, before this woman moved to the United States. It was very difficult for her to leave her mother behind but she stayed in touch as well as she could.

One day she received a phone call from her sister who informed her that their mother was very sick and she needed to come see her. She immediately bought a plane ticket, but before she could board the plane she received another phone call from her sister who told her that her mother had already died. This woman never got to see her mother before she died, and she never got any closure with her.

I shared with her how she could resolve and release her grief by making a list of everything that she missed about her mother and then praying and giving it to the Lord. I listened and wrote out a list as she talked about her mother and told me everything that she missed about her. She said that she was a Christian, so I led her in a prayer and read off each item on her grief list. She repeated each item after me, in her native language, and cried through the entire prayer. When we reached the last item on her list she asked the Lord to take her grief and carry it for her.

I asked her how she felt now. She wiped her tears and smiled and said she felt peaceful and calm. She exclaimed, "I can't believe that I have been carrying this for 16 years and no one has told me how to do this!" She was very excited and thanked me for praying with her, then she gave me a hug.

The following week when I returned to this clinic, I went to her office to check on her. I knocked at her door and she opened it. She was wearing a Santa hat! I asked her how she felt and she just smiled and pointed up at the hat. She told me that she went out and bought a Christmas tree and that she was looking forward to Christmas.

A month after Christmas I checked on her again. She told me that she had had a wonderful Christmas and had no sadness or grief or depression. She said she was happy to have her life back and her husband said he was happy to have his wife back. Then she said, "this week my husband went outside to take down our Christmas lights and I told him, 'No, leave them up!'" She was still wanting to celebrate Christmas a month later, as if she was making up for the 16 years she had gone without celebrating Christmas.

The Biblical Basis

When I began counseling 40 years ago I wanted to learn how to help people by using biblical principles. The first model that I used as my counseling theory was a "Biblical counseling" approach. I believed that "All Scripture is inspired by God and profitable for teaching, for reproof, for correction, for training in righteousness; so that the man of God may be adequate, equipped for every good work," as the apostle Paul stated in 2 Timothy 3:16-17. I enjoyed it and found it helpful in giving people biblical advice, but I was unable to help with clinical issues that I encountered in my practice. I still believed the Bible to be inspired and the source of all truth, but I came to believe that there was something missing from my understanding of the Bible, so I continued examining other approaches.

I first began using behavior therapy, then various forms of cognitive therapy, then family therapy, and spiritual warfare counseling. But after twenty-five years I was still unable to help people with grief, until I learned that they needed to be honest, make a thorough list of the reasons for their grief, then give them to the Lord and let Him carry them for them. As I carefully reexamined the scriptures, I concluded that there were many verses that supported these principles for resolving grief.

Paul told the church at Thessalonica to "not grieve as the rest who have no hope" (1 Thessalonians 4:13), so he was implying that we can find relief from our grief through the Lord, but he did not explain how to do this. Other scriptures also suggested that believers can overcome their grief, such as Isaiah 53:4 which says, "Surely He has borne our grief and carried our sorrows," and Matthew 5:4 where Jesus said, "Blessed are those who mourn, for they shall be comforted." He promised to send us a "Comforter" (John 14:16, KJV) to help us and comfort us in all our afflictions (2 Corinthians 1:4). Then in 1 Peter 5:7 Peter exhorts us be in the practice of, "Casting all your care upon Him, for He careth for you" (KJV).

Set Free Prayer Ministry teaches people to cast their emotional burdens of grief upon the Lord, by specifically identifying the things they miss about a person, and letting the Lord carry them. The same principle is taught in the Old Testament where we are told in Psalm 55:22 to "Cast your burdens upon the Lord, and He will sustain you." Many people know this principle and are quick to advise others to give their burdens to the Lord, but they do not tell them how to do that.

Assessing the Presence of Grief

When you encounter people who have had a loss, you may wonder how to approach them to offer this ministry. I have found that it is very simple to approach people about their grief because I know that I can help them, and where many people would be afraid to venture, I feel very comfortable asking them questions such as "How are you handling your loss?" or "How often you think about the person you lost?" Many people respond by saying they have good days and bad days, but when they respond like this I like to follow-up by asking, "How do you feel when you think about them?" This is more direct and personal than most people get with them and if they do not want to talk about their feelings they can always say so. I find that most people are willing to talk about their feelings and glad to talk to someone who cares. Many times I will also ask them, "Does it affect your sleep?" These questions are all helpful in identifying whether the person is struggling with feelings of grief over their loss.

Once they respond to these questions I like to ask the following key question: "If you could get rid of your painful sadness and grief while keeping the memories, would you want to?" Most people will say that they would, although a few will say that they would not. If they say they would like to get rid of it, I tell them that I can show them how to do that. I may explain that I have helped many people find freedom from painful grief and that I have found relief from my own losses, then ask them if they would like to learn how.

The Church and Grief

Churches do not teach this simple prayer principle, and every church is full of grieving people who need to learn how to be set free. Many of them are depressed and taking "antidepressants" due to their unresolved grief over some losses in their lives, including many pastors and church leaders. Most people would be amazed to learn how many of their Christian friends are depressed and struggling with grief.

Every believer needs to learn how to be set free from grief and help others be set free from grief, because it will impair their lives and prevent them from being fruitful. This is a basic discipleship matter that should be taught to each new believer so that they can live a victorious life of joy and peace. Grief leads to depression, anger at God, anger at others, and marital problems. Unresolved grief makes people unhappy and very vulnerable to sinful activities that make them feel better but keep them in bondage.

As the Church steps up to share this truth with others and sees people being set free, God will be glorified, and Christians will become more excited about the Lord and openly share their excitement about the Lord. The more that these miracles are seen, the more we will see radical change in the lives of people, and the more people will be attracted to the Church.

"It's Too Simple"

One of the most common objections raised to this ministry is that "It's too simple." I spoke to a group of pastors one time at a luncheon and shared briefly how the Lord is able to set people free from anger and grief through prayer. They were very attentive and many of them thanked me afterwards. But several weeks later I spoke with the pastor who organized the luncheon and asked him if he received any feedback from the pastors. He said, "Yes, several of them told me they thought it was too simple."

I have heard this numerous times while speaking to churches and Christian organizations. My response, when I have a chance to respond, is that I tried the hard way for 25 years and that did not work, so I am glad to find a simple way that works. I also like to point out that God does things in a very simple way, usually. He didn't make salvation complicated or hard; He simply says "whoever believes in Him should not perish, but have eternal life" (John 3:16).

This principle is illustrated for us in the Bible, in 2 Kings 5:10-14, when Naaman, the captain of the army of a neighboring country, was struck with leprosy. An Israelite slave girl spoke up and told her master about the prophet Elisha and said that the prophet could heal Naaman of his leprosy. So Naaman took a caravan and traveled to the land of Israel to see Elisha. When he arrived at Elisha's house, Elisha sent one of his servants to the door and told him, "Go and wash in the Jordan seven times, and your flesh will be restored to you and you will be clean." But Naaman was furious that Elisha did not come out to meet him or come outside and pray for him or wave his hands over him, so he left enraged.

Then one of his servants came near and spoke to him and said, "My father, had the prophet told you to do some great thing, would you not have done it? How much more then, when he says to you, 'Wash, and be clean?'" So he went down and dipped himself seven times in the Jordan, according to the word of the man of God; and his flesh was restored like the flesh of a little child, and he was clean."

Naaman expected it to be complicated and he felt foolish to do something so simple as dipping himself in the Jordan river seven times. But when he obeyed the prophet and did as he instructed he found that God did, indeed, heal him. God likes to do things in a simple way so that we know that He is the source of the change, and so that our "faith should not rest on the wisdom of man, but on the power of God" (1 Corinthians 2:5).

The same is true in dealing with human emotions. We can either trust in the wisdom of men, who have found nothing that heals grief after approximately forty years of research, or we can be honest with God, tell Him specifically what we miss about our loved ones who have passed away, and ask Him to take it and carry it for us.

The Lord has given us the powerful privilege of prayer and the comfort of the Holy Spirit, so that we will see that Jesus does indeed heal the brokenhearted and He wants to set the emotional captives free from their emotional bondage (Isaiah 61:1). The doctors and wisest researchers today will tell you that nothing heals grief, but Jesus will heal your broken heart and set you free from grief if you simply give it to Him, as He has instructed us to do.

In spite of what the world tells us about how complicated emotional healing is, the fact is that Jesus can do for you what no counselor, psychologist, psychiatrist, doctor, or medication can do for you. He can heal your emotions, including your grief, and give you His peace because He is the "Wonderful Counselor, Mighty God, Eternal Father, Prince of Peace" (Isaiah 9:6).

8

IDENTIFYING AND RESOLVING OTHER LOSSES

Many people experience losses but do not recognize them as losses, and others admit they have had losses but deny that they continue to bother them or affect them. They often say that it does not bother them as long as they don't think about them, but that is nothing more than suppression of feelings.

I was working in an inpatient treatment program for substance abusers and was evaluating a man who was about to complete the program. I asked him if he had any significant losses prior to the onset of his drinking and he said he did not. Then he said, "Well, I did lose my uncle and that was difficult." I asked him if there were any other losses and he thought for a moment and said, "Yeah, there was my grandfather who died when I was 8 years old, and then I lost my grandmother a few years later." He continued to think about his losses and ended up identifying ten significant losses that he had experienced prior to his drinking, and yet he initially stated that he had no significant losses. He left the program without having resolved any of these losses, so the chances were slim that he would be able to stay sober for long, even though he said he felt very good.

Grief is a common experience that everyone experiences eventually, so most people seem to disregard it as insignificant, and yet it can have a profound impact on them. The last chapter briefly discussed the various types of losses and how they can impact us. In this chapter we will discuss some specific examples of losses and illustrate how to resolve them using the principle outlined previously.

RELATIONSHIP LOSSES

Usually, when someone speaks about grief, they are talking about the loss of an individual through death. However, there are other forms of loss that are just as painful, such as divorce, romantic breakups, and loss of health. There are support groups for grief, but most of them deal only with losses by death, and they don't do a very good job of helping with that because there are no other techniques that work. These groups allow people to talk about their losses and ventilate, and the sharing with others who have had similar experiences provides them some social support and opportunity to talk about their grief without irritating others. But it does not, ultimately, speed up the grieving process or decrease the emotional pain of the loss. Set Free Prayer Ministry quickly resolves grief, and works for people with all types of losses. We will consider several forms of relationship losses, including divorces, romantic breakups, children leaving home, loss of custody of children, and obsessive relationships.

Set Free from Divorce

A woman came to me for help after her husband of forty-three years divorced her. He just told her one day that he was tired of being married, and he divorced her when he retired. She was devastated! During the divorce proceedings she discovered that he did not even include her name in his retirement, and two weeks after the divorce she learned that he was living with another woman whom he had been seeing for several years.

She was understandably very angry at him because of his lying and deceit, and she was very hurt that he would leave her after so many years for another woman, and not even care about what happened to her. He even told her that God told him to leave her and now he was spending time with their grandchildren, and his new companion. She made a list of eight reasons for her anger and gave it to the Lord. I prayed and asked the Lord what He wanted her to know and she said, "He is with me all the time, He wants me to be happy, and I'm going to be alright." She missed many things about her husband, and made a list of eight major things she missed about him, then prayed and asked the Lord to take her grief from her. Afterwards she said she felt calm, and felt no anger, and she truly felt that he was the one who lost out from the divorce. She said that her heart felt lighter.

The next time I saw her she said that she felt good but she felt lonely and hurt. I asked her what made her feel hurt and she said that she felt unloved, unwanted, rejected and felt she didn't measure up. Since these are belief-based feelings, which we will discuss in a later chapter, I asked her when she first felt such feelings, and after some thought she said she felt this way growing up, because she had a handicapped sister whom her mother spent a lot of time with. I asked permission to pray for her then prayed, "Lord, what do You want her to know about this belief that she was unloved and unwanted by her mother?" Tears came to her eyes and she said, "Momma loved me so much; she had to depend upon me. She was always there for me." After receiving these insights from the Lord, she said she understood why her mother spent more time with her sister, and she said she felt calm and peaceful. Her feelings of hurt from her husband were gone, as well.

She also had some sadness regarding her ex-husband, and prayed about her sadness and gave it all to the Lord, and got rid of it. We then talked about her feelings of loneliness, and I prayed and asked the Lord what He wanted her to know about her belief that she was all alone. The thoughts that came to her were, "I'm not alone; I have family. I know that I am not alone." She became tearful so I asked her why. She said, "I had a vision of smiles." She told me that she visualized the smiling faces of her grandchildren who love her so much. When we finished she felt peaceful and calm in spite of the loss of her forty-three year marriage, and she left smiling.

People who go through divorces often feel anger, grief, sadness, guilt, and hurt, like this woman did. What an amazing thing it is to see people like this release all these feelings, and the Lord simply takes them and replaces them with His peace. Imagine what would happen if every divorced person found this kind of healing from the Lord and turned back to Him, and the Church got the reputation as a place where people can find healing and restoration like this! What a revolution would occur if all believers did this and simply released their anger and grief! May God bring about a revival and use His Body to bring healing to the brokenhearted.

Romantic Breakups

Romantic breakups are just like divorces; they can lead to a lot of anguish, sadness, hurt, and depression. Many people, young or old, get depressed and have suicidal thoughts after a romantic breakup. A young man was referred to me who was eighteen years old and was cutting on himself superficially. He had lost his mother four years earlier, and then his girlfriend broke up with him a few weeks earlier and he became very depressed. I shared with him how he could be set free through this prayer process and asked him if he would be comfortable trying this he said, "I don't know; I'm not even sure that I believe in God. I think of myself as a scientific person." I said to him, "Well, if you're a scientific person would you be willing to do an experiment and try it?" He said that he would be willing to try.

This young man said he was angry at his grandfather, and he asked me to help him make up a list of the reasons for his anger so I did. When we finished the list I asked him if he wanted me to lead him in a prayer, but he said he wanted to do it on his own. The following week when he returned I asked him how it worked. He said, "Well, I don't want to spend time with him but I don't feel angry toward him anymore." I asked him if he wanted to get rid of any more feelings, and he said he needed to get rid of his feelings toward his ex-girlfriend. So, we talked about his former girlfriend and made a list of the reasons for his anger toward her, and made another list of the things he missed about her. I volunteered to lead him in a prayer but he, again, wanted to do it by himself.

When he returned the following week I asked him how it went. He said, "I had to do it three times but it worked. I don't feel angry at her anymore and I haven't even thought about her since then." I asked him what he thought about that and he said, "Well, it has strengthened my faith as a Christian."

"I thought you said you were an atheist," I responded. "When did you become a Christian?" "Oh, somewhere between last Saturday and this Saturday," he replied. I asked him how that happened and he said, "When I saw how God answered my prayer so quickly, that was the physical evidence I needed to know that God was real, and I just prayed and asked Him to forgive me for my sins and be my Savior."

This young man was not even a Christian, but became a believer in Jesus after he saw how powerful prayer was and he saw how good God is. Jesus said in Matthew 5:45 "He causes His sun to rise on the evil and the good, and sends rain on the righteous and the unrighteous." In John 5 Jesus healed a lame man and then slipped away in the crowd (John 5:13) so the man didn't even know who he was. When the Jews asked him who healed him on the Sabbath, he did not know. Jesus healed this man, not because of his faith, but because of his compassion for this man. Later He saw him in the temple and told him, "Behold, you have become well; do not sin anymore, so that nothing worse may befall you" (John 5:14). Jesus can heal people today of their grief and anger, and then use this to draw them to Him for salvation.

Another young man told me that he was depressed and thought he might be bipolar and said, "I have rage." He lived with his parents who he said treated him well, and he got along well with his three siblings, but he said he had been throwing fits at home for the last year. I asked him if anything had happened to make him depressed and he told me that he had a friend who accidentally shot herself but he felt he had resolved this and was no longer upset about it. I asked if he had any other losses and he said he had not, but when I asked if he had any relationship problems he told me that his girlfriend broke up with him the previous year. He was upset with her because he liked her a lot, but he was always working and she enjoyed sports and wanted to spend more time with him. Then one day she told him that they should quit seeing each other. This made him very upset, and he missed her and thought about her a lot, but then she got another boyfriend two days later.

I shared with this young man how he could get rid of his anger and grief by being honest about the reasons for his anger and his grief, and then asking God to take these feelings from him. He said he was willing to try this, so he set up an appointment to come back the following week. When he returned, we first made a list of the reasons for his grief. He said he missed her sweetness, her phone calls, her love and affection, their conversations, and spending time together watching movies. He also missed the fun times they had together, eating out together, fishing, mudding, and going to her house every day. He identified ten things he missed about her, then prayed and asked the Lord to take his grief from him and carry it for him. I asked him how he felt about her after praying and he said he felt nothing; he just felt neutral. His feelings of grief and missing her were gone but he admitted that he still felt some irritation and anger.

He told me that she got a boyfriend two days after breaking up with him, but then she continued to call him which just upset him. He felt that she was "two-timing" him. In addition to this anger he added that he missed seeing her, hearing her voice, and hearing her say sweet things to him. We made a list of seven things that irritated him about her and that he missed about her, then he prayed and gave all these resentments and losses to the Lord. Afterwards, he said he felt calm and was no longer angry or sad about her.

When I saw him a week later he said he was doing well. He felt a lot better, he was no longer angry or having outbursts, and he didn't feel depressed. He said that he had not even thought about his former girlfriend in the last week, and when she tried to call him one time he just ignored it, but did not feel angry. He felt that he could talk to her and be friendly, but he no longer had any deep longings to be with her. His friends noticed that he was being more active and having fun with them, and they asked him how he got over his feelings for her. He told them that he had prayed with his counselor about his anger and grief and given it to the Lord. They were amazed, and he was pleased to share with them how he was set free from his anger and broken heart through prayer.

This young man thought he was "bipolar" but found that he was just angry and brokenhearted, and the Lord took away this anger and grief and replaced it with His peace. Thankfully he did not start taking any dangerous medications for a bipolar disorder. When someone is brokenhearted over a relationship they usually have feelings of grief, anger, and shame, but the Lord "heals the brokenhearted" when they give their feelings to him and ask Him to take them and carry them for Him.

Set Free from Obsessive Relationship

I met a Christian woman who was carrying strong feelings of guilt and shame about her emotional involvement with a married man. Both she and the gentleman were strong Christians who were knowledgeable about the Bible and were leaders in their churches. She consulted with him about some family issues and he gave her some helpful advice and showed her some kindness. They had been friends for years, and their friendship had always been wholesome and appropriate until one day she started to fall and he caught her. While holding her he kissed her and she felt an overpowering rush of feelings for him. She had never been involved with another man or desired it, but the affection he gave her was overwhelming because she was so lonely. Her husband never showed her any affection, held her hand or said kind things to her. He was an honest and good Christian man, but was emotionally cold to her and never even hugged her, leaving her to cry herself to sleep many nights out of loneliness. This other man was also lonely and felt unfulfilled in his marriage because his wife was emotionally cold to him and had never experienced physical pleasure in their marriage.

After the kiss, they began to meet together secretly to talk and go for walks. Although they never engaged in any sexual contact, she enjoyed sitting with him with his arm around her while saying sweet things to her. They both knew it was wrong, but the excitement they felt was so strong that it was overpowering their consciences. She said that she had always been lonely and had never experienced such strong feelings or felt this kind of "young love." It made her feel wonderfully loved for the first time in her life! For months they continued this secret relationship, and both of them felt guilty and shameful. Her prayer life was destroyed and she couldn't lead Bible studies anymore because she felt like such a hypocrite.

Both of them were so overwhelmed with guilt that they decided they had to end the relationship. Although she knew it was the right thing to do, she could not quit thinking about him and longing to see him and talk with him. She prayed desperately and begged the Lord to take him out of her mind and life, but every time she tried to pray he jumped into her mind. I explained to this woman that she was experiencing grief over the loss of her relationship and that she needed to do two things: First, she needed to be honest and identify what she missed about this gentleman, and then second, she needed to tell the Lord what she missed about him and ask the Lord to take her grief and sadness from her. She said she missed his love and affection, his kind words, his hugs and comfort, him sitting with his arm around her, and their intimate conversations each week. She also missed his occasional phone calls, hearing him call her sweet names, and the feeling of "fire" of being in love for the first time.

After making this list she sincerely prayed for the Lord to take her grief and sadness away. I asked her how she felt and she said she still longed to see him, and wanted him out of her heart but not out of her life. She still felt some longing for him so I knew we had missed something. She said she also missed spending time with him, going for walks with him at night, and going to his house when his wife was gone. We prayed again and she gave these additional losses to the Lord. When I asked her how she felt, she said she now felt sad because she met him so late in life and this intimate relationship happened innocently without any intention. She also was sad to know that there was no future with him and they had to ignore each other when around mutual friends, to avoid any suspicion of their feelings for one another. She said she wanted to be able to witness again and to have a clean heart.

We prayed about these feelings of sadness and gave them to the Lord, just as we would with any other loss, and then I asked the Lord what He wanted her to know. "Peace will come; I was disobedient so God wouldn't hear me but we have an advocate with the Father." These thoughts felt true to her because they were whispered to her by the Lord, but then she said, "You reap what you sow and you deserve to be miserable." I knew that this thought was not from the Lord so I prayed and asked the Lord if that was true, and asked what He wanted her to know about that thought. She then said, "God is a loving God; He forgives me. I know I'm forgiven; He doesn't want me to be miserable. He is a loving God. He wants me to rejoice and be glad. He loves me even though I failed." She told me that these thoughts felt true, and they were.

I asked her to think about her gentleman friend again and tell me how she felt. This time she said that she felt better and she felt some hope. Then she said, "The Lord has a plan for my life." Now she could think about her friend without the painful longing for him that she had felt before, and she said she felt "good, peaceful, and restful." The next day she told me with excitement that she was free! She still felt peaceful, and calm, and free of the deep longing she had had before and the constant, painful obsession with this man. She was no longer thinking about him or longing to see him again. She thanked me for my help and praised God for His goodness, love, and power. When I saw her several weeks later she reaffirmed that she was doing well and was free from her obsession with this man.

Relationships can be very addictive and powerful, even without sexual involvement, and can be very difficult to break. But Jesus heals the brokenhearted, including those who become emotionally trapped in an unholy relationship and are unable to break those bonds. He is able to heal our broken hearts, and to fill us with His love and joy and peace when we learn to be completely honest with him and give our burdens to Him in prayer. What a mighty God we have who is worthy of our praise!

Set Free From Custody Loss

I was invited to a Christian recovery meeting and asked to share about Set Free Prayer Ministry. I explained how the Lord had taught me how he can set people free from addictions as they release their feelings of grief, anger, and shame through prayer. The group was very attentive and when I asked for a volunteer, a man threw his hand up immediately and volunteered. He said that he would like some prayer about his divorce. He stated that he had been married fourteen years, and then three years previously his wife had divorced him and taken their three children with her, and he began using drugs heavily. He broke down and began sobbing in front of the group; he was obviously very emotionally torn about this divorce.

I asked the man what emotions he felt as he thought about his divorce, and he said that he felt guilt and grief. He felt very guilty and shameful for not visiting his children, because it was so painful for him to see them and not be able to live with them and raise them. He denied initially that he was angry and said that he had already forgiven his ex-wife, but as he talked it was apparent that he still had some anger. I suggested to him that we start with his anger, because anger prevents us from hearing from the Lord, and he agreed. I asked him what made him angry at his wife and he told me that she cheated on him, she lied about the other man and said that he was a homosexual, and then she left him for this other man. It also made him angry that she took their children from him, and coached them to lie to him about the other man, and then she took everything from him in the divorce.

I led him in a prayer and he told the Lord these six resentments he had, and he asked the Lord to take away his anger from him. Then I prayed and asked the Lord if there was anything that He wanted this man to know. "He wants me to forgive her; the babies need us to get along," he said. "He forgives me for overlooking them and not paying attention to them, and for using drugs. They miss me and love me," he said. His mood suddenly changed and he quit crying and began smiling as he talked. I asked him how he felt now as he thought about his divorce and he said, "I love her; she's a good mother to them." He said that he had no more anger.

The entire group was amazed at his dramatic change of mood and attitude. He felt no more anger or shame from his divorce, but he still felt sad and missed his children, so I asked him what he missed about them. He told me that he missed their smiles and laughter, watching them play, looking into their eyes and telling them that he loved them, being with them, and hearing their childish noises. He talked about the youngest child and her sweetness, and he said that he missed the love and affection of the kids, and them climbing in bed with him and his wife, and he missed just watching them grow up each day. We made a list of twelve things he missed about his children, then I led him in another prayer and he gave his grief and sadness to the Lord. I asked the Lord, again, what He wanted this man to know and he said, "He wants me to know they are okay and they miss me and love me. He wants me to do well." After this I asked him how he felt as he thought about his children and he said, "I love them. I feel peace. I feel great!"

This man who was so distraught over his divorce and the loss of his wife and children was transformed from brokenness and bitterness to peace and joy in just a few minutes. The Lord heard his cry and took his burden of anger and grief from him and replaced it with His perfect peace and joy! What a joy it is to see the Lord setting captives free!

OTHER TYPES OF LOSSES

Grief over Ending Affair

A woman came to me for help with feelings of depression and anger toward her husband. I shared with her how she could be set free through prayer and she was receptive, so I asked her if she would like to get rid of her anger toward her husband. She hesitated and then finally admitted that she was having an affair and did not want to release her anger toward her husband because she would then have to break off her affair. I appreciated her honesty and did not push her to release this anger yet, but I did talk with her about how she could be set free from all her negative feelings when she was ready. I saw her three weeks later and she told me that she was getting along "great" with her husband and said he was "an incredible man." He had realized how he had neglected her for a long time and began loving her and showering her with gratitude and affection until she finally repented of her affair and ended it.

She told me that she was no longer mad at him but now was mad at the other man, and she also had some grief and guilt regarding her affair. I asked her if she would like to get rid of these feelings, and she said that she wanted to get this man out of her head completely so that it would not interfere with her marriage any more. We began with her anger at this man who pursued her, pushed her to end her marriage, then left her hanging and never divorced his wife as he had promised. We made a list of seven resentments she had toward him, and she prayed and asked the Lord to take her anger from her and carry it for her. She immediately lost her anger and felt better.

I then asked her what she missed about this man, because it is difficult for individuals in affairs to end them due to the enjoyable times they had and lost. She honestly admitted that she missed this man's attention, his affection, his sense of humor, and the talks and pleasant times they spent together. We made a list of twelve things she missed about him, then gave this grief to the Lord and asked Him to take it from her. Her grief and longing for him stopped immediately, though she felt some more anger, but she also gave it to the Lord.

I asked the Lord if there was anything that He wanted her to know and she said, "I put this man above God. The loss of my close relationship with the Lord is far greater than the loss of this man." "So, how do you feel now?" I asked her. She said that she felt very shameful. She told me that she had already confessed her sin to the Lord but she still felt shameful and bad, so I prayed and asked the Lord what He wanted her to know about her belief that she is shameful and bad. I asked her if any thoughts came to her mind and she said, "I know God loves me and I'm His child." She said that made her feel good, so I asked her how she felt now as she thought about her affair and about the other man. She said that she had no more anger, grief for losing the man, or feelings of shame. She had no more negative feelings; the Lord had lifted all her negative feelings and she had no interest in, or feelings for the other man.

I asked her what she thought about this sudden change and she smiled a big smile and said, "It's awesome!" We have an awesome God who forgives us, loves us, and sets us free from all our emotional bondage when we give it to Him!

Unfortunately, affairs do occur among Christian couples and this often destroys the marriage, but healing can occur when the individuals give the Lord their feelings of anger, grief, and shame that need to be released. The devil loves to destroy marriages but the Lord loves to bring healing and to restore marriages to protect the family and bring glory to Himself. Affairs and divorces can be avoided when couples learn to give the Lord their anger and emotional burdens so that they have joy and peace.

Grief over Retirement

A woman came for counseling with her husband and said she had recently become very depressed. She had previously received a lot of emotional healing and was doing well when last seen, but became so depressed that her husband was fearful that she could harm herself. She and her husband were very close and they had no financial stressors, and their children were doing well but she said she had "no joy in life."

I asked her when she first remembered being depressed, and she stated that she became depressed after her mother died 11 years earlier, but she had prayed about this loss and received healing for her grief. Her husband said that she began to act depressed about a year or 18 months ago, so I asked if she had any losses around that time. Initially, she said she did not but I asked her when she quit working full-time with her husband on their home business, and she said it was about a year and a half ago. This was about the same time that she "retired" and spent more time at home.

This woman told me that she spends a lot of time alone during the day while her husband is working, and she thinks about her children and grandchildren. She also admitted that she feels bad about being a wife who stays home and does not work hard at cleaning the house or preparing meals. She felt that she "should be doing more" and that she was a "lazy, worthless person." I recognized these as feelings of shame and asked this woman when she first felt like a lazy, worthless person. She told me that her first husband came home one day when she was pregnant and had morning sickness, and found her lying on the couch and commented to her, contemptuously, about how she was lazy. I prayed and asked the Lord what He wanted her to know about that belief that she was lazy and that she should be doing more. She told me that the thought that came to her was, "I was not lazy or worthless," and "my husband, now, is okay with what I do." Her feelings of shame were immediately gone after that thought came to her.

We talked about her grief over the loss of her full-time work with her husband and she identified the things she missed. She missed staying busy, working with her husband, having fun together as they worked, feeling needed, talking with one another, joking around, having coffee together, and companionship. She then prayed and gave her grief to the Lord and asked Him to take it from her. Afterwards, I asked the Lord if there was anything that He wanted her to know, and she said, "It'll be okay. There are other things in life I can do. I'm not worthless or lazy."

I asked her how she felt after we prayed about these losses, and she said, "I feel pretty good. I'm not depressed. God is so wonderful!" The deep depression she had felt suddenly disappeared when she resolved her feelings of shame and her grief over the loss of her full-time work. Many people experience similar feelings when they retire, but the Lord can set them free from their depression so that they can live productive, happy lives.

Grief over Loss of Job

A man came to see me after losing his job, which he had held for twenty-seven years. He enjoyed his job and took great pride in doing it well, but the company ran into financial difficulties and closed its doors that year, leaving him without a job. This loss compounded other losses he had previously had in his life, and led him into a deeper state of depression. He had been taking psychiatric medications, but he was still deeply depressed until he began praying about his losses over the last four years. His depression decreased dramatically after several prayers but he was still depressed about his unemployment.

I asked him what he missed about his job and he told me how he missed being around his co-workers who were like a family to him. Of course he missed his paycheck, insurance, and benefits, but he had sufficient savings to last him a long time; it was the intangible benefits he enjoyed that he missed the most, such as the feeling of satisfaction at doing a good job, feeling needed, and enjoying his job. He got along well with his co-workers who never argued or got into personal conflicts. He missed the barbecues they had, the fish fries, and throwing horse shoes with them. We made a list of seventeen things he missed about his job, and then he said a simple prayer, telling God what he missed about it, and asking Him to carry his grief and sadness for him. When we were finished praying I asked the Lord what He wanted this man to know. He said, "He wants me to know everything is going to be okay. He is there for me; it's going to be okay."

I asked him how he felt now as he thought about his job. He said that he felt no more sadness or grief; he was confident that he would find another job. The following week he told me that his depression was completely gone; he had had a good week and was busy working on his house and doing various outdoor projects. He said that he was ready to get off his medications that were not helping his depression anyway. He said about the medicine, "It is no fix; it just numbs you." This man had been taking antidepressants for over eighteen years and it had never taken away his depression; he was still so sad and depressed that he cried all the time and was lying around doing nothing. But with a few prayers to release his grief he was set free completely from his depression. Apparently it wasn't a brain disorder or chemical imbalance; it resulted from his losses, and when the Lord set him free from his grief, he was free from his depression, also. He is now free, indeed.

Grief over Suicide of Husband

Suicides lead to grief, but they often lead to feelings of anger and shame, as well. When I deal with suicides I first try to help the individual identify the various feelings they have, and then take them one by one and pray about each emotion. Usually, I prefer to begin with anger because it can interfere with the person's healing of feelings of shame and guilt.

A Christian woman came to me whose husband had committed suicide several months earlier. They had been married twenty-three years, and he had some serious health problems and began verbally abusing her and acting strangely, so she moved out for several days. When she returned home she found his body in the back yard where he had shot himself. The carnage he left was shocking to her, and he left a suicide note in which he blamed her for his suicide.

When he died he left her with no money or source of income, so she had to borrow money to bury him, and then she had to quickly find a job to support herself. She said that she prayed and read her Bible every day, but in spite of that she was so full of sorrow that she "howled with grief." She asked her pastor to anoint her and pray for her healing, which he did, and that gave her some relief, but she was still full of a lot of emotional pain when she came to me.

I asked her what emotions she felt as she thought about her husband. She said that she felt anger, grief, shame, and some sadness. Since she was clearly a Christian woman I explained to her how she could get rid of her anger, grief, and sadness by doing two things: first, she needed to make a list of the reasons for her anger, and then she needed to pray and tell God why she was angry and ask Him to take it from her. She was willing to try this.

I asked her what made her angry. She told me that it made her angry that her husband killed himself, she had to see the carnage in her back yard, he left her no income, he blamed her for his suicide, and she had to borrow money to have him buried. She identified seven reasons for her anger, and then I led her in a prayer and she asked the Lord to take her anger from her and carry it for her. After giving her anger to the Lord she said that she felt "more mellow" and had no more anger toward her husband.

She said that she mostly felt grief, now, and just missed him. She talked about their twenty-three years together and said she missed the way he held her hand, the way he liked to scare her, his laughter and sense of humor, his love and affection, his companionship, and studying the Bible together. She also missed watching TV together with him, cooking for him, hearing his voice, feeling protected by him, and hearing him pray. She identified twenty things she missed about her husband, then she prayed and told the Lord all these things, and asked Him to take her grief from her.

I asked the Lord if there was anything that He wanted her to know. She said, "I'll see him again." She said that she felt better, but she felt it was her fault that he killed himself, so I prayed and asked the Lord for truth. The thought that came to her mind after my prayer was, "It's not true and he wouldn't want me to feel this way." I asked her how she felt now, and she said she felt no more anger, sadness, or guilt. She laughed and said, "I want to go home and put his pictures back up." She had taken them all down after he killed himself, due to her anger at him.

When I saw this woman the following week she told me that she had been doing very well and was feeling good. She did, indeed, put his pictures back up, and she had no anger toward her husband, and cried only "one tear" while remembering some good times they had together. She said she felt "relaxed and peaceful," and she had been sleeping well and eating better. She was thrilled to share her prayer experience with a friend of hers who was still grieving deeply after losing her husband one and a half years ago. She said she was excited to begin using this prayer ministry with her friends and her church.

Grief over Suicide of Brother

A Set Free ministry team went to Kansas to provide some training to group of youth workers. After the first hour in which I gave an overview of the ministry principles I asked for a volunteer who would like to resolve some feelings of grief. A young woman came forward for prayer. She said that her brother had committed suicide three years earlier, and she was the last one he called before taking his life. As she spoke the tears began to flow and the audience became silent and attentive. I explained that when there is a suicide the surviving friends and family members often have mixed feelings of grief, sadness, anger, and shame, and I asked what emotion she felt. She stated that she felt sadness and missed her brother.

I asked the young woman what she missed about him and she began tearfully talking about how she missed his presence, watching him play with her children and being a good uncle to them, hearing his jokes and laughter, witnessing his friendliness to people, and seeing his big, brown eyes. She also missed hanging out with him, talking with him, and mothering him since he was much younger than her. After completing the list of things she missed about him, I led her in a prayer and she told the Lord what she missed about her brother and asked Him to carry her pain for her. Then I asked the Lord if there was anything that He wanted her to know. She said, "It's okay." She said she felt "calm and blank."

She still looked a little tearful, so I asked if she felt some sadness, and she said that she did. She was sad because she was helpless to do anything to prevent his suicide, he was too young to die, her children lost their uncle, he wouldn't get to see her kids grow up, and she would never see him get married and have a family. We prayed about these feelings of sadness and she gave them to the Lord; then I asked the Lord again if there was anything that He wanted her to know. "There's nothing I could have done" was the response she received. She never stated that she felt any feelings of shame or guilt or thought that she should have been able to do something, but she apparently felt this way, and this thought removed that feeling. Then she said she felt "peace and calm."

I asked if there were any other negative feelings she had and she admitted that she felt some anger at her parents and brother because her father was not a good father to them, her mother did nothing when warned about her brother's mental state, and her other brother was such a poor model to this brother who died and did nothing to help him when asked for help. We prayed and she gave her anger to the Lord.

After this prayer she said that her anger was gone and now she felt complete peace and calm. Immediately after the session she and her husband drove to her brother's grave site, which she had been avoiding since his death. The Youth Minister asked her how her visit went and all that she said was, "God is amazing! Thank you!" The Lord had taken all her grief, sadness, anger, and shame and replaced it with His peace.

Suicides can be devastating to the family and friends of the deceased and lead to depression, anger, and substance abuse. The

Lord set this young woman free from her feelings of grief, sadness, shame and anger that resulted from her brother's suicide and now she can pray with her children and family to see them set free. God truly is amazing!

Grief over Loss of Pet

Grief can occur for any type of loss, including the loss of a pet. Many people will undoubtedly scoff at this notion and consider it trivial or childish, but it can seriously affect some individuals and must be addressed. I saw a woman who told me that she had been depressed since age 8 or 9 when she tried to kill herself but she was fearful that if she just talked about her past that she would break down emotionally and would not be able to stop crying. Rather than do my usual social-history on her to learn about her background, I talked with her about the two steps for resolving grief, and gave her an illustration of how it works. She was very receptive to prayer and told me that God had taken her desire for drugs from her, but she still struggled with a lot of depression. She told me that she had just lost her puppy a few months ago when he was run over by a car and this had been very traumatic for her, but she said that she felt she had gotten over this loss and resolved it.

I asked her for more details about what had happened to her dog and she told me that it was run over by a neighbor. As she talked about this she became very emotional, so it was obvious that she still had a lot of grief and sadness about the puppy. I asked her if she would like to get rid of this grief, if possible, and she said she would, so I explained that the first step to overcoming grief is to be completely honest about the loss and identify everything she misses about the puppy. She told me how she had taken care of this puppy since his birth and how special he was to her. She felt like she was the pup's momma; he came to her for comfort when he was in pain or when he was scared. Since she never got to be a mother to her own children it was especially meaningful to her to take care of this puppy. She told me how the puppy loved her, how he playfully nipped at her, ran around her, needed her, and missed her. We made a list of fifteen things she missed about her puppy and she expressed guilt and shame that she should have been watching him more closely to prevent him from being run over.

I explained the second step to overcoming grief; to say a simple prayer, telling the Lord what she missed about the puppy and asking the Lord to take the sadness from her. I led her in a prayer and with tears rolling down her cheeks she gave her grief to the Lord and asked Him to take it from her. I prayed and asked the Lord if there was anything that He wanted her to know; "It's okay," was all that came to her mind. I asked her how she felt now and she wiped away her tears and said, "I'm more at ease. God gave him to me for a reason; I couldn't have watched him all the time. He was happy." She said that she felt relieved and peaceful, and even her feelings of guilt and shame were gone.

This woman was peaceful and calm afterwards, even while thinking about her puppy being run over, and she saw how quickly the Lord was able to take her grief from her. We talked about her need to talk about her other losses and life traumas so that the Lord can take them from her as well. Having just experienced the Lord's deliverance from some grief, she said she was ready to meet for counseling again, and start getting healing for her other life traumas. She had other larger losses and traumas, but the loss of her pet allowed the Lord to show her the path to freedom. All losses can be painful, and even the loss of a pet, as trivial as it may seem, can be very painful and needs to be resolved, especially when it triggers off feelings of guilt and shame, as it did in this woman. But the Lord can set us free from all our grief and guilt when we learn to take them to Him in prayer.

Grief over Loss of Dream

Another type of loss that is easily overlooked is the loss of dreams. A middle-age man was arrested for possession of methamphetamines and shocked his family, who had no idea he used drugs. He admitted himself into a treatment program where I worked and I began to counsel him and explore the reasons for his addiction.

He said that he played baseball in high school and had the dream of becoming a major league baseball player until he permanently injured his throwing arm. This made him very depressed until he and some friends developed a band and sought to become successful musicians. After years of playing in bars and not making progress toward his dream, he began to use drugs and eventually gave up his band and began working a regular blue-collar job. He got married and had two sons, but continued using meth until the day he was finally caught with illegal drugs in his possession.

I prayed with him about the loss of his dream of becoming a major league baseball player. He identified the things he missed about his dream and prayed and asked the Lord to take his grief from him. He felt so much better that the next time we talked he told me that he had come to realize that his wife was a wonderful woman and he had two awesome children. He gave up his unhealthy relationship with a drug-using girlfriend and returned to his family after he released his grief over the loss of his vocational dream.

Resolving All our Griefs

"Surely our griefs He Himself bore, and our sorrows He carried," the prophet Isaiah wrote about Jesus in Isaiah 53:4. The Lord Jesus Himself said, "Blessed are those who mourn, for they shall be comforted" (Matthew 5:4). The Lord promises that He will carry all our grief, but we must be willing to give it to Him and ask Him to carry it for us. In order to do that we must first recognize when we are experiencing grief, and be honest about it, then ask Him to take it and carry it for us.

Grief comes in many forms, as we have been illustrating in this chapter. Even as we grow older and begin gradually losing our abilities, we begin to experience grief, and when we have medical problems and lose our health, we also may experience grief. We must recognize these feelings so that we can give them to the Lord. The good news is that He is able and willing to carry all our griefs and sorrows.

Grief is a major source of emotional pain that leads to many types of emotional problems, and we must know how to release it. The secular world has no way of resolving grief, so they try to numb it through medications that not only numb the grief but numb all our feelings, the good ones and the bad ones. A woman told me that she had taken medications for fifteen years and it took away her "happy" feelings. In addition, those medications have many adverse side effects including depression, aggression, violence, and suicide. Thankfully, the Lord has given us a simple way to be set free through honesty and prayer because He does, indeed, want to carry our grief for us and give us His peace.

The most important point in this chapter is that we must recognize when we are experiencing grief, in any form, so that we can overcome it by listing those things that we miss, and then give our grief to the Lord. It doesn't matter if the loss is a death or a relationship loss, or some other form of loss, the Lord is able to take it from us and replace it with peace. With any form of grief or loss we will receive emotional relief from the Lord when we do this and cast "all [our] cares upon Him" (1 Peter 5:7), knowing that He cares for us.

9

OVERCOMING SADNESS AND MAKING THE SECOND PLEDGE: "DO NOT GRIEVE AS THE REST"

A woman bravely sat at the bedside of a close friend as she lay dying in a hospital from cancer. Her friend was unsure of her salvation, and although this woman tried to help her find assurance, she was terrified about going to hell as she passed away. This left the woman very traumatized. The dying woman left behind her husband and two young children, to be raised by their father. Several months later this woman came to a class that I did on grief and she shared her experience with the class. I offered to pray with her about her grief over this loss.

I asked this woman what she missed most about her friend who had died, and she burst out in tears and shared her grief. We made a list of these items, then I led her in a prayer, and she gave them to the Lord. After the prayer I asked her how she felt, and she burst into tears again, saying she still felt badly. I asked her what thoughts were connected to her feelings, and she said, "The thought that her children are going to have to grow up without their mother; the thought that her husband is going to have to raise the children all alone; and the thought that she will not get to see her children grow up."

These thoughts were all symptomatic of feelings of sadness, so I suggested that we pray again and give her sadness to the Lord. We bowed our heads and I led her in another prayer, telling the Lord what made her feel sad, then giving her sadness to Him and asking Him to carry her sadness for her. When we finished praying I asked her, "How do you feel now?"

This time she said, "I feel a lot better. The strong emotions I felt before are gone and I feel calm now." A week later she confirmed that she still felt peaceful and calm, and then a year later she told me that she had participated in a memorial service for the deceased woman and she was totally calm. She was even able to sing a song at the service and felt perfectly calm. The Lord removed both her grief and her sadness, so that reminders of the trauma did not cause her any more difficulties.

Steps for Overcoming Sadness

The steps for overcoming sadness are the same as the two steps for overcoming anger and grief.

> **Step One**: Be completely honest about the sadness by making a list of the reasons for the sadness.
>
> **Step Two**: Pray and tell God why you feel sad, then ask Him to take your sadness and carry it for you.

All fact-based emotions can be released in the same manner, with these same two steps. The main four fact-based emotions are grief, anger, sadness, and disappointment. It is important to learn to discern your emotions, and the emotions of others, so that you can take yourself or others through these two steps and find freedom and release from these feelings.

The Difference between Grief and Sadness

Many people have difficulty differentiating between grief and sadness, but it is important to know the difference when dealing with your own feelings or when helping others with theirs. Grief is the feeling of missing someone or something, and having a longing to be with them again or see them again. However, the story just told illustrates that after people release their feelings of grief, they may still feel deep sadness about the loss.

The most common reasons for feelings of sadness over the loss of a friend or loved one are that they died too young, they suffered too much, their death could have been prevented, their life was wasted, their family members suffered from their loss, or they died in a violent or frightening manner. Sadness is a fact-based, or reality-based, emotion just like grief and anger. When a young person dies for any reason it is truly sad. When someone dies due to a tragic medical mistake, it is very sad and can also lead to feelings of anger at the medical practitioner.

In the previous chapter I shared about a woman whose husband shot himself in the head and she had to clean up the carnage and blood and body tissues. This was a profoundly sad experience that left her with post-traumatic stress disorder (PTSD) and led her to have flashbacks about the experience. Such violent deaths leave individuals deeply and profoundly sad. Whatever, the reasons for the sadness, however, the sadness can be released by using the same two steps identified above for resolving grief.

Sadness over the Death of an Unsaved Person

Many times when I pray for someone who is grieving over the loss of a close friend or family member I pray and ask the Lord what He wants them to know. Frequently, but not always, the individual says, "I know that I will see them again." When I hear this response I usually believe that the Lord has spoken this into their mind and I don't question it; I just leave it to the Lord to bring other words of comfort to them if this is not the truth. Even individuals who lived like an unbeliever, abusing drugs or alcohol, and going to jail repeatedly, are sometimes born again, but never were set free from their emotional bondage.

Sometimes it is clear that the deceased person was not a believer, and the Lord's response is very different to the grieving person. He can comfort the person with other thoughts or insights. One night a man came to a Set Free meeting and listened quietly throughout the meeting as various members shared stories of being set free. I asked this man and his partner if they had any questions for us and he said that his best friend had recently died, and he was an atheist.

I asked him if he would like to pray about the loss of his friend and he said that he would, so we began making a list of the things he enjoyed about his friend and missed about him. We then prayed and he asked the Lord to take his grief from him and carry it. I asked him how he felt and he said, "I feel better but I still feel some sadness." He said that he felt sad because his friend was an atheist, and this man feared that he was in hell. We made a list of several other reasons for his sadness, then I led him in a prayer and he gave his sadness to the Lord and asked Him to take it from him.

After this prayer I asked the Lord what He wanted this man to know. He said, "It was his choice. That's not for you to worry about." I asked him how he felt now as he thought about his friend possibly being in hell and he said that he was calm and was no longer weighed down with sadness. He felt peace in his heart, because the Lord brought words of truth and comfort that took away his sadness and gave him peace.

It truly is sad to think about some of our friends and loved ones going to hell when they die, but the Lord does not want us to be weighed down with sadness while we are enjoying eternity with Him. He will take it from us so that we can enjoy His perfect joy and peace for all eternity.

Sadness over Seeing a Parent Cry

I prayed with a woman several times regarding her abusive father, and she had already released her anger toward him, but on the 17th anniversary of his death she felt a lot of sadness for him. She said she felt that she needed to tell him she was sorry, too, and never got to do so; he died before she could tell him. Her father was an extremely abusive alcoholic who singled her out for abuse because she tried to protect her mother from him, and ending up being abused herself.

In his last years he developed Alzheimer's and began losing his mind, getting lost, and seeing people who didn't exist. She quit her job to help take care of him, and she prayed for her daddy that he would get right with God before he died (such amazing love for an abusive father). One day he had a clear mind, and as she lovingly ministered to his needs he began crying and told her that he was sorry for all the mean things he did to her. As he cried he told her that he wanted to ask God for forgiveness and she told him that he needed to talk to the Lord, so he cried out to the Lord and begged for God's forgiveness.

She had never seen her daddy cry or pray and was deeply touched by his tearful confession, but after his prayer he immediately went into a coma and then died two days later; she never got to tell him that she was sorry for holding such resentment and anger toward him. This woman was carrying deep sorrow and sadness because she had never had a close relationship with her daddy, she felt sad that he was so disabled by Alzheimer's, and she was sad that she never got to tell him that she was sorry. We made a list of thirteen reasons for her sadness, then she prayed and gave her sadness to the Lord.

After her prayer, I prayed for her and asked the Lord what He wanted her to know. She said that her daddy was at peace, God answered her prayer, he knew that his time had come, and God put her there that morning so she could see that he turned to Him before he passed away into eternity. I asked her how she felt and she said, "Glad. He got right with God. I never saw daddy cry or pray but he cried out and asked God to forgive him. If God forgave him then I knew that I needed to, also." I asked her how she felt and she said she felt "relieved and calm."

Isn't God wonderful to answer this woman's prayers for her abusive father? He gave her dad clarity of mind just before he died so that he had one last chance to get right with Him; and she said that she knows her daddy forgives her and they will one day enjoy the closeness that they never had in this life. And He also took her sadness from her and replaced it with His awesome, awesome peace! How can we be quiet about a God like that? Let's share with everyone what a God we have!

Sadness over the Father she never Met

I saw a woman who had a history of alcohol abuse and depression and had experienced a great deal of trauma, abuse, and loss in her lifetime. She had been sober for three months but was fighting the urge to drink after a recent relationship break-up. In order to begin the ministry process I asked her what was the most traumatic loss she had experienced. To my surprise she told me that the death of her father prior to her birth was the greatest loss for her and created the greatest emotional pain for her. It is not uncommon for individuals to grow up without a parent like this, but it is surprising to have someone say it was their greatest loss.

I asked this woman how she felt when she thought about her biological father whom she had never met, and she told me she felt lonely and sad. She said she felt sad because she never got to know him, he was murdered and his murderer was never convicted, and she wished that she knew the truth about his murderer. She also said that she was sad because she believes her life would have been very different if she had grown up with him, because she always felt alone and had to fight for herself and had no one to defend her or protect her. I had never seen someone who was so emotional about the loss of someone prior to their birth but I led her in a prayer to tell the Lord why she was so sad about the loss of her father and to give her sadness to Him. After we prayed I asked her how she felt and she said, "Sad but good." She said she felt better but still felt some sadness because she did not know the truth about the death of her father. I led her in another prayer saying, "Lord, it makes me sad that I do not know how my father died. But Lord, I am tired of carrying this sadness, so right now I choose to give it to you and ask You to carry it for me. In Jesus' name I pray."

I then prayed and asked the Lord to carry her sadness for her and replace it with His peace. I also asked the Lord if there was anything that He wanted her to know. Immediately, she opened her eyes and said, "Let it go; put it in His hands." I asked her how she felt and she said she felt "blank." Then she said, "I felt a lot of pressure lifted off. My heart is not heavy like it was! I feel peace. That's awesome!" I asked her if there was any more sadness or any negative feelings and she said, "It's all good; it's all clear. No more sadness; I feel happy! I'm smiling. There's no more sadness in my heart anymore! That's awesome! Wow! I've prayed and prayed for relief and never got any till now. My heart is fuzzy with joy! It's like God just took the heaviness off my head and just pulled it off! I can feel the Holy Spirit all over me; look at the hair on my arm; it's standing up! Wow!"

Sadness at the Thought of Dying

A woman came to me who had received much healing previously but who had become very fearful of dying and leaving her three children motherless. She was healthy and had no known medical problems, but knew a thirteen-year-old girl who had died a few weeks earlier, and this triggered off obsessive thoughts about dying and not being able to see her children grow up. I asked her if she knew anyone else who had died early like this and she said that she had lost five close relatives as a child and that she felt some sadness about their losses. When she was fifteen years old her father died, also, so she grew up without him and she felt sad that her children never met him. We prayed about her sadness over these losses and she gave them to the Lord and got rid of them.

Since she was feeling fearful I had difficulty deciding whether I needed to pray about her fear or sadness. She said that she first felt this fear when her kids were removed from her one time by DHS when she was in a hospital. She panicked when she didn't know where they were taken, and she was very fearful that something terrible was going to happen to them and they would be scarred and emotionally damaged. I prayed about this fear that something terrible was going to happen and she had no thoughts come to her mind, but she did feel more calm. She then said, "It would be terrible if I died young when my kids are so young. I don't want to miss out on seeing them grow up and see them have families of their own." It made her very sad to think about dying young and leaving her children behind, so I decided to pray about her sadness. I led her in a prayer saying, "Lord, it makes me sad to think about dying young and leaving my kids without a mother. It makes me sad to think about missing out on seeing them grow up and raising their own families. But Lord, I'm tired of feeling this sadness, so right now I choose to give it to You, and I ask You to take my sadness from me."

After we finished praying this time, she said that she felt "Okay." She said she that she felt no more sadness or fear, and she felt calm. I thought that her primary emotion was fear, but when she did not respond to praying about her fear, then I looked for another emotion and prayed about her sadness. It worked; she left smiling and feeling peaceful and calm.

Sometimes I run into cases that puzzle me, but as I continue praying the Lord shows me what to do and sets people free. I'm still learning! We have to discern whether we are dealing with a belief-based emotion like fear, or a fact-based emotion like sadness. When we have bad feelings, we either need to give them to the Lord to carry, or we need to pray for truth. All of our negative feelings can be resolved using these two prayer principles, and when we pray for the right emotion and in the right way, He sets people free!

Sadness over Anticipatory Grief

Sometimes people become anxious and depressed about the prospect of losing someone they love. I prayed with a woman about some grief and anger she had, and she felt a lot better, but when I asked her how she would rate her depression on a 10-point scale she rated it a four. When I asked her what she was depressed about, she told me that she missed her mother who had come for a visit, and she was worried about her health. Her mother had multiple health problems, lost 20 pounds in about a month, and she wasn't eating right, and it upset her to think about losing her mother even though she was still alive. She was worried about losing her and it made her sad to contemplate her death. This is "anticipatory grief" and it is a form of sadness; the person becomes sad when they think about what life will be like without the loved one.

I asked this woman what made her sad in thinking about losing her mother and what she would miss the most about her. She said that her mother was her best friend and she would miss being able to call her, talk to her, hear her laughter, go visit her, feel her love and affection, and spend time with her. It also made her sad that her mother lived alone and she could die and no one would know it. We made a list of twelve things that made her sad, then she prayed and asked God to take her sadness from her and carry it for her. I asked the Lord what He wanted her to know and she said, "He's going to be there with me when the day comes. Everything will be okay. I need to learn to give my burdens to Him."

After this I asked her how she felt when she thought about losing her mother. She said, "I'm ok with it. I'm not sad anymore." I asked her what emotion she felt and she said, "Peace." When I asked her to rate her depression again on a 10-point scale she rated it a one. She was smiling as she left and she said, "I look forward to these visits." It's wonderful to see how the Lord wants to take all of our burdens and carry them for us.

Don't settle for being better; give all your negative emotions to the Lord until your depression or other negative feelings are completely gone, and you experience the peace of God that passes all comprehension. The Lord wants you to have 100% peace.

Sadness over a Suicide

An elderly lady came to me and told me that her doctor said that she was depressed. Two days earlier she had a relative who had shot herself in the head, and she was still upset about it. The doctor told her that she needed to be on an antidepressant even though she had just lost her relative the day before and she was experiencing normal feelings of grief. I asked her if she was depressed and she said that she was just sad. She felt much better that day because her friends at church had prayed for her. She was concerned about whether this woman had gone to heaven or not, but she was not very close to her so she really didn't miss her.

I asked this woman about her sadness and she rated it as a two on a 10-point scale. We talked about her sadness and she said that it was sad to see this woman pass away because she was such a wonderful musician, pianist, and song writer. It was also sad to her because the lady was so unhappy and distraught about something that she shot herself. She identified four reasons for her sadness, and I led her in a prayer to give her sadness to the Lord and ask Him to take it from her. After praying I asked her how she felt. She said, "I feel peaceful; it just lifted from me." She said she felt no more sadness.

We talked about the possible adverse side effects of the antidepressant that she had taken for one day and she said, "I didn't want to take those pills anyway. I'm just going to throw them away." Many doctors are quick to place people on pills and to tell their patients that they are depressed, as if they can know their feelings better than the patients. This doctor didn't even inform this woman of the many possible adverse side effects of her medications, and the pharmacy did not even provide her a list of the potential side effects which can include depression, suicidality, insomnia, agitation and hallucinations. Furthermore, diagnosing someone as depressed who has no history of depression and who just lost a loved one is completely inappropriate.

Dr. Peter Breggin, in his book *Medication Madness*, documents approximately fifty cases of individuals who innocently took mind-altering medications and became suicidal or violent as a result. This does not happen to everyone who takes these medications but it happens far more often than most doctors admit. Christians need to realize that their emotional struggles are not the result of a broken brain or a chemical imbalance, and they cannot be solved with a pill, but Jesus is able to heal their broken heart. This woman left feeling peaceful, with a smile on her face and her sadness released, because she took her sadness to the Lord and He lifted it from her.

Sadness over a Tragedy

A man told me that he does not participate in Halloween activities because his daughter died on Halloween and he gets sad on Halloween and does not like to think about it. I shared with him the story of the woman I prayed with who became depressed around Christmas because her mother died on Christmas day sixteen years earlier. I told him how she made a list of what she missed about her mother, then prayed through the list and gave it to the Lord, and was immediately set free and began celebrating Christmas again.

After I shared this story he looked directly at me and told me that he also had had a bad experience on Christmas day. He served in the military during the Iraq war in the 1990s, and on Christmas day about 200 Iraqis surrendered to him and several dozen American soldiers. He stated that they were shaking them down one-by-one when a young woman pulled out a pistol and shot his sergeant. He immediately opened fire on the woman and shot and killed her. As he described this scene he became tearful. I asked him how he felt and he said he wasn't sure, but he did not feel guilty. He knew that he was just doing his job. He said that it was upsetting because this happened on Christmas day, the day of "peace on earth," and it was senseless and unnecessary, because if they had followed procedures taught to them they would have made all the POWs lie down on the ground as they inspected them one-by-one. It also bothered him that this young woman died, and this was his first killing as a soldier.

I wrote out a list of six reasons for his sadness and he agreed to give his sadness to the Lord in prayer. He repeated after me as I led him in a prayer and asked the Lord to take his sadness and carry it for him. Afterwards, I asked the Lord if there was anything that He wanted this man to know. All he heard was, "It's not true." I asked him what that meant and he didn't know, so I asked the Lord to clarify what that meant. The man immediately said, "It's not my fault." I asked him if that felt true and he said that it did. Then I asked him how he felt and he said, "A lot better." I instructed him to think about the incident and visualize it and tell me how he felt now as he remembered it. He took a few seconds to think about it and said. "It's gone; it's okay now." He could remember the incident now without feeling any sadness or tearfulness. He just needed the Lord to speak to him and bring truth to him to set him free.

What this man experienced was posttraumatic stress disorder, and this was just one incident that he had experienced. PTSD victims often have feelings of sadness and shame, like this man did, as well as feelings of anger and fear, and each of these feelings needs to be discussed and resolved through prayer. This prayer process does work to resolve PTSD if the victim is willing to work through each of his emotions and give them to the Lord in prayer.

Recognizing our Sadness and Giving it to the Lord

Life is full of trials, struggles, and disappointments. Even strong Christians encounter discouragements and have experiences that make them sad. Many Christian parents experience sadness when their children make poor decisions or abandon their faith. They become sad when they witness their children going through difficulties, divorces, medical problems, and many other unpleasant experiences. They would like to take those burdens from them and see them full of joy and peace.

As these feelings surface, we have to be aware of our feelings and recognize when we are feeling sad. Once we do identify feelings of sadness we can then take steps to release them by praying, telling the Lord why we are sad, and asking Him to take our sadness from us. I have occasions when I hear about something that is disappointing or upsetting to me, and my initial response is to just dismiss it from my mind. I sometimes wake up at about 2:00 am from a disturbing dream, and find myself thinking about the events of the day that upset me. When this happens I have learned to simply talk to the Lord, tell Him what makes me sad, and then give my sadness to Him. Once I have done this I generally feel very calm and am able to go back to sleep immediately.

Each of us needs to learn to recognize our negative feelings and release them quickly, so that we can enjoy God's peace and joy. If we do not do this, those feelings can build up and make us depressed or angry and rob us of our peace. May the Lord help each person reading this chapter to develop a close relationship with Him, and to learn to walk with Him and talk with Him moment by moment, casting all your cares upon Him. He is, indeed, our friend and our Wonderful Counselor, and He wants us to be in constant communication with Him throughout our day. This is why the apostle Paul tells us in 1 Thessalonians 5:17 "pray without ceasing."

Releasing Grief and Sadness Immediately

Grief and sadness are both reality-based, or fact-based, emotions and can be released in the same way as anger. They are also very common and can be caused by many different circumstances and rob people of their joy, so it is critical that we learn to recognize them when they occur and release them very quickly.

Grief may be just as common as anger, and the impact of grief and sadness may be as profound as that of anger. When I interviewed all the clients that entered an inpatient treatment program for six months, I found that 69% of them had experienced some form of traumatic grief and loss just prior to the onset of their substance abuse, which was the most common childhood trauma leading to substance abuse. Physical abuse, emotional abuse, and sexual abuse were significantly less common than grief, but cumulatively they may lead to more angry clients than grieving clients.

The scriptures tell us clearly to "let not the sun go down on your anger" (Ephesians 4:26), but this could just as well be applied to the elimination of our grief and sadness as well, so that we would be wise to not let the sun go down on our grief or sadness. A more direct scripture on this might be the words of the Lord Jesus when he said in John 14:27, "Let not your heart be troubled [agitated]." Or perhaps, even more directly, we can heed the words of Paul in 1Thessalonians 4:13 that we should "not grieve as the rest who have no hope."

Making Pledge No. 2: "Do not grieve as the rest"

Just as we cannot afford to hold onto our anger overnight, we cannot afford to hold onto our feelings of grief or sadness overnight either. Once you learn how to give all your grief and sadness to the Lord, you would be wise to give it all to Him quickly and systematically so that it will not damage your mood and gradually interfere with your life. Many people are unconscious of how much past losses continue to affect them on a daily basis.

Each reader is strongly encouraged to make this second pledge to "not grieve as the rest who have no hope." Make a list of all significant losses you have had, and then one by one, make a list of what you miss about each one and give all your grief and sadness to the Lord. Once you complete this task and eliminate all past losses, then it is critical that you maintain your freedom and peace by recognizing each new loss that occurs and quickly eliminating it before it can damage you.

As with the first pledge, if you are ready to make this pledge do not do it flippantly. Realize that you must immediately identify all unresolved grief and sadness from your past and systematically and thoroughly release it all to the Lord. Then commit yourself to recognizing any new losses and sadness that occur in your current life, and release them immediately, committing yourself to doing this every evening before the day is done.

If you do this you can enjoy "love, joy, and peace" in your life, as you continue with the other pledges you will learn about in this book. As you learn to make these commitments and to "pray without ceasing" (1 Thessalonians 5:17), the "peace of God, which surpasses all comprehension, shall guard your hearts and your minds in Christ Jesus" (Philippians 4:7). What an awesome promise and an awesome goal to pursue in your life. After all, that is what Jesus said He desire for each of us: "Peace I leave with you; my peace I give to you" (John 14:27).

10

OVERCOMING DEPRESSION

You have undoubtedly heard that depression is caused by a chemical imbalance; that's what the pharmaceutical industry has been telling us for almost two decades and wants us to believe. However, there is no credible evidence of this, but rather research indicates that it is "stressful life events" that cause depression, not chemical imbalances or brain disorders.

The Cause of Depression

Dr. Peter Breggin states in his book *Medication Madness*, that it is a marketing myth created by pharmaceutical companies that depression is the result of a biochemical imbalance, and that there is no evidence that this is true (p. 269-270). One of the theories of depression that has been advanced by pharmaceutical companies is that depressed individuals have a deficiency of serotonin, and that antidepressant medications resolve this. However, studies have found that individuals who are depressed may have a deficiency of serotonin or an overabundance of serotonin. The serotonin levels do not correlate with depression and cannot be used to diagnose depression. In fact there are no blood tests or objective medical tests to diagnose depression.

Joseph Glenmullen, clinical instructor in psychiatry at Harvard Medical School wrote in his book *Prozac Backlash*, "A serotonin deficiency for depression has not been found… Still, patients are often given the impression that a definitive serotonin deficiency in depression is firmly established. ... The result is an undue inflation of the drug market, as well as an unfortunate downplaying of the need for psychological treatments for many patients" (Glenmullen, 2000, p. 197-198).

Brain scans are sometimes alleged to differentiate between depressed and non-depressed individuals, and give the impression that depression is a brain disorder. However, Peter Breggin states in his book, *Reclaiming Our Children* (Perseus Books, Cambridge, Mass., 2000, page 293),

> Brain scans cannot distinguish a depressed person from a nondepressed person and they have not located a cause for any psychiatric disorder. Indeed, they are mainly used in biopsychiatry to promote the profession to lay audiences by giving the false impression that radiological technology can distinguish between normal people and those with psychiatric diagnoses. The usual sleight of hand involves comparing photographs of a brain scan of a depressed patient and a nondepressed patient where there happen to be other differences between the two brains. Sometimes the differences simply reflect normal variation and sometimes they reflect drug damage. Brain scans cannot show differences between the brains of depressed and normal patients because no such differences have been demonstrated.

An impressive study referred to as the "Virginia Twin Study" was conducted to determine whether mental disorders are genetically based or environmentally based. With regard to depression, the researchers found that 87.4% of all depression is caused by "Stressful Life Events" involving loss of a loved one, job, health, or other relationships. This left only 12.6% of all depressive episodes that were not "apparently" precipitated by some type of loss (Kendler, Myers, & Zisook, 2008). My own clinical experience suggests that sexual abuse is another cause of depression that may account for the other cases of depression.

In the December 2010 issue of *Psychology Today*, author and psychologist Jonathan Rottenberg, Ph.D. wrote an article called, "The Road to Depression Runs through Bereavement." In this brief article he asserted that depression usually results from bereavement. If this is true, which I have concluded is true from my own clinical experience, then bereavement-related depression, which includes about 87% of all depression, can only be successfully treated by those who know how to help individuals resolve their grief. Believers who know this ministry can help those with depression by helping them with their grief, if the individuals are receptive.

Grief and Depression

When the apostle Paul wrote to the church at Thessalonica, "do not grieve as the rest who have no hope" (1 Thessalonians 4:13) he was clearly indicating that believers should not be as impacted, or overwhelmed, with grief as unbelievers are, because of their hope of eternal life and seeing their loved ones again. Even though Christians do grieve, their hope in the Lord should provide them an anchor in times of loss and prevent them from becoming completely disabled by their losses.

The important point being made in this verse is that we should not "grieve as the rest," meaning that believers should not have to grieve as long or heavily as unbelievers. This is very similar to the words of Jesus in John 14:27 when He said, "Peace I leave with you… not as the world gives do I give to you." Jesus was saying that the peace that He provides us is different from the peace we can get from the world. His peace is so different from the world's peace because it comforts us and lifts us above our circumstances in times of serious losses. That is precisely what Paul said in 2 Thessalonians

3:16 when he wrote, "May the Lord of peace Himself, continually grant you peace, in every circumstance." "Every circumstance" includes the loss of our loved ones, even when it is tragic and unexpected. It is normal to feel grief and deep sorrow, but the Lord does not want us to be stuck in those feelings for a long time or to become disabled by them. He wants us to experience His peace in "every circumstance."

There is nothing that the world has to offer those who are suffering from loss that can compare with what the Lord offers. The world offers peace in a pill that is very ineffective and has serious adverse side effects, including depression, suicidal impulses, and violence. At best they might numb feelings slightly, including the good ones, and at worst they may lead to homicide or suicide. Since loss is something that all humans encounter frequently, we need to be prepared to deal with grief on a day-by-day basis.

No One is Laughing Now

On Aug. 11, 2014 comedian and actor Robin Williams hung himself by a belt in his home. He was known to have struggled with drug and alcohol abuse in the 1970s and 1980s, and then was sober for twenty years, but relapsed in 2006 and 2014. After his last episode he entered the famed Hazelden inpatient substance abuse program on July 1, 2014 and was given a cocktail of medications for his depression. Family members reported that after being discharged from the program he slept 20 hours per day and kept his window shades drawn to keep out the light. Several weeks later he was found dead in his bedroom and the authorities ruled his cause of death to be suicide by hanging.

Robin Williams had the best treatment that money could buy, but he received the same treatment that so many others with depression receive. He was given psychiatric medications for his depression, most of which contain black-box warnings required by the FDA that warn about the possibility of depression worsening and suicidal thinking resulting from these medications.

One writer stated that "Robin Williams made us all laugh, but no one is laughing now." It illustrates the truth found in Proverbs 14:13 that, "Even in laughter the heart may be in pain, and the end of joy may be grief." It is sad that Mr. Williams ended his life in such a tragic and painful way, but it is also sad that his story is so common. Many people commit suicide as a result of their medications that are supposed to decrease their depression and suicidal thoughts, and yet churches and pastors continue to rely upon the same solution.

Just prior to writing this chapter a mother and father came to me for help in dealing with the loss of their 14-year-old daughter who hung herself four weeks earlier. They were a normal family who loved their daughter and neither parent used drugs or alcohol or had any problems with anger or abuse. When she became depressed they referred her to a local mental health counselor and the counselor referred her to a psychiatrist for medications, the standard practice of mental health professionals.

Several months later this young lady told her counselor that she had "overwhelming suicidal impulses" and her counselor believed that it was caused by her "antidepressant" medications and recommended that she see her doctor to change her medications. Her parents scheduled an appointment with the doctor, but before she could see the doctor she became upset one day and ran out of the house. Her mother and father went into the woods around their country home, looking for her, and her father found her hanging from a tree by her scarf. The sad thing is that this suicide was completely avoidable if her doctor and counselor had heeded the warning of the FDA about the dangers of these medications.

In the first chapter of this book I shared that author/pastor Rick Warren of Saddleback Church had prayed for 27 years for his son and provided him the best counselors, psychiatrists, and treatment that were available, but he concluded that his son had a "brain disorder" that could not be changed. Pastor Warren is now encouraging other pastors and churches, and those involved in Celebrate

Recovery which he co-founded, to join with him in embracing the mental health profession and psychiatric profession in medicating those like his son with depression.

I also shared the story about the former policeman who told how he became so deeply depressed and suicidal that he was given electro-convulsive shock treatments repeatedly and placed upon multiple medications for his depression. He ended his personal testimony saying, "I take six medications every day and have suicidal thoughts every day. I will have to take them the rest of my life because I have a brain disorder." This man stated that he is now a pastor, and he is teaching everyone that his depression is a "brain disorder" and that there is no solution for it, other than taking psychiatric medications for the rest of his life.

Hope for Depression

In spite of these voices of doom and despair, there is good news to share about depression. Those who proclaim the belief that depression is a "brain disorder" have never seen individuals set free from depression by any method, and after a while it is easy to conclude that nothing helps. But I have seen many people completely set free from depression, and now I see this on a routine basis.

The first case occurred shortly after I learned this prayer ministry and had a private practice where I began using it. In chapter 7 I told about a pastor was referred to me by an insurance agency which stated that he was being released from a psychiatric hospital where he had received electroconvulsive shock treatments and needed outpatient counseling.

He told me that he became deeply depressed after his wife committed suicide, and he also had a son who had committed suicide previously. He became very depressed and suicidal and his doctor medicated him with psychiatric drugs that did not help, so he was admitted into a hospital for shock treatments. When I first met him it was obvious that he suffered a lot of memory loss and brain damage from the shock treatments, but he still had depressive thoughts.

He responded to prayer-based sessions, and after a series of sessions his depression diminished until he reported no depression. I had opportunities to see him for the next several years and he continued to report that his depression was gone.

In the last fourteen years I have seen many depressed people set free through prayer, and yet we are being told that depression is a "brain disorder." However, if depression is truly a "brain disorder," then it would not respond to counseling or prayer ministry. I would not expect individuals with traumatic brain injuries to be healed by participating in counseling, although they might receive some emotional healing of their anger or grief that resulted from their loss of their health. When anger, grief, shame, addiction, and depression respond to prayer ministry it demonstrates that these disorders are not "brain disorders" at all, but are emotional disorders that can be healed through prayer.

Man Set Free from Depression

In chapter 8 I described a man who was referred to me by his doctor after he lost the job that he had held for 27 years and became very depressed. When I met him he stated that his depression began nineteen years earlier when he lost his first wife through divorce. He subsequently remarried and then his second wife died four years before I saw him, and his mother and father also died that same month.

He stated that he had been taking antidepressant medications for nineteen years and was still depressed. I explained that depression was primarily caused by unresolved grief, and that he could be set free by praying for each of his significant losses. He was willing to do this, so we prayed first about the loss of his second wife. He was surprised at the relief he experienced from this prayer. We prayed in our second session about the loss of his mother and father. Afterwards, he felt so much better that he said he felt like going home and working on his parents' home that he had been neglecting since their deaths.

In our third session, we prayed about the loss of his first wife and he was set free from this loss and continued to feel even better. Then we prayed about the loss of his job and he found freedom from this loss. By this time he was feeling so good that he came to his sessions smiling and said that he no longer felt depressed. After several months his doctor weaned him off all his medications and he continued to do well and had no more depression. After nineteen years of taking medications that did not help, he was completely set free from his depression through prayer, in just a few weeks.

Man's Solution to Mental Disorders

A $20-million study of U.S. adults, called the National Co-morbidity Replication Survey, estimated in 2005 that 48% of all Americans will experience some form of mental illness in their lifetime and 3/4 of them will do so by age 24, using their broad definition of "mental disorders." The solution recommended for these disorders is early screening and "treatment" (medication). Some mental health leaders believe that the purpose of the study was to market psychiatric drugs for the pharmaceutical industry.

The director of the study, Thomas Insel, M.D., was disappointed to learn from the study that about 1/3 of people rely solely on nonprofessional sources and spiritual advisers. He wrote, "You wouldn't rely on your priest for treatment if you had breast cancer. Why would you go to your priest for a major depressive disorder? These are real medical and brain disorders, and they need to be treated that way" (Weis, 2005). More and more, this sentiment is being spread across the medical field, reflecting the success of the marketing strategy of the pharmaceutical industry to convince more people to buy their drugs.

It's always appropriate to seek a second opinion on medical questions of importance, and is certainly important in this case where psychiatrists and pharmaceutical companies are working jointly to persuade everyone that our mental struggles are all "brain disorders."

Dr. Peter Breggin is a Harvard-trained psychiatrist who has been in private practice in Ithaca, NY, since 1968, and has been used as an expert witness in many court cases dealing with pharmaceutical cases. He has been called "the conscience of psychiatry" for his efforts to expose the harmful side-effects and abuses of psychiatric medications, electroshock, lobotomies, and drugging of children. He has written dozens of scientific articles and more than 20 books, including *Medication Madness* and *Brain-Disabling Treatments in Psychiatry.*

He also has a website which shares videos and articles regarding the adverse side effects of psychiatric medications (www.breggin.com).

In his books "*Medication Madness*" (2008) and "*Brain-Disabling Treatments in Psychiatry*" (2008) he says that many psychiatric medications cause depression, suicidality, hallucinations, delusions, panic attacks and severe mania. He recommends that doctors never use these drugs due to their dangerous and tragic side-effects. He states that the latest research indicates that antidepressants do not work any better than placebos, and often cause depression and other serious problems.

I learned about Dr. Breggin as the result of a personal experience with a client who experienced serious, adverse side-effects from her medication. I met with a woman who was experiencing some intense anxiety as a result of her ex-husband harassing her and her children. I conducted a thorough social history on her and found that she had never experienced any serious mental health problems previously, but I was very concerned about her level of anxiety. I referred her to a Christian psychiatrist who put her on a low dose of Ativan/Lorazepam and scheduled her for a follow-up session the following week. She did well that week, so when she returned the following week the psychiatrist increased her dosage, which is a common practice. The following day, she became very delusional and aggressive and had to be restrained by four men in a gas station.

She went to another medical clinic, since her original clinic was closed, and a nurse told her that her violent reaction was probably caused by the Lorazepam, so she took herself off it suddenly. The sudden withdrawal from this medication caused her to have seizures, but all of her delusions and aggressive reactions stopped immediately. She returned to see me and told me about this event. I was shocked and spoke with a nurse at our clinic, who was a mature, Christian woman, and I asked her if that medication could have caused that reaction. She said to me, "No, that woman is just crazy! She needs to be locked up in a psychiatric facility."

I was standing in the doorway of her office and asked her if she would look it up for me on the internet, so she looked up Lorazepam side effects on the internet. I looked over her shoulder at the list of side effects on this website (drugs.com) and saw that delusions, violence, and aggression were possible side effects of this medication, and I pointed this out to the nurse who grudgingly agreed. I then began searching the internet to learn more about the side-effects of psychiatric medications and found the name of Dr. Peter Breggin. I learned that he had just finished writing two new books and I ordered them immediately. As I began reading *Medication Madness* I was amazed at his first-hand stories of people who had severe, tragic side-effects from taking psychiatric medications, even at low doses for a short period of time.

Since that time I have had the opportunity to meet Dr. Breggin personally and heard him speak on numerous occasions, and I have learned that he is a very knowledgeable scientist and researcher who has fought with the psychiatric community for over forty years. He has almost single-handedly fought the psychiatric community to oppose biologic psychiatry that believes human emotional struggles are the result of biochemical problems that can be solved with pills, electroconvulsive shock, and brain surgery. These interventions destroy people's lives and do not solve their problems, and yet the entire medical establishment has embraced their views and harmful treatments. Although the vast majority of physicians accept the mechanistic view of the establishment, other researchers have begun to join Dr. Breggin in opposition of these doctors and their brain-disabling treatments.

Nurse Set Free from Depression

A woman was referred to me who had lost her mother a year earlier. She was a nurse and she had been taking antidepressants for an entire year, but she continued to have crying spells each day when she began thinking about her mother. She was afraid that she was going to lose her job, and that her husband was getting tired of her emotional displays and might leave her if she couldn't get her emotions under control.

We talked about her mother and I explained that she could get rid of her grief by making a list of the things she missed about her mother, and then praying and asking God to take her grief from her. She was receptive to this, so we prayed about her grief and it was suddenly lifted. When I saw her the following week she told me she felt fine but was worried, so we prayed about some anxieties she had and then she felt better.

When I saw this woman two weeks later she was still doing well. I asked her what she attributed her improvement to, and she said that she had changed her medications recently and she thought that it finally began working. I was dumbfounded, because her depression had instantly lifted after we prayed, and she had been taking medications for a year with no results. We talked about this and I tried to persuade her that it was the prayer, not the medications, that had led to her emotional improvement.

This experience demonstrated to me how deeply ingrained this thinking is in our culture, especially in the medical profession. When God performs a miracle and sets a person free, they can very quickly attribute the miracle to a medication, rather than recognizing the hand of God in the change.

The Adverse Childhood Experiences Study

Around 2000 a study was conducted by a group of doctors in California who were trying to help obese individuals lose weight. They found that many of their patients made some significant progress in their weight loss, but then it began to unravel and the patients regained their weight. They began to suspect that there were underlying emotional issues from their childhood experiences that were interfering with their weight loss.

They designed a simple study in which they asked all of the patients in an HMO group to complete a one-page, eight-item questionnaire regarding adverse childhood experiences such as physical abuse, sexual abuse, and being placed outside of their home during their childhood. There were approximately 17,000 subjects in this study and the researchers were able to correlate their scores on this one-page questionnaire with many social and health problems these individuals had experienced.

The results were fascinating and impressive. This study demonstrated that there was a strong, graded correlation between early childhood adversities/traumas and the person's abuse of alcohol or drugs, involvement in criminal behavior, abortions, out-of-wedlock pregnancies, and many other conditions, including having prescriptions for antidepressants, anti-anxiety medications, and antipsychotic medications. The higher the score of an individual was on the ACE test (with the highest possible score being 8), the stronger the likelihood was that he/she would experience these other medical and social problems.

This study provided some powerful evidence that depression and other "mental disorders" are related to traumatic childhood experiences. The director of the study, Dr. Vincent J. Fellitti, M.D., said, "We propose giving up our old mechanistic explanation of addiction in favor of one that explains it in terms of ... decisions being made to seek chemical relief from the ongoing effects of old trauma" (Felitti, 2004, p. 8). "Addiction is <u>not</u> a brain disease, nor is it caused by chemical imbalance or genetics" (Felitti, 2004, p. 9).

By the same reasoning it could also be said that this study demonstrates that depression and other mental disorders are not brain diseases, nor are they caused by chemical imbalance or genetics.

Strong Christian Set Free from Depression

A woman was referred to me due to her depression that was affecting her health. She was a Christian woman who faithfully attended church with her husband and had never been on antidepressants; she said that she refused to give in to the pressure of her doctors to take medications for her depression.

I asked her when she first became depressed and she told me that she became depressed as a child. She had a little boyfriend at age 7 whom she liked a lot, and one day he laid his head down on his desk in class and died of a brain aneurism. This led to her first bout of depression. Then at age 19 she was engaged to a young man who joined the military and died in Vietnam. She met another man and married him when she was 26 years old, and he died in a car accident. She married her second husband in her 40s and he died a few years later from cancer. Then she met another man whom she became romantically involved with and he died from cancer at age 48. When she was 50 years old her mother, father, and grandfather all died. In addition, she told me that her brother had been diagnosed with cancer and she anticipated losing him in the near future.

I shared with this woman how she could get healing for these losses by making a list of the things she missed about each person, and then praying and asking the Lord to take it and carry it for her. The most painful loss was the loss of her mother, so we made a list of twenty-one things she missed about her mother and she prayed and asked the Lord to take her anger from her and carry it.

After she gave her grief to the Lord, I prayed and asked the Lord if there was anything that He wanted her to know. She said, "I see her smiling; I just see her smiling with her big, brown eyes." I asked her how she felt while thinking about her mother and she said, "I feel happy; no sadness; very calm." I asked her what she thought about this process and she said, "It's so simple! I want to help my brother with his grief over my mother."

This woman began praying about some of her losses on her own. Three weeks later, when she came back to see me she stated that she had no depression, in spite of having been depressed all her life. She said, "I feel everything is lifted off. I don't feel the urge to crawl up in bed or hide and tell people to leave me alone."

She was so excited about her freedom from depression that she gave her sisters a copy of the Set Free Grief Booklet and they wrote down their losses also and said they felt much better. One day she saw a woman in Walmart with white hair, and from the back of this woman it looked like her mother, and it made her smile instead of feeling sad. When I last saw her she said that on most Tuesdays she had been in a "black mood," because her mother died on a Tuesday, but she said, "Now I feel good on Tuesdays and I have begun doing some visitation." She laughed and told me, "My husband is blown away! He told the men at church that he had a brand new wife. Everyone should know about this!" Even though she was already free of her depression, she continued praying about some more sadness and the loss of her first husband, and she continued praying about all her other losses on her own.

Woman Loses Husband

Another woman said that she had been depressed for nine years due to the loss of her husband to whom she had been married for thirty-five years, and she had been taking antidepressants. The medications had not helped her, and she began crying all the time and wanted to get off her medications. I shared with her how she could resolve her grief, and we made a list of twenty-one things she missed about her husband and things that made her sad about him, and she gave her grief and sadness to the Lord. Immediately, the grief and sadness lifted and she felt calm and no longer wanted to cry. Two weeks later she said her depression was gone.

We continued meeting to pray about the other items on her prayer plan. She identified fourteen resentments she had toward her abusive mother and she released her anger. Afterwards she said that she felt "nothing" and had no more anger toward her. A month later when I saw her again she still had no depression or anger toward her mother. Then we prayed about the loss of her son ten years earlier and she was able to release her feelings of grief and sadness and felt peaceful when thinking about him. A month later she still was doing well and had no depression, anger, or grief.

I asked this woman what she thought about this prayer process. She replied, "I'm amazed that it worked so well!" A month later she said with excitement, "It worked!" When people have lived with grief or depression for a long time and then suddenly are released from it, they are often shocked and excited about prayer and about the Lord. It strengthens or renews their faith in God.

Doctors and Medications

Doctors have been so indoctrinated in their training and by the pharmaceutical representatives that they are very quick to recommend psychiatric medications in spite of the serious, documented side effects of these medications. Most of these doctors know very little about mental health treatments and have never known anyone to overcome their grief or depression, so they just prescribe medications to their patients.

In chapter 9 I told about an elderly woman who came to me just two days after her cousin shot herself. Her doctor told her she was depressed and needed an antidepressant, even though it was one day after the incident had occurred. This is both incompetent and unethical for a physician to misdiagnose depression a day after a patient experienced a death of a friend. She was not depressed, but her doctor insisted that she was depressed and should take an antidepressant. She felt a little sadness, so we made a list of the reasons for her sadness and she gave her sadness to the Lord. After we prayed, her sadness was completely gone and she said, "I think I'll just throw those pills away."

The Goal: 100% Peace

When I pray with people with grief, my goals is to see them have 100% peace regarding their loss. This means that they can think about their loved one, talk about them, and look at pictures of them and not feel tearful or sad, but just peaceful. This is a standard that no mental health professionals use because they do not believe it is realistically achievable. But I see this goal reached most of the time when praying with grieving people.

A woman came to me whom I had seen previously and who had received healing before. But she had since lost her father and was returning for more help. We made a list of twenty-one things she missed about her father, and she prayed and asked the Lord to take her grief from her. When she returned the following week she said she felt "great," but when I asked her how strong her depression was she still rated it as a 4 on a 10-point scale.

I asked her what made her feel depressed still. She said she was sad about her mother leaving after a visit, about her mother not eating right and losing 20 pounds, and about losing her best friend. I led her in a prayer about the twelve reasons she identified for her sadness, then I asked the Lord what He wanted her to know. She said, "He's going to be there with me when the day comes; everything is going to be ok." I asked her how she felt now and she said, "I'm ok with it now; I feel no more sadness." I continued with her until her grief and sadness were completely gone, as well as her depression.

Depression and the Church

The psychiatric and pharmaceutical professions want us to believe that all of our emotional struggles are just brain disorders and that we need their medications to overcome our emotional struggles. But this flatly contradicts the words of Jesus who said, "Peace I leave with you; My peace I give to you; not as the world gives do I give to you. Let not your heart be troubled, nor let it be fearful" (John 14:27). If all our emotional struggles are caused by brain disorders, then we cannot have peace as Jesus promised we can have, because we have no control over our feelings. The Lord says that we can have His peace, so our emotional struggles are not due to brain disorders.

Unfortunately, there is little evidence of the power of God in the lives of most Christians and, consequently, there is no excitement about Jesus. There is as much divorce, substance abuse, immorality, anger and depression among Christians as there is in the world. And yet, God desires to show His power in the church so that men will be drawn to it. He has given us the Holy Spirit as our Comforter, and the power to set people free through prayer, as we learn how to pray about our emotions.

Most pastors have been persuaded that the doctors are right, especially pastors of large churches where there are many doctors whom the pastor trusts, who tell them authoritatively that depression is a chemical imbalance. Not only do they believe that depression is a chemical imbalance, but even anger is a chemical problem or brain problem. A Christian man came to me who wanted help with his anger because he had been too harsh with his daughter. He spoke with his pastor who told him that he should see a doctor about some medication to help him with his anger, because his pastor had a problem with anger and took medications which he thought helped him reduce his anger.

The apostle Paul wrote to the Christians in Galatia that, "the fruit of the Spirit is love, joy, peace, patience, kindness, goodness, faithfulness, gentleness and self-control" (Galatians 5:22-33). This passage states that self-control is a result, or fruit, of the Spirit, which one could conclude occurs when we are set free from our negative emotions. The first three fruits mentioned are love, joy, and peace, which are three emotions, and then the last six fruits are character qualities. I believe that this means that as the Lord takes away our negative emotions, like anger and grief, and replaces them with His peace, it leads us to have more love and joy as well. And when our lives are ruled by love, joy, and peace we will alsodevelop the six character qualities, including self-control. Control of our anger comes not through anger management or through a pill, but from learning to pray effectively about our emotions and allowing the Lord to take our anger and grief. Once we have His peace, we also have self-control over our anger.

Exposing the Medication Lies

This battle with the psychiatric and pharmaceutical industries is a major spiritual and philosophical battle. The world teaches us that all that our emotions are the result of brain disorders and chemical imbalances. It is obvious from observing the growing amount of violence in our society that mental health professionals do not know how to help people with anger. It is also obvious from the growing number of people with depression who are already taking antidepressants and antipsychotic medications to help them overcome their depression, and the growing interest in use of electroconvulsive shock treatment, that they do not know how to help people with depression. Since they cannot help people overcome their grief, they are also unable to help people with depression.

This is a major stronghold of our society that needs to be opposed and exposed by the Church. This is one of the philosophies of our day that Paul was referring to in Colossians 2:8 when he said, "See to it that no one takes you captive through philosophy and empty deception, according to the tradition of men, according to the elementary principles of the world, rather than according to Christ." The church needs to teach about the hope that is found only in Christ. Men and women can be set free from depression, anger, and addiction. We have to firmly oppose the lie that you can find peace in a pill and demonstrate through our lives that peace comes only from the Lord.

The early New Testament church exploded into history due to the radical change that they saw in the lives of people who were being healed and changed. In Acts 3:2-10 we read about the lame man who asked Peter and John for charity, and in verse 6 Peter said, "I do not possess silver and gold, but what I do have I give to you: In the name of Jesus Christ the Nazarene—walk!" Verse 8-10 says, "With a leap he stood upright and began to walk; and he entered the temple with them, walking and leaping and praising God…And all the people saw him walking and praising God…and they were filled with wonder and amazement!"

As we begin to pray with people in our communities and see large numbers of people set free from anger, grief, and depression, the same excitement will occur today as happened in the New Testament church. Many people will be filled with wonder and amazement and become excited about the Lord, and the church will grow in strength and numbers. May God use each reader and participant in this program to demonstrate His awesome power and be a part of the revival that the Lord wants to bring to our country.

A Word of Caution

Some people who are on psychiatric medications and hear about the dangers of the medications and how they can be set free from their emotional bondage, want to take themselves off of them immediately. It is very important to understand that there can be dangerous withdrawal effects when coming off of these medications. Once your body and brain become adjusted to these medications they can be very difficult to withdraw from, and can result in serious, life-threatening emotional and physical withdrawal reactions. Methods for safely withdrawing from psychiatric drugs are discussed in Dr. Breggin's 2013 book, *Psychiatric Drug Withdrawal: A Guide for Prescribers, Therapists, Patients, and Their Families.* Therefore, it is important to include a caution such as the following to those who are considering withdrawing from their medications.

WARNING: Most psychiatric drugs can cause withdrawal reactions, sometimes including life-threatening emotional and physical withdrawal problems. In short, it is not only dangerous to start taking psychiatric drugs, it can also be dangerous to stop them. Withdrawal from psychiatric drugs should be done carefully under experienced clinical supervision.

11

UNDERSTANDING MEDICATIONS

Jesus was going with a man named Jairus to heal his daughter, and a large group of people were following Him. The following account is given in Mark 5:25-34 of what happened on the way.

> *A woman who had had a hemorrhage for twelve years, and had endured much at the hands of many physicians, and had spent all that she had and was not helped at all, but rather had grown worse— after hearing about Jesus, she came up in the crowd behind Him and touched His cloak. For she thought,*
>
> *"If I just touch His garments, I will get well." Immediately the flow of her blood was dried up; and she felt in her body that she was healed of her affliction.*
>
> *Immediately Jesus, perceiving in Himself that the power proceeding from Him had gone forth, turned around in the crowd and said, "Who touched My garments?" And His disciples said to Him, "You see the crowd pressing in on You, and You say, 'Who touched Me?'" And He looked around to see the woman who had done this. But the woman fearing and trembling, aware of what had happened to her, came and fell down before Him and told Him the whole*

> *truth. And He said to her, "Daughter, your faith has made you well; go in peace and be healed of your affliction.*

This story is such a fascinating story because it demonstrates that stark contrast between the healing that the world offers and the healing that the Lord Jesus offers. This woman had exhausted all of her personal resources and had tried every medical treatment available, and this passage says that she "had spent all that she had and was not helped at all, but rather had grown worse."

This same scenario is being acted out today in the lives of countless individuals who have sought out medical and mental health treatments with secular methods, but who have found no help. I see many people who have tried psychiatric medications for years and they have not been helped at all, but rather "had grown worse."

Mary's Story

Mary was a Christian woman came for counseling after her adult daughter died suddenly. She was overwhelmed with grief at her loss and could not get past her grief and guilt. I prayed with her about her grief and guilt several times and she was able to get peace. Her husband came with her each time and waited in the waiting room while she was in the counseling session, and he noticed that she left my office smiling each time and feeling better.

But Mary had a lot more issues than just grief. She had been on heavy psychiatric medications most of her adult life due to her difficult childhood. Her parents were extremely abusive to her and her siblings, and even murdered two of them by starving them to death. She had experienced a lot of trauma and had a great deal of grief, anger, fear, and feelings of shame even though she was a Christian. In 1992 she started taking the antidepressant Paxil, then she was prescribed a heavy dosage of Seraquel, an antipsychotic medication. She was later prescribed Effexor, another antidepressant, and she was given Valium to help her sleep. We developed a prayer plan for dealing with her emotions and then systematically prayed through each issue. The more we prayed the more she smiled, and then her husband asked for help and wanted prayer for his issues, since he had had an abusive family upbringing also. Eventually, both Mary and her husband had resolved most of their underlying emotional issues, and they quit having serious marital problems. They also became excited about the ministry and began praying with others about their emotions, and helping other people find freedom.

Mary was doing well emotionally but she had been taking heavy psychiatric medications for a long time, and her doctors told her that she would have to take them the rest of her life. However, she wanted to get off them, so she slowly began to withdraw from them on her own. She was a nurse and knew how to slowly lower her dosage on these medications, and continued doing so until she was completely off them. She told her psychiatrist and he was amazed that she could do this. It took her many months to completely wean herself off her medications but with much patience and determination she succeeded. She is now free from her medications, and doing very well, a task that her psychiatrist did not believe was possible.

Miracles of Modern Medicine

The medical treatments that were available in the days of Jesus were poor, in comparison to what is available today. Today, we have a lot of advanced technology to assist doctors in making a diagnosis and in prescribing treatments to correct medical problems. We have x-rays, sonograms, MRIs, lab tests, and many other ways of assessing and treating physical problems. Doctors can now do heart transplants, by-pass heart surgery, and many other procedures in saving lives that are remarkable. However, they are very limited when it comes to treating the common cold and helping with other medical issues.

I had triple by-pass surgery several years ago when my arteries were so clogged that I could not sweep the floor with a broom for more than 30 seconds without my chest hurting. I was hospitalized one day and recommended for immediate heart surgery. I was sedated and anaesthetized while a team of doctors and nurses attached me to a heart machine, stopped my heart, and removed arteries from my leg and arm to use to replace the clogged arteries around my heart. A week later I began a new job and have been doing well ever since. I would not be alive to write this book today if it was not for the amazing medical technology that we have available today.

However, a few years later I developed a neuroma on the bottom of my foot that hurt so bad that I could barely walk. For months I was barely able to walk and felt that I had suddenly aged 20 years, because elderly people who were in their 80s and 90s were able to do laps around me while I hobbled through a local mall. I went to several competent podiatrists who diagnosed my condition and offered surgery to correct this condition, but they also informed me that another neuroma might develop before the first one healed. I was facing the prospect that I might never be able to go for healthy walks again.

In my desperation I looked on the internet and found a doctor who claimed that he could correct neuromas through a simple shoe insert that corrects the arch of my foot. I spoke with him and he sounded sensible, and I had some inserts custom made for my foot that slowly raised the arch of my foot to the desired level. That was about five years ago, but I have been functioning normally, walking as much as I desire without any pain, and even playing racquetball again. The advice of my original podiatrists would have left me as an invalid, unable to walk any distance, but when I sought a second opinion I found some solutions that were very effective, but were not common knowledge or practice in the medical community.

There are many, many medical problems that modern medicine cannot treat, in spite of their advanced knowledge and technology, and when we find these areas we need to seek a second opinion and look to other sources for help. There is no area that is more in need of assistance than the area of psychiatry and mental health treatment. Doctors will claim that there have been great advances in medical science and in the understanding of the brain, and then they will confidently declare that they can solve our mental health problems with pills, electroconvulsive shock, or with surgery. All of these are brain-disabling techniques that attempt to solve emotional problems by disabling the brain in some fashion.

Other Medical Opinions

In the previous chapter I introduced the readers to Dr. Peter Breggin, the Harvard-trained psychiatrist who has been writing about the dangers of psychiatric medicines for over forty years. Dr. Breggin has taught at numerous universities, including Johns Hopkins and George Mason, was a former full-time consultant at the National Institute of Mental Health, and has testified as a medical expert in many criminal and civil cases, including product-liability suits against pharmaceutical companies. He has also written dozens of scientific articles and more than twenty books.

Very few of his psychiatric colleagues will dare to debate the issues associated with psychiatric medications with him, because of the overwhelming evidence he has of the dangers of psychiatric drugs. In *Medication Madness* Dr. Breggin describes his debate with a respected British colleague in April 2006 on the question, "Do psychiatric drugs do more harm than good?" He focused on the data from his medical books and from scientific literature, and his opponent had little familiarity with this research. When the audience voted on the question of whose presentation was more convincing, the vote was 85 to 3 in favor of the proposition that Dr. Breggin was arguing (Breggin, 2008b, p. 318).

Dr. Breggin has written dozens of books as well as many professional articles on psychiatric drugs. In addition to *Medication Madness* 2008b), he also wrote *Brain-disabling Treatments in Psychiatry* (2008a), *Toxic Psychiatry* (1991), and *Psychiatric Drug Withdrawal* (2013). Other brave researchers have begun to join Dr. Breggin in his opposition to psychiatric medications, such as Danish physician Peter Gotzsche, MD, the director of the Nordic Cochrane Center at Rigs Hospital in Copenhagen, Denmark. In his 2015 book, *Deadly Medicines and Organised Crime: How Big Pharma Has Corrupted Healthcare,* he clearly presents the scientific evidence for the inefficacy and harmfulness of psychiatric drugs.

Robert Whitaker, a medical journalist and finalist for the Pulitzer Prize in 1999, began writing about the dangers of psychiatric medications. He began exploring psychiatry with his 2001 book, *Mad in America: Bad Science, Bad Medicine, and the Enduring Mistreatment of the Mentally Ill,* and then expanded on it in his 2010 book, *Anatomy of an Epidemic: Magic Bullets, Psychiatric Drugs, and the Astonishing Rise of Mental Illness in America.* He travels internationally to share his findings and has a website that he uses to share new information with his readers (MadinAmerica.com).

Joanna Moncrieff, a practicing psychiatrist and Senior Lecturer in the Department of Mental Health Sciences at University College London, UK, has also written a devastating critique about the use of psychiatric drugs. In her 2009 book, *The Myth of the Chemical Cure,* she presents a concise critique of psychiatric drug treatment and provides a well-referenced source of information about the various classes of psychiatric drugs.

Church Elder Assaults Cop

In his book, *Medication Madness,* Dr. Breggin tells true stories of fifty individuals who committed violent acts or suicide as a result of taking psychiatric medication. He tells the story of a man by the name of Harry Henderson (pp. 5-11) who went to the doctor one day regarding a minor medical problem, and he read a flyer about depression while in the waiting room. He was an elder in his church and taught frequently, was a solid family man with his own business, and had no history of mental problems or arrests. He told his doctor that he felt "blue" on and off, throughout his life, so his doctor wrote him a prescription for Paxil. A month later his dosage was increased and his behavior gradually began to change. His wife noticed that he sometimes became irritable and he gestured obscenely to another driver who had cut him off, which was totally out of character for him. At other times he cried uncontrollably, and he began buying worthless and extravagant items, which was also very untypical for him.

After eight months his dosage was doubled and his mental state grew worse. He felt a strange pain in his head, which is known as "akathisia." Akathisia means the inability to sit still, but it is discussed in the American Psychiatric Association's *Diagnostic and Statistical Manual of Mental Disorders*, fourth edition (1994) where it states that "Akathisia may be associated with dysphoria, irritability, aggression, or suicide attempts." It also states that the newer antidepressants, called SSRIs, can cause akathisia (p. 801). In 1990, the Public Citizen Health Research Group estimated Prozac-induced akathisia to occur at a rate of 15 to 25 percent of the time with patients.

In 2002 Harry Henderson felt so tortured by this painful sensation that he developed a desperate desire to stop the pain inside his head, and he began contemplating killing himself. Then he thought it would be wrong to put his wife through such a trauma and he began thinking it would be the "morally right" thing to kill her first before killing himself. He began searching for a way to obtain a gun to kill himself, and he considered breaking into a police car to get a shotgun so he would not harm anyone else.

Harry drove around town looking for an opportunity and eventually spotted a police officer who was writing a ticket for another driver. He sat and waited until the officer opened his door and got out, then he rammed his car into the officer's car, knocking him down and injuring him. He then ran to the officer and tried to get his gun from him to kill himself, and two men helped subdue Harry and get help for the injured officer.

All of this was uncharacteristic for Harry, who had never done anything like this before. He had no history of violence, or suicidality, and he did not even know how to operate a gun or how to take the safety off the gun. He thought only about killing himself. When the effects of the Paxil began to wear off he began to understand what he had done and became extremely remorseful and depressed. When Dr. Breggin interviewed him and his wife and friends, and examined his medical records he wrote a detailed scientific report on the ability of Paxil to cause compulsive, violent acts and suicide, and Harry was allowed to plead guilty to a lesser charge with a short jail sentence. The injured officer even requested that the court show leniency to Harry after he read Dr. Breggin's report and was convinced that Harry was the victim of "medication madness."

Dr. Breggin relates approximately 50 such real cases that he has investigated in his work as a psychiatrist and expert witness. While sharing such cases he discusses various types of psychiatric medications and their dangers and adverse side effects. His books are highly recommended to the readers, especially his books, *Medication Madness, Toxic Psychiatry*, and *Psychiatric Drug Withdrawal: A Guide for Prescribers, Therapists, Patients and Their Families* and *Brain-Disabling Treatments in Psychiatry*.

Facts about Psychiatric Medications

There are five main types of psychiatric medications, but all psychiatric drugs operate by disabling the brain in some way. The following is a brief summary of these medications, their adverse side effects, their effectiveness or ineffectiveness, and their withdrawal problems, as described by Dr. Breggin in *Medication Madness (2008b), Brain-Disabling Treatments in Psychiatry (2008a),* and *Psychiatric Drug Withdrawal (2013)* and in Robert Whitaker's book, *Anatomy of an Epidemic (2010).*

<u>Antidepressants</u>

- "In 2006, according to IMS Health (2007), antidepressants were the most prescribed among all classes of drugs, with a total of 227.3 million prescriptions. They were third in revenue, with a total of $13.5 billion" (Breggin, 2008a, p. 116).

- The FDA requires a Black Box warning for children and adults who take antidepressants, to warn consumers that they can cause "anxiety, agitation, panic attacks, insomnia, irritability, hostility, aggressiveness, impulsivity, akathisia (psychomotor restlessness), hypomania, and mania" (Breggin 2008b, p. 46).
- Many patients receiving antidepressants experience "akathisia," a painful sensation in the brain that often leads to suicide or homicide (Breggin 2008b, p. 15).
- Between 30% and 80% of patients taking an antidepressant also suffer from sexual dysfunction as a result of taking SSRI antidepressants (Breggin, 2008a, p. 174).
- Recent studies of antidepressant effectiveness have failed to demonstrate their effectiveness to be greater than that of placebos. A 2008 analysis of research studies demonstrated the ineffectiveness of antidepressants (Breggin 2008b, p. 53) and studies have shown that 80% of depressed individuals will get better without any treatment.
- Antidepressant "drugs can cause severe withdrawal problems, including a variety of neurological symptoms, agitation, and a worsening of depression.... Sometimes these withdrawal symptoms persist for months or even years after stopping antidepressants" (Breggin 2008b, p. 54). These withdrawal symptoms often lead individuals to believe they need to take these medications the rest of their lives, even though they are not reducing their depression.
- Antidepressants have been shown to cause patients to relapse into depression after they discontinue their medications, leading them to a state of chronic depression, in contrast to placebos and no treatments that lead to spontaneous recoveries up to 85% of the time and to no relapses (Whitaker, 2015, p. 158, 169).
- Antidepressants are known to cause mania, and frequently lead to a diagnosis of bipolar disorders, which then results

in the use of other medications to treat that condition and turning bipolar disorders from a rare disorder to a very common one (Whitaker, 2015, p. 180, 192).

- "It's impossible to prove that antidepressants actually relieve depression but it's relatively easy to demonstrate that they can worsen depression and cause mania, murder, and suicide" (Breggin 2008b, p. 53).

Antipsychotics

- "All antipsychotic drugs clog the brain and mind by performing a chemical disruption of frontal lobe function, the equivalent of a pharmacological lobotomy" (Breggin 2008b, p. 225).
- "Antipsychotic drugs do make patients and inmates more compliant and numb in the short term, thereby easing management problems, but they end up doing much more harm than good" (Breggin 2008b, p. 303).
- A study published by researchers in Psychological Medicine (Harrow, Jobe, and Faull, 2015, p. 1) on a 20-year follow-up study of schizophrenics taking antipsychotic medications, found that antipsychotic medications led to chronic psychosis, and that those who never took antipsychotic medications had significantly less psychotic activities than those who did take these medications.
- From 40% to 50% of patients taking antipsychotics experience tardive dyskinesia (Breggin 2013, p. 42), "a persistent and usually irreversible disorder that causes disfiguring grimaces and tics and potentially disabling abnormal movement of arms, hands, legs, and neck, as well as the muscles of speaking, swallowing, and breathing" (Breggin 2008b, p. 134, 135).
- In 20 to 75% of patients they also cause akathisia, "an experience of inner torture with a compulsion to move" which "can "produce suicidal and violent behavior" (Breggin 2008b, p. 236).

- "Withdrawing from antipsychotic drugs can be extremely difficult and sometimes impossible" ... "children or adults who have taken these drugs for months or years often become more psychotic than ever when they try to withdraw" (Breggin 2008b, p 302).
- Treatment programs around the world have shown that acutely psychotic patients have better outcomes when treated without antipsychotic drugs (Breggin 2013, p. 55).

Anti-anxiety Medications

- "The benzodiazepines were tenth in sales, with over 80 million prescriptions written" in 1999 (Breggin, 2008a).
- "SSRI antidepressants frequently cause agitation, anxiety, and insomnia" (Breggin 2008b, p. 168).
- Suicide and Violence: "One or two doses of a benzodiazepine can lead to violence that is wholly out of character for the individual" (Breggin, 2013, p. 90).
- Tolerance: The original studies for panic disorder showed that at 8-10 weeks of exposure the patients were more phobic, more anxious, and had a 350 percent increase in the panic attacks for which they were being treated (Breggin, 1991, p.252-254).
- Benzos result in "a generalized suppression of ... electrical activity of the large neurons throughout all regions of the brain and spinal cord" (Breggin, 2008a, p. 323) and cause a range of effects from "relaxation through sleep, and, in the extreme, coma" (Breggin, 2008a, p. 322).
- Anti-anxiety medications can quickly provide relief of anxiety, but they are extremely addictive and their benefits wear off quickly, leaving the individual more anxious than ever before (Breggin 2013, p. 96).
- Adverse side effects of anti-anxiety medications include euphoria, restlessness, hallucinations, bizarre uninhibited

behavior, hostility, rage, paranoia, depression, and suicidal ideation (Breggin, 2008b, p. 159).

- They can also "cause persistent or irreversible harm to the brain in the form of persisting memory dysfunction and dementia" (Breggin, 2008a, p. 328).
- "These drugs commonly cause abuse and dependence (addiction), and even in relatively short-term use at relatively small doses, they can produce withdrawal syndromes. Because the withdrawal symptoms are so distressing, many patients cannot stop taking these drugs" (Breggin, 2008a, p. 345).

Mood Stabilizers

- "Lithium for the treatment of manic episodes or bipolar disorder was originally promoted to the public and to the mental health profession as the ultimate example of a specific biochemical treatment for a specific psychiatric disorder" (Breggin, 2008a, p. 193).
- "Mood stabilizers... act by suppressing overall emotional responsiveness. Individuals become less able to feel and less able to identify and express their feelings" (Breggin, 2013, p. 107).
- "Between 1994 and 2003, there was a 40-fold increase in diagnosing bipolar disorder in children, and the trend has been escalating since then" (Breggin, 2008a, p. 239).
- Lithium has a generalized brain-disabling, deactivating effect. "This effect may at times reduce the occurrence of manic episodes, but it does so by reducing overall brain function. Even in regard to reducing the frequency of manic episodes, its efficacy is doubtful and it causes manic withdrawal reactions" (Breggin, 2008a, p. 200).
- Researchers in 1995 conducted a study of patients treated with lithium for bipolar disorder who were carefully monitored for compliance, and "despite this, 73% of the patients relapsed into mania or depression within 5 years" (Breggin, 2008a, p. 211).

- "Mood stabilizers, when prescribed for months and years, can cause chronic brain impairment" (Breggin 2013, p. 107)
- "Several studies have shown cognitive impairment in short-term memory, long-term memory and psychomotor speed in bipolar patients taking lithium" (Breggin, 2008a, p. 204).
- Researchers at the University of Wisconsin "found that many patients became demented or otherwise deteriorate severely when abruptly withdrawn from lithium" (Breggin, 2008a, p. 212).

<u>Stimulants</u>

- In 2009 12.3% of boys and 5.5% of girls aged 5-17 were diagnosed with ADHD according to the CDC (PDW, p. 73).
- Stimulants are prescribed for ADHD which is not a valid medical syndrome (Breggin 2013, p. 83-84)
- "Parents are seldom told that methylphenidate (Ritalin) is speed" (Breggin, 2008a, p. 300).
- Stimulant drugs used for ADHD are extremely addictive and make children exposed to it much more likely to abuse cocaine in early adulthood (Breggin 2013, p. 78).
- The FDA stated, "Long term effects of Ritalin in children have not been well established (BDTIP, p. 285) but "within an hour after taking a single dose of a stimulant drug, any child tends to become more obedient, narrower in focus, and more willing to concentrate on humdrum tasks and instructions" (Breggin, 2008a, p. 303).
- A U.S. Department of Education review reported that "Long-term beneficial effects have not been verified by research" and concluded, "Teachers and parents should not expect long-term improvement in academic achievement or reduced antisocial behavior" (Breggin, 2008b, 198).
- An NIMH -funded 36-month study concluded that there were no long-term positive effects from stimulant drugs, and that stimulant drugs stunt growth (Breggin, 2008b, 198).

- "Stimulant medications… cause potentially irreversible tics, insomnia, depression and suicidality, OCD, apathy, overstimulated behavior, cardiovascular risks, and mania and psychosis" (Breggin 2013, p. 84)

Facts about Mental Health Treatment

One of the main reasons why so many people turn to psychiatric drugs for help with their emotions is that mental health counselors are so ineffective in helping them.

When discussing mental health treatments it is important to understand certain basic facts. First, it is important to understand that having a master's degree and being licensed as a mental health professional does not equip anyone to help others with their emotional struggles. Most master's level training programs teach students approximately twelve of the most popular counseling theories currently being used. They are then encouraged to select one that appeals to them, not based upon any scientific evidence that one works better than another. Most students emerge from their training very confused and having no particular skills to enable them to help someone else.

Second, there are no clinical criteria that therapists must meet. They must demonstrate that they have a certain base of knowledge about counseling theories and ethical principles, but they do not need to demonstrate any level of competence or skill in helping others. Very few counselors or therapists have any knowledge of the research on treatment effectiveness or ineffectiveness, but the following are three facts that every counselor or therapist should know, although very few do.

Third, research has clearly shown that grief therapies do not work. Twenty-three of the top researchers in the field of grief counseling wrote a "Report on Bereavement and Grief Therapy" and concluded that nothing works, and half of the time clients feel worse after their counseling session than they did before it (Genevro, Marshall, and Miller, 2003). One writer classified Grief

Counseling as a therapy that may damage clients. Since that report was written a new form of grief therapy has surfaced for treatment of "complex grief" but it requires 16 weeks, is so painful to endure that 25% of the subjects drop out, and is marginally effective. In contrast, this prayer ministry leads to rapid and complete healing of grief for both complex grief and normal grief.

Fourth, research has shown that anger management does not work. As quoted previously, one of the top researchers in the field of anger management, Ray DiGuiseppe, stated that "anger management is like a Bandaid. It makes people feel like they have done something but they have not had any real treatment" (Carey, 2004). The research has consistently demonstrated that anger management does not reduce the recidivism rate of inmates in prison, or show any significant change in their behavior and yet this is the primary tool used by therapist for those with anger difficulties.

Fifth, most posttraumatic stress disorder treatments do not work. While there are many therapies that claim to be effective in resolving posttraumatic stress, an examination of the research by The National Academy of Sciences, a neutral scientific group, found insufficient evidence that any treatment helps, other than "exposure therapy" (National Academy of Sciences, 2008). Exposure therapy involves the repeated exposure of patients to their traumatic memories by recalling a traumatic event repeatedly until their emotional reaction decreases. Although, these researchers concluded that exposure therapy works, they did not indicate that there is a clinically significant effect, just that it works better than no treatment at all. The truth is that the primary emotions involved in posttraumatic stress disorder are anger, grief, shame, and fear, and since therapists are unable to effectively reduce these feelings, they are also ineffective in helping most people with PTSD.

Finally, it is a well-established fact that there is very little evidence that psychotherapy is effective. A reputable psychologist by the name of Martin Seligman was commissioned by Consumer Reports in 1995 to conduct a study for them to evaluate consumer satisfaction of various types of psychological treatments. He found that there was no difference in levels of satisfaction for those who were treated by doctoral level psychologists, by social workers, or professional counselors, and there was no difference in outcomes based up treatment models used by the therapists. Interestingly, there were significantly higher levels of satisfaction by those who attended AA than those who receive standard psychological treatments (Seligman, 1995).

General Facts about Psychiatric Medications

In chapter 19 of his book *Medication Madness*, Dr. Breggin talks about the "Marketing Myths and the Truth about Psychiatric Medication." The following facts about psychiatric medications are drawn from this chapter.

Fact One: Psychiatric drugs do not correct chemical imbalances in the brain that cause mental health problems. The chemical-imbalance theory was promoted by pharmaceutical companies like Eli Lilly as a marketing tool for their medications, but there has never been any evidence of a chemical imbalance in individuals experiencing mental health problems. *The Textbook of Clinical Psychiatry* (2003) that is printed by the American Psychiatric Publishing company in Washington, D.C. laid this chemical imbalance theory to rest in 2003. The editors wrote, "Additional experience has not confirmed the monoamine depletion hypothesis" (p. 479). In other words, the belief that mental health problems are caused by the depletion of monoamines like Serotonin is no longer believed by those who are aware of the latest research. Editor-in-chief of *Psychiatric Times*, psychiatrist Ronald Pies wrote, "In the past 30 years, I don't believe I have ever heard a knowledgeable, well-trained psychiatrist make such a preposterous claim, except perhaps to mock" (Pies, 2011).

In spite of this admission, however, the belief continues and can be found in literature about psychiatric medications. Award-winning journalist and author of *Mad in America*, Robert Whitaker, has stated that "87% of Americans still believe mental problems are caused by chemical imbalances" (Whitaker, 2016). Even in television advertisements about these medications they often say "many physicians believe that depression is caused by chemical imbalances," which is true. Most doctors are not aware of the latest research and continue to repeat this obsolete theory.

Fact Two: Many psychiatric medications can lead to "medication madness" and have serious, adverse side-effects, including suicide and homicide, and carry FDA Black-box Warnings and label warnings, such as SSRI antidepressants and Ritalin. These FDA warnings are required on television advertisements because of the serious, adverse side-effects of these medications.

Fact Three: Psychiatric medications can permanently damage the brain. There is growing evidence that psychiatric drugs can create permanent brain damage. The anti-psychotic drugs cause uncontrollable body movements called "tardive dyskinesia" which is usually irreversible and believed to be evidence of brain damage. Likewise, there is growing evidence that the stimulants prescribed for children for ADHD can permanently damage the brain. There is also mounting evidence that the use of SSRI antidepressants can permanently damage the brain cells and the physical structure of the brain (Breggin, *Medication Madness*, p. 274).

Fact Four: Psychiatric medications can be harmful even in small doses. Dr. Breggin describes a case in *Medication Madness* involving a man who drowned himself and his two children in a bathtub after taking only two or three doses of the smallest available dose of Paxil (Breggin, 2008b, p. 263). He also points out that the ill and elderly are more susceptible to adverse drug reactions, and that up to 10 percent of the population are "poor metabolizers" due to the lack of some liver enzymes. The size of the dose that is dangerous for an individual also depends upon whether the individual is taking other medications at the same time.

Fact Five: Your psychiatrist is not a brain expert. Most physicians and psychiatrists who push psychiatric medications on patients have gained their knowledge from pharmaceutical representatives during medical meetings and dinners, where they are given a sales pitch. These representatives cater in meals and provide doctors with all sorts of free items, to win the acceptance of the doctors and clinic administrators for their new medications. The brain is probably the most complex object in the universe, and those who are brain experts recognize how very little they truly understand the brain. Beware when a doctor begins talking like a brain expert or telling you how there has been a revolution in brain science and you need to listen to his recommendations!

Fact Six: Psychiatric medications are not needed for the rest of your life. In fact, there are no clinical studies of the long-term effects of taking psychiatric medication, other than one study on the long-term use of anti-psychotics that demonstrated that long-term use of anti-psychotic medications leads to chronic psychosis (Harrow, Jobe, and Faull, 2014). A typical psychiatric drug study lasts only four to six weeks, because the drugs are so ineffective and cause so many adverse side effects that patients drop out before the study can last six weeks. Psychiatrists often complain that their patients are not "compliant" with their medication regimen, and solicit the help of their nurses and the mental health staff to try to keep them on their medications.

There are no long-term studies to demonstrate that long-term use of psychiatric medications is effective. In fact, there are more studies surfacing over time that demonstrate serious physical harm to the brains of patients who remain on these medications for a long time. MRI studies of monkeys given antipsychotic drugs have shown that after two years their brains shrunk 10% in volume.

Fact Seven: Psychiatric disorders are not like diabetes. Diabetes has biological markers, known physical causes, and rational treatments, such as diet, medication, and insulin replacement. Psychiatric disorders have none of these characteristics. Doctors who treat diabetes encouraged patients to change their lifestyle and diet, to exercise, and to reduce their stress. Interestingly, psychiatrists rarely talk with their patients about such lifestyle changes. Mostly they just push their drugs on their patients and show them far less respect and care than the typical diabetic doctor.

Fact Eight: Psychiatric drugs can be both dangerous to start and difficult to stop, due to their serious withdrawal effects. Because of this it is important that everyone taking psychiatric drugs is strongly cautioned to withdraw from these medications only under the close supervision of an experienced clinician. In some cases, due to prolonged use of the medications, individuals may be unable to withdraw completely from these medications.

Genuine Brain Disorders

There are some genuine brain disorders that are caused by a disease, such as Alzheimer's and brain tumors, and there are many biological or medical disorders that cause psychiatric symptoms, including "thyroid disorder, sleep apnea, Lyme disease, diabetes, encephalitis, and head injury, but in their mistaken emphasis on mythical biochemical imbalances, some clinicians are likely to miss these real physical disorders" (Breggin, *Psychiatric Drug Withdrawal*, 2013, p. 32).

In addition, there are mood disorders that are caused by antidepressants, stimulants, and anti-anxiety medications that are recognized in the official psychiatric diagnostic manual. These disorders are, properly, diagnosed as "Substance-induced mood disorders" but it is rare for physicians to use this proper diagnostic label. Clients should never be given any additional diagnoses when they are already on medications that have the potential for creating psychiatric problems, but this is also a very common practice.

The Church and Psychiatric Medications

A youth minister learned this prayer ministry and began using it with the young people in his church. He became very excited about it and saw remarkable changes occur in the lives of many of the young people in their church. One day he was visiting with a woman from his church about the exciting changes he was witnessing with the young people and this woman was employed as a pharmaceutical representative. She was very impressed with what she was hearing from the youth minister and commented that "maybe I need to change to another line of work." When the senior pastor heard about this he became angry at the youth minister and told him not to discuss this anymore with people in the church.

The Church is called the "pillar and support of truth" by the apostle Paul in 1 Timothy 3:15, and Jesus called believers "the light of the world" in Matthew 5:14. As such, the Church must lead in showing the world the truth in the area of moral truth and in the area of philosophical beliefs, and when it fails to do so it results in a world that is full of darkness.

The Bible strongly teaches the responsibility of man for his behavior, and when so-called scientists begin telling us that men evolved from primates, we should not be swayed by such teachings but hold firmly to our belief in creation. Likewise, when so-called scientists tell us that we are not responsible for our behavior, or our depression, or anger, we should be very skeptical and oppose such false teachings. Even if we do not know how to overcome anger, grief, shame, and fear, we should pursue an understanding of how to be set free from bondage to our emotions.

Many Christians stand firm in opposition to secular counseling approaches that are based upon worldly belief systems, which is appropriate. Most churches and Christians recognize that Freudian psychoanalysis is based upon philosophies and beliefs that are unbiblical, but this does not necessarily mean that everything Freud taught was untrue. But the beliefs of biological psychiatry that are now dominating our culture and society and leading to shock treatments, psychosurgery, and the drugging of people with emotional problems is far more unbiblical and contradictory to Christian thinking than anything that Freud believed and practiced. At least Freud believed that talk therapy could be helpful to individuals and he did not simply try to medicate them or disable their brains to make them feel better. Psychiatrists today seldom attempt any form of verbal therapy; they simply see clients for 15 minutes and prescribe them a medication to solve their problems.

I grew up in a Christian home and believed with all my heart that the Bible is God's Word and is the truth, and I devoted my life to learning how to help people find freedom through the Lord. After 25 years of seeking solutions from the secular world I learned that they did not know how to help individuals overcome these basic emotions that lead to most forms of mental health problems. I am excited now to see people being set free from addiction, grief, anger, shame, and fear on a regular basis.

Pastors and Bible teachers should not be surprised that the world has no answers for these emotional problems, but they must remain firmly committed to learning how to help people through the use of biblical principles. With my firm belief that the Lord is able to set us free, I eventually found something that worked. I was open-minded to it because I believed the Bible to be true and was willing to "let God be found true, though every man be found a liar" (Romans 3:4).

WARNING: Most psychiatric drugs can cause withdrawal reactions, sometimes including life-threatening emotional and physical withdrawal problems. In short, it is not only dangerous to start taking psychiatric drugs, it can also be dangerous to stop them. Withdrawal from psychiatric drugs should be done carefully under experienced clinical supervision.

12

OVERCOMING SHAME AND OTHER BELIEF-BASED EMOTIONS

I was conducting a brief, two-hour seminar in Arkansas and had spoken about how to overcome grief and anger. There were about thirty people in attendance, and I told them that I would like to do a demonstration of the prayer process if someone would volunteer for prayer. During the break a woman spoke with me and told me that she would like prayer about the loss of her husband who had died nine days earlier.

When we reassembled, I asked her what the strongest emotion was that she felt about the loss of her husband, and she said it was shame. I had not spoken about shame so I knew that the audience would not understand what I was about to do, but I asked her why she felt shame. She told me that her husband had walked down the hallway to their bathroom, and when he got inside the bathroom he collapsed against the door, blocking it so that she could not get inside. This woman tried desperately to get inside to help him but could not. When she finally called for help her husband was dead. She felt guilt and shame, believing that it was her fault that he had died because she failed to act quickly enough in calling for help.

These feelings of shame were due to her belief that if she had acted appropriately he would still be alive. I asked her permission to pray for her, then I prayed and asked the Lord what He wanted her to know about that belief that it was her fault that her husband died. I told her to be quiet and let me know if any thoughts came to her mind. She said, "It wasn't my fault; it was his time to go." I asked her, again, how she felt and she said that she no longer felt guilty or shameful; she just missed him. Her feelings of shame were gone so we made a list of the things she missed about her husband and then prayed and gave them to the Lord. Afterwards, she said she felt peaceful and calm. She was able to think and talk about her husband, without any painful emotions.

This woman had three teenage children she now had to raise on her own, but she was able to handle this with calmness after resolving her feelings of grief and shame. I saw her several times after this and she was still doing well and feeling peaceful, even though we had prayed only nine days after the death of her husband.

Two Kinds of Emotions

So far in this book we have spoken about grief, sadness, anger, and disappointment. These four emotions are all "fact-based emotions" that are primarily caused by unpleasant events in our lives, rather than by our beliefs. I like to call them fact-based because they occur naturally as the result of events that occur around us. For example, when someone dies suddenly with whom you are very close, it is very painful even for emotionally mature individuals. Their grief is not a sign of weakness; it is normal to experience emotional pain in the form of grief when you lose someone close to you, and you realize that you will never see them again in this life.

Even strong Christians who lose their spouse and know that they will see them again one day, can experience strong feelings of grief. Their emotional pain is not a sign of lack of faith. They simply miss their loved one, and it is difficult to adjust to the reality that they will not see them again. When my father died I was very sad even though I knew that I would see him again and I knew that he was in a much better place. It was sad to realize that I would never see him again or talk with him in this lifetime.

Grief, anger, sadness, and disappointment are the four primary fact-based emotions and they can all be resolved through the simple two-step process identified in the preceding chapters. First, be completely honest about your sadness, anger, or grief by making a list of the reasons for your feelings. Second, say a prayer, telling the Lord the reasons for your feelings, then ask Him to take your feelings and carry them for you. This simple process is following the Scriptures that tell us to "Cast your burdens upon the Lord and He will sustain you" (Psalms 55:22) and 1 Peter 5:7, which exhorts us to be in the practice of "casting all your cares upon Him."

Belief-based Emotions

There are other emotions that are caused by our thinking or our beliefs, in contrast to the fact-based emotions. Shame is an example of a belief-based emotion. Shame is a feeling of false guilt and self-blame for something that was not your fault or is already forgiven. It can also be defined as "a false feeling of guilt that you should have done something, that something is your fault, or that you are dirty, bad or shameful because of something that you did or did not do, or because of something that happened to you." In the example just given, the woman felt shame because she falsely blamed herself for her husband's death, which is very common with losses. She was not truly guilty of any wrongdoing, but she falsely believed the lie that she was bad and shameful and responsible for her husband's death.

Shame is a very powerful emotion that Satan uses to destroy lives. When a child is sexually abused he or she often believes that he is dirty, shameful, and bad because of what happened to him. These beliefs can make him feel dirty and bad and act in a self-destructive way. Sexually abused people often become suicidal, self-injurious, or they feel that they deserve to be punished and they surround themselves with people who will punish them.

One of the most popular forms of therapy used by secular counselors and psychologists is cognitive therapy, which teaches that ALL negative emotions are cause by irrational or distorted thinking. Cognitive therapists look for the underlying beliefs that are upsetting people, and try to persuade them of the wrongness of their thinking. There are many emotions that are caused by irrational thinking, or distorted thinking, but it is very difficult to challenge these beliefs through logic because these beliefs are deeply rooted in childhood experiences and cannot be changed through simple logic or persuasion, but require prayer and the Holy Spirit for change.

The "Jesus" Emotions

The fact-based emotions of grief, anger, sadness and disappointment reason are not caused by irrational thinking or distorted thinking. We know this because Jesus experienced each of these, and we know that He had no irrational thinking, so these emotions are not caused by distorted thinking. Because Jesus experienced these feelings, I sometimes like to call them the "Jesus" emotions.

Jesus experienced each of these four emotions, and since He was the Son of God He did not have any irrational thoughts. In John 11 we read about the death of a friend of Jesus' named Lazarus. Jesus was told that he was sick, but He waited four more days before going to see him, so that God would be glorified. When He heard that Lazarus had died, he then went to Bethany where Lazarus had died, and his sisters came out to greet Him. They both fell at His feet and wept over their brother and said, "If you had been here my brother would not have died" (John 11:21, 32). In John 11:35 we are told that "Jesus wept." This short verse is one of the most profound scriptures and it raises many theological issues, but the simplest interpretation of it is that Jesus empathized with Lazarus' sisters in their emotional pain, and He felt their sadness and grief, even though He knew He was going to raise him from the dead in a few minutes. His sadness and grief tells us that grief is not based upon any distorted thinking.

We also see in the gospel accounts of the life of Jesus that on several occasions He became angry. In John 2:15 he went to the temple and saw the money-changers who were in the temple making money from the poor. The scriptures say that He wove a cord and began overturning their tables and, "He drove them all out" (John 2:15). His anger was not due to distorted thinking, but to observing the evil that was occurring. He had righteous and justified anger.

In Luke 19:41 we read that Jesus was going to Jerusalem with His disciples and that "He saw the city and wept" as He began to think about the coming destruction of Jerusalem. He felt sadness as He contemplated this city that He loved, being destroyed due to their stubbornness of heart. His sadness was justified and was not caused by any irrational thinking.

Finally, in Mark 16:14 we are told that Jesus appeared to His disciples after His resurrection, and "He rebuked them for their hardness of heart" in not believing those who had seen Him and told them that He was alive. He was disappointed in their hardness of heart and not understanding that He had told them He would be crucified and that He would be raised up again on the third day. His disappointment was not due to any irrational thinking or distorted thinking, but due to a disappointing event. Disappointment can be released in the same way as anger and grief, by identifying the reasons for your disappointment and then giving it to the Lord and asking Him to take it from you.

Overcoming Feelings of Shame

A sincere Christian man came to see me for counseling. He told me that he had been to prison for two- and-a-half years and he was saved while in prison, and began reading his Bible every day and going to church services. Once he was released from prison he continued getting up every morning at 4:30 a.m. to read his Bible and pray, because he was so hungry for the Lord.

One day he said that he needed to talk with me about something that had been bothering him. He said that as a young man he did something that he felt badly about, and every time he thought about it he felt shameful. I asked him if he had confessed this to God, and he said he had. When I asked him if he believed he was forgiven by the Lord, he said that he believed that God was a forgiving God and had forgiven him. I asked him if he felt forgiven and first he hesitated, then he said he didn't feel forgiven.

I asked this man if he would like to feel forgiven and he said he would, so I prayed and asked the Lord what he wanted this man to know about his belief that he was bad, dirty, and shameful because of what he had done as a young man (which he had not disclosed). He immediately burst into tears and began sobbing, so I asked him what thoughts had come to his mind. "You are my son," he said. "Does that feel true?" I asked him. He affirmed that it did, and he said that it made him feel good.

I asked if I could pray for him again, and he gave me permission so I prayed, "Lord, is there anything else that you want this man to know about his belief that he is bad and shameful because of what he did as a young man?" He suddenly burst into tears again and began sobbing. I asked him what thoughts had come to his mind this time and he said the thought that suddenly popped into his mind was, "You're already clean, whiter than snow." I asked him if that felt true and he said it did. Then I asked how it made him feel. He replied that it made him feel good and forgiven.

I told this man to think about what he had done as a young man that made him feel so bad, and asked him how he felt now about it. He said, "I know that what I did was wrong, but I also know that the Lord has forgiven me, and I am clean in God's eyes." "How does that make you feel?" I asked. He broke into a smile and said "that makes me feel wonderful!"

I saw this man many more times after this and he continued to feel good and to do well. He was able to talk openly about his past sins without being overwhelmed with feelings of shame. He had been forgiven long before I met him, but he didn't feel forgiven because he was full of shame.

Steps for Overcoming Shame

There are three simple steps for resolving feelings of shame, which are as follows:

> **Step One**: Identify the original source of the feelings.
>
> **Step Two:** Identify the beliefs underlying the feelings of shame that resulted from this past experience.
>
> **Step Three**: Pray for truth and ask the Lord what He wants you (or the other person) to know about these beliefs.

The process for resolving belief-based emotions is very simple and is illustrated by this man. He felt guilt and shame because of his false beliefs that he was still dirty and shameful, even though the Lord had forgiven him. Such irrational beliefs can be very difficult to change as you attempt to challenge the person's wrong beliefs. If I had attempted to persuade him through logic and by quoting scriptures that he was not shameful or bad, he would probably have agreed with my logic but continued to feel guilty and shameful.

Such beliefs are difficult to change, mostly because they are rooted in earlier experiences. In the case described I simply identified the beliefs underlying his feelings, that he was still shameful and bad, and then prayed for truth and asked the Lord what He wanted this man to know. The Lord brought truth to him and set him free. There are many scriptures that give support to this principle but the most direct one is John 8:32, "You will know the truth, and the truth will set you free." James 1:5 also supports this principle, which says "If any of you lacks wisdom, let him ask of God, who gives generously and without reproach, and it will be given to him."

Three Sources of Thoughts

When I prayed for this man and he immediately burst into tears, I knew that a thought had come to his mind, but not all thoughts that come into our minds are from the Lord. There are three possible sources from which our thoughts can come.

First, the thought might come from the Lord, but when thoughts are from the Lord they must be fully consistent with the Scriptures. In addition, they will change the person's life and bring healing. Isaiah 55:11-12 says, "So will My word be which goes forth from My mouth; It will not return to Me empty, without accomplishing what I desire and without succeeding in the matter for which I sent it. For you will go out with joy and be led forth with peace." It's very interesting that this scripture says that "you will go out with joy and be led forth with peace" when God's word comes to you. That is exactly what happens when a person hears from the Lord while praying sincerely for truth. They feel the peace of God in their life.

Second, the thought could come from the person's own mind. Usually they can tell if it is a thought that is coming from them, and just asking them where their thought came from can reveal this. When the thought is new to them or foreign to them they will immediately tell you that it didn't come from their own mind. If it didn't come from their mind, then it either came from the Lord or from the devil, and this can be discerned by noting if it is consistent with the Word of God.

The third possible source of thoughts is from the enemy. You can usually recognize it immediately because the devil will say, "God says He wants to punish you" or "you can never be forgiven" which is contradictory to the Word. It is important for prayer ministers to be very familiar with the Word so that they can quickly recognize the voice of God and the voice of the enemy.

An interesting biblical example of this is found in Matthew 16: 15-23 when Jesus asked his disciples, "Who do you say that I am?" Peter immediately responded with, "You are the Christ, the Son of the Living God" and Jesus said, "flesh and blood did not reveal that to you." Then a few minutes later Jesus began telling His disciples that he was going to be crucified and Peter said, "No, Lord. That will never happen." Jesus rebuked him saying, "Get behind me Satan! You are not setting your mind on God's interests, but man's." (Matthew 16:16, 23). In the first instance, Peter received thoughts from the Lord which were revealed to him directly from the Father, and in the second instance he received thoughts from the devil, which the Lord rebuked. We, too, must learn to discern the voice of God and the voice of the devil when we pray for truth for ourselves or for others.

The Impact of Shame

The Bible describes Satan "a liar and the father of lies" (John 8:44), so it is clear that he uses lies and deceptions to put people in bondage, just as he did Adam and Eve in the garden of Eden. Shame is a very powerful emotion that Satan uses to destroy lives.

Sexually abused children are often devastated by shame. They frequently believe that they are shameful and bad because of what happened to them, because they didn't tell anyone, or because they believe they should have resisted more. These are all lies that are placed in their minds by their abuser and by the devil, but it can lead to self-abuse, anger, depression, substance abuse, and relationship problems. Shame that is rooted in early-life experiences like sexual abuse is difficult to remove, but through prayer the Lord is able to remove it easily and replace it with truth to set us free (John 8:32).

Ann Jennings, a psychologist from the state of Maine, documented the sad story of her daughter's sexual abuse as a child and the impact it had on her childhood and adult life (Jennings, 1994). From age 13 until her death at age 32, her daughter, Anna, was treated by the mental health system and given many different diagnoses. While hospitalized at age 22 she disclosed to her mother that her emotional problems began when she was sadistically raped by a male babysitter at age 2 ½ which led to many different symptoms over the years. She was repeatedly hospitalized, medicated, and given shock treatments. At times she was homeless, and her feelings of shame led her to prostitute herself, and mutilate herself, because of her belief that she was evil and shameful. Tragically, at age 32 she committed suicide by hanging.

This sad story is repeated time after time in the lives of countless individuals who are full of anger and shame due to sexual abuse. The usual underlying beliefs behind feelings of shame are: "I am dirty, bad, and shameful; I should have done more; I should have resisted more; If I had done more my wife, mother, or friend would still be alive; It's my fault that this happened; I am dirty and nasty because of what happened to me." Satan uses these lies to cripple and enslave people. It is one of his favorite tools for holding people in bondage and destroying them.

Three Forms of Truth

When the Lord speaks to individuals, it comes in one of three forms. The man described earlier had the thought come to his mind, "You're already clean, whiter than snow." That thought was clearly from the Lord because it was consistent with the Word of God which says in Isaiah 1:18, "'Come now, and let us reason together,' Says the LORD, 'Though your sins are as scarlet, They will be as white as snow; Though they are red like crimson, They will be like wool.'" Sometimes there is a clear thought like this that comes to the persons' mind after they pray for truth.

At other times, individuals have a visual picture that conveys a truth to them. Sometimes people say that they are visualizing Jesus standing before them with a smile, or with tears in His eyes, and this leads them to believe the Lord is sharing their sadness or is showing His love and concern for them.

When I first learned this ministry I requested ten hours of prayer sessions with the man who introduced me to this ministry. I was experiencing a great deal of stress at work where I was the director of a state program and had to deal single-handedly with rebellious employees and their unions. I felt very alone, and my prayer minister asked me when the first time was that I could remember feeling alone. I shared with him that I felt alone in high school one time, when I took my Bible to school with me and during a study hall I had no homework to complete so I took out my Bible and tried to read. However, I felt very alone and felt that everyone was looking at me (which was probably not true).

The prayer minister prayed for me and asked the Lord what He wanted me to know. I had my eyes closed and in my mind I turned to my right side in the study hall and visualized, to my great surprise, Jesus sitting beside me smiling. Immediately my anxiety and feelings of aloneness lifted because I realized that I was not alone, the Lord was with me, and He was pleased with me. This was my first experience in hearing from the Lord through prayer, and it was through a visual picture that came into my mind.

At other times, individuals do not have any thoughts come to their mind and they do not have any visual pictures come to them, but they suddenly acquire a new insight into their situation. If they had previously expressed the belief that it was their fault that someone died, I might ask them if it still feels true, and their response may be, "No, that's not true." They may not have a thought come to their mind or a visual image come to them, but they simply have a quiet realization of the truth.

Biblical Basis: Praying for Truth

I did not grow up in a church that regularly spoke of the Lord speaking to believers, so I initially wondered if there was any biblical basis for this belief that the Lord will speak into the hearts of believers as they pray for truth. The first scripture that came to mind was John 8:32 where Jesus said, "You shall know the truth, and the truth will set you free." This scripture can be interpreted to apply to this situation, but it could be interpreted as applying to a number of other circumstances as well.

However, in John 16:13 Jesus spoke of the Holy Spirit, saying, "When He, the Spirit of truth comes, He will guide you into all the truth." This scripture is much more direct in suggesting that the Holy Spirit will guide us to know truth that we need to know. James 1:5 is a very interesting scripture that I had previously interpreted very differently, primarily to mean that we should pray for direction from the Lord when trying to make an important decision. However, it is given in the context of trials, because in James 1:2 James says, "Consider it all joy, my brethren, when you encounter various trials." Then in verse 5 he writes, "But if any of you lacks wisdom, let him ask of God, who gives to all generously and without reproach, and it will be given to him."

There have been many different definitions of "wisdom" but Bible scholar W.E. Vine, author of the *Expository Dictionary of New Testament* Words, defines it as "Insight into the true nature of things." This is a very helpful definition which fits well into this discussion about the role of the Holy Spirit in our lives during trials and tribulations. When we are distressed due to our wrong thinking or beliefs, He provides us "insight into the true nature of things" in our past and present experiences, that sets us free from our fear, shame, hurt, helplessness, and hopelessness.

A wonderful example of this principle in operation can be found in 2 Kings 6 when Elisha was surrounded by the armies of the Arameans, and his servant cried out to him in fear. Elisha said to him, "Do not fear, for those who are with us are more than those who are with them," (2 Kings 6:16) but these words were of no apparent comfort to him. Verse 17 says, "Then Elisha prayed and said, 'O Lord, I pray, open his eyes that he may see.' And the Lord opened the servant's eyes and he saw; and behold, the mountain was full of horses and chariots of fire all around Elisha." When Elisha prayed for the Lord to open the eyes of his attendant, then he saw the truth that there were, indeed, more with them than those against them. That took away his fear and gave him peace.

This is exactly what happens when believers pray for truth about something that is distressing them due to their false beliefs. The Lord responds to their request and gives them peace and calm once they know the truth, just as the prophet's attendant did. This is sometimes referred to as the "still, small voice of God," based upon 1 Kings 19:12 (KJV) when the Lord spoke to the prophet Elijah with a "still, small voice" rather than in a wind, fire, and earthquake.

Hymns of Truth

There are many traditional hymns that bear witness of how the Lord speaks to believers to comfort them. As a child I remember singing a well-known hymn called, "He Keeps Me Singing." The first stanza says, "There's within my heart a melody, Jesus whispers sweet and low, 'Fear not, I am with thee, peace, be still, in all of life's ebb and flow.'" The concept that Jesus whispers to us the words, "Fear not, I am with thee, peace, be still," is very consistent with this ministry and with the way the Lord speaks to us to comfort us.

Another classic old hymn titled, "Jesus Paid it All," begins with the words, "I hear the Savior say, 'Thy strength indeed is small, child of weakness, watch and pray, find in Me thine all in all.'" Once again the hymn states the theme that the Lord is personally speaking to the hymn writer who wrote, "I hear the Savior say."

A beautiful, but less well-known hymn that I heard often as a child is titled, "I heard the voice of Jesus say." The beginning stanza to this hymn says, "I heard the voice of Jesus say, 'Come unto Me and rest; Lay down, thou weary one, lay down Thy head upon My breast'."

Many hymns of invitation express the thought that the Lord is calling unbelievers to them, through His Holy Spirit. The hymn, "Softly and Tenderly" says, "Softly and tenderly, Jesus is calling, calling for you and for me." These many classic hymns casually and unapologetically speak of how the Lord speaks to us, in our hearts, when we listen to Him and give testimony to the long-standing belief of the Christian community that the Lord does speak to us, brings truth to our minds to comfort us, and gives us peace.

A Father's Story

A man came for help with his long-held addiction problem. He was clean and sober but had a long history of drug abuse, and had been incarcerated and completed many treatments, and always returned eventually to his addiction. I asked him what was the most emotionally difficult experience for him and he said that the most difficult thing for him to deal with was his guilt and shame about his children. He had neglected his children and had never been a good father to them; this weighed heavily on his conscience and he felt shameful about it.

This man had a clear testimony of salvation and said he had confessed his sin and failure to the Lord, but still felt very badly about his failure as a father. I prayed about his belief that he was bad and shameful and asked the Lord what He wanted this man to know about his belief that he was still bad and shameful. The thought that came immediately to his mind from the Lord was, "You are my child; you are a new creature; I love you." This made him feel comforted, but he then confessed that he participated in the abortion of one of his children, which he witnessed. I asked the Lord what He wanted this man to know about his belief that he was bad and shameful because of this abortion. The Lord brought a thought that came to his mind to give him comfort, and he left our session feeling peace and freedom from feelings of guilt and shame for the first time in his life.

Set Free from Sexual Abuse

A man told me that he had always felt something was different about him, and from a very young age he believed he was a homosexual. As an adult he sought counseling, and he told me that three years previously he suddenly had a clear memory of being sexually abused by his father. He remembered as a young child thinking, "he's not supposed to be doing this," and he remembered feeling strong feelings of shame. His father told him, "You're going to tell mom and I'll never see you again." He replied to his father, "No, I'm not."

I prayed and asked the Lord what he wanted this man to know about his belief that he was guilty and shameful. The thought that he said immediately came to his mind was, "I'm innocent; I'm not guilty; I have no need to be ashamed. I was afraid to not see my dad so I immediately blocked it out of my mind." After we finished praying I asked him to think about the sexual abuse and tell me how he felt now. He said, "I see myself as guiltless and innocent. I don't feel guilty any more. I feel free!" He left my office a free man because the Lord brought truth to him to set him free.

Most mental health counselors try to talk clients out of such feelings, but these feelings are so deeply rooted in childhood events and memories that they cannot be removed through simple reason. However, the Lord can easily remove the lies when we identify them and pray for the truth. The Holy Spirit gives us "insight into the true nature" of our childhood experiences, and sets us free from feelings of shame that can hold us in bondage our entire life. Earthly counselors cannot set you free from these lies, but the Lord can because He is the "Wonderful Counselor."

Other Belief-Based Emotions

In this chapter we have introduced the concept of belief-based emotions and shared steps to freedom. We have focused on the feeling of shame, but all other belief-based emotions are resolved using the same simple steps.

In contrast to the "fact-based" emotions, belief-based emotions cannot be simply given to God. They are based on false beliefs and they require truth for individuals to be released from them, but even logical truth is insufficient when these beliefs are rooted in early-life experiences. Such beliefs require finding the original source, then receiving truth from the Holy Spirit into "the true nature of things." This necessitates both the utilization of prayer, and reliance upon the Holy Spirit for freedom from belief-based emotions.

The primary emotions that are belief-based include shame, fear, aloneness, hurt, helplessness, and hopelessness. Each one of these emotions has some basic beliefs connected to them that must be identified. Once these beliefs are identified, one must then pray and ask the Lord for truth regarding the underlying beliefs behind your emotions. It is also generally necessary to identify the historical source of your feelings so that the Lord can then speak truth into that memory.

The following are the beliefs most commonly associated with the emotions identified:

> *Helplessness*: I am powerless, weak, and unable to do anything.
> *Hopelessness*: There is no way out of this, it will never change, it will never end, I am trapped.
> *Hurt:* I am unacceptable, unloved, unwanted, or I do not measure up.
> *Aloneness*: I'm all alone, unprotected, abandoned, no one understands me.
> *Fear*: Something terrible is going to happen.
> *Shame*: It is my fault, I failed, I'm a bad person, I'm dirty, bad, or shameful.

These other belief-based emotions will be discussed in more detail in later chapters of this book. Particularly, fear will be discussed more thoroughly because so many people struggle with feelings of anxiety and fear that disable them. Regardless of which of these emotions you are experiencing, however, the Lord can set you free from all of these negative emotions through the three simple steps identified earlier.

Dealing with Genuine Guilt

It is very important to understand the differences and the relationship between shame and genuine guilt. Everyone falls short of God's standards according to the Bible which says, "All have sinned and fall short of the glory of God" (Romans 3:23). When individuals fail morally they experience feelings of genuine guilt. The apostle Paul says that "they show the work of the Law written in their hearts, their conscience bearing witness" (Romans 2:15).

When a woman has an abortion, it creates a strong sense of shame, usually because she has an innate awareness of the life that she is carrying within her. This is why women often struggle with grief when they have miscarriages, and when they deliberately choose to abort a child, it leaves deep and lasting emotional scars and a guilty conscience. The same is true for individuals who have affairs, even though immorality is so common and accepted in our society. Many people feel guilty about their affairs, even though they may deny this.

Genuine guilt results when we break God's laws, and do things that we know are wrong. Such guilt cannot be resolved through psychotherapy or through medications. It is a strictly spiritual matter to resolve guilt, because only God can forgive us for our sins. The only way to find true freedom from guilt is to confess our sins to the Lord and ask for His forgiveness through the blood of Jesus. Jesus died for our sins, according to the Bible, and everyone who sincerely confesses their sins will be forgiven through Him (1 John 1:9).

Ephesians 1:7 says, "In Him we have redemption through His blood, the forgiveness of our trespasses," and 1 John 1:9 says, "If we confess our sins, He is faithful and just to forgive us our sins, and to cleanse us from all unrighteousness." Those who have received Jesus as their Savior will continue to sin after they are saved, but they need to learn to confess their sins on a daily basis so that their relationship with the Lord is restored. If they fail to do this they will grow further and further from the Lord and can become utterly miserable.

King David was described as "a man after God's own heart" and yet he cried out in Psalm 32:1-5, declaring how wonderful it was to be forgiven for his sins, and how terrible it was to carry guilt in his heart.

> *How blessed is he whose transgression is forgiven, Whose sin is covered! How blessed is the man to whom the LORD*

> *does not impute iniquity, And in whose spirit there is no deceit!*
> *When I kept silent about my sin, my body wasted away, Through my groaning all day long. For day and night Your hand was heavy upon me; My vitality was drained away as with the fever heat of summer. Selah.*
> *I acknowledged my sin to You, And my iniquity I did not hide; I said, "I will confess my transgressions to the LORD," And You forgave the guilt of my sin.*

Guilt is a terrible burden to carry, and secular counselors have no way to help people find release from feelings of guilt! But Jesus wants to carry it for you, just as He gave Himself for you so that you could have eternal life and forgiveness of all of your sins. If you want to be forgiven for your sins and be free of your genuine guilt, you need to confess your sins to the Lord and ask for His forgiveness through the blood of Jesus.

If you are not 100% sure that you are forgiven for all your sins and that you are going to heaven, let me encourage you to call upon the Lord now and receive Him as your Savior. John 1:12 says, "As many as received Him, to them He gave the right to become children of God, even to those who believe in His name." The Lord Jesus said in Revelation 3:20, "Behold, I stand at the door and knock; if anyone hears My voice and opens the door, I will come in to him." If you will answer His call and receive Him into your life now, He will forgive you for your sins and make you a child of God. If you wish to do this sincerely say the following prayer and receive Him as your Savior.

Suggested Prayer:
"Thank you, Lord, for loving me and sending your Son Jesus to die in my place. I confess to You, Lord, that I am a sinner and have fallen short of your standards. I ask You to forgive me through the blood of Jesus and take control of my life so that I can serve You and follow You. I pray this in Jesus' name. Amen."

SECTION C:

Letting the Truth Set You Free

13

OVERCOMING SEXUAL ABUSE

In the previous chapter, I made reference to the sad story of psychologist Ann Jennings whose daughter, Anna, was sexually abused as a child and it had a devastating impact upon her adult life (Jennings, 2004). From age 13 to 32 she was repeatedly hospitalized in psychiatric hospitals, treated by mental health professionals, and given many different diagnoses. Psychiatric drugs comprised 95% of the treatment approach given to her. While hospitalized at age 22 she disclosed to her mother that her emotional problems began when she was sadistically raped by a male babysitter at age 2 ½, which led to many different symptoms over the years. She was repeatedly hospitalized, medicated, and given shock treatments. At times she was homeless, and her feelings of shame led her to prostitute herself, and mutilate herself with the belief that she was evil and shameful. Then tragically, at age 32, she committed suicide by hanging.

Reading such stories is heart-breaking, and hearing individuals tell such stories is extremely sad. Unfortunately, this sad story is repeated time after time in the lives of countless individuals who are full of anger and shame due to sexual abuse. Many lives have been damaged and destroyed by the effects of childhood sexual abuse, and the Church must be able to help such individuals in order to be relevant to the emotional needs of those in our society.

Research on Sexual Abuse

Many research studies have documented a strong connection between childhood sexual abuse and adult psychological problems. Individuals who report childhood sexual abuse are much more likely to have significant problems with depression, anxiety, eating disorders and substance abuse. Studies of women have found that between 20% and 35% received some kind of unwanted sexual attention before age 16, and between 5% and 15% had experienced severe forms of sexual abuse, such as attempted or completed intercourse (Kendler and Prescott, 2006, p. 142).

The Adverse Childhood Experiences (ACE) Study is one of the largest investigations of its kind ever conducted, with approximately 17,000 subjects included. They found that 16% of men and 25% of women in their sample had experienced childhood sexual abuse. The number of males who are sexually abused is less than that of females but there are still many men who suffer similar adult psychological problems as a result of sexual abuse.

The "Virginia Twin Study" found that individuals who experienced childhood sexual abuse were from three to six times more likely to experience some form of psychological problems during their adulthood (Kendler and Prescott, 2006, p. 146). In twin studies, where the twins shared the same family environment, identical genes, and exposure to other environmental risk factors, the twin who experienced childhood sexual abuse had a consistently higher risk for emotional or psychological problems over the twin who did not experience sexual abuse. This same relationship was found in two other large Australian twin studies (Kendler and Prescott, 2006, p. 284).

Set Free from Childhood Sexual Abuse

A woman asked for help with her anger and admitted that she had been angry since childhood. She stated that she became angry after age 10 when she was molested by a young man, and she began to hurt others due to her anger, having recently hit a friend. I explained to her that she could get rid of her anger through prayer, and she said that she believed in prayer and was willing to give this a try. She told me that she had forgiven the man who had abused her but was still angry at him because he hurt her emotionally and physically, he took advantage of her, and he later took advantage of other young girls. This sexual abuse led her to become mean to her sister and damaged her relationship with other men. We made a list of seven resentments she had toward the young man, and she prayed and asked the Lord to take all her anger from her and carry it for her. Then I prayed and asked the Lord what He wanted her to know. She said, "It's okay; it's not my fault but I was wrong to hurt my sister." She said she felt no more anger at the man who molested her. The thought that "it's not my fault" felt true to her and took away her feelings of shame about her sexual abuse.

I asked this woman if she would like to get rid of her guilt and shame over her mistreatment of her sister and she said she would, so I led her in a prayer, and she confessed her guilt and shame and asked the Lord to forgive her. After that she said that she felt no more guilt or shame over the molestation or over her mistreatment of her sister, but she felt some sadness that she had hurt her sister and contributed to her personal problems. She was also sad that she did not have a good relationship with her sister, her sister wouldn't talk about her problems and had been treated badly by others, and she did not take good care of her children. We made a list of five reasons for her sadness, then she prayed and asked the Lord to take her sadness from her. After praying she said that she felt no sadness, anger, or shame. She just felt peaceful and calm when thinking about her molestation.

This sexual abuse had affected her entire life, made her angry at others, damaged her relationships with men, and robbed her of joy and peace, but after this brief prayer session she was set free from her anger, shame, and sadness. Most people who have been sexually abused carry the effects of their abuse for the rest of their lives, but the Lord is able to set them free from their anger, sadness, shame and fear. Like this young woman, they can be set free in just a few minutes as they learn to cast all their cares upon the Lord and let Him carry them for them.

Emotional Impact of Sexual Abuse

This case illustrates how to help those who have been sexually abused. Sexual abuse is a very personal, private matter which many people do not want to discuss, so it should be approached with sensitivity. In my work as a professional counselor this is facilitated by my work setting, because people come to me for help with their emotions and expect to talk about personal experiences. If you are functioning as a prayer minister and someone is coming to you for help, it may be similar, but it is always advisable to ask their permission before asking personal questions about their traumatic childhood experiences. Even in my counseling office I generally ask permission before delving into personal background issues. I usually say, "Do you mind if I ask some more background questions about your family so that I can understand you better?" Everyone gives me approval when I do this, and it gives me permission to probe into their background to learn about their past, including any possible sexual abuse.

To be able to help a sexually abused individual, it is important to help them identify the various emotions they feel when they think about the abuse. Sexual abuse is a form of posttraumatic stress disorder (PTSD), and trauma and trauma healing will be discussed in a later chapter of this book. I usually ask several key questions when I begin to explore an individual's sexual abuse trauma. First, I ask "If you could resolve your sexual abuse so that it no longer affects you emotionally, would you like to?" That question opens up the conversation and obtains the person's cooperation, since you are now in a position to help them achieve their personal goals.

A second question that I generally ask is, "Was this a one-time incident or did it happen repeatedly? Were there other times that you were sexually abused?" The obvious intent here is to determine if there are multiple traumas that need to be resolved, or just one incident. The third question I ask is, "When you think about your sexual abuse, what are the main emotions you feel?"

Sexual abuse has a lasting impact on individuals because of the negative emotions that result from the incident or incidents. It may make the individual angry at the offender, it may make them feel dirty and shameful, or it may make them fearful of men, women, or adults. The main emotions that are experienced from sexual abuse are anger and shame, but they may also feel some sadness and fear. The process of resolving their sexual abuse is to help them find emotional healing for each negative emotion they have from the sexual abuse. As you pray with the individual about each emotion they have about their abuse and they resolve these emotions, they will feel peaceful and be able to talk about their abuse without any negative feelings.

I had two young boys brought to me by their father after their older brother had molested them. The older boy was 13 years old and he was having anger problems. When I asked about his sexual abuse by his brother he repeatedly said that he didn't like to talk about it, which is a clear indication that it was stirring up strong feelings of shame and anger. His younger brother was 10 years old and when I spoke to him separately he responded very differently. When I asked about his feelings about the sexual abuse he told me that he wasn't really angry because he had forgiven him. I asked him how he was able to forgive him and he said, "Through God." He said that he goes to church and he knew he had to forgive his brother. Then I asked him if he felt embarrassed about what happened or felt like he was dirty or like it was his fault. He said he did not; he was not embarrassed about it at all and he was able to talk about the incident without any discomfort.

This is the best test of healing: the individual can talk about the incident without any embarrassment, because there are no negative emotions connected to the memory and it is completely resolved. All of this can be accomplished, frequently, in a single counseling or prayer session. Once you identify the various emotions about the sexual abuse incident, then you simply begin praying about each one until they are all resolved. If the individual was sexually abused by other individuals, these can also be discussed one-by-one until they are completely resolved.

When Prayer Doesn't Work

A woman came to me for help in dealing with her separation from her husband who was having an affair with another woman. She had previously given her anger at her husband to the Lord but she still felt guilty and blamed herself for the emotional struggles that her children were experiencing as a result of the separation, and she felt that she was being selfish. She said that she had made a list and tried to pray about her guilt and give it to God, but it didn't work. The reason why it didn't work was because she was treating her feelings like genuine guilt but she was actually dealing with feelings of shame. You cannot just give your shame to the Lord, you need truth to set you free from false guilt, or shame.

Recognizing that her feelings of shame were probably rooted in a childhood experience, like most strong feelings, I asked her when was the first time that she could remember feeling such feelings of shame and blame. She said that at age 5 she was molested by her stepfather for several years, and when she resisted his continuing advances he screamed, hollered, threw things and beat her mother. She told her mother about the sexual abuse but her mother ignored it, because she was only concerned about losing her husband and being alone. This woman believed it was her fault that her mother was being beaten and that she was being selfish. I prayed and asked the Lord what He wanted her to know about her belief that it was her fault that her mother was being beaten. She immediately said, "I shouldn't feel guilty; it was not my fault. I was just a kid." This was the truth that she needed to be set free from her feelings of shame.

I asked this woman how she felt now, and she said she no longer felt guilty or selfish, but she felt angry at her mother for not protecting her. She said that her mother never acknowledged her wrong in this matter or apologized to her, and her mother continues to believe that women have to do whatever it takes to keep their men. This woman also said that her mother was never a good mother to her, she never protected her or provided her emotional comfort, and yet she expects this daughter to take care of her. She identified 19 reasons for her anger toward her mother, then she prayed and gave all her anger to the Lord and asked Him to carry it for her. When we were finished praying I asked her how she felt toward her mother, and she said she forgave her and had no more anger. She even said, "She does care about me but doesn't have the capacity to realize what she is doing. I feel pity for her."

With her anger out of the way, I prayed and asked the Lord what He wanted this woman to know about her belief that it was her fault that her children were suffering from the separation, and that she was being selfish. She reflected quietly for a few moments then said, "They're not suffering as much as I thought. It's not my fault; it's their daddy's fault. I have tried to save my marriage and can't allow my son to believe it's ok to treat his wife this way, or my daughter to believe she has to let her husband have affairs." She said that she needs to teach her children how to be at peace and be strong. When I asked her again how she felt, she said she had no more feelings of guilt or hurt feelings. I explained how she first released some feelings of shame, then she had released her anger, and then the Lord brought truth to her to set her free from more feelings of shame. Prayer did work when she prayed for truth. I asked her what she thought about this. She smiled and said, "It's amazing!"

Woman Set Free from Sexual Abuse

I prayed with a woman who lost her husband and was so depressed that she cried all the time and secluded herself, not wanting to ever leave the house. Her doctor prescribed an antidepressant for her but it made her feel worse so she quit taking it. I talked with her about how to overcome grief by being honest and making a list of the reasons for her grief, and then praying and giving it to the Lord. She was very receptive to this idea and was eager to get started with overcoming the loss of her husband. Her strongest feelings about her husband were feelings of guilt and shame, so we prayed first about these feelings. Then we prayed about her anger toward her husband for his years of abuse. After releasing her guilt, shame and anger she said she felt calm and she began getting out and meeting people again. The following week she said she was still doing well but she felt some sadness and missed her husband. These were feelings of grief so we identified 15 things she missed about him and then I led her in a prayer. She gave her grief and sadness to the Lord and then had 100% peace about the loss of her husband of 43 years.

The next time I saw this woman she said that her father had called her, and was insisting that she come to visit him for Christmas, but she had a lot of resentments toward him because of his years of abuse. Her father was an angry alcoholic who had abused her mother and her for the first eight years of her life before her parents divorced. He was very controlling, and treated her mother as inferior. After the divorce, this woman lived with her mother and grandparents until age 16, and her father never paid any child support to help raise his children. At age 16 she went to live with her father, and he continued to drink, and he verbally and physically abused her stepmother like he had her mother.

One night while intoxicated he sexually abused her, and she told her mother but he denied it. He never admitted having abused her in any way and always insisted that he was a good father. However, she understandably resented his physical, verbal, and sexual abuse all her life, and it led her to become depressed and to drink.

She said that she was tired of being angry toward her father, who was now elderly and posed no threat to her, so I led her in a prayer. She told the Lord 16 reasons for her anger, and asked Him to take her anger and carry it for her. After giving her anger to the Lord, I asked her how she felt. She said that she felt sorry for him, and pity, but felt no more anger toward him. She said, "I carried it too long and should let it go. It's in the past. It's taken care of. He has to carry that load. I did nothing wrong, it wasn't my fault." I asked again how she felt as she thought about her father. She smiled a big smile and said, "I'm at peace. It does't bother me any more to talk about it. I feel like I can do anything." She left with a huge grin on her face and joy in her heart, and felt sorry for her father rather than angry. She was completely free from the anger and shame of her physical and sexual abuse by her father.

How can someone feel sorry for someone who has harmed them so deeply? It's a supernatural work of God in the person's life when they honestly tell the Lord why they are angry and ask Him to take their anger and carry it for them. It's the same response Jesus had when he was hanging on the cross and said, "Father, forgive them, for they know not what they are doing" (Luke 23:34). This woman had justified anger toward her father, but the Lord does not want us to carry this anger for long. He wants us to give it all to Him so that we can experience His supernatural peace and joy in our lives and be set free from our past traumas.

If this woman was younger and her father was still emotionally abusive and posed a threat to her, I would have discouraged her from seeing him. Emotional release and forgiveness do not require that an abuse victim must reconcile to their abuser; it simply means they have released their negative feelings toward the person so that they harbor no resentments or anger toward them. When they are emotionally neutral about their abuser, they are capable of listening to the Lord to determine if it is wise for them to be around the abuser or not. The Lord can, and will, guide you into the truth and enable you to make a wise decision about the extent of involvement you can safely have with your former abuser, if any.

Thirty Years of Bondage to Sexual Abuse Released

A young woman came for help after she exploded in anger one day at her son's school. She became combative with the police and was incarcerated, then she was sent to a psychiatric facility where she was so heavily medicated that she slept all day and could not function as a mother. She was desperate for help, and I was able to pray with her about her feelings of shame and guilt over this situation. She also prayed about three significant losses she had had, and was able to release her grief, and her depression lifted. She came one day prepared to talk about her sexual abuse as a child.

This woman told me that she was sexually abused from age 3-5 by a stepfather, and then at age 14 she was raped by a 21-year-old man. She said that the second incident was more upsetting to her than the earlier one so we talked about it first. She was angry at this man for taking advantage of her as a child and for how this had such a traumatic impact on her life. She later found out that the same man had abused her best friend and other young girls, and was never arrested nor experienced any consequences for his actions. He caused her, and these other girls, immense emotional, physical, and relational harm, and when she saw his picture on Facebook it upset her.

She identified nine reasons for her anger toward this man, and then she prayed and asked the Lord to take her anger and carry it for her. I prayed and asked the Lord what He wanted her to know. She said, "God loves me anyway and I don't have to be ashamed." After giving her anger to the Lord and receiving these truths from Him I asked her how she felt. She said, "I don't feel anything; just neutral. I hope that he gets help. I have been angry at him for 20 years. God will handle it in His own time and way; it's not my responsibility to dole out punishment." Her feelings of anger and shame were completely gone and she smiled and laughed and said she felt "Pretty good!"

We then talked about her being sexually abused from age 3 to 5 by her stepfather. She told me that she was sad as she recalled how this man drugged her mother and beat her in their basement and broke her down emotionally. She felt sad as she recalled how sadistic and cruel this man was to her and her mother, and how he kept them confined in a house with bars on the windows and with an attack dog that frightened them. He threatened that he would kill them if they ever left him. She spent a lot of time alone, in her room, while he entertained other drug addicts in their home.

She had blocked all of these memories from her mind for 31 years, but recently had begun remembering these early childhood experiences. This woman denied any anger, but identified 16 reasons for her sadness, and she prayed and gave it all to the Lord. Afterwards she told me that her sadness was gone, but then her anger began to well up inside her and she became so angry that she said she felt like punching something. She identified nine reasons for her anger toward her stepfather, then prayed and gave it all to the Lord. I asked her how she felt afterwards and she said, "Peaceful; there's no anger at all." Her anger was instantly gone! She then said, "My overprotectiveness with my son was based on knowing that my mother did not protect me and could not protect me."

She smiled with peace and joy in her heart. The anger and shame she had carried from these childhood sexual abuse experiences for 30 years was suddenly gone, and she was able to think and talk about them without any anger or shame. It was this anger that had led her to be so explosive, and to become combative with the police and get incarcerated. She left my office rejoicing. What an awesome privilege it is to watch the Lord heal people of such trauma in their lives as they learn to cast all their cares upon him and to listen to the comforting truths of the Holy Spirit who sets us free!

Set Free from Sexual Abuse Fear, Anger, and Guilt

A man came for help with his anger. He said that he grew up in an abusive home with alcoholic parents who were violent with each other and with their children. He began drinking at age nine as a way of coping with his feelings. When he got married he became violent with his wife, so she left him and took the children and he gave up hope and began living on the streets. He went to prison twice, and while in prison he received Jesus as his Savior. After leaving prison he stayed free of all drugs and alcohol and became actively involved in church and ministry, but he admitted that he had a lot of anger and anxiety still that he wanted help in resolving.

I shared with this man how he could be set free from his anger by making a list of his resentments toward those who had wronged him. I asked him who he resented the most, and he told me he resented his brother for being so emotionally and physically abusive to him. His brother was eight years older than him and beat him every day, laughed at him when he cried, slapped him on his back as hard as he could, and almost drowned him, so that he was afraid of water. One night this man was awakened by his brother who put his hand over his mouth and nose and almost smothered him while he raped him. Since then he had had nightmares, anxiety, and woke up shaking and crying and feeling like he was suffocating. He told me that he had plotted what he would do to his brother to get even with him when he got too old to defend himself. Now that he was a Christian he knew that was wrong and he wanted to release his anger.

We made a list of 16 reasons for his anger, then he prayed and told the Lord why he was angry, and asked Him to take it from him. After praying I asked him how he felt, and he smiled and said that he had no feelings of anger toward his brother. He felt remorse for things he had done to hurt his brother, so he confessed it to the Lord and asked for His forgiveness. I prayed and asked the Lord what He wanted this man to know. He suddenly began crying and shaking and said he heard the words, "I love you." I asked him how he felt about his brother now, and he said he felt relieved, and felt compassion for his brother, and was sad that he doesn't know the Lord.

I asked this man to think about his sexual abuse and tell me how he felt. He said he had no anger, but he still felt fearful and felt like he was going to suffocate and die. I prayed and asked the Lord what He wanted this man to know about his belief that he was going to suffocate and die. He began crying again and said, "He (God) is with me; I'm not alone." This made him feel good, and he was no longer fearful while thinking about his sexual abuse.

He told me that he had a lot of anger at himself for things he had done, and he confessed it all to the Lord and asked for forgiveness. I prayed, again, and asked the Lord what He wanted this man to know, and he said, "It's alright; I'm forgiven." At the end of our session I asked him how he felt and he smiled and laughed and said, "I feel like shouting to the Lord!" He had no more anger or fear from his brother's sexual or physical abuse. The Lord set him completely free from his physical and sexual abuse by his brother!

Prayer Minister Helps Sexually Abused Woman

Sexual abuse victims are typically referred to mental health professionals, who are believed to have specialized training and skills for helping them. The truth is that professional counselors have no special training for helping sexually abused individuals and spend years and years with them in individual counseling sessions and group therapy sessions, with very poor results. When I deal with sexually abused individuals, they receive complete healing of their sexual abuse, usually in a single session, unless they have had multiple abuse experiences that require additional sessions for resolving each additional incident. Individuals who have been trained in this prayer ministry are just as capable of helping sexually abused individuals, and are far more effective than professional mental health counselors.

A woman sought help from a prayer minister about her anxiety. She told the prayer minister that she had been taking anxiety medicine most of her life and recently had stopped the medicine, but she was still having anxiety attacks. The prayer minister asked her if she could remember a time in her life that she had experienced a traumatic incident that caused her to first feel anxiety. The woman told her of a time when she was in high school and she found a letter to her father from his girlfriend. This made her very angry, hurt, scared, disappointed, and empty; her parents were still married and living together, and he had been having an affair with another woman. As they started to pray about that event, she informed the minister that she remembered a previous traumatic event that had occurred when she was 10 years old. She said that she had never told anyone about this event, and that it still caused her a lot of anxiety when she thought about it.

When this woman was in the 5th grade, she and a few other girls stayed after school to help the janitor clean the bus. He took the girls aside and sexually molested them; touching them inappropriately. The minister asked her to think about that event and tell her what emotion she felt. She said that she felt "fear." The prayer minister asked her if she would like to give that fear over to the Lord and ask Him what He wanted her to know about that event. She said she would, so the minister led her in this prayer: "Lord, when I think about the time when I was in the 5th grade and the janitor sexually molested me, it makes me afraid and anxious. Lord, I don't want to be afraid and anxious anymore. I choose to give it to you. Please take it and carry it for me in Jesus' name, AMEN!!"

She then asked the Lord what He wanted this woman to know, and as she sat quietly and listened to the Lord, He spoke truth to her: "It's OK, It's OK. It's not my fault, He loves me." She then stated, "I don't have to be scared anymore. I can breathe, it doesn't scare me or take my breath away when I think about it, I'm OK, I'm OK!!" The prayer minister asked her to think about the event one more time and try to stir up those feelings. She stated, "I'm OK, I can breathe." Those thoughts from the Lord took away her fears, and some feelings of shame, as well.

She then made a list of all the reasons she was angry with her father for the note she found from his girlfriend. She said she was angry at her dad because she felt like he tore their family apart, she thought she and her mother would not be together anymore, she was disappointed in him because she knew her father was not supposed to do those things. She then prayed: "Lord, I'm angry with my dad because of all these things. But Lord, I don't want to be angry with my dad anymore, so please take my anger and carry it for me. I choose to give it to you in Jesus' name." She then sat quietly and listened for the truth from the Lord. The Lord told her, "Don't be mad at your dad anymore, He loves you." She said, "I'm OK, I'm going to be at peace; no more consuming thoughts." She then looked up at the prayer minister and said, "I feel like a big weight has lifted off my shoulders." The minister asked her to think about the sexual abuse again. She stated, "I don't feel anything, I can breathe."

For years this woman had been taking anxiety medicine for her panic attacks, all the while still carrying around the memories and emotions of two major traumatic events that took place in her life at a very young age. For the first time, she was able to "breathe" deeply while thinking about her sexual abuse, and to feel at peace, a feeling she had never experienced before, even on the anxiety medicine. She also had some issues of grief over loved ones she had lost. The prayer minister explained to her how to pray about her grief in the same way, by making a list of what she misses about the person and giving these things to the Lord. She was excited about continuing the healing process through prayer.

Healing from the Church

This story was contributed by a prayer minister who learned this ministry by simply attending Set Free meetings week by week, and then going to the local jail to minister to women. Many people who never thought they could minister so effectively to sexually abused people have learned how to do it very effectively, and they become excited to see the power of God working through them in the lives of other people. As believers learn how to pray effectively with those who have been sexually abused, the world will see that prayer is powerful, and that God can heal them of their emotional struggles.

The world has no solution to the emotional traumas that people experience in life, but the Lord does, and He wants to use the Church to bring healing to the lives of individuals. As more and more believers learn how to help people with their emotional difficulties, the Church will quit referring individuals to "the professionals" and begin using believers in their own church to minister to them.

How exciting it is to see individuals who have been damaged by sexual abuse traumas being set free so quickly through prayer, when they have already exhausted the world's resources. Medications do not bring healing, and secular therapy does not bring complete healing, even after years of therapy. But the Lord sets captives free from sexual trauma so that they can live healthy, productive lives unhindered by the sinful actions of others.

14

OVERCOMING TRAUMAS

In January of 2010 a serious earthquake struck Port au Prince, the capital city of Haiti in southern Haiti. I had already been to Haiti several times on short-term mission trips and wanted to return to help some believers learn how to be set free from traumas. I contacted a Haitian pastor I knew in the northern city of Cap Haitian and arranged to visit his church to present a conference on how to overcome traumas.

On my first day at the Haitian church I spoke about how to overcome grief and how to overcome anger. We had a question-and-answer session after the second session, and a young woman shared that she had been in Port au Prince during the earthquake and had been trapped in the rubble and experienced some trauma from it. I asked her if she would like to have me pray with her about her feelings and she said she would.

At our next meeting this young woman sat up front in the church with me and my translator, and I asked her what happened to her during the earthquake. She said that she was with her nephew when the earthquake struck, and the concrete house she was in collapsed on top of her and her 8-year-old nephew. The nephew was trapped underneath her for 8 hours and they lay there helplessly until some rescuers were able to extract them from the rubble. She was not seriously injured but her nephew was and he was hospitalized and was still in the hospital 8 months later.

I asked this woman what emotions she felt while thinking about the earthquake. She said that she had some friends who had died, but she had already prayed about her grief on her own, after my first lesson on how to overcome grief, and she felt her grief was resolved. She said that she felt sad about a pregnant woman she knew who died and about her nephew who was still in the hospital and not doing well medically. I made a list of the reasons for her sadness, then led her in a prayer, and she asked the Lord to take her sadness from her. After the prayer, I asked her how she felt, and she began smiling and said she felt calm and peaceful. I could see her well because I was sitting next to her, but I told the audience to look at her face, and everyone stood up to see the peaceful smile on her face after giving her sadness to the Lord.

She also said that she was fearful about her nephew and worrying that he might not survive. I prayed for her and asked the Lord what He wanted her to know about her belief that "he was not going to recover." I told her to be quiet and let me know if any thoughts came to her mind. She said, "I'm taking care of him; it's not for you to worry about." Those thoughts relieved her of her fears and gave her peace. The Haitian believers were excited to witness this immediate transformation in this woman's emotions. She was set free from the emotional trauma of the earthquake.

Another Haitian pastor from Port au Prince was present for this conference and told me that I needed to go to Port au Prince with him to speak to his church, so I volunteered to go that weekend before returning home. On Sunday morning I spoke in his church about how to overcome grief and anger, I invited anyone who wanted prayer to come to the front of the church after the service, and I agreed to stay and pray with them.

After the service I had about a dozen people sitting in the front row of the church waiting for prayer. One by one I spoke with each one through a translator, identified their feelings about the earthquake, and prayed for them. I spent the entire afternoon praying with people and was exhausted, but each one left smiling and feeling peace in his or her heart. Some had grief over the loss of friends or family members, some had sadness, some had fears, and some had survivor's guilt. Each of them found healing, however, for their emotional trauma from the earthquake, and left with peace in their heart. It was a wonderful experience, and I was thrilled to have the opportunity to teach these Christians how to overcome traumas.

Posttraumatic Stress Disorder

The official term used for trauma reactions such as this is "posttraumatic stress disorder." Posttraumatic stress disorder is when "A person has been exposed to a traumatic event that involved actual or threatened death or serious injury, or a threat to the physical integrity of self or others, and the person's response involved intense fear, helplessness, or horror" (DSM-IVR). Any event that involves death or serious injury or threat can lead to PTSD.

There are many natural events that can qualify as traumas and lead to serious emotional struggles, such as tornadoes, earthquakes, tsunamis, floods, and so forth. There are also many types of man-made traumas such as violence, sexual abuse, and wars, and there are many types of accidents such as car wrecks, fires, and explosions that can lead to emotional difficulties in individuals. Each one of these can cause serious emotional problems, interfere with sleep, and affect the individual's ability to function well in life.

It is helpful to distinguish between "simple PTSD" that occurs as the result of a single incident, such as a rape or witnessing violence, and "complex PTSD" that occurs when multiple events occur over a period of years or over an entire childhood. Simple PTSD can be very traumatic and cause profound disruption in a person's life, but is generally easier to resolve than complex PTSD, such as occurs when an individual has had a lifetime of physical abuse or when a soldier is traumatized day after day during combat. Some types of interventions may help an individual overcome their simple PTSD by simply talking about it with a counselor who is a good listener, but the more complex forms of PTSD are not likely to be resolved by simply talking about them.

Resolving Traumatic Events

When helping people who have experienced a trauma, it is necessary to help them identify their emotions and then systematically resolve each one of them. The first step is to help them identify the emotions that the trauma caused by simply asking them how they feel when they think about the trauma. The young Haitian woman said she felt grief, sadness, and fear. The second step is to help the individual select an emotion to work on first. Usually it is good to start with the strongest emotion they feel and help them resolve it. Once this emotion is resolved, then select another emotion to focus on and help them resolve it. Continue this process, focusing on one emotion at a time until all emotions connected to the traumatic event are resolved, and the victim can think about the trauma without any emotional distress.

The most common emotions that occur from a trauma are grief, anger, sadness, shame, and fear. Grief may be present when the trauma involved a death, like a car accident, tornado, or earthquake, but not with traumas like sexual abuse or witnessing violence. Anger is very common, toward God or others involved in the event, such as when the person witnesses some violence or experiences violence. Sadness is frequently present because of the tragedy, the suffering, or the shock over what happened. Feelings of shame or guilt may be present when the individual questions how they responded, or believes they could have, or should have, done more. Fear may be present if the individual was threatened by someone, or develops anxiety about the event happening again, or worries that the perpetrator will return to harm them again. Each of these feelings needs to be discussed and fully resolved for the individual to be set free from their PTSD.

Impact of Traumas

Traumas can have a serious impact on individuals and affect their lives for a long time. There are many individuals, for example, who experienced sexual abuse one time in their childhood and it led to permanent damage to their relationships, and to many forms of self-abuse. Even Christian men and women who love the Lord and are committed to following him, can be affected by early childhood sexual abuse. This is not a reflection on their maturity or the strength of their faith, it is simply a reflection of their lack of knowledge of how to pray effectively about their emotions.

Physical abuse can also lead to long-term emotional damage and cause the individual to have explosive angry outbursts, emotional overreactions, and relationship difficulties. As a child I was deeply influenced by a preacher who loved young people and was the director of a youth ministry. I was very shy and withdrawn, but he went out of his way to befriend me and make me feel loved. Every summer, however, he would get upset at least once and go into a rage and begin yelling at the young people and swatting them with a ping pong paddle, never doing any harm but simply overreacting in anger. Everyone knew he was going to have these fits of anger but they learned to overlook it because it was just part of his personality.

I was told that this man went to a psychiatrist one time to get help for his anger and was told that nothing was wrong with him. However, it was clear that he had had a traumatic childhood because he frequently told stories about his childhood while preaching, and these angry outbursts were simply the result of unresolved anger that he had from physical abuse and trauma he had experienced in his childhood. No one could tell him how to resolve these, so he lived with them his entire life in spite of his genuine love for the Lord and knowledge of the Word of God.

Individuals who have gone to war and been involved in active combat are often very traumatized by their experiences, and these experiences can follow them the rest of their lives without help from a prayer minister. Combat veterans have often witnessed a lot of violence, experienced the traumatic loss of close friends, and had to do things that haunt them the rest of their lives. Christians are not exempt from the long-range impact of combat PTSD, although their faith may protect them from some fears and feelings of guilt.

I knew another preacher while growing up who was a World War II veteran, and he had posttraumatic stress. He was a very gentle, loving, pleasant man and a good friend of my family, and I had a great deal of respect and admiration for him, but it was well known that he had night terrors and flashbacks that caused him problems his entire life. Individuals with combat trauma have multiple traumas, and the major traumatic events need to be examined and resolved individually in order for them to be set free from them.

Soldier Set Free from War Trauma

In chapter 9 I related the story of a soldier who had some strong feelings of sadness as a result of a traumatic event he experienced on Christmas day in Iraq. He served in the military during the Iraq war in the 1990s, and on Christmas day about 200 Iraqis surrendered to him and several dozen American soldiers. He stated that they were searching each captive one by one when a young woman pulled out a pistol and shot his sergeant. He immediately opened fire on the woman and shot and killed her.

As he described this scene he became tearful. I asked him how he felt and he said he wasn't sure, but he said he did not feel any shame or guilt. He knew that he was just doing his job. He said that it was upsetting because this happened on Christmas day, the day of "peace on earth," and it was senseless and unnecessary, because if they had followed procedures taught to them they would have made all the POWs lie down on the ground as they inspected them one by one. It also bothered him that this young woman died, and this was his first killing as a soldier.

He identified six reasons for his sadness and then prayed and gave his sadness to the Lord in prayer. Afterwards, I asked the Lord if there was anything that He wanted this man to know. All he heard was, "It's not true." I asked him what that meant and he didn't know, so I asked the Lord to clarify what that meant. The man immediately said, "It's not my fault." I asked him if that felt true and he said that it did. These were feelings of shame that he had, even though he stated that he felt no shame or guilt. Then I asked him how he felt and he said, "A lot better." I instructed him to think about the incident and visualize it, and tell me how he felt now as he remembered it. He took a few seconds to think about it and said, "It's gone; it's okay now." He could remember the incident now without feeling any sadness or tearfulness. He just needed the Lord to speak to him and bring truth to him to set him free.

What this man experienced was posttraumatic stress disorder, and this was just one incident that he had experienced. PTSD victims often have feelings of sadness and shame, like this man did, as well as feelings of anger and fear, and each of these feelings needs to be resolved through prayer. This prayer process does work to resolve PTSD if the victim is willing to work through each emotion of each traumatic memory, and give it to the Lord in prayer. Unfortunately, the trauma is so intense that many soldiers will not talk about their trauma so they can pray about it and find release from their PTSD.

Set Free from Severe Domestic Violence

A Christian woman requested to see me, saying that she felt like she was going crazy. She had received some significant healing previously, but she had found two bullets in her purse which reawakened some traumatic memories of a former boyfriend. She began having flashbacks and night terrors of this man forcing her to take drugs by holding a knife to her neck, playing Russian Roulette with her, sending her out walking to the store at night to get things for him, tying her up, beating her, choking her, and torturing her for three months. As she vividly remembered these events, it terrorized her and she could not sleep. She had posttraumatic stress disorder (PTSD).

I asked how she felt while remembering these events and what she believed at the time. She said that she was fearful and believed "he is going to kill me and leave my kids without a mother." Since fear is a belief-based emotion, I prayed for her and asked the Lord what He wanted her to know about these beliefs. She immediately said, "God protected me and my kids, and He will judge him for what he did." She said her fear left, but she worried that he would come back to retaliate toward her for leaving him. I prayed again and asked the Lord what He wanted her to know about that. This time she said, "He's probably in jail because he beat up a woman. I have to trust God to protect me; He is protecting my family." These thoughts from the Holy Spirit comforted her and resolved her fears. I asked her how she felt now and she said, "Hatred; I hate him." "Would you like to get rid of that hatred if you could?" I asked, and she said, "Of course." We talked about everything this man did to her, how he terrorized her, beat her, forced her to take drugs, and got her children taken from her. She also hated him because of some permanent injuries she suffered from his abuse. We made a list of twelve reasons for her hatred and she prayed and asked the Lord to take her anger from her.

I prayed and asked the Lord if there was anything He wanted her to know. "I'm going to be okay" she said. "I have faith and I'm a strong woman. God protected me and my children, and He's going to get me through this. I'm not going to let this man steal my peace and joy anymore. I'm going to be a good mother." After having these thoughts I asked her how she felt now about this man. She still had some anger toward him for taking her personal property from her, so she told the Lord about this and asked Him to take this anger from her. Then she said, "God is telling me I will be set free. These were just material things that can be replaced. I have a lot to be thankful for." I asked, again, how she felt toward this man and she said she felt "nothing; just neutral." All her anger, hatred and fear were gone. We reviewed each traumatic event, and she had no more emotion about them. She said, "I lived; I'm here." The next day she texted me and said she had slept well and had no more night terrors, and was no longer bothered by the memories.

Two weeks later I saw her again and she told me that she had no more problems with these memories and traumas, and she had no more fears. Her PTSD was completely gone after an hour of praying. She was amazed and thankful to the Lord for His goodness and ability to set her free from the torture she had received over a three-month period. It is truly amazing and wonderful how God gives us the Holy Spirit to comfort us and give us His peace, when we learn to give Him our burdens and listen to His voice of comfort.

Sharon's Story

A woman came for help who was very unhappy, depressed, couldn't sleep well, and was having nightmares and flashbacks from some previous abuse, and from a car wreck she had experienced recently. She had multiple traumas that were affecting her emotionally, and she had been prescribed some medication to help her sleep, but it wasn't working well. She lived with her Christian husband, whom she said treated her well, but she still lived in fear of a former boyfriend who had abused her for thirteen years, and these emotions were making it difficult for her to enjoy her time with her husband and to appreciate him for his patience and loving support.

When I begin ministering with people I usually gather some background information on them so that I can understand them better and create a prayer plan for them (See Chapter 3). As I obtained information from her, I learned that she had been abused by her father and molested as a child. She married a good, Christian man but was unhappy, probably due to her history of abuse, and ran off with another man, who brutally abused her for thirteen years until he was incarcerated for almost killing another man. She then escaped and returned to her husband, who graciously welcomed her back home. He was very forgiving of her and treated her well, but she was full of guilt, shame, and fear. Then she had a car wreck that almost killed her, and she became afraid of driving.

After my initial session with this woman I created a prayer plan for her that included her anger toward her father, her mother, her boyfriend, and her grandson. She had unresolved grief over the loss of her father and her mother, unresolved feelings of fear over her former boyfriend and her car wreck, and feelings of shame from her childhood sexual abuse and abuse by her boyfriend. These were the components of her prayer plan.

I shared with this woman how she could be released from her fear, shame, and anger through prayer and she was receptive to this, so we began meeting regularly to pray about each of these issues. After her initial session, we talked about some anger she had toward her grandson, who was treating her badly, and she made a list of the reasons for her anger, and then she released it through prayer.

In our third session we discussed her anger toward the abusive boyfriend, and she identified 27 reasons for her anger. She prayed about her anger and gave it to the Lord, and found immediate relief of her anger. Then we prayed about her guilt and shame over her relationship with this man and she released it. Finally, she prayed about her fear and she was able to resolve it in the same session. She left this session with no anger, shame, or fear but feeling "peaceful" and smiling. Her sexual abuse and trauma over this violent relationship was completely resolved at the end of this session.

In the next session she identified 14 reasons for her anger toward her abusive father, and she prayed about it and was able to release it. Then she also prayed about some sadness and grief she felt about her father, and she said she felt "peaceful," afterwards.

In our fifth session we prayed about her car wreck and her fear of trucks. She told me that she was driving on a 4-lane highway behind an 18-wheeler that was driving slowly so she decided to pass it. She moved into the passing lane and began accelerating on a curve, when suddenly she saw a car stopped in her lane. She couldn't stop quickly enough to avoid hitting the car, so she pulled over close to the truck to avoid rear-ending the stopped car, and the truck's wheels lifted her car off the ground and flipped her over. Her car flew off the highway into the median and she found herself hanging upside down by her seat belt, and bleeding profusely. She later learned that half of her head was scalped, but she survived without any serious injuries.

She recovered quickly and her husband replaced her car before she left the hospital, but for the following year she was fearful of driving, and especially of passing trucks on the highway. Her post-traumatic stress primarily consisted of anxiety about driving and passing trucks on the highway. Each time she approached a truck on the highway and thought about passing it she felt fearful that "it's going to happen again." Fears will be discussed in the next chapter, but suffice it to say that fears are belief-based emotions and that the only way to remove fears is to receive truth to replace the person's false beliefs. I prayed and asked the Lord what He wanted this woman to know about her belief that "it's going to happen again."

As she quietly listened, the thought that came to her mind was, "It was a one-time thing; have no fear of driving." She then said, "Something told me what to do, and we all lived through it." She came to realize that the Lord had told her how to avoid rear-ending the other car so that no one was seriously hurt or killed. I asked her to visualize the scene again and tell me how she felt. She said she felt calm and had no more anxiety about it. As I set up her next appointment she chuckled and said, "It's gone. I've been trying to think about the accident and it's like an empty spot up there. There's no more fear."

This woman was seen for two more sessions. In the sixth session she prayed about her anger at a friend, which she released, then on her seventh and final session she indicated that she was doing well and had no anger, shame, fear or depression. She did not specifically pray about some of her losses, but she was no longer depressed or experiencing overwhelming fears, and she was getting along well with her husband. The Lord set her free of the many traumas that she had experienced from her childhood and as an adult.

PTSD Treatment Efficacy

There are various types of treatments for PTSD that claim they are effective, including cognitive-behavior therapy, exposure therapy, eye-movement desensitization and reprocessing (EMDR), and pharmacotherapy. Most of the studies on the effectiveness of drugs are funded by pharmaceutical companies whose medications are being tested, and the majority of psychotherapy studies are conducted by the individuals who developed the techniques, or by close associates. This creates a conflict of interest and leads to biased findings. Because of all the controversy over the treatment of PTSD in the VA hospitals, Congress consulted with an independent research group to assist in the evaluation of PTSD research.

The National Academy of Sciences was commissioned by Congress to study the efficacy of PTSD treatments and present their findings and recommendations, which they did in 2008. They found many problems in the design and performance of most studies, due to small sample sizes, high dropout rates, and poor handling of missing data, but they evaluated 89 studies that included randomized controlled trials. Based upon these studies, this independent committee of scientists came to some conclusions (National Academy of Sciences, 2008).

With regard to the use of all drug classes used for treatment of PTSD, they concluded that "the evidence is inadequate to determine efficacy in the treatment of PTSD." With regard to the use of psychotherapy treatments for PTSD, they wrote, "The committee concludes that the evidence is inadequate to determine the efficacy of the following psychotherapy modalities in the treatment of PTSD: EMDR, cognitive restructuring, coping skills training." With regard to the use of exposure therapy involving the repeated exposure of the individual to the traumatic memories and stimuli, they wrote: "The committee finds that the evidence is sufficient to conclude the efficacy of exposure therapies in the treatment of PTSD." Although they found evidence for the "efficacy" of exposure therapies, they did not state how effective they were, but simply that they are more effective than no treatment at all (National Academy of Sciences, 2008).

Because of the lack of evidence that PTSD treatment programs were effective, the VA withdrew support for PTSD programs in 2000, after 20 years of futile attempts. The Veterans Affairs and the Department of Defense now spend $3.3 billion a year on psychiatric medications and therapy for US veterans diagnosed with post-traumatic stress disorder, without any proof that their efforts are "successfully treating" our military.

Woman Traumatized by Mental Health Treatment

In 2013 I attended a conference sponsored by Dr. Peter Breggin. During a lunch break I was in line behind an attractive young couple, and after we loaded up our trays with food I began looking for a place to sit. I decided to be friendly and asked the young couple if I could join them at their table, and they cordially invited me.

As we began eating our lunch, I asked where they were from and what had brought them to the conference. They looked at each other hesitantly and finally the young woman told me that she had been held up at gunpoint a year earlier and was traumatized by the experience. She decided to seek counseling at a local clinic she had seen, and they informed her that they only provided inpatient counseling. They persuaded her to voluntarily admit herself into the facility, and she began to receive psychotherapy for her post-traumatic stress. She was also given psychotropic medications, then they recommended that she receive electroconvulsive shock treatments (ECT). When she objected, she learned that she was unable to leave the facility against medical orders, so she continued receiving ECT treatments until she had suffered severe brain injury. By the time she was finally released from the facility, she had suffered so much brain damage that she was unable to read. She seemed to be very articulate and intelligent, but she was actually very damaged by this treatment, and she had come to hear Dr. Breggin speak more about the dangers of psychiatric treatment.

The medications used most frequently for treatment of PTSD are SSRI antidepressants. I attended a workshop on PTSD that was led by a so-called "trauma expert." She was a very nice woman and was probably a Christian, but during her presentation she stated that "SSRIs can heal people of PTSD." I was so shocked to hear this statement in front of a large group of people that would be influenced to believe this falsehood, that I immediately spoke up, in a very uncharacteristic manner for me, and commented that I had seen many people with PTSD treated with SSRIs, but had never seen anyone "healed" of PTSD. She paused and reworded her statement to say, "SSRIs can be helpful."

The Inefficacy of Psychiatric Medications

The National Academy of Sciences examined not only the claims made by practitioners of various psychological treatments, but also the claims of psychiatrists and pharmaceutical companies that antidepressants are effective in helping those with PTSD. Their conclusion, in contrast to that of the so-called expert cited above was, "With regard to the use of all drug classes used for treatment of PTSD, they concluded that "the evidence is inadequate to determine efficacy in the treatment of PTSD."

This is the conclusion of a neutral, third-party scientific group who examined the evidence carefully, without any bias or financial interests. They concluded from their examination that there was inadequate evidence to conclude that antidepressants or drugs of any classification are effective in treating PTSD. Although there are physicians who will prescribe antidepressants, and SSRIs in particular for PTSD, there is no clear and convincing scientific evidence that they are effective. The Los Angeles Times reported on June 20, 2014 that the government spent $3 billion in 2014 in providing these medications for veterans with PTSD but there is little evidence that its efforts are working, according to a new report commissioned by Congress.

Natural Disaster Traumas

There are many natural disasters that can lead to posttraumatic stress, including earthquakes, tornadoes, floods, and tsunamis. Every year there are natural disasters that occur around the world that gain world-wide attention, and rescue teams converge from around the world to provide assistance. When dealing with the emotional and psychological components of the traumas, the most common emotions involved are grief, sadness, anger, shame, and fears. Prayer ministers who are involved in providing emotional and spiritual assistance should know how to identify each of these emotions and pray with the individual to release them.

A woman came for counseling who had a fear of storms that she had had for over twenty years, and she was fearful that she was going to pass her fear on to her children. She told me that at five years of age she was at a friend's house and her mother had gone shopping, when a storm came. Dark clouds blew in and the winds became strong, then the tornado sirens began to sound. She and her girlfriend climbed into a bath tub, and her friend was terrified and began screaming. She said, "I believed we were all going to die."

While she was telling this story I told her to visualize the scene so that she felt the fear, then I prayed for her and asked the Lord what He wanted her to know about her belief that she was going to die. I told her to listen quietly and tell me if any thoughts came into her mind. She said, "Nothing happened; He kept us safe." Then she quoted the Bible where Jesus said, "Which of you by worrying can add a single hour to his life?" I prayed again and asked the Lord if there was anything else that He wanted her to know. She said, "God keeps us safe; we always have some warning when a tornado comes; I have to straighten up for the sake of my kids."

I asked her if it felt true that God kept her safe, and she said that it did. I asked her how she felt now while thinking about that memory. She said, "It was silly and weird. We were safe." Her feelings of fear over the storm were gone once she received the truth from the Lord that He had protected her and no one was hurt. Her fear of storms was gone. The next time I saw her she said that she used to become very anxious every time it became stormy, but since we had prayed she remained calm when it became dark and stormy outdoors.

Man-made Traumas

In addition to natural disasters, there are many man-made disasters that can cause posttraumatic stress. This includes childhood sexual abuse, rape, criminal assaults, murders, abortions, military conflicts, wars, and physical abuse. Each one of these events can lead to strong feelings of grief, anger, sadness, fear, and shame. Those who are ministering to individuals who have been traumatized by these events need to help the victims identify their feelings, and then teach them how to release each emotion connected to the event.

A prayer minister had a friend of hers call one evening to tell her that her husband had gone crazy and became violent and killed her father. She met with her friend to be with her and help calm her, and help her deal with her feelings of sadness, grief, and anger. Her friend responded so well that in the midst of this crisis she was able to maintain a high level of calm for the benefit of her family and her children.

This murder was a high-profile crime in her city and she had to face reporters and appear in court on numerous occasions. She handled the crisis with such grace and calmness that the media interviewed her and asked her how she was able to remain so calm. She told them that the Lord had given her peace to deal with this crisis and they were amazed at her serenity. The Lord used this prayer minister to help this woman deal with this serious trauma.

The marvelous thing is that any believer can learn how to do this ministry. It is not a complicated process that needs to be handled by "the professionals," because most professionals do not know how to help someone deal with such traumas. But any believer who learns how to pray about their emotions effectively can help fellow believers in times of crisis.

Accident Traumas

There are many types of accidents that occur that can cause posttraumatic stress. Car wrecks are one of the most common accidents that lead to traumas, but there are many other accidents such as industrial accidents, explosions, fires, and plane crashes that can lead to posttraumatic stress.

A woman was driving to work and witnessed a helicopter crash. Some of the debris from the helicopter flew through her windshield and she stopped her car quickly and took cover. She thought she was going to die. When I met with her I asked her what emotions she felt when she thought about the accident. She said she had feelings of anger, grief, sadness, fear and shame.

First, we prayed about her anger at the helicopter crew, and the ground crew who had misinformed them about where to land the craft and caused the accident. She was also angry that no one would take responsibility for the damage to her car, and she was without a vehicle for days. We made a list of the reasons for her anger and she was able to release her anger.

Next, we prayed about her feelings of shame over her reaction. She felt she should have done something to help the victims, but instead, she was so frightened that she just took cover. We prayed about her belief that she failed and should have assisted the injured individuals in the helicopter. She was able to release her feelings of shame and guilt.

We also prayed about her feelings of grief and sadness over the death of several individuals. She identified the reasons for her sadness, and gave them to the Lord, and her sadness was lifted from her. We prayed through each of her feelings about the helicopter crash and when we finished she had no more anger, grief, sadness, fear, or shame. She was able to talk about, and think about the accident, without any more negative feelings, and she was able to drive to work at night without any more feelings of anxiety.

Violence Trauma

I spoke a woman who had been traumatized while serving as a missionary in Africa. She had been working on a translation of the Bible into the native language of a tribe, and had developed some close relationships with the local natives. She said that one day a group of violent men raided the village and began shooting people, and she and her colleagues were hurriedly evacuated from the village for their safety. As she talked about the event, it was very difficult for her to think or talk about it due to the extreme sadness, grief, and fear she felt. I asked her what was the main emotion she felt. She said that the main emotion was sadness about all her friends and colleagues that she left behind, especially a local woman who was helping her learn their language. She loved this woman and missed her greatly, so we talked and she identified 23 things she missed about her. I led her in a prayer and she prayed and told the Lord what she missed about her friend, then asked the Lord to take her grief and carry it for her. After giving her grief to the Lord, I asked the Lord if there was anything that He wanted her to know. She said, “My time there was not a failure or loss; she knew I loved her.” I asked her how she felt, and she said, “I just see her smiling; it makes me happy.” Her grief and sadness were both gone.

I asked her how she felt now, and she said she felt some guilt and sadness because she never had a chance to talk with her friend about the Lord. I asked the Lord what He wanted her to know about her guilt feelings, and she told me that the thought came to her that, “all is forgiven.” She smiled and said she felt “Peace.”

I asked her again how she felt and she said she felt some fear because she was worried about her friends who stayed behind. She worried that “something terrible is going to happen.” Her fear seemed fairly intense, so I suspected that it was coming from an earlier source in her life. I asked her if she had felt this kind of fear previously, and she said that she felt this way as a child when storms came.

She told me that her father was deathly afraid of tornadoes, and one time when she was five years old a storm came and her father was terrified, and hurried her downstairs to their basement in a panic. She felt very fearful that "something terrible was going to happen." I prayed and asked the Lord what He wanted her to know about this belief. She listened quietly and said, "He's in control." I asked her if that felt true, and she affirmed that it did. Then I asked her to think about the incident and tell me how she felt. She said, "Factual; it's just facts without feelings." All her feelings of fear that were connected to her memory of the storm were gone. With this early memory resolved, I asked her to think again about her African friends and tell me how she felt. She said she felt "peaceful and safe" and her African friends, she said, "are safe in the Lord's hands. It doesn't turn my stomach any more. He's in control. I'm happy they're at peace and safe."

A week later this woman e-mailed me and said the following: "We had a pretty good thunderstorm the other night & I was completely unfazed and was able to sleep through the night without being conscious of the noise outside. Wow! Haven't ever had that happen. PTL! Pretty awesome!" All her grief, sadness, guilt, shame, and fear about her trauma were resolved, and even her childhood trauma was resolved from one prayer session. The Lord is truly awesome and able to comfort us and give us peace in all of our circumstances, when we learn how to pray about our emotions.

Trauma from Religious Persecution

Many Christians are being persecuted and executed in Muslim parts of the world, and believers everywhere need to learn how to pray with one another for emotional healing from these traumas. The major source of executions and persecutions are devout Muslims who are called "radical Islamic terrorists." Brother Andrew and his nonprofit organization, Open Doors USA, compiles an annual list of the world's worst persecutors of Christians. He has stated that the Muslim countries with stringent Shari'ah law comprise 8 of the top 10 worst persecutors of Christians.

Journalist John Allen has said that the followers of Jesus are "indisputably…the most persecuted religious body on the planet." In his latest book, *The Global War on Christians* (Random House, 2013), he cites such authorities as the International Society for Human Rights, noting that the group identifies 80 percent of religious freedom violations worldwide as targeting Christians. Believers must become more involved in prayer for those being persecuted, around the world, because of their Christian faith. To learn more about religious persecution around the world, the reader is encouraged to subscribe to "Voice of the Martyrs" newsletter.

The scriptures warn us that, "All who desire to live godly in Christ Jesus, will be persecuted" (2 Timothy 3:12), and Jesus told his disciples, "A slave is not greater than his master. If they persecuted Me, they will also persecute you" (John 15:20). He also told them, in the Sermon on the Mount, "Blessed are you when men cast insults at you, and persecute you, and say all kinds of evil against you falsely, on account of me. Rejoice and be glad, for your reward in heaven is great, for so they persecuted the prophets who were before you" (Matt. 5:11-12). It should not surprise us that persecution is increasing against Christians, but we must equip ourselves to know how to pray for one another for emotional healing as this increases.

Franklin Graham spoke out openly about Islam shortly after the twin towers were attacked in New York City in 2001. He said, "Islam is an evil & wicked religion." As a result of his open denouncement of Islam, the Pentagon disinvited him to a meeting there for the National Day of Prayer on May 6, 2010. In defense of this comment others have given justifications for his statement. The following article was written about Islam by Bryan Fischer, a guest columnist for "Renew America" on May 23, 2010 (Fischer, 2010).

Its founder, whom all his followers are taught to scrupulously imitate, married a girl at age six and began having sex with her at age nine. Taking child brides is routine all across the Muslim world. So, what do you think about pedophilia? "Evil and wicked" or not?

Its founder made his fortune plundering caravans in the Arabian peninsula. He was a land pirate. So, what about piracy, pillage, and plunder? "Evil and wicked" or not?

He taught his followers that it is permissible for a man literally to beat his wife into submission. Even today imams deliver entire televised sermons on exactly how husbands may go about administering this beat down. So, what about wife-beating? "Evil and wicked" or not? It's a terrible thing when it happens at all. It's entirely another thing to be taught that it's good. So, what about killing victims of rape and shooting, burning or cutting the heads off Westernized females? "Evil and wicked" or not?

Women in general are second class citizens who are forbidden in many Muslim countries from getting an education or even showing their faces in public. So, what about severe and unrelenting sexism? "Evil and wicked" or not?

Honor killings are widely practiced in the Islamic world. According to the U.N., at least 5000 females are brutally murdered every year because they have brought dishonor to their families by, in many cases, being the victims of rape. In America, one Muslim in New York cut off the head of his wife (he was hosting a television program at the time designed to improve the image of Islam), a Muslim in Arizona ran down his daughter with the family station wagon, and another in Houston shot his two teenage daughters to death in the back of a taxi cab. In my hometown of Boise, Idaho a Muslim man burned down his home with his Westernized wife and daughters inside. So what about killing victims of rape and shooting, burning or cutting the heads off Westernized females? "Evil and wicked" or not?

Muhammad taught his followers to "slay the idolaters wherever you find them" and decapitate them. There are 109 verses in the Koran commanding Muslims to kill the infidel Jews and Christians. His followers, as demonstrated by the events of 9/11 and Fort Hood, and the gruesome deaths of Daniel Pearl and Nick Berg, are still faithful to his teaching. So, what about the mass murder and decapitation of innocent people? "Evil and wicked" or not?

There is no freedom of religion in Islam. Christians are given three choices and three choices only, where Islam has the power to impose its will: convert, submit or die. Conversion from Islam to Christianity is a capital offense in most Muslim countries. So what about the complete and total absence of religious liberty? "Evil and wicked" or not?

Islam is determined to subdue the entire world at the point of a sword. Christian Europe was forced to turn back the armies of Islam in 732 at Tours and again in 1683 at Vienna to preserve its freedom. So, what about militaristic totalitarianism? "Evil and wicked" or not? We might want to ask the Europeans of the 1930s for an answer to that question.

Muslims are specifically forbidden by their founder from assimilating into Western cultures. They are prohibited from taking friends from the Jews and Christians around them. So much for the American

> ideal, "Out of many, one." Of course, many followers of Islam do in fact make friends of Westerners. This, according to Muhammad, makes them bad Muslims."

It is no surprise that devout Muslims who know the Koran and seek to follow it and the example of their prophet, Muhammad, acted out violently against "the infidels." Muslims consider Muhammad the perfect man, in the same way that Christians believe Jesus was the perfect man and God, and believe that they must follow his example in every way. Radical Islam is actually "devout Islam," and is comprised of individuals who seriously want to follow their leader. Thus, the members of ISIS were systematically going from house to house in Iraq where they had taken over, and asking children to denounce Jesus or be killed. In spite of these atrocities, the United Nations and the U.S. government did nothing to protect Christians in these countries.

In addition to these increasing acts of violence toward Christians around the world, Christians are being attacked in the United States for their moral belief, and for exercising their freedom of speech. Donald Knapp and his wife Evelyn were sentenced to spend 180 days in jail and be fined $1000 a day for politely declining to perform a sodomy-based marriage ceremony in Idaho. City officials in this Idaho city fined this couple $180,000 for refusing to marry a homosexual couple. Declining to perform a homosexual wedding is now a crime in America.

Preparing for Persecution

The Lord Jesus said in Matthew 24:6-8,

> *You will be hearing of wars and rumors of wars; see that you are not frightened, for those things must take place, but that is not yet the end. For nation will rise against nation, and kingdom against kingdom, and in various places there will be famines and earthquakes. But all these things are merely the beginning of birth pangs.*

He tells us "see that you are not frightened." We must learn to take refuge in His Word and in His promises, and to understand that He is still fully in control. Everything is going according to His plan, and in the end, His plan will be fulfilled.

However, we cannot afford to be complacent and passive. We must be prepared for persecution and learn how to support and encourage one another. Prayer is the key for the church to learn how to remain strong and victorious in these times. The apostle Paul told us, "Be anxious for nothing but in everything through prayer and supplications, with thanksgiving, let your requests be made known unto God. And the peace of God, which surpasses all comprehension, shall guard your hearts and your minds in Christ Jesus" (Philippians 4:6-7).

The early New Testament church was persecuted, but this just strengthened them and motivated them to be more devoted to the Lord and to one another. We're told in Acts that the apostles, "were continually devoting themselves to prayer" (Acts 1:14, 2:42). Paul also instructed believers, "Be devoted to prayer…rejoice with those who rejoice, weep with those who weep" (Romans 12:12, 15). James, the Lord's brother, entreated the church, "Confess your faults to one another and pray for one another that you may be healed" (James 5:16).

When the early church was persecuted by the authorities, "They shook off the dust of their feet…And the disciples were continually filled with joy and with the Holy Spirit" (Acts 13:51-52). In spite of their persecution they were "filled with joy and with the Holy Spirit"! What a testimony to us, and what an example for us to look at so that we do not lose heart or become intimidated by the world.

Final Challenges

The world and our country are in desperate need of the Lord; they need the Lord to save them and to set them free. The greatest evidence of this is the growing violence and drug problems in society, plus the booming pharmaceutical industry, that is getting rich off of emotional problems. The secular authorities and medical experts have concluded that no counseling works because these personal struggles are all caused by brain disorders, and they push their drugs as the best solution. The Lord has a much better solution: "Come unto Me; all who are weary and heavy-laden, and I will give you rest" (Matthew 11:28).

The Bible tells us that a time is coming when Christians will be persecuted and killed by those who think they are serving God (John 16:2). He has provided us a way to deal with this coming persecution through prayer and the Holy Spirit (Luke 12:12). As this chapter ends, the reader is challenged to do three things to prepare yourself for this persecution. First, learn to apply these principles to your own life so that you live in genuine peace and get excited about Jesus. Second, share these prayer principles with friends, family, and others in your church on a daily basis and pray with them. Third, meet with others in a Set Free meeting to spread this good news across our society and throughout our churches.

Remember, Jesus can do for you what no counselor, psychologist, doctor or medication can do; He can set you free from emotional bondage and give you His peace. May you learn to cast all your cares upon Him and devote yourself to prayer during these last days, so that you are "continually filled with joy and with the Holy Spirit" (Acts 13:52) like the early Christians were in times of persecution, and "may the Lord of peace Himself continually grant you peace in every circumstance" (2 Thessalonians 3:16).

15

OVERCOMING FEARS AND MAKING THE THIRD PLEDGE: "DO NOT LET YOUR HEART BE AGITATED OR FEARFUL"

In John 14:27 the Lord Jesus told His disciples, "Let not your heart be troubled, nor let it be fearful." One of the most repeated phrases in the Bible is "Do not fear," which can be found 59 times in the Bible. It is clear that the Lord does not want us to be afraid or to live in fear, and yet many people experience overwhelming fears in their lives that disable them, even Christians.

Jesus had been teaching his disciples and a multitude of people in parables, then in Mark 4:35-41 He told His disciples to go to the other side of the Sea of Galilee. They got into a boat with Him to cross over to the other side and Jesus lay down to sleep. As He slept, a storm arose and the waves began to fill the boat with water so that it began to sink. In a panic, the apostles woke the Lord and said in verse 38, "Teacher, do You not care that we are perishing?"

Peter and the other disciples were very fearful and believed that they were going to die, but their fear was not caused by the storm, because Jesus was calm and sleeping through the storm. The cause of their fear was their false beliefs. Three of these beliefs are revealed in this single statement. First, they believed that Jesus was just a good teacher, because that's how they addressed him, as "teacher." Second, they believed that He did not care, because if He cared He would be awake and doing something to help them. The third lie they believed is revealed in the words "we are perishing." They believed they were going to die, when the truth was they were just being tested and taught an important lesson.

Mark 4:39 (KJV) says, "And He arose, and rebuked the wind, and said unto the sea, 'Peace, be still.'" When He spoke, the waves and wind immediately subsided so that the sea was completely calm. The disciples were amazed and learned, experientially, that Jesus had power over all earthly forces, and that as long as He was with them, nothing could harm them. This was a very important lesson for them to learn, because they would later face threats and persecution, and this lesson taught them that they had nothing to fear as long as they were with the Lord and in His hands. The same is true for each of us, as we walk with the Lord and learn experientially to trust Him to protect us and allow nothing to harm us, so that He can fulfill His purpose for us in our lives. Our fears and anxieties are also based upon our beliefs, and can quickly be overcome as we learn to replace the lies we believe with His truth.

Types of Fears and Anxieties

There are many different ways that people experience fears. Sometimes they are exaggerated reactions to something. These are called "phobias," and there are many such phobias, such as a phobia of water, wasps, heights, darkness, elevators, closed rooms, or crowds. Some fears are more general, like social situations, test taking, and public speaking. At other times, people have panic attacks or anxiety attacks that occur unpredictably, and are so intense that the person feels they are going to die. Generalized anxiety occurs sometimes with people who are always anxious and worried.

Whatever type of anxiety or fear that occurs, the steps for overcoming the fears are the same. Fear is a belief-based emotion, which means that you must identify the underlying beliefs that are causing the fear, such as "something terrible is going to happen; it's going to happen again; I'm going to die; he's going to come back and hurt me." In order to resolve the fear, truth is needed from the Lord to replace the person's lies about the event... "The truth will set you free."

Woman Set Free from Water Phobia

A woman came for help with her depression and relationship problems. She had been physically abused and sexually abused as a child, and she prayed several times with me and was able to release her anger and grief from her physical and sexual abuse. I asked her what else bothered her that she would like to pray about. She told me that she had a fear of water that she would like to talk about.

When she was about 8 years old she found a baby possum, and she took it home and gave it a bath, like she had seen her mother do with her children. She accidentally drowned the baby possum and when her stepfather found out about it he was furious. He filled the bath tub with water and held her head under water to teach her what it felt like to drown. She couldn't breathe and thought she was going to die. Ever since then she had been afraid of water and could not even take a shower without having a panic attack and feeling like she was going to die.

I told this woman to remember the emotions she felt while being held under water, and remember the thoughts she had at the time. She said that she thought she was going to die so I prayed for her, "Lord, what do You want her to know about her belief that she is going to drown and die?" She said, "I have to be calm. I'm not going to die." She said that this felt true, that she wasn't going to die. I instructed her to picture herself being held under water and to tell me how she felt now. She said that she felt calm and that it didn't bother her anymore.

We discussed how the Lord can set us free from belief-based emotions like fear and shame by speaking to us and replacing our lies with His truth. This young woman, who had been so depressed a month earlier, indicated that she was no longer depressed and she had released a lot of anger and grief, as well by simply praying and giving God her emotions. In about 15 minutes she was set free from her fear of water that she had had for over 15 years. The Lord is able to set us free of all our fears when we learn how to pray about them and let Him speak truth into our hearts through his Spirit.

Steps for Overcoming Fears

This story illustrates the three steps for overcoming fears:

> **Step One:** Identify the source of the fear, where it first occurred or originated.
>
> **Step Two:** Identify the underlying beliefs at the time of the original incident: I'm going to die…something terrible will happen, he's coming back, it will happen again.
>
> **Step Three:** Pray for truth and listen. When the person listens quietly, the Lord will bring truth to their mind which will set them free from their fears, if they do not harbor anger in their heart.

OVERCOMING PHOBIAS

Child Set Free From Fear of Dark

A woman who had learned this ministry went to visit her daughter and grandchildren in another state. While she was visiting them, her 4-year-old granddaughter said she was afraid of the dark and couldn't go to sleep. The woman lay down with the child in the bed and asked her if they could pray about her fear. The girl agreed, and said that she was afraid that something bad was going to happen to her in the dark. She said that she knew God could protect her but He was in heaven and was too far away to do anything to help her.

This woman asked her granddaughter if she could pray with her about that belief. She prayed that Jesus would show her the truth about God being so far away in heaven. The granddaughter immediately responded that He was in her heart, not far away, and that with Him there, there wasn't anything to be afraid of! The woman asked her granddaughter how she felt. She paused a bit and then said. "Happy!"

The child then asked her grandmother that if Jesus was in her heart, did that mean that heaven was right there with her? She hadn't thought about it like that before but was amazed at how profound the thoughts of little children could be. She answered, "Yes," and asked her how that made her feel to know that heaven was so close. She said, "Happy!" This woman was thrilled to see how Jesus could talk with little children and trade their pain for His peace, in even His little ones. She was also excited to be able to help her grandchildren to learn to pray to the Lord about their feelings.

Set Free from Claustrophobia

Once a week I go to the local county jail and visit with men in jail and talk with them about the Lord and about being set free from anger and addiction. I had a ministry partner who frequently went with me and we had a good time speaking with the inmates and praying with them. We are usually encouraged by these visits, and we enjoy ministering to these men and taking inspirational books to them on a book cart. One day, as we were about to leave, a man asked for a copy of the New International Version of the Bible, and we found an NIV New Testament but could not find a copy of the entire Bible, so I told him that I would look for a copy in the library and bring it to him.

We wheeled the cart down the hallway into a "multi-purpose room" which was unlocked, so we went inside it to the back of the room where the "library" was located. This room is a small storage room with a heavy 500 pound metal door that is usually kept locked. However, the door was still unlocked from when we had been there earlier to get the cart, so I pushed the cart inside and began looking for the NIV Bible while my partner held the door. He thought he saw an NIV Bible so he stepped inside to get it for me, and I heard the door click behind him, locking us both securely inside this small concrete closet. There was no intercom system in this room or any other way to communicate from inside this room, and there was no way to unlock the door from either side of the door. It was operated remotely by an officer in the control room who is responsible for operating about 50 doors in the institution and who was responsible for watching about 100 cameras in the jail.

I was shocked but remained calm initially. I told my partner that we were locked inside, and he chuckled nervously and began shaking the door gently so that someone could hear us, but the sound could not be heard anywhere in the institution, and we were locked inside this vault with no way to get out and no way to communicate. Even if we shouted and kicked the door no one would hear us unless they were on the other side of the door. I began thinking to myself that we were probably going to be there for at least 2 or 3 hours before anyone was likely to come into the multi-purpose room, and we might be trapped there all night!

As I thought about this, I began feeling panicky; I remained calm on the outside, but my heart was racing and I began to feel light-headed. I told my partner that I was wasn't feel well and needed to sit down. I sat on a chair and talked to the Lord. I knew that my fears were belief-based and that I need truth, so I prayed, "Lord, what do you want me to know right now?" I listened quietly and the thought came into my mind, "You're going to get out; it's going to be okay." Immediately my heart calmed and the light-headedness left me and I felt peaceful. I prayed again and said, "Lord, please send someone down here to let us out."

I stood up and my partner and I talked as he continued rattling the door. I knew that after a couple of hours the air would get thin inside but we could probably lie on the floor where there was a slit between the floor and the door to get some fresh air if necessary.

After about thirty seconds the door buzzed and we pushed on the door and it opened. The guard operating the controls had noticed that we had disappeared and wondered where we were. He buzzed the door in case we were inside. I was thrilled! We were set free and I was so elated and grateful to the Lord for being with us and watching over us. It was a miracle that the officer would even notice us going into that room since we had not buzzed him earlier to get inside but I believe the Lord told him to check on us.

What an awesome God who never sleeps or slumbers! Many men and women are trapped in circumstances and in their emotions and He wants to set them free in the same way that we were set free from this vault. What a joy it is to be able to call upon Him in times of need. As King David said in Psalm 3:4, "I was crying to the Lord with my voice, and H answered me."

Girls Set Free from Fears

Two young girls were living with their grandmother after being removed from their mother due to neglect and suspected abuse. Their grandmother began taking them to church with her and they responded quickly to her loving care and discipline and began behaving better and doing well in school. The oldest girl was 11 years old and she was afraid to sleep by herself in spite of her declaration that she was going to start sleeping in her own bed. I asked her, "If you could get rid of your fear of sleeping alone would you like to?" She said she would, so I told her that I needed to know how her fear started to know how to pray for her.

The girl told me that her stepfather used to scare her by knocking on her bedroom window at night and getting a neighbor to look in her window with a mask on. She was afraid that something bad was going to happen or that her stepfather was going to come back and scare her again. I prayed and asked the Lord what He wanted her to know about that belief. "I know he won't do it again," she said. "Jesus will protect me." I asked her how she felt when thinking about her stepfather coming back to scare her and she said, "Not scared." "So what happened to that fear you had a few minutes ago?" I asked her. She said, "Jesus is carrying it for me."

Her younger sister was 9 years old and she let me pray with her about her loss of her father, and her grief and sadness were taken away from her. But her grandmother told me that she was afraid to go to the bathroom by herself and always cried and insisted that her grandmother go with her. I asked her if she would like to get rid of her fear of going to the bathroom alone. She said that she would and I told her that I needed to know how her fear got started so I would know how to pray for her.

She told me that her stepfather thought it was funny to try to scare them. He hid in her bedroom, made scary noises, jumped out at her, and hid under her bed to scare her. When she went to the bathroom he would wait for her to come out and then he would jump out at her, wearing a mask. I prayed and asked the Lord what He wanted her to know about her belief that he was going to come back and scare them. "He's not going to be around to scare me," she said. I asked her how that made her feel and she said, "Not scared; not much; just a little bit." "Why do you feel a little scared?" I asked. She said, "Because he wore a mask with horns like the devil and I was afraid that the devil could get hold of me."

I prayed and asked the Lord what he wanted her to know about this. "He's not going to hurt me because I'm one of God's children and angels are all around me." "So, how do you feel now about going to the bathroom by yourself?" I asked. "I'm not scared; I know He can't hurt me because I'm one of God's children." The grandmother was ecstatic to hear how the Lord had spoken to the girls and set them free from their fears. Jesus does love the little children, and when they learn how to take their burdens to Him and to listen to His comforting Spirit they will grow to love Him and rely upon Him.

Set Free from Fear of Confinement

A woman told me that she went for a medical exam earlier in the week and was asked to lie down in a small "coffin-like" device. When she got into it she began to panic, and became very fearful and couldn't breathe, and she thought she was going to die in there. She told the technicians to get her out of there, so they helped her out and they offered to use a larger device which was much less confining and she did fine. I asked this woman if she would like to overcome her irrational fear and she said she would, so I told her to visualize being inside the apparatus and remember how she felt and what she thought at the time. She closed her eyes and recalled what it felt like, then I asked her if she had ever felt this way previously. She began crying and said, "Yes, when I was sexually abused at age 12. I thought that I had already dealt with that." "Would you like for me to help you get rid of that fear?" I asked her. She said that she would so I told her to remember what happened during the abuse and remember how she felt and what she believed. "I couldn't breathe and I thought I was going to die," she said. I prayed for her and said, "Lord, what do you want this 12-year-old girl to know about this belief that she is going to die?" I told her to let me know if she had any thoughts come to her mind. "He has always been with me; He's my protector," she said. "How does that make you feel?" I asked. She said that her fear left her and she suddenly felt calm. Even when she visualized the sexual abuse she said that she no longer felt fearful or unable to breathe and she had no other negative emotions connected to the sexual abuse. Those thoughts from the Lord set her free from her fear.

In order to test whether this had removed her fear of the medical device I asked her to visualize climbing back into it and tell me how she felt. She closed her eyes and visualized it and said that she felt calm and it did not upset her to think about it. Her fear of the device was gone because she went to the original source of the fear, prayed about it, and the Lord brought truth to her mind to set her free. Fears can be removed through three simple steps: 1) Identify the original source of the fear, 2) Identify the underlying beliefs, and 3) Pray for truth. When you pray and listen to the Lord He will bring truths to your mind to set you free from your fear.

The Lord does not want us to be controlled by fear but to let His peace fill our hearts. Jesus is the "Prince of Peace" (Isaiah 9:6), so whenever you fear, learn to use these three steps to replace your fears with His peace and "let the peace of Christ rule in your hearts" (Colossians 3:15).

Girl Set Free from Fear of Deadly Disease

A woman brought her daughter for counseling because she had developed an irrational fear that she had a terrible disease and was going to die. She had gone to the doctor many times concerning physical problems that she thought were symptomatic of some terrible disease. She was fearful that she had cancer because she knew a boy at school who had died from cancer the previous year, and then a young man whom she knew had been shot recently and died. She also had a grandmother who had died of cancer ten years earlier, and an aunt who had a panic attack recently. She had begun fearing that she had cancer and was going to die.

I prayed with her that the Lord would take her to the source and origin of her fears, and she began having a panic attack and could not remember when this started. Her mother remembered a time when she was about 3 years old and she choked on some food and almost died. This girl could not remember this, however, so I encouraged her mother to wait until the anxieties occurred again and to pray with her about her fears and her beliefs.

A week later it did happen again when she was at home, and her mother prayed and asked the Lord to bring to her mind what had happened. Her daughter remembered being at a party and the babysitter made her eat a hot dog which lodged in her throat. She thought she was going to die, so her mother prayed and asked the Lord what He wanted her to know. She said, "I didn't die. The Lord protected me and I'm okay." This resolved her fears and panic attacks which quit happening.

OVERCOMING ANXIETIES

Man Set Free from Social Anxiety

A man came to me for help with his social anxiety. He was very intelligent and had a college degree, but had never held a job due to his social anxiety. He stated that he had not had any panic attacks for a year, but he felt anxiety every time he ventured outdoors. The last time he felt it was when coming to his counseling appointment with me. I asked him what he was afraid of, and he said, "I might say something to embarrass myself."

I asked this young man when was the first time he could remember having this kind of anxiety and he recalled a time in the fourth grade when he had to give a report in his class. He was very shy and when he stood before the class he turned beet-red and the entire class laughed at him. The teacher not only laughed but made fun of him also, and he was very embarrassed and believed that he was shameful and weak and did not measure up to the other children.

I had never seen this man before and had not talked with him about how to pray about his emotions, so I was hesitant to introduce it so quickly. As I spoke with him I learned that he also had fears of losing family members or pets, and he had panic attacks that made him fearful of dying. He told me that he had had a dog for 12 years that died and he couldn't stop crying because he was overwhelmed with sadness and the thought that he would never see him again. This gave me the chance to explain how to get rid of grief through prayer, and he said he would like to get rid of his grief over his dog. We made a list of 11 things he enjoyed about his dog, then I led him in a prayer in which he told the Lord what he missed about the dog, and asked the Lord to take the grief from him. I asked him how he felt about the dog and he said, "Peace. I just feel peace." I asked him what he thought about this and he said, "I think it's amazing!"

I then explained how the Lord can also take away feelings of anxiety and I asked him if he would like to try. He said that he would, so I told him to think about his fourth grade class while I prayed, "Lord, what do you want this man to know about his belief that he was "shameful and weak and did not measure up to others." I told him to be quiet and let me know if he had any thoughts come to his mind. He very quickly said, "I'm not weak. My strength comes from other sources." I asked him how he felt, now, as he thought about his fourth grade class and teacher, and he said, "Nothing; neutral." I asked him what he thought about that and he said, "That's amazing!"

I told this man to visualize himself leaving his house to go to the store or to a social event, and tell me how he felt. He said, "I don't have to be afraid. Even if I do say something wrong, it's not the end of the world. I'll get over it. I might not be loud but I have worth." I asked him where those thoughts came from and he said, "It came from God." When I asked him how he was feeling, now, he said, "Okay. Calm, neutral, no anxiety."

This man continued to pray about his fears and eventually began going into public regularly and living a normal life. Fears that we acquire in our childhood can have a life-long impact on us. It's amazing how a little lie in our childhood can put us in bondage to fear, but it is more amazing how the Lord can set us free as we learn to identify the source of our lies, identify the lies we believe, and then pray for truth. As we listen quietly to the Lord speaking His truth, it will set us free, indeed!

Man Set Free from Anxiety Attacks

A man came for counseling who had anxiety attacks, angry outbursts, and had abused alcohol. He was an extremely angry man, but he desperately desired to be set free, and he came regularly to our appointments. He was temporarily unemployed due to health problems, so he was able to come to two or three appointments each week. It was with great difficulty that he finally prayed and gave all his anger to the Lord and released it. He immediately became much more calm and felt much better.

However, he continued to experience anxiety each morning. I asked him what was happening when he became anxious and what thoughts were going through his mind. He told me that when he woke up in the morning and had nothing to do while his wife got ready for work, he became breathless, hyperventilated, and felt that he should be working. He said, "I should be bringing in income;

I'm a bad husband since I am not working." I asked him to try to remember the first time he felt that he was failing because he wasn't working and he said that he always felt this way as a child, because he always had work to do at home and he got a whipping if he failed to get his work done. If he forgot to take the laundry out of the dryer, or if he didn't have dinner ready when his parents got home from work, or if the house was not clean or the horses weren't fed, then he got whipped. He got whipped frequently as a child and he believed, "I deserve to be whipped; I was a bad child to not get my work done."

I prayed for this man and asked the Lord what He wanted him to know about this belief. The thoughts that came to him were, "Those are just memories; I was never allowed a childhood; I was not a bad child who deserved to be punished; It's not true that when I'm not working I am just taking up space." After these thoughts came to him (from the Lord) he relaxed and smiled and said he no longer felt so burdened by his unemployment. The following week when I saw him he stated that he had had no more anxiety attacks since our last session and he felt "real good." He agreed that the Lord had lifted his burden and his anxiety and given him peace through our prayer.

The world says that we need drugs to eliminate our anxiety, but the Lord says, "Be anxious for nothing but in everything, through prayers and supplications, with thanksgiving, let your request be known. And the peace of God that passes comprehension will guard your hearts and minds in Christ Jesus" (Philippians 4:6-7). And when the Lord brings His truth into our minds through prayer and the Holy Spirit, the truth does indeed set us free from our anxiety and fears.

Man Set Free from Panic Attacks

A man told me that he had panic attacks every morning about 3:00 am that were waking him up. He said that he felt overwhelming anxiety and couldn't breathe until he got out of bed, which left him feeling tired and sleepy throughout the day. Since he was having marital problems, I assumed that he was probably worrying about his wife leaving him.

I asked him to focus on the feelings he had that morning when he woke up at 3:00 am and to try to remember the first time he felt those feelings. He told me the first time was probably when he had an accident 18 years ago. He suffered a head injury that broke his neck and blinded him in one eye. When he came to consciousness he was in restraints to prevent him from moving his head and to prevent him from rubbing his face, which had been badly mangled. He felt helpless, trapped, and fearful that he was going to choke to death and die. I told him to focus on this memory and I prayed, "Lord, what do you want this man to know about his belief that he is trapped and helpless and going to die?" I told him to be quiet and let me know if any thoughts came to his mind. He said, "I'm making some progress. I'm going to be alright." He said he felt better, but he was afraid it was going to happen again.

This man said he had the same overwhelming feelings one other time, after he had neck surgery to repair his broken neck. When he woke up after surgery, he was strapped down and couldn't move began choking on his saliva and couldn't turn his head. He felt helpless, and thought he was going to choke to death until his wife noticed him and went to help him. I instructed him to focus on this memory and then I prayed and asked the Lord what He wanted this man to know. He immediately said, "I'm still here; it didn't happen. It's just in my head, and my wife is still here." I asked him how he felt as he remembered that moment. He said that his anxiety was gone and he was calm. He said, "I'm glad it's over." He told me that his anxiety about remembering the accident was gone, and his anxiety about remembering the surgery was also gone. He also felt more grateful to his wife for being with him through his long recovery, which made him feel more loving toward her.

After receiving relief from these two incidents, I told him to think about how he felt that morning at 3:00 am when he woke up and felt overwhelmed and unable to breathe. He said that he felt calm now and had no more anxiety about it. He even said that he suddenly felt sleepy; he was ready to go back to bed! We discussed how he had PTSD from his accident, and how the Lord took his anxious beliefs that he was trapped and going to die, and replace them with His truth that it was over and he was okay now. He smiled and said that he didn't understand how it worked, but he knew that our prayers were helping him feel better.

The remarkable thing is that this man was not a believer yet, but the Lord was healing him of his fears and emotional bondage through prayer, because he was willing to cry out to Him. Many times the Lord uses such healing to bring people to salvation as they experience the grace and kindness of God in healing them and it softens their heart to Him. This affirms what the apostle Paul said in Romans 2:4 that "the kindness of God leads you to repentance."

The World's Solution for Fear

Panic attacks are manifested in symptoms such as hyperventilation, heart palpitations, perspiration, and fear of dying. When individuals experience persistent, intense anxiety they become desperate for help and for quick relief, and they turn to their physician for help. A study published in 2012 found that about 10% of US adults took sleeping pills in 2010 due to poor sleep, and that there was a three-fold increase in mortality risk from taking these pills (*British Medical Journal*, 2012). Physicians are quick to prescribe anti-anxiety medications and sleeping pills, which can quickly remove the symptoms (temporarily) and make the individual feel better. But they are also extremely addictive and after 8-10 weeks of usage their effectiveness wears off leaving the individual more phobic and anxious than ever. There are other serious risks associated with these medications, including the following:

Dangers of Anti-anxiety Meds

Addictiveness :

"After only brief therapy" in the "recommended" dose range Xanax can cause withdrawal symptoms, and interdose rebound leads to a craving for more before the next dose is due ("Xanax XR," 2011).

Adverse Side Effects :

"As with ALL benzodiazepines, paradoxical reactions such as stimulation, increased muscle spasticity, sleep disturbances, hallucinations, and other adverse behavioral effects such as agitation, rage, irritability, and aggressive or hostile behavior have been reported" ("Xanax XR," 2011, pp. 17-18).

Suicide and Violence:

"One or two doses of a benzodiazepine can lead to violence that is wholly out of character for the individual" (Breggin, 2013, p. 90).

Tolerance:

The original studies for panic disorder showed that at 8-10 weeks of exposure the patients were more phobic, more anxious, and had a 350 percent increase in the panic attacks for which they were being treated (Breggin, 1991, p.252-254).

Withdrawal Effects:

"It's not only dangerous to start Xanax, it's dangerous to stop it… Withdrawal can become far worse than withdrawal from morphine, hydrocodone, oxycodone, or heroin" (Breggin, 2012, blog).

Chronic Brain Impairment :

"In long-term use, benzodiazepines cause CBI with severe and potentially disabling cognitive deficits and neurological abnormalities including paresthesias, atrophy of the brain, and dementia" (Breggin, 2013, p.97).

Doctors are quick to prescribe anti-anxiety medications and sleeping pills to clients, because they do not fully appreciate the serious potential side-effects of these medications, and because it is a simple solution to take a pill to resolve anxiety and sleep disorders. Sometimes, they even prescribe these medications for themselves, or engage fellow-physicians to prescribe for them.

One physician with whom I was familiar was having difficulty sleeping, because he was so conscientious and compulsive in his practice that his heavy work load began interfering with his ability to sleep. He was aware of some of the literature regarding the dangerous adverse side-effects of these drugs, but did not really believe it because he had never personally experienced it. He spoke with another doctor about his sleep difficulties and got him to prescribe a sleeping aid for him. The day after he began taking the sleeping pills he made some extremely inappropriate comments to a female at his office, which was totally out of character for him, and his comments were reported to the clinic administration. He was almost fired, but due to his long history of outstanding work for this institution, he was required to seek psychiatric treatment and to follow the psychiatrist's recommendations.

The psychiatrist diagnosed him as having a bipolar disorder, based upon this one incident, and prescribed lithium for him. He dutifully took the medications for a few days, but it caused him to become so mentally impaired that he could not perform his job adequately. In the meantime, his sleeping had improved so he discontinued the lithium against medical advice, but his psychiatrist was unusually accommodating to him and allowed him to do what he thought was best. This doctor learned first-hand, how dangerous anti-anxiety medications can be, and how damaging mood stabilizers can be, as well.

If all physicians were required to try a dose or two of all psychiatric medications they intend to prescribe to their patients before being permitted to prescribe them, it would drastically change their prescribing patterns. Of course, most of them would never do this, because they have enough knowledge of the potential dangers of these medications that they would not want to jeopardize their health and their careers by taking these dangerous drugs.

Secular researchers, doctors, and therapists do not know how to effectively help individuals suffering from mental disorders, whether it is anxiety, anger, grief, depression, sadness, or any other emotional or psychological problem. We turn to physicians for help with medical disorders, but emotional problems are not medical disorders, in spite of the efforts of the psychiatric profession to persuade us that they are. Of course, they make a strong effort to convince their medical colleagues that they are a legitimate branch of medical science, and so physicians have come to believe them.

Christian doctors need to examine the questionable claims and examine the research by those who have challenged the psychiatric and pharmaceutical advocates, and exposed the false, underlying claims of effective, safe pharmaceutical solutions to human problems. Pastors and Christian leaders need to examine the underlying beliefs of biological psychiatry, challenge them with biblical truths about human nature, and teach their church members how to deal with emotional struggles without medications. One of the purposes of this ministry is to equip pastors to do exactly that.

The Bible clearly holds each of us responsible for our behavior. There are some medical conditions that can cause hallucinations, delusions, and emotional problems, such as brain tumors and drug-induced emotional reactions, but these are very rare and few in number, compared to the large number of people with depression, anger problems, and anxiety. The solution to these problems is not a pill, but finding peace through effective prayer. We must pay heed to the Scriptures that warn against turning to doctors, instead of turning to the Lord, for help with serious problems, for which there is no medical solution (2 Chronicles 16:12).

Making the Third Pledge: Let Not your Heart be Troubled Nor Let it be Fearful

The Scriptures not only tell believers to "not let the sun go down on your anger" (Ephesians 4:26), and "do not grieve as the rest" (1 Thessalonians 4:13), but it also says "Let not your heart be troubled, nor let it be fearful" (John 14:27). We cannot afford to hold onto any of these emotions for long or they will lead us to do or say things that we regret. Once you learn how to give all your grief and sadness to the Lord, you would be wise to give it all to Him quickly and systematically so that it will not damage your mood and gradually interfere with your life. Many people are unconscious of how much past losses continue to affect them on a daily basis. Believers must learn to daily cast their cares upon the Lord and to not be agitated in order to experience God's peace and joy.

Each believer is strongly encouraged to make this third pledge to "not let your heart be [agitated], nor let it be fearful." Identify any other sources of agitation besides anger and grief, and begin praying about them so that you can eliminate them. Identify any persistent, regular sources of fear or shame that hinder you in your life and begin praying about them. If you have a fear of water, or rejection, or persecution, begin praying about it to overcome it. If you have any sources of shame from your past, pray about them until they are completely eliminated from your life. If necessary, find a prayer partner to help you explore these fears and feelings of shame so that you can overcome them. The Lord instructs us in Hebrews 12:1 "let us also lay aside every encumbrance, and the sin which so easily entangles us, and let us run with endurance the race that is set before us."

As with the first and second pledges, this pledge should be made seriously and not flippantly. Realize that you must honestly identify all fears that are hindering you, or encumbering you, and ask the Lord for His grace to identify the source, identify the underlying beliefs, and then pray for truth to set you free. Once you have removed all known hindrances, then commit yourself to recognizing any additional feelings of shame or fear that may surface in your life, and seek to overcome them so that you will be fully productive in your life.

The removal of these encumbrances will enable you to have the fruit of the Spirit in your life so that you will enjoy love, joy, and peace. This will also enable you to be a true disciple of the Lord Jesus and go wherever He sends you to accomplish His work for you, without fear or any impediments. You will be fruitful as a disciple and be able to enjoy the exciting task of spreading the gospel throughout the world and helping to expand God's kingdom.

16

OVERCOMING ADDICTIONS

A woman came for counseling regarding the loss of her son. He was her only son and he suffered from some depression and low self-esteem as a teenager, which led him to develop a drug and alcohol abuse problem. After he graduated from high school, his drug abuse worsened until he decided that he needed to enter a treatment program. During this 60-day treatment program, he began attending church and received Jesus as his Savior. After completing the program he continued attending church, reading his Bible, and praying, and his mother was ecstatic.

This young man remained clean and sober for five years but then he began to slip back into his depression, and the urges to drink and use drugs returned. He lived with his mother, who was very close to him and prayed for him and spoke to him daily. One day while she was out of the house, he called the local police and gave them his address, and told them he was going to kill himself. He didn't want his mother to come home and find him dead.

A police officer happened to be next door to where the young man and his mother lived, and he quickly went next door to talk with the young man, who answered the door. He went out on the porch to speak with the officer, but after a few minutes he pulled out a gun and shot himself on his mother's porch, in front of the officer. The mother was heartbroken, of course. I prayed with her about her grief, anger, and feelings of shame, and she was set free from this traumatic loss through prayer.

This is a very sad story but it illustrates a very important principle. This young man had gone through treatment and even got saved, which helped him feel better and stay sober, but he eventually relapsed because he never released the underlying emotions that led him to abuse drugs and alcohol.

Why Treatments Fail

The failure of drug treatment programs is legendary, but most people do not understand why treatments are so ineffective. Most treatment programs are 12-step programs, modeled after the 12 steps of Alcoholics Anonymous, and they are educational programs that focus on persuading the person that they have a problem and need AA or NA to stay sober. The primary help given in these treatment programs is "intellectual," rather than "emotional" change.

Strongly addicted individuals need a safe place to go where there is little or no access to drugs or alcohol, so they can acquire a period of sobriety. During this time they are taught about the dangers of drugs and alcohol and they learn some strategies for trying to stay sober. But, if the underlying emotional pain is not healed, they remain vulnerable to drugs or alcohol abuse, and will likely return to their substance abuse when their negative feelings are triggered off again.

Salvation and Addiction

When I first began working in the mental health field, I genuinely believed that if I could lead an addicted person to salvation that they would be able to stay sober and drug free. I was dismayed to learn that many people who were genuinely saved continued to struggle with drinking, drug abuse, and other vices and problems. I then began devoting myself to trying to understand what it takes for believers to be set free from their strong urges for their addiction.

Salvation is, of course, the most important decision an individual can make in their life, because it determines their eternal destiny. Jesus asked the question, "For what does it profit a man to gain the whole world, and forfeit his soul?" (Mark 8:36). It would be better to be a saved man who struggles with addictions, than to be a sober man who goes to hell. However, it is clear from an examination of the scriptures that salvation does not automatically renew the individual's mind. In Romans 12:2 the apostle Paul says, "Do not be conformed to this world, but be transformed by the renewing of your mind." New believers still have the same old mind they had before salvation and need to have their mind renewed.

There are many people who are genuinely saved and going to heaven, but they have never been set free. The process of having our minds renewed to become more and more like Jesus is what the Bible calls "sanctification," and we are frequently challenged in the Bible to be renewed in our minds and to become more like the Lord. Salvation is very important and can be a tremendous aid to helping people find purpose, joy, and peace, but it does not automatically lead to freedom from old habits and behaviors. Some of our old habits and behaviors are deeply rooted in past experiences, and we need to learn how to resolve these experiences and the feelings connected to them so that we are less tempted to turn back to our old ways.

The Strengths and Limitations of AA

I spoke with a man who came to me for help with his drinking. He told me that he used to be involved in Alcoholics Anonymous but he no longer believed in it. He said that he had a sponsor who had been sober for ten years and was well liked and respected by other AA members. New members often turned to him for advice and asked him to be their sponsor. But one day, after ten years of sobriety, he put a gun in his mouth and pulled the trigger, taking his life and shocking his AA friends. He was, by all appearances, a successful recovering alcoholic, but he had a daily battle with his emotions and urges to drink, and he ended it suddenly and violently.

Of course, not all AA members do this, and there are some who maintain their sobriety with the help of AA, but it exposes some of the limitations of this organization. Just like drug treatment programs, AA does not teach their members how to overcome feelings of grief, anger, or shame, so most recovering alcoholics in AA struggle with these emotions on a daily basis. The AA social network and support system provides a support group as members seek to break their pattern of addiction, and this is helpful, but not sufficient. The AA Twelve Steps are biblical principles for living, but do not provide emotional healing.

Some AA members learn how to release their anger and grief, but there is nothing in the AA Big Book or official literature that systematically teaches members how to overcome grief, anger, or shame. Remaining clean and sober is a daily battle of staying sober just one day at a time for most AA members. Those who work hard, attend a lot of meetings, and seek help from one another when they are struggling, may stay sober.

Underlying Emotions of Addicts

The most common underlying emotions that addicts have that lead them to abuse drugs and alcohol are grief, anger, and shame. When addicts are asked when they started abusing drugs or alcohol and what happened just prior to the onset of their substance abuse, most of them will admit that they experienced some type of loss prior to their substance abuse. Usually, the loss of a parent, a sibling, a close friend, or some other significant loss led them to depression or anger, which made them vulnerable to substance abuse.

When I worked in a treatment program, I interviewed every client admitted and collected data for six months, asking each client what traumatic events occurred in their life prior to the start of their substance abuse. These clients reported the following events occurring prior to their substance abuse: 68% reported a traumatic loss, 52% reported emotional abuse, 41% witnessed violence in their home, 36% experienced physical abuse, 23% experienced sexual abuse, and only 4% reported no traumas. Thus, the most frequently cited cause of substance abuse was the experience of a significant loss in their life.

Loss leads to grief, sadness, and depression, but emotional, physical, and sexual abuse can lead to feelings of anger, which my survey indicated were also high probability events in the lives of addicts that contributed to their substance abuse. This is consistent with the AA Big Book, which states that "resentment is the number one offender" for alcoholics. There is no doubt that most addicts are full of anger toward parents, siblings, and abusive people in their lives, and that anger leads them to start abusing substances, triggering many of them to relapse once they have some sobriety.

The third major emotion that leads to substance abuse is shame, over sexual abuse or over other events in their lives that lead them to feel guilt or self-loathing. As described previously in this book, guilt and shame are related but separate emotions. Feelings of genuine guilt are important contributors to addictions, and these are discussed in detail in steps 4-10 of the Twelve Steps of AA, where the individual is instructed to conduct a thorough moral inventory of themselves, and to confess to God, to themselves, and to another human being the exact nature of their offenses, and seek to make amends whenever possible. This is an important process that can do a lot of good for the individual, and help them to be honest and to try to clear their conscience. But the only way to truly find forgiveness is to confess our faults to the Lord, and to ask forgiveness for all our sins.

Groups like Celebrate Recovery, that help people go through this "moral inventory," can help addicts to confess their sins and find true forgiveness from the Lord. But feelings of shame may remain after all of this confession and continue to destroy the individual. Shame is a belief that you are dirty, bad, or shameful and you deserve to be punished, and this belief frequently remains after going through the moral inventory steps of AA. Set Free Prayer Ministry teaches individuals how to overcome feelings of guilt and shame, so that the addict will not continue to have urges to drink or use drugs in order to mask their feelings of shame.

The Basic Addiction Principle

Many young people experiment with alcohol and drugs, but most people do not like feeling drunk or high, so they do not become addicted. But when someone has underlying emotional pain of any type, they like the numb feeling that drugs and alcohol provide, so they are vulnerable to becoming addicted.

Having worked with addicts for forty years, I have learned that there are always underlying emotional reasons why people become addicted to alcohol or drugs. On the other hand, when addicts get rid of their underlying emotional pain they feel good and don't want to use drugs. The urges to drink or use drugs go away and then it is not difficult for them to stay clean and sober.

This is what I call the "Basic Addiction Principle," that when individuals have underlying negative feelings they are vulnerable to using drugs in order to feel better, but when they overcome their feelings of grief, anger, and shame their urges to abuse drugs stop.

What Research Says about Addiction

The "Basic Addiction Principle" has been documented in the Adverse Childhood Experiences (ACE) study described previously in this book. In this study a group of doctors in 2000 in California did a study of 17,000 people in an HMO. They had each person fill out a 1-page form with 8 questions about childhood adversities. The adversities included physical abuse, emotional abuse, sexual abuse, absence of a biological parent in childhood, living with a substance abuser, living with a chronically depressed or mentally-ill person, living with a person who had been incarcerated, or witnessing violence in the home.

Where these eight childhood adversities existed they were found to correlate with a wide range of subsequent social and medical problems. A strong, graded correlation existed between the number of childhood traumas a person experienced, and all kinds of mental disorders and social problems they later developed. This did not even include what is probably the highest risk factor, significant personal losses in an individual's life.

The Origins of Addiction

The director of the ACE study, Vincent J. Felitti, MD, stated, "In our detailed study of over 17,000 middle-class American adults of diverse ethnicity, we found that the compulsive use of nicotine, alcohol, and injected street drugs increases proportionally in a strong, graded, dose-response manner that closely parallels the intensity of adverse life experiences during childhood" (Felitti, 2003, p. 3). Only about 2% of the individuals in the study who indicated that they had no adverse childhood experiences and received an ACE score of 0, became alcoholics as adults, in contrast to almost 6% of those who received a score of 1 for having experienced one of the adverse childhood experiences identified on the questionnaire. Ten percent of those with a score of 2 were alcoholics, almost 12% of those with a score of 3, and 16% of those with a score of 4 on the questionnaire became alcoholics, and were 8 times more likely to do so than those with a score of 0. The larger the number of types of childhood traumas an individual had, the higher their risk was of becoming an alcoholic.

The same relationship was found between intravenous drug use and ACE scores. About .25% of those subjects who reported having had none of the eight types of childhood adversities became intravenous drug users as adults. Twice as many of those who experienced one type of childhood trauma, became intravenous drug users as adults. Those with an ACE score of 2 were six times more likely, those with a score of 3 were eight times more likely, and those with an ACE score of 4 or more were almost 12 times more likely to become intravenous drug users as adults, than those who had experienced none of these childhood traumas (Felitti, 2002, p. 5).

Conclusions by Vincent J. Fellitti, MD

Dr. Fellitti summarized the findings of the study by saying, "Our findings show that childhood experiences profoundly and causally shape adult life." With regard to addictions he concluded that, "The major factor underlying addiction is adverse childhood experiences that have not healed with time," and "unrecognized adverse childhood experiences are a major...determinant of who turns to psychoactive materials and becomes 'addicted.'" (Felitti, 2003, p.9).

He went further to say, "We propose giving up our old mechanistic explanation of addiction in favor of one that explains it in terms of ... decisions being made to seek chemical relief from the ongoing effects of old trauma" (Felitti, 2003, p.9). In other words, he is saying that this data leads one to conclude that individuals who have experienced childhood traumas use drugs and alcohol in order to receive relief from the negative emotions they have experienced from past traumas.

Based upon the data from this huge research project, Dr. Felitti confidently concluded, "Addiction is <u>not</u> a brain disease, nor is it caused by chemical imbalance or genetics." The evidence is very clear from the ACE study that childhood traumas lead to long-range emotional reactions that lead the traumatized persons to seek relief through the use of alcohol and illegal drugs. In light of this finding, it is very interesting to note that most substance abuse programs, nowadays, place clients on psychiatric medications for "co-occurring disorders" before they begin the program. The treatment providers force their clients to use psychiatric medications to numb their feelings, rather than using their illegal drugs.

Underlying Causes of Addictions

This study leads to the unavoidable conclusion that early-life traumas lead people to feel emotional pain, which then leads them to turn to drugs, alcohol, promiscuity and risk-taking behaviors to numb their feelings. This has profound implications for treatment providers and for churches who want to help those struggling with addictions. Churches need to teach addicted individuals how to release or resolve their emotional pain through Biblical principles in order to free them from their destructive behaviors. If indeed the Bible can help us to experience love, joy, and peace through prayer and our relationship with the Lord Jesus, then we should be able to help people with addictions to find freedom through the Lord.

It is also important to notice that people who experienced childhood traumas are much more likely to abuse drugs and alcohol than those who did not, but most people who experience traumas do not become addicted to substances as adult. Only 16% of individuals who experienced four or more ACE events in childhood became alcoholics as adults. Although childhood traumas do not invariably lead to, or cause, alcoholism or drug abuse, they do cause negative feelings of grief, anger, shame and sadness that predispose people to abuse drugs or alcohol to feel better.

Sexual abuse often leads the victims to have feelings of anger and shame that continue to exert a negative impact on them into adulthood. Those who experience physical abuse or witness violence are prone to have feelings of anger and fear, and if the violence led to death they may also have unresolved feelings of grief that can affect them as adults. Emotional abuse also leads frequently to feelings of anger, hurt, and sadness, and those who experience traumatic losses in childhood often have unresolved feelings of grief, anger, and sadness that linger long into their adulthood and affect their relationships and lives. Even though these individuals may not abuse drugs or alcohol, they may experience anxiety or depression that can seriously affect their lives.

Basic Causes of Addictions

Summarizing the ACE study, we can say that underlying emotional pain often leads individuals to compulsively seek relief through the addictive activity. This is confirmed by the Scriptures that say in Proverbs 31:6-7, "Give strong drink to him who is perishing, and wine to him whose life is bitter. Let him drink and forget his poverty and remember his trouble no more." The Bible recorded this truth thousands of years before the ACE study, but it is helpful to find, once again, that the Scriptures are very accurate in their observations about human struggles, and that their accuracy is verified by good research.

The ACE study also found a strong correlation between childhood traumas and social problems, as well as all sorts of mental disorders. There was a high correlation between childhood traumas and depression, hallucinations, suicide attempts, abortions, unintended pregnancies, and poor life expectancy. There was also a high correlation between childhood traumas and adult prescriptions of antidepressants, anti-anxiety medications, and antipsychotic medications.

The clear evidence from this study and other recent studies is that mental health problems are not caused by genetic or chemical problems, but are the result of traumatic childhood experiences and losses that create long-lasting feelings of grief, anger, sadness and shame. Psychiatric medications do not correct chemical imbalances or cure problems. They simply numb feelings and disable the brain, but are also at high risk of permanently damaging it and causing mental and social problems.

Emotional Healing Prayer

The Lord not only wants us to be saved but to be set free from emotional bondage through prayer, Scriptures, and the Holy Spirit. There are very few believers who know how to pray effectively about their emotions, or how to help other believers who struggle with past traumas like sexual abuse, physical abuse, divorce, trauma, and death. There are some support groups available for those who suffer with these issues, but they mostly use techniques derived from secular counseling approaches, and they are not effective. Individuals who attend these support groups seem to enjoy them and return faithfully for months and years, but they never find freedom from their struggles.

There is a relatively new movement, created by Rick Warren of Saddleback church, that attempts to teach churches how to create counseling programs within their church to help those with mental disorders. The program is called "Hope for Mental Health," but it only encourages Christians to embrace traditional mental health counseling and to take psychiatric medications, which does not offer any true hope. Being told that you have to take medications for the rest of your life that blunts your emotions, diminishes your cognitive abilities, and destroys your sex life is not very hope-engendering.

In Set Free Prayer Ministry we want to teach churches and individuals how to overcome grief, anger, shame, fear, and depression, and how to be set free from addictions and compulsive behaviors. We provide booklets and literature on these topics so that people can find freedom and experience genuine joy, peace, and hope through the Lord Jesus.

The bottom line in this ministry is that Jesus can set you free. He said, "Come unto Me, all who are weary and heavy-laden, and I will give you rest" (Matthew 11:28), and He can take away your grief, anger, sadness, and shame and give you His peace. Secular counselors, psychologists, psychiatrists, and medications cannot do this for you, but Jesus can. When you are full of grief, anger, sadness, or shame, you cannot have God's peace and it is very difficult to stay clean and sober. However, when you get rid of those negative feelings that lead you to want to drink or use drugs, it is not hard to stay clean and sober; you don't want to get drunk or high when you already feel good.

Multiple Causes of Addictive Behavior

In an earlier chapter I made reference to a woman who was referred to me by a friend. She had been drinking for twenty-five years and had gone to treatment programs and AA, but she continued to struggle with drinking. She told me that she began drinking after her husband left her for another woman, and she still missed him twenty-five years later. We first prayed about her grief and she was able to release it in one session; then we prayed about her anger toward him in the second session. She quit drinking and continued to do well five years later. She had one major source of her grief, anger, and depression, namely her divorce, but once she resolved the underlying emotional issues that led her to drink, she quit and remained sober.

However, this is rather unusual, because most addicts have multiple feelings that lead them to drink or use drugs, and most addicts have multiple sources of grief, anger, and shame that need to be resolved before they are set free from their addiction. For example, I met a young man in the jail who was a drug dealer and a repeat offender who had been to prison many times. He was never interested in talking about spiritual matters while in jail, but when he was released he sought admission into a treatment program to please the courts. The treatment program rejected him, however, due to his criminal history and history of violence, and they referred him to me for outpatient drug counseling.

When he walked into my office, he was shocked to recognize me from the jail, but we had a good talk. I asked him when he began using drugs and fighting, and he told me that he began after the death of his grandmother at age 15. He said that his grandmother raised him, and when she died he was so angry that he began drinking heavily and using drugs, and committing crimes. He went to prison several times and began fighting regularly to entertain the other inmates. I asked him how he felt when he thought about his grandmother, and he admitted that he still missed her and felt very sad about her death.

I asked this young man if he would like to get rid of his feelings of anger and grief over the loss of his grandmother, and he said he would. I then explained how he could be set free from his grief by making a list of the things he missed about his grandmother and giving them to the Lord in prayer. As I led him in this prayer, he sobbed heavily and gave all his grief to the Lord, and was set free from this loss. He was amazed and began attending a Set Free meeting, but he still had a lot of other losses and traumas he needed to address. He returned to jail, and while he was incarcerated he gave his life to the Lord and asked forgiveness for his sins. He then began praying on his own about ten other significant losses he had experienced in the previous ten years. While he was still in jail he was set free from his anger and grief, and when he was released from jail he began serving the Lord and started up a recovery program.

This man was not set free after releasing his grief over the loss of his grandmother, but that was what got him started. He prayed a lot on his own about other losses and had other sources of anger that needed prayer as well. This is much more typical for addicts; they need to identify the major sources of their grief, anger, and shame in order to be completely released from their addiction. The best way to identify these issues is through the creation of a Prayer Plan, as discussed in Chapter 3.

Identifying the Source of the Emotional Pain

When interviewing individuals who struggle with addictions, I try to identify the underlying, root emotions of grief, anger, and shame that led them to start using, and that continue to motivate them to abuse drugs or alcohol. This usually begins as I ask the person, "When did you begin to use drugs regularly or begin to get drunk regularly?" After identifying the age of onset, I then ask them if anything traumatic or significant happened just before they began abusing drugs. If they struggle with this question or comment that they just did it because their friends did, I will ask them to recall how they felt at that period of their life; were they angry about anything, or depressed about anything. I may ask them specifically, if they lost anyone or anything prior to the beginning of their substance abuse. If they admit to some significant loss or anger, I usually ask permission to ask more questions about their background in order to better understand them, and then I do a social history as described in Chapter Three.

In Chapter Three I also shared the story about a woman named Nola who grew up in a Christian home and was actively involved in her youth group as an adolescent and never drank or used drugs. After she got married and had three children she became addicted to pain medications after breaking her leg. She began drinking compulsively when her pain medications were withdrawn. I interviewed her and created a prayer plan for her to help her pray about the underlying emotions she had from prior experiences that were leading her to crave drugs to feel better. After just four prayer sessions with this woman and her husband, she was doing extremely well, and was able to remain clean and sober without any further treatment. All four of the prayer sessions with this woman were videotaped, by permission, and are available through the Set Free website: tradingpain.com.

Set Free from Drugs and Gambling: Joanna's Story

A young woman came for counseling after her children were removed from her custody by the department of social services. She went to a hospital for some medical treatment and she tested positive for methamphetamines in her system, which led the authorities to remove her three children from her care, and she was charged with drug abuse. She was very distraught about the loss of her children, but was so addicted to the meth that she could not stop using it. In the first session, I gathered background information from her and learned that she had experienced seven significant losses and was angry at two individuals, so these were included in her prayer plan. I explained how she could release her feelings of grief and anger through prayer, and how the release of these emotions would set her free from her addiction, and she was very receptive to this.

This woman had been raised by both parents, who got along well and provided her a stable home. She enjoyed school, made good grades, behaved well, and had plenty of friends, but her favorite uncle died when she was 7 years old. Another close aunt of hers died when she was 10 years old, another aunt died when she was

11 years old, and her maternal grandmother died when she was 12 years old. These losses made her sad and depressed, but then her father died when she was 15 years old, and her paternal grandmother died when she was 18 years old. She began gambling at age 18 to "take her mind off things," and at age 20 she began using meth and drinking to feel better. When her favorite cousin died at age 21, she began using meth regularly.

In addition, she had some unresolved anger toward a former boyfriend and toward her brother, so all seven losses and two sources of anger were placed on her prayer plan.

During our second session we prayed about the loss of her cousin at age 21, which was a major loss for her that led to a lot of grief and emotional pain. She experienced relief from her grief during the first session, and when she returned the following week, she said that her urge to use drugs had stopped. However, she admitted she had a gambling problem in addition to her drug addiction. She had gone to a casino one night and lost about $900 which she and her boyfriend could not afford to lose. I asked her how she felt the night that she went gambling. She told me that she was angry at her brother who was "being a jerk." She often went gambling to take her mind off of other issues. We made a list of the reasons for her anger and she prayed about her anger toward her brother and released it. She was amazed at how quickly she was able to release her anger toward him after only one session.

The following week she said that she had done no more gambling, and she had not become angry about anything. We prayed about two more losses from her prayer plan, and she was able to release her grief over these two losses in her childhood. She also said, "I feel a lot better," and her mother and boyfriend told her they were proud of her. She stated that she had prayed about four losses on her own and was feeling very well. During our fourth session her boyfriend began coming with her to the sessions, and she had used no more drugs and had no more urges to use. He said he could tell a big difference in her. She always came in smiling after that, and her boyfriend began referring his friends who were using drugs to me, because he saw how quickly she had overcome her drug use.

This young lady continued doing well and stayed clean of all drug usage, and after several months her children were returned to her custody and she was thrilled. She and her boyfriend even got married so they could give their children a more stable environment. At our last session I asked her husband if he could tell any difference in her. He said, "She is a whole lot easier to get along with; she used to do things to make me mad, and now she tries to keep me happy." She just smiled at that remark and giggled. She was always eager to share her story with others about how the Lord set her free from her addiction.

Sandra's Story

Another woman came for help after completing a 4-month inpatient substance abuse program. Everyone else in her class had already relapsed, and she admitted that she was also feeling the urge to drink. I explained to her how addictions are caused by unresolved feelings of grief, anger, and shame, and I shared with her how she could resolve these feelings through prayer. She was receptive to this suggestion so we talked about her background to identify the emotions she needed to resolve. We identified six unresolved losses and four sources of anger that needed to be resolved.

She told me that she was raised until age 9 by her mother, who drank heavily. At age 8 she was sexually abused, which made her very angry and depressed. Then at age 9, her father was released from prison and wanted to take over as her father immediately, which she resented. He was very strict, and became violent when he drank and she reacted by beginning to drink at age 11, fighting, and being rebellious. At age 14 she joined a gang and then a year later her maternal grandmother died and her drug abuse increased. When she was 17 years old she met her husband, got pregnant, and had a miscarriage, which further depressed her. At age 21 she gave birth to her son, but resumed her drug abuse as soon as she could. At age 25 she lost her father and an aunt, and at age 30 she lost another aunt and an uncle. We included a total of six losses, four sources of anger, and feelings of shame from a sexual abuse event on her prayer plan.

We began praying about her loss of her father during our second session, and she identified 17 things she missed about him. Then she prayed and released her grief. In our third session we prayed about the loss of her uncle, and she identified 17 things she missed about him, and prayed and gave these feelings to the Lord. After the first three prayer sessions she began praying on her own, and released grief over loss of an uncle, two aunts, and her grandmother. On our fourth session we prayed about her sexual abuse by a family friend, and she released her feelings of anger toward this man, and her feelings of shame, and she was set free from her sexual abuse. During the next two sessions we prayed about her anger toward her father, mother and her husband, and she released all her anger toward them.

When I saw this woman on week 7 she said she was doing great, was no longer angry at her mother or husband, or her abuser, and she had no unresolved feelings of grief over her losses. She continued to do well and went back to school and received a degree so she could get a better job and provide well for her and her son. I saw her several times after that, and each time she affirmed that she was still clean and sober and had no more urges to drink or use drugs. The treatment program she completed did not set her free from her negative feelings, but she was set free over a period of seven prayer sessions.

Overcoming Other Addictions

There are many forms of addiction, but all of them operate on "The Basic Addiction Principle." The addiction principle is: Any behavior that makes you feel good temporarily and covers up your emotional pain can become an addiction. The solution to all forms of addictions is the same: identify the underlying emotional issues that drive the addicted person to engage in their addiction, resolve them through prayer, and the addiction will stop.

Some people are addicted to pain pills and prescription medications, and it is still the unresolved emotions of grief, anger, and shame that lead most people to become addicted. As illustrated in Joanna's story, gambling can become addictive to individuals who like to get their mind off their life troubles and their unpleasant feelings. One Christian man I knew had a severe gambling problem that led to him losing his job, family, and home. He had grown up in a severely abusive home, and yet he insisted that he had resolved all his feelings on his own. He died having never resolved those feelings, and having never even admitted that they were the cause of his gambling.

More and more people are struggling with pornography addictions and sexual addictions. Whenever they feel lonely, depressed, angry, or shameful, they feel a compulsive desire to use pornography to make them feel better. Even many Christian men struggle with this and have difficulty finding help for their addiction. Some people compulsively, and repeatedly, have affairs, even when they are professing Christians. They need others to help them understand the nature of addiction, and to show them how to find freedom through prayer about the underlying emotions they experience that lead them to seek sexual relations to make them feel better.

Finally, some people have an addiction to tobacco products which make them feel better, and many people in our society turn to food to make them feel better. Obesity is a serious health problem in our society, and is probably the addiction of choice for most Christians. This was the focus of the Adverse Childhood Experiences study: understanding why it is that so many obese people sabotage their treatment when they are seeking help with their obesity that is ruining their health. Each of these addictions has the same underlying cause and the same solution: resolving the underlying emotions that led the individual to engage in the addictive behavior.

Complex Cases

Each of the cases presented in this chapter involved people with addictions who were truly set free through prayer. But it is important to understand that each of these individuals had some resources that enabled them to get back on their feet. Each of them had jobs, homes, cars, supportive families, and driver's licenses. There are some individuals who are much more difficult to help because they lack these resources. Homeless people have none of these resources and are much more difficult to help. If you manage to get them to return for prayer sessions long enough to resolve their issues and overcome their addiction, they still do not have income, driver's licenses, or vehicles to support themselves.

The same is true for incarcerated people who have few of these resources. When I minister to inmates in the jail, some of them have families and jobs, but many of them do not. If they genuinely get saved and set free from their addictions and mental issues, they may have felony offenses that make it very difficult for them to find jobs, and to get a vehicle again.

This is further complicated by the number of homeless and incarcerated people who receive disability from the government for some type of psychological disability. If they succeed in overcoming their depression or emotional problems, they are likely to lose their source of income, so the government basically pays them to stay sick. Sometimes family members also enable individuals and provide them food and shelter when they do not work, and they just sit around and use drugs. Homeless individuals will often spend their monthly check on drugs and alcohol and then have nothing left to provide a shelter for themselves. Those who continuously support such individuals usually do so out of feelings of guilt and shame, and do so to the detriment of the addicted person. They would do well to observe the words of the apostle Paul in 2 Thessalonians 3:10 where he said, "if anyone is not willing to work, then he is not to eat, either."

Set Free Indeed!
It is very difficult for addicts to stay clean and sober when they still have strong, underlying feelings of grief, anger, sadness, or shame. But when addicts resolve their underlying feelings of grief, anger, and shame, it is not hard to stay clean and sober, because the urges to use drugs or to drink stop. It is no longer a daily battle for them to stay sober or clean! Jesus does, indeed, set the captives free as they learn to turn to Him for help and learn to pray effectively about the underlying emotions that keep them in bondage. John 8:36 tells us, "If the Son makes you free, you will be free indeed."

Ten Steps to Spiritual Maturity and Freedom
Most addiction programs are based upon the AA 12 Steps but Set Free Prayer Ministry is not. However, some people will find it helpful to have a series of steps outlined to guide them in their path toward freedom. The following ten steps summarize the process to spiritual maturity that is recommended in this ministry:

1) Come to recognize that you cannot be set free from sin and emotional bondage apart from the power of God, and confess all your guilt and moral failures to God, asking for forgiveness and cleansing through the blood of Jesus.
2) Turn to Jesus as the Wonderful Counselor and meet with a prayer minister to be completely honest about your life experiences and underlying feelings that might give the devil a foothold in your life, and develop a prayer plan for resolving these feelings.
3) Identify all sources of anger from the past, making a list of the resentments you have towards those who have wronged you, giving them to God one-by-one through prayer, asking Him to take them from you, then making a solemn pledge to the Lord to "not let the sun go down on your anger" anymore.

4) Identify all losses, making a list of everything that you miss about each one, then giving them to God one-by-one through prayer and asking Him to take them from you.
5) Recognize any feelings of shame and fear you may have, identifying the source and origin of these feelings, identifying the underlying beliefs to these feelings, praying for truth, and allowing the Holy Spirit to bring truth to your mind to set you free from your shame and fear.
6) Learn to talk with the Lord as your friend and comforter throughout each day, identifying and resolving other negative feelings as they surface, and listening to and obeying His promptings each day so that He can lead you and fill you with His Spirit and with His joy and peace in all circumstances.
7) Spend time each day studying God's Word, prayerfully asking the Lord what He wants you to know or do based upon the Scriptures you read, and walking in the Spirit by allowing Him to lead you through His Word and through His Spirit to do His will.
8) Share your newfound peace and excitement about the Lord and use it as an opportunity to share the gospel with others so they can experience God's peace and freedom as well.
9) Unite together on a regular basis with others who are seriously pursuing a close walk with the Lord, to encourage them, pray with them, and to be encouraged and challenged by them in your daily walk, while avoiding close relationships with those who do not love the Lord or follow Him.
10) Seek the kingdom of God above everything else in your life, obeying Him, following Him, allowing Him to develop the fruits of the Spirit within you, and seeking to spread His kingdom through the use of your personal gifts and experiences.

17

OVERCOMING HURTS, HELPLESSNESS, HOPELESSNESS AND ALONENESS

In the previous chapter we talked about how to overcome addictions, and how the three major emotions that most addicts experience are feelings of grief, anger, and shame. Fear is probably the next most common emotion experienced by addicts, so it is important for everyone who wants to minister to addicts to be able to identify these four emotions and know how to resolve them using the prayer principles presented by this ministry.

Chapters 2-11 discussed how to overcome feelings of grief, anger, sadness, and disappointment through two steps: 1) Identifying the reasons for your anger or grief, and 2) Praying and asking the Lord to take your grief or anger and carry them for you. These four emotions are fact-based emotions because they are not based upon your thoughts or interpretations.

Chapter 12 introduced the concept of belief-based emotions and focused on one such emotion, the emotion of shame. Belief-based emotions require truth to be released. The three steps given previously for resolving feelings of shame are: 1) Identify the original source of the shame, 2) Identify the underlying beliefs connected to the shame, and 3) Pray for truth regarding your underlying beliefs. These same steps apply to the resolution of feelings of fear, which was discussed in Chapter 15, because fear is also a belief-based emotion.

There are other belief-based emotions that require the same prayer process, including feelings of hurt, helplessness, hopelessness, and aloneness. When ministering to people with addictions, trauma, or any other type of disorder, you must learn to recognize their feelings and deal with them as they surface. Once you recognize the presence of one of these emotions, you simply need to follow the three steps for resolving belief-based emotions to help the individual find freedom and peace.

Overcoming Feelings of Hurt

Many people say that they are not angry at anyone but they say they just feel "hurt," when I ask them how they feel. Usually, they mean that they feel unloved, unwanted, unimportant, or worthless. I like to just use the word "hurt" in talking about these feelings. This feeling is very common and it is a belief-based emotion. The underlying beliefs connected to it are usually beliefs like "I am unimportant, I am not wanted, loved, or valued, my feelings are not important, I am worthless, no one cares for me, I cannot measure up no matter how hard I try, I am unacceptable, I am a burden, I am in the way, and I cannot please others because of ____________." Sometimes people say they are hurt, but they are really just angry, and you can make a list of the reasons for their anger and they can just give it to the Lord to be set free. But if they also have feelings of worthlessness and feeling unloved, then they need help in identifying these beliefs and praying for truth to be set free.

When I first saw Jerry he was abusing meth and he was desperate for some medications to calm him. He told me that he was so angry that he was afraid that he might kill someone. As we talked I learned that he had good reason to be angry. He had been badly abused by his stepfather, who also was extremely violent to his mother until Jerry was old enough to fight back and to protect her. Not surprisingly he became addicted to drugs as an adolescent, and he had a lot of anger inside. We met for several sessions and discussed his anger toward his wife for her infidelity, his anger toward his brother, and his anger toward his stepfather who had abused him and his mother. Each time we met he was able to release his anger and to gain more peace. After several sessions his anger was gone and his depression had dropped from a rating of 10 to a rating of 2.

But there was one person whom he never mentioned in our sessions, his biological father. When I asked him what was causing his low-level depression, he stated that he felt hurt and rejected by his former wife, so I asked him the first time he felt such rejection and he said it was at age 8. His parents were divorced, and when his mother met his stepfather, Jerry could tell that he was unwanted by the stepfather. Once his mother married him they often fought about Jerry. But his mother became ill and could not care for him, so Jerry hoped that he would be able to live with his real father because his stepfather was abusive and did not want him. He had been seeing his father about once per month prior to this, but when his father was asked to take care of Jerry he began making excuses. Jerry felt that his dad didn't want him and so he began to feel that he was an inconvenience and was in the way. These feelings were still very strong, as if this had happened yesterday.

I asked permission to pray for him, then I prayed, "Lord, what do you want Jerry to know about this belief that he was an inconvenience and was in the way?" He told me the following thoughts came into his mind: "I know I'm not an inconvenience. I am important; I'm not in the way. I am a good person. I'm not a burden." I asked him if these thoughts felt true and he said they did. I asked him what changed his mind from a few minutes earlier when it felt true that he was inconvenient and a burden and he said that God had put the truth in his mind after we had prayed. He said, "The words just popped in my head like flash cards."

I asked him to think about his former wife who left him and had an affair, and asked him how he felt while thinking about her. He said that it didn't upset him anymore, since he had resolved his feelings about his father. He knew that he was important and that her rejection was just due to her own issues. His depression was completely gone after having prayed about his feelings of hurt and rejection.

We reviewed our previous sessions and how the Lord had removed all of his anger and hurt feelings and replaced it with His peace. Jerry was smiling, relaxed, and appeared to be truly at peace. He began attending church faithfully, praying, reading his Bible, and feeling positive about his family and his future. When I first saw him he was so violently angry that he was afraid that he could kill someone, but after several sessions he was a completely new person. What a difference it makes when the Lord renews our minds, carries our burdens for us, and replaces our inner lies with the truth. Today Jerry is indeed a "new creature" in Christ!

Regardless of whether you call these feelings hurt, rejection, worthlessness, or anything else, they are caused by underlying beliefs, and these beliefs are lies that must be replaced with truth. Simply identify the source of the beliefs, like Jerry did when tracing his feelings to how he felt toward his father, identify the beliefs, and pray for truth. As the person listens quietly, the Lord can give them the truth they need to set them free.

Overcoming Feelings of Helplessness

A young man told me he was feeling overwhelmed with his new job. He had always been involved in manual labor, then he was promoted to a new position that involved writing reports and using a computer. He had always been good at what he did, but he felt very overwhelmed at the thought of having to learn how to use a computer, which he had always avoided previously, and this was placing a strain on his marriage. Feeling overwhelmed is usually a feeling of helplessness, which is a belief-based emotion, so I asked him if he had ever felt overwhelmed like this before (to identify the source of his emotions). He couldn't remember ever feeling this overwhelmed but he told me that he had always avoided computers in high school and had his friends help him with reports.

I inquired more about his high school experiences, and he told me that he avoided computers because he had tried to use them once in the sixth grade, and became so aggravated and irritated when he couldn't figure it out that he wanted to cuss and throw it down. He said that everyone else could do it but he couldn't and it made him feel very helpless and overwhelmed. This sounded like a "source" to me so I asked him to reflect on this experience and remember how he had felt, while I prayed for him. I prayed, "Lord, what do you want this boy to know about his belief that everyone else could do it but he couldn't." I told him to be quiet and let me know if he had any thoughts come to his mind. He said no thoughts came to his mind, but when I asked him if it still felt true he said, "No. It was just something that happened. I know I can do it; I just have to try." I asked him to think about going to work and learning how to use the computer to do his reports and to tell me if he still felt overwhelmed. He said that he no longer felt overwhelmed or fearful that he would not be able to do the job. He was confident that he could learn how to use the computer.

I explained to this man that feeling overwhelmed was due to his belief that everyone else could do it but he couldn't, and when I prayed for truth the Lord brought truth to his mind to set him free from his feelings of helplessness. The Lord brings truth to people in three different ways: some people have a thought enter their mind that comes from the Lord, some people have a visual picture that brings a truth to them, and others just have a "quiet realization of truth" (Smith, 1996, p. 143). This man had a "quiet realization of truth" that set him free. The Lord said He would send us His Holy Spirit to "guide you into all truth" (John 16:13) and we are instructed in James 1:5 "If any of you lacks wisdom [insight into the true nature of things], let him ask of God... and it will be given to him." That's all we did; asked God for truth and He gave it to this man, and he was set free. Each believer has the Holy Spirit available to guide them into all truth and set them free from anxiety and feelings of helplessness, if they will identify the source of their feelings, identify the false belief they have, and pray for truth.

A woman became extremely anxious when she heard that her husband's ex-wife was coming to town. The ex- had made threats against her previously, and the prospect of her coming to town made this woman very fearful, helpless, and nauseous. She begged her husband to take her away from their town where she had so many memories of abuse, but her husband insisted that she could not run from her problems.

I encouraged her to focus on her feelings of anxiety and asked her when was the first time she had felt such feelings. She said the first time was when she was a child and her father yelled at her and threatened to beat her. She felt fearful and helpless, and these bad feelings began to flood her mind, and she began to feel anger at her father and at God for allowing her to experience such terrible things as a child. I asked her if she would like to get rid of her anger and she said she would, so we made a list of her resentments toward her father and toward God. We prayed about her anger and she was able to release it, then she said she still felt fearful, so I prayed, "Lord, what is the truth that you want her to know about her belief that she is helpless, is going to be hurt, and something terrible is going to happen?"

She stated that the thoughts that came to her were, "He is here with me; He will protect me." "Do those thoughts feel true?" I asked. She said they did. As we reviewed her emotions she indicated that she no longer felt any anger or fear about meeting her husband's ex-wife.

The following week went well, she had no more anger toward her father or God, and she was no longer fearful of confronting her husband's ex-wife. She stated that she felt so good during the week that her husband asked her at one point, "Are you on drugs?" She laughed and said that she was not but she felt good because she had been able to resolve her anxieties and release her anger.

Both of these stories illustrate how to deal with feelings of helplessness. Helplessness, is based upon beliefs such as, "I am weak, I am powerless, I cannot do anything to resist him, I'm too small to do anything about it, I'm overwhelmed, everything is out of control, I'm trapped, and there is no way out." These types of beliefs lead to feelings of helplessness, but once you identify the original source of these feelings, you then can express these beliefs and pray for truth, to be set free.

Overcoming Feelings of Hopelessness

Hopelessness is similar to helplessness, but they are different feelings. Helplessness is a feeling that you are weak and unable to do anything to change your situation, but hopelessness is a feeling that there is no way out and your situation will never get any better. Feelings of hopelessness are based upon beliefs like, "There is no hope for me, it's never going to get better, there is no way out, not even God can help me, nothing good can ever come from this, I have no reason to live." A feeling of hopelessness is a fundamental component of depression. It often occurs when an individual has lost someone important to them, believes they can never be happy again without that person, and believes there is no hope of ever feeling happy again.

One of the negative consequences of psychiatric treatment is that when people are told that they have a disorder that will never end, and they will need to take medications for the rest of their life, this creates a strong sense of hopelessness. A teenager drove a long distance with her mother to see me after being diagnosed as bipolar. She came from a stable family and got along well with both parents and her siblings, but during the last three years she had been involved with a young man who repeatedly became involved with other girls. She struggled with this up-and-down relationship for several years, and at times became depressed due to this unstable relationship. She eventually broke up with her boyfriend, but in the past eight months she had lost three close friends, including one who committed suicide and one who was murdered. When she went to a psychiatrist she was told she was "bipolar" and would have to be on medication the rest of her life. This announcement further depressed her and made her feel hopeless. She disliked the medications, which had unpleasant side effects including manic feelings. I encouraged her to educate herself about the medications she was taking so she could discuss them with her doctor.

Her intake form stated that she was "unsure" about any religious beliefs, so I was very cautious about suggesting prayer as an intervention for her anger and grief. I gave her an example of another teenager her age who released his grief through prayer and assured her that I did not want to push any religious beliefs on her. However, she and her mother both lit up and smiled and said they had recently returned to their faith. The girl told me that she had been "on fire for God" when she was younger but had not been to church for five years. She stated that she had begun praying again over the last three weeks and had found it helpful. She was eager to try anything that might help her feel better, and she stated that her strongest pain was at the loss of a close friend two weeks earlier.

I encouraged her to talk about her friend and what she missed about him. I made a list as she tearfully spoke about him, then I led her in a prayer in which she was completely honest with the Lord about her feelings. When we finished praying and asked God to take her grief from her, I asked the Lord if there was anything He wanted her to know. She told me, "He's okay. I'm happy he's not in this sinful world and I'm glad I got to spend time with him while he was still here." I asked her if it felt true to say "He's okay" and she said it did. That thought brought peace to her heart.

She said she felt peaceful and calm while thinking about her friend who had died, and she and her mother were both beaming with joy when they left. Her mother said that it was worth the long trip they had made to come to the appointment. The girl had found relief from her intense grief, and she promised to pray about the other grief and anger issues on her own. She was also thrilled to not feel the hopelessness any more of believing that she would be stuck with these negative emotions and have to be on medication the rest of her life.

The Lord replaced her emotional pain with peace, joy, and hope in the short time we spent praying. What a wonderful God we have who comforts the brokenhearted and sets the captives free. Any message that gives people a feeling of hopelessness is contrary to the Word of God, because He does not want us to feel hopeless, but to have hope. In Romans 15:13 the apostle Paul ends his letter with these words: "Now may the God of hope fill you with all joy and peace in believing, so that you will abound in hope by the power of the Holy Spirit." Ultimately, our hope comes from the Lord, who is able to rescue us out of our despair and to give us hope and peace.

Overcoming Feelings of Aloneness

Another belief-based emotion that many people experience is a feeling of aloneness. This is one of the most painful, excruciating feelings you can experience, when you feel utterly and completely alone in your pain. It is based upon beliefs such as, "I'm all alone, no one cares about me, I'm abandoned, not even God cares about me, I will always be alone, no one understands me, God has forsaken me, there is no one to protect me, and they will never come back for me." These beliefs can become anchored in childhood experiences and lead to a lifetime of feelings of aloneness, but once they are overcome an individual can feel good even when they are alone, because they know that the Lord is always with them.

A young mother of four children was deeply hurt by her husband when she discovered that he was spending private time with a female fellow employee, and had become emotionally involved with her. He admitted his emotional infidelity and was embarrassed and apologized to his wife about it. He admitted also that he felt depressed and this had made him vulnerable to the attentions of his female co-worker.

His wife met with a counselor and discussed her anger. She was willing to release her anger, and after making a list of her resentments toward her husband she asked the Lord to take them from her and replace it with His peace. When the counselor asked her how she felt afterwards she stated that she no longer felt any anger toward her husband, but she felt alone.

"When is the first time that you can remember feeling such feelings of aloneness?" the counselor asked. "When I was 9 years old my father was depressed and committed suicide," she replied. "I felt all alone with no one to comfort me or talk with me."

"Could I say a prayer for you?" her counselor asked. With her permission he prayed and asked the Lord what He wanted her to know about her belief as a child that she was all alone with no one to care for her. Then he asked her if any thoughts had come into her mind. She answered, "I wasn't alone; God was with me and He took care of me. He is going to take care of me now; He is in control."

"Do those thoughts feel true?" the counselor asked. She said that they did. She told him that she felt comforted and peaceful. All her feelings of anger were released first, and then her feelings of aloneness were released. Once she prayed, she knew the truth that she was never alone and it felt true to her.

Gary's Story

Gary was a young man who was seen several times for counseling. In the first session he focused on his anger toward his biological father, who had been abusive to his mother and had abandoned the children after his mother divorced his father. This young man made a list of his resentments toward his father and released it in the first session. In the second session he talked about the loss of his grandmother, who was very loving to him and taught him about the Lord. She died when he was a teenager, and this devastated him, so we made a list of 21 things he missed about her, and then we prayed about this list and gave it to the Lord. When he was seen again he indicated that he no longer felt any anger toward his father, just pity, and he said that he was able to think about his grandmother without any emotional pain.

Gary reported that in the previous week he had been calm and content. He said his depression dropped to about a level 3 on a

10-point scale, whereas it had been an 8 for the previous six months. But he stated that he sometimes felt unimportant and lonely, and he felt that he did not deserve to have a partner in his life. He explained that as a child his parents often went out partying and left him behind, and he cried and felt unwanted and alone. I asked Gary to concentrate on these memories and to try to remember how he felt. Then I prayed for him, "Lord, what do you want Gary to know about his belief that he is unwanted and all alone?"

He immediately began to pucker up as if he wanted to cry, and the following string of thoughts came to his mind. "I've always wanted you; I've always been there with you; you're never alone. I am wanted; God wants me; when I thought I was alone, God was with me and grandmother was there; she wanted me. I will never be alone." I asked him if these thoughts felt true and he nodded his head. "Lord, is there anything else that you want Gary to know?" I prayed. He began reporting other thoughts coming into his mind. "I will never be alone. I always hold back with people because I'm afraid they will leave me; my parents didn't abandon me; they left me with my grandmother who loved me; I had my grandmother there to love me; I am important and needed."

We talked about these insights and Gary was smiling. He was amazed at how good he felt as these insights sank into his mind. I explained that it is not necessary for him to remember each separate incident when he felt alone, because once the initial memory was healed, many others will also be healed, like dominoes falling. "Yes," he said. "I'm remembering other incidents when my parents left me, but I feel some emotion for just a second then it disappears." He smiled even bigger. "Other memories are being cleaned out as they flash through my mind."

We talked about the goodness of God and how much He loves us. Watching Gary light up as God brought truth into his mind was an awesome experience, and left me filled with excitement the rest of the day. God is so good, and He wants to carry all our grief and sorrow. There is no need to feel alone when you know the truth that the Lord is always with you and has promised "I will never desert you, nor will I forsake you" (Hebrews 13:5).

Truth-Based Aloneness

When we feel alone it is based upon a lie we believe, because the truth is that the Lord is always with us if we are believers, and even with unbelievers the Lord is near to them so they simply need to call out to Him (Acts 17:27). The only One who has ever been truly alone was the Lord Jesus when He was forsaken by everyone, including God the Father, as He hung on the cross to pay for our sins. When he cried out, "My God, My God, why have You forsaken Me?" (Mark 15:34), I believe He was crying out due to the extreme pain of being alone in His suffering. The Heavenly Father abandoned Him while He was bearing our sins and dying in our place, and even the angels were unavailable to minister to Him in that period of time. It was His anticipation of this aloneness that led him to sweat "drops of blood" (Luke 22:44) in the Garden of Gethsemane when He prayed to the Father, "My Father, if it is possible, let this cup pass from Me; yet not as I will, but as you will" (Matthew 26:39).

Thank God that Jesus experienced such utter aloneness so that we would never have to experience it. His aloneness was truth-based, but our feelings of aloneness are lie-based, and He wants to take these feelings from us and give us His peace by giving us the truth that we are never truly alone.

Jesus was the Son of God, and therefore did not have any distorted thinking or any belief-based emotions like fear, shame, helplessness or hopelessness, but He did experience the painful feeling of genuine aloneness. Because of this He does understand our feelings and is able to sympathize with us and comfort us. Hebrews 5:7 says, "He offered up both prayers and supplications with loud crying and tears to the One able to save Him from death, and He was heard because of His piety." Hebrews 4:15-16 tells us, "We do not have a high priest who cannot sympathize with our weaknesses, but One who has been tempted in all things as we are, yet without sin. Therefore let us draw near with confidence to the throne of grace, so that we may receive mercy and find grace to help in time of need."

Because Jesus can sympathize with our weaknesses, and understands how we feel, He wants us to go to Him to receive mercy and grace in times of need. As we learn to regularly cast all our cares upon Him, we will learn that He is able to carry all our emotional burdens for us and give us His peace. Even though He never experienced feelings of fear, shame, helplessness, or hopelessness, He did experience the physical pain which He bore for us, and the extremely painful feelings of grief, anger, sadness, disappointment and aloneness. This enables Him to feel our pain, to empathize with us, and to be able to comfort us through His Holy Spirit.

18

OVERCOMING SINFUL HABITS: SANCTIFICATION AND FRUITFULNESS

The English author Robert Louis Stevenson wrote a classic story about a Dr. Jekyll, who was a skilled, competent, caring physician in the day time, but in the evenings he liked to go to bars and girlie shows, and he went by the name Mr. Hyde. His conscience bothered him about this dual lifestyle so that he could not fully enjoy his nighttime adventures, so he sought to find a potion that would dull his senses and enable him to engage in his nefarious outings after hours without any twinges of conscience during the day. He did indeed find a potion that enabled him to enjoy himself more in the evening hours, and for a while he enjoyed living this double life. But he became progressively more angry, selfish, and violent, and eventually the potion quit working so that he was unable to return to his physician personality. In a drunken rage one evening he became violent and murdered a child, and the police began looking for him and eventually caught him. He was divided by two opposite personalities, a good one and a bad, selfish one, that ultimately destroyed him.

Theologian Anthony Hoekema wrote a theological article in which he stated, "Most of us would indignantly resent the suggestion that we bear any resemblance to the notorious Dr. Jekyll and

Mr. Hyde. However much we may dislike admitting this fact, however, there is a sense in which every converted person is a kind of Jekyll-Hyde combination. The Scriptures clearly affirm that there is a continual struggle within every converted man between his old nature and his new" (Hoekema, 1962, p. 42).

Dr. Hoekema is referring to Romans 7:19 where the apostle Paul said, "What I want to do, I do not do, but I do the very thing I hate!" And yet Paul also said in 2 Cor. 5:17 "If any man is in Christ he is a new creation." Reconciling these two concepts theologically is what the doctrine of sanctification is all about. How can a Christian renew his or her mind to allow him or her to progressively become more and more like Christ, and to less frequently live in sin?

This struggle is, unfortunately, illustrated all too often in the lives of modern day religious and public figures who live double lives. There are many respected preachers and public figures who have taken a strong stand for conservative moral values, but who have later been found to have struggles with pornography, prostitution, homosexuality, and affairs. When these struggles are exposed, it brings a great deal of disappointment and shame to the Church, or to the conservative organizations that supported these individuals.

The apostle Paul never experienced any serious moral failures like this in his life, and yet he admitted to a deep, inner struggle. If you are a believer, then you want to do what is right and serve the Lord, but you may repeatedly do things you dislike. Perhaps it is your anger, or jealousy, lust, or some addictive behavior. In Rom. 7:24 Paul asked the question, "Who will set me free from the body of this death?" Then, he answered his own question with, "Thanks be to God through Jesus Christ!" (Verse 25). It is fortunate that he did not leave us hopelessly pondering that question, but he declared that God through Christ Jesus could set us free from this bondage. He does not explicitly identify the path to freedom, but there are hints given in the following chapter of Romans.

The Fruit of the Spirit

Another hint to the answer to this question can be found in Galatians 5:22-23, where Paul talks about the fruit of the Spirit and the deeds of the flesh. He is obviously speaking to believers, and challenging them to walk in the Spirit so they will not engage in the "deeds of the flesh," because this letter was written to the believers in the churches in Galatia which he established in an earlier missionary journey. When he speaks about the fruit of the Spirit, the first three fruits he mentions are emotions: love, joy, and peace. The last six fruits are character qualities. The significance of this is that it suggests we must first have love, joy, and peace in our lives, and the result will be the development of patience, kindness, goodness, faithfulness, gentleness, and self-control.

If this is, indeed, the intention of this passage, it is very helpful and consistent with the teachings of this ministry, because when we learn how to experience peace in our lives, then love and joy increase, and the other fruits of the Spirit are able to develop. But when we do not have peace, we cannot have self-control or the other character qualities. Thus, the development of peace, love, and joy is a very important aspect of the sanctification process.

The three primary emotions that rob people of peace in their lives are grief, anger, and shame. When we are full of anger, grief or depression, we are not at peace, and when we are not at peace, we are very vulnerable to the temptations of the devil to do things that briefly make us feel better. In the long run, however, these behaviors lead to more problems and negative consequences. The Bible says that "there is a way that seems right to a man, but its end is the way of death" (Proverbs 14:12) and there are "passing pleasures of sin" (Hebrews 11:25). We have shown in previous chapters how the

Lord can set us free from these negative emotions and that as He does so, we will become progressively more fruitful and less prone to compulsive behaviors.

The Doctrine of Sanctification

The theological term for this struggle is "sanctification." In a book entitled *Five Views of Sanctification* five theologians discuss this topic and present five different theological perspectives on the subject. The word "sanctify" means "to make holy" and "sanctification" means being able to live lives that are pleasing to God. Dr. Anthony A. Hoekema, a reformed theologian, defines sanctification as, "that gracious operation of the Holy Spirit, involving our responsible participation, by which He delivers us as justified sinners from the pollution of sin, renews our entire nature according to the image of God, and enables us to live lives that are pleasing to Him" (Dieter and Hoekema, 1987, p. 61).

Christians from all denominations and theological persuasions struggle with their behaviors. It is clear that there are no churches or theological groups that are exempt from such struggles, so it is also clear that they all lack a practical theology of sanctification to help their members overcome these struggles. Some churches work hard to provide practical help in dealing with their emotions, but few or none of them has a clear doctrine of sanctification to equip their members to overcome their personal struggles.

When problematic behaviors occur, most pastors and church leaders simply refer them to Christian or secular counselors, because they consider this to be out of their realm of expertise. But the mental health profession has no answers for these behaviors either, although they try hard to present themselves as the experts in human behavior and the only ones who can help people with their deep emotional struggles.

During my forty years of experience as a mental health counselor, I studied the scriptures, and I looked for practical suggestions from Christian writers and secular writers to learn how to help others gain victory in their lives over their emotional struggles. When I had exhausted my efforts and found nothing that truly worked to help people with grief, anger, and shame, I was thrilled to learn how the Lord could set people free from these feelings through simple specific prayer. I was receptive to this because I truly believed the Word of God was adequate and held the answers to life's problems. The more I used prayer ministry to help people, the more I modified my personal doctrine of sanctification, and I offer some suggestions on this matter in this chapter.

The process of sanctification requires at least four fundamental components in the lives of believers. First, the individual needs to pursue a close walk with the Lord through reading the Word, prayer, and fellowship with other believers. Second, believers need to learn to pray effectively about their emotions and to cast all their cares upon Him. Third, believers must learn to "walk in the Spirit" (Galatians 5:16) and pray for truth to enable them to experience the peace of God in their daily lives. As they do this, the Lord promises to bring them truth to set them free of their negative emotions. Fourth, as believers learn to do these three things habitually and daily, they will manifest the fruits of the Spirit, first by experiencing the emotions of love, joy, and peace, and then by developing the character qualities of patience, kindness, gentleness, goodness, faithfulness, and self-control.

Sanctification is not the result of simply acquiring doctrinal knowledge or Biblical information, because there are many people who are very knowledgeable of the Bible and yet they struggle deeply with sinful impulses. If biblical knowledge was all that was required for sanctification, then the attendance of a seminary or Bible college should be sufficient to enable believers to have victory in their lives. There are even some believers who have committed large portions of the Scriptures to memory in an effort to find freedom, but memorization of the Word of God does not bring victory to their lives either, although it is a good thing to do. Neither is sanctification the result of a one-time experience with the Spirit that permanently changes the individual. It is the result of walking in the Spirit daily, praying without ceasing, casting our cares upon the Lord, and allowing the Holy Spirit to daily renew our mind. This will result in frequent fillings of the Spirit to give us joy and peace in our lives.

Overcoming Sinful Compulsions

Most of this book has focused on teaching us how to pray about our emotions so that we overcome negative feelings like grief, anger, shame, depression, and fear. But many times people seek help, not to overcome negative emotions, but to learn how to overcome compulsive, destructive, or sinful behaviors. In Chapter 16 we talked about how to overcome addictions, and there are many types of addictions that this covers, including addictions to alcohol, drugs, gambling, sex, and food. Other behaviors that people engage in that lead them to seek help from counselors and pastors include repeated affairs, sexual compulsions, obsessive-compulsive behaviors, and compulsive stealing. How do the principles of emotional healing prayer apply to these types of problems?

Over my forty years of practice as a Christian counselor I have encountered many believers who struggled with sinful behaviors and compulsions, including sexual impulses, lust, affairs, compulsive masturbation, exhibitionism, cross-dressing, homosexuality, gambling, compulsive spending, hoarding, obsessive-compulsive behaviors, pornography, and compulsive stealing. In this chapter I want to briefly discuss some of these behaviors and provide some general principles to help the reader understand the origins of these behaviors and the way to find freedom from them.

There is no question that these behaviors are sinful, and in some case they are even illegal. Certainly it is appropriate to confess these sinful behaviors and ask for forgiveness and strength to overcome them, based upon 1 John 1:9. However, there are many people who compulsively continue in these sinful behaviors even when they sincerely confess their sins and desire to overcome them.

The primary reason why such behaviors are difficult to change is because of the underlying emotions the individuals have that drive them to engage in the behavior to feel better. If these underlying emotions are not recognized and resolved, the individual will continue to struggle with their impulses, even if they remain victorious for a period of time. This principle was illustrated in Chapter 7 when talking about addictions, and it was shown how the compulsion to use drugs or to drink stops, when we resolve these underlying feelings.

Sin and Emotions

All of us are sinners and are tempted to do things out of selfishness that harm others. Therefore, we can be tempted with evil, and it is important to have a strong walk with the Lord by reading His Word and meditating on it, learning to "pray without ceasing" (1Thessalonians 5:17), and being in fellowship with other believers. But even with these elements in our lives, we are very vulnerable to sin when we feel badly due to things that happen in our lives. When we harbor anger in our hearts we are very vulnerable to sin, and it creates a separation between us and God (Isaiah 59:2) and gives the devil an opportunity (Ephesians 4:26-27). When we have unresolved grief, depression or sadness, we are also vulnerable to temptations.

A good example of how our feelings can lead us into sin is found in the life of David, who is described in the Bible as "a man after God's own heart" (Acts 13:22) and who wrote many psalms expressing his sincere love for the Lord. He was a devout follower of God, and yet he fell into gross immorality when he committed adultery with Bathsheba, which led to the death of his child and the murder of her husband to cover up his sin. 2 Samuel 11:1 says that this sin occurred in the spring when kings normally go out to battle, and David remained in Jerusalem. Verse 2 says that one evening he arose from his bed and walked around on the roof of his house, and he saw Bathsheba bathing. He sent for her and committed adultery with her, and she became pregnant.

It is important to notice several significant circumstances that led David to this situation and to his temptation. First, he had six wives, and children from each wife, so it is not surprising that he was alone this evening and could not sleep. It is highly likely that he did not have a good relationship with his wives because of the number of wives and children he had, so he was probably very lonely. Second, he would normally have been with his army during this time period, so he was probably feeling somewhat bored and useless. Third, he had some significant conflicts with his wives and children who rebelled against him, so he probably was unhappy about his family life. David was very vulnerable to Satan's temptations, given the negative feelings that he felt at the time.

When David saw that Bathsheba was beautiful, he sent for her and she came to him at his house. His selfish, sinful relationship with Bathsheba was surely exciting and made him feel good at the moment, but led to a great number of problems later. The fact that he could do this without any of his wives noticing or complaining supports the view that he was estranged from them and was, indeed, very alone in his own house. Although he was esteemed highly by his nation and he sincerely loved the Lord, he was not happy at home with his family, probably due to his sin of taking more than one wife to himself. In this emotional condition he was very weak and vulnerable to sin.

The same principle applies to each believer. When we allow ourselves to become resentful, or we become depressed or feel guilty, we become very vulnerable to anything that makes us feel good. That means that we are especially vulnerable to affairs, pornography, drugs, and alcohol when we fail to resolve our negative feelings. The devil knows that we are weak at such times, and is ready to provide temptations to sinful activities that will make us feel good for the moment. We must learn to guard our hearts and to cast all our cares upon Him so that we do not give in to temptations.

ADDICTIVE BEHAVIORS

In Chapter 7 we discussed how to overcome addictions, and we focused primarily on drug and alcohol addictions. To summarize this chapter, the key to understanding alcohol and drug addictions is to realize that abusive use of drugs and alcohol occurs when individuals have strong underlying feelings of grief, anger, or shame which make them feel bad. They then use addictive substances to make them feel better, and it becomes addictive because they want to use them every time they feel bad, since they know no other way to resolve these feelings. However, when they identify their underlying negative emotions and resolve them, they feel good most of the time, and do not have strong urges to use substances again to feel better. This same principle can help us understand other forms of compulsive behaviors, such as pornography, sexual fetishes or behaviors, deviant forms of sexuality, infidelity, and gambling.

SEXUAL IMPULSES

Pornography

Perhaps one of the most common struggles of believers with sin is the sin of pornography usage. Many Christian men struggle with this, and pastors are at a loss to know how to help them. A man came to me to discuss his struggle with pornography and lust, and to seek counsel on how to overcome it. He was a mature, sincere believer who faithfully attended his church and studied his Bible. He admitted that he had struggled with his sexual impulses all his life, and he had recently had some struggles with pornography and was caught by his wife. She was very upset and told their pastor about it, which embarrassed him, but he humbly admitted his struggle and requested prayer.

This man asked me if it was normal to struggle with pornography because the sexual drive in men is so strong. I explained that the temptation to look at women and to lust for them is very normal and will last for a lifetime, but that when it begins to manifest itself in an addiction to pornography, phone sex, affairs, or seeking relationships with prostitutes, then this is not normal. When people become so fixated on sex that they engage in these immoral and risky behaviors, there are underlying emotional reasons that need to be identified and resolved through prayer.

I asked him what had triggered him off the last time he had turned to pornography, and he told me that he and his wife had had an argument. He felt sad and angry, and when they didn't get along well it damaged their sexual life and made him tempted to look at pornography. He looked at some pornography on the Internet, and his wife had caught him, which made their problems worse. I asked him when was the first time he could remember when he felt so alone. He said that when he grew up his father was seldom around and he felt lonely and unwanted.

On another occasion he called me and shared with me that while he was traveling he had a strong urge to look at some pornography on his cell phone. I asked him how he was feeling just prior to this, and he said that he felt alone. I asked him when the first time was that he remembered feeling this way, and he recalled times as a child when his mother had left him home with his father who was emotionally unhealthy, and this man was fearful of his father. Many times as a child he felt alone and wanted to talk to someone. He prayed about this memory and the Lord told him, "You were never alone; I was always with you." This truth gave him peace and removed his feelings of aloneness, which took away the temptation to use pornography, which gave him a false feeling of intimacy. He admitted that he still had occasional temptations to look at pornography because it is so easily accessible and free on his phone, but as long as he recognized the emotions he had and gave them to the Lord, he continued to do well and avoided pornography.

Compulsive Promiscuity

A young man came for counseling regarding his struggle with compulsive infidelity. He was 21 years old, said he was a Christian and had never been married, and had four children from four different women. He was distraught about the growing financial burden it was to be supporting these women and their children.

We discussed his background so that I could understand what had happened to him to make him so vulnerable to sexual temptations, and I was surprised to learn that he had a normal family upbringing and went to church as a child. But at age 19 his father died, and he began drinking and getting involved in illicit relationships. We prayed about his grief over the loss of his father, and he was able to release it. He admitted that he still had some anger toward several of the women he had dated, so we prayed about them and he was able to release his anger. Afterwards, he said that he no longer felt any anger toward either of them, and he still cared about them and hoped they were doing well.

When people are full of anger and grief they are very vulnerable to using drugs or alcohol to feel better, and to getting involved in unhealthy relationships to feel better. This is what Paul said in Eph. 4:26-27, "Do not let the sun go down on your anger, and do not give the devil an opportunity." When we have unresolved feelings such as anger or grief we feel badly, and the devil tempts us to do things to feel better. As this young man received healing from all his anger and grief and shame, he was able to avoid unhealthy relationships and drugs and serve the Lord.

This young man was very cooperative and motivated to break this pattern because he was a believer, and after a series of prayer sessions he was able to resolve his anger and grief and avoid any more premarital sexual relationships. There are many unsaved men who engage in such selfish lifestyles and have no conviction about their behavior, but this young man did want help, because he was a genuine believer who did not know how to overcome his compulsion to have sexual relations in order to overcome his negative feelings.

Inappropriate Sexual Contact

A young man came for counseling due to feelings of depression. He stated that he had been angry for several years, had developed an addiction to pornography, and was so depressed that he had suicidal thoughts. He came from a good family, but had been traumatized by witnessing a sexual act as a very young child, and then developed an obsession with pornography after discovering some pornography. He also had several significant losses in his childhood that were very painful to him, and he became angry at some relatives for fighting and arguing all the time while he was visiting them. Shortly before coming to see me, he touched a relative inappropriately, which upset her terribly, and he was so ashamed about it that he began to have suicidal thoughts and even some homicidal thoughts.

I met with this young man and explained how he could be set free from his grief, anger, and feelings of shame through prayer. He was receptive and said that he would like to get rid of these feelings. We began with his losses. We made a list of what he missed about these people, then prayed and told the Lord what he missed about them and asked the Lord to carry this grief for him. He reported afterwards that he felt peaceful and calm, and he was receptive to meeting again and doing some more praying.

The second time I met him he was looking much better and had had no more suicidal thoughts. We talked about his anger toward his relatives and made a list of what they did that made him angry at them. Then we prayed, and asked the Lord to take his anger from him and carry it for him, and he immediately felt relief. He said that his anger toward them was gone. The next time we met he talked about his feelings of shame for witnessing a sexual act between his parents when he was a very young child. We prayed about his belief that he was dirty, bad, and shameful for watching and asked the Lord what he wanted this young man to know. "You were just a child; I love you" was the response he received, and his feelings of shame immediately left.

The next time I saw this young man he looked good, he said that he had no more depression or anger, and he no longer had any obsession with pornography. He was doing great! I saw him again a month or two later and he was still doing great! His coach told him that he was a "role model to his teammates," and he was excited about his life. We discussed how the Lord had set him free from his grief, anger, and pornography addiction through prayer, and he was eager to share these prayer principles with his teammates and friends. After just five prayer sessions he was set free from all those negative emotions and behaviors that were destroying him.

"Johnny's" Story

A man told me that he had just been released from prison where he had given his life to Jesus. He studied the Bible, took Bible correspondence courses, and took every class available in his effort to break free from his past, but the first day that he was free he fell into sexual sin and was devastated, because he thought he had changed. He poured out his heart and wept and told me very candidly about his past, how he had been molested several times as a child and had been beaten violently by his father and hurt by women. In spite of his sincere desire to follow Jesus, he was struggling with feelings of anxiety, guilt, anger, and shame. He said that he knew that his wife loved him and was faithful to him, but he sometimes was overwhelmed with suspicions that she was seeing another man. He told me that it was causing him to doubt his faith, and he poured out his heart and pleaded for help from me.

Many people, like this man, struggle with sinful urges and are overwhelmed by their emotions, even after they have genuinely received Jesus as their Savior and dedicated their lives to following Him. Even the apostle Paul said, "For what I am doing I do not understand; for I am not practicing what I would like to do, but I am doing the very thing I hate" (Romans 7:15). He then explains in the following chapter that we must learn to walk in the Spirit and set our minds on the Spirit in order to overcome our "flesh."

I shared with this man that he was indeed a "new creature," and this was reflected in his desire to do right and to follow the Lord, but that he still had the old mind which needed to be renewed. I explained how the Lord wanted to renew his mind and set him free from his past so that he would no longer be in bondage to it, and I encouraged him to begin by eliminating all anger from his past. We discussed his feelings toward his father who had been so abusive to him, who never showed him any love or told him that he loved him, who broke his mother's heart through his infidelity, and who verbally abused him every day of his life. We made a list of his resentments toward his father, and he tearfully identified 30 specific resentments he had; then we prayed and he asked the Lord to take his anger from him and carry it for him.

When we finished praying, I asked him how he felt as he thought about his father. He said that he felt no anger toward him; he just felt "sorry for him" because he was so unhappy and had so many problems. He laughed as he recalled trying to be honest with his father as an adult and his father blamed him for the harmful things that happened to him. He began to smile as he talked about his freedom from his anger toward his father. He commented about how simple it was, and he was filled with hope that he could be set free from his past and his emotional bondage through Jesus and prayer.

This man's struggle is typical for many believers who sincerely desire to break free from their past and from emotional bondage. Many believers turn to the Church and to their spiritual leaders but find no help from them, and they begin having doubts about their own salvation. Then they turn to mental health professionals, who tell them that they have a brain disorder or chemical imbalance and need to be on psychiatric medications. But the Lord is the Wonderful Counselor, and He heals broken hearts and sets the captives free as they learn to cast all their cares upon Him and turn to Him for truth to set them free.

SEXUAL IDENTITY PROBLEMS

Individuals who have sexual identity problems usually have underlying emotional problems with their mother figures and father figures. Homosexual men frequently have a lot of anger toward females due to having been hurt by their mothers and other females, and have a poor relationship with their fathers, so they crave male attention. The reverse is usually true with lesbians; they have been hurt by men and long for acceptance from females. These emotional feelings make them feel hostility toward the opposite sex and crave for acceptance from same-sex individuals. As they receive healing for their anger and shame, their natural biological attraction toward the opposite sex usually returns, and this can happen unintentionally as the prayer minister helps them experience healing of their underlying relationship issues and emotions.

Homosexual Releases Anger toward Mother

I asked an inmate in the local county jail if he was 100% sure that he was going to heaven. He said that he was about 80% sure because he had received Jesus into his heart, but he told me that he was a practicing homosexual. He said that he had tried to give up his sexual interest and had prayed about it, but God had never delivered him from his interest in other men, and he was not sure he wanted to give it up now.

We discussed the most common underlying emotional issues that lead to such "gender confusion." He told me that his father left when he was about 4 years old, and then his stepfather also left his mother when this man was very young, so he felt a lack of male acceptance, and admitted that he held some "grudges" against his mother. He also admitted that he had been molested as a child, which affected his attitude toward himself and males.

I asked him if he would like to get rid of his resentments toward his mother and he initially said he would not, because he felt he needed to protect himself, but then he said that he would like to. He told me that he resented his mother for being married seven times and failing at each marriage, but continuing to pursue men. She refused to admit that she was the problem in her marriages; she blamed this son for her pregnancy with him and resented him for being a burden on her. She even told this man that she tried to abort him but failed, then she abandoned him when he was 15 years old and chose another man over him. We made a list of 14 resentments he held toward her, then I led him in a prayer in which he asked the Lord to take his anger from him.

When I asked him how he felt toward his mother he said that he felt "disgusted" toward her because of her lack of responsibility, her increasing irresponsibility, her loss of her job due to stealing, her feelings of entitlement, and her lack of desire to change. We prayed a second time and gave these five resentments to the Lord. I asked him, again, how he felt toward his mother. He said that he still felt angry because his mother was still trying to run her children's lives even though she had failed so miserably at her own life, she had told her children that they should never get married because they are incapable of handling it, and she seemed to want her children to fail in their marriages. We prayed a third time and he gave these three additional resentments to the Lord.

After this third prayer I asked him how he felt toward his mother and he said, "I feel bad for her. She's not happy. She has missed out on her life." He said that he was no longer angry at her; he just felt sorry for her! He said that he felt very peaceful and calm when thinking about his mother, and no longer felt any anger or disgust toward her. He also said that he realized that she was a very unhappy person whose mother was a very poor mother to her.

We talked about how the Lord wants to set him free from his negative emotions, and that as he is set free he will be able to have normal emotions for women and not be disgusted at the thought of being affectionate toward them. He also admitted that he lost his father and stepfather and had many other losses that made him fearful of being close to people and losing them. We talked about his need to resolve these losses so that he would not be afraid of an intimate relationship with a woman, and his need to resolve the feelings of shame that resulted from his molestation as a child.

Homosexuality is not a genetic condition; it is rooted in unresolved feelings of grief, anger, and shame that disrupt a person's natural attraction toward the opposite sex and leads them to crave love and acceptance from their same-sex acquaintances. Sexual attention from a same-sex friend is easily mistaken for love and acceptance when a person lacks a good relationship with their same-sex parent. This man acknowledged that his sexual behavior was not pleasing to the Lord, and he may be saved, but he can never have joy or peace in his life when he is living in sin, any more than a heterosexual man can enjoy a close walk with the Lord if he is living in adultery or is in bondage to pornography. He was encouraged to continue to pray about his anger, his grief, and his feelings of shame, so he could be set free from his negative feelings and from his compulsive sexual behavior that made him feel good momentarily but increased his feelings of shame and guilt. The Lord is capable of setting homosexuals free from their guilt, shame, anger and grief and filling them with joy and peace and a normal desire for intimacy with the opposite sex.

Cross Dresser Set Free

A Christian man came for help with a cross-dressing problem that had baffled doctors and psychiatrists for many years. As a child he began dressing in women's clothing and his parents permitted this, but eventually they decided that it needed to stop, so they took him to a psychiatrist who administered repeated shock treatments to try to help him get rid of this impulse. Eventually the doctor told his parents that he would never change and they needed to raise him like a girl, so they did. He was saved as a teenager, but the behavior continued, and he hid it from his Christian friends, but continued going to various counselors over the years to try to stop this compulsive behavior.

While in his twenties he married a Christian woman, and had three children with her, but the behavior continued in secret. When she learned about it, his wife became so distressed that she tried to shame him into stopping, and even told his children about his behavior, leading one of them to become very disrespectful to him. He began to live in separate quarters so that he could be away from his wife's frequent criticism and negativity, due to her anger toward him. In a counseling session with him he denied having any negative emotions, but I have learned that whenever there is a compulsive behavior there is always an underlying emotion that is driving the behavior, so we began working on one emotion at a time.

The first emotion we dealt with was his feelings of anger toward his wife, so we made up a list of the reasons for his anger at her and he gave it to the Lord. Then we prayed about some anger he had toward a relative, and he made a list of his resentments toward this man and gave them to the Lord. In another session we prayed about some strong feelings of grief at losing his college dreams, and some anger toward God. In our last session we prayed about some anger and resentment he had toward his parents. He reported feeling better after releasing these emotions, but he continued to cross-dress whenever he was angry or frustrated. However, he said that he was amazed to see what strong emotions he had from his childhood that he had been suppressing, and he saw that this prayer process was working, so he felt some hope and he was no longer angry at God.

One day he was feeling frustrated and I was not available so he called another man to ventilate about his feelings and this man prayed with him and led him to confess his attitude to the Lord and ask for forgiveness. He said that he felt an "incredible, empty sadness," but he felt he got his heart right with God. His impulses to cross dress stopped completely at that time. He said that he continued to do "a lot of repenting" during that week, and he told his wife that he wanted to move back in with her. This took some time, however, due to the resentments she has had toward him for so many years because he had totally disregarded her for so long. The following Sunday he went forward in church to testify publicly that he was rededicating his life to the Lord. He reported months after that that he had no more impulses to dress in women's clothing since that last prayer.

What an amazing testimony of God's grace and healing power. Jesus can do for us what no psychologist, psychiatrist, doctor or medication can do! He can set us free from our negative emotions and give us peace, which changes our lives completely.

Homosexual Relationships

We are being told by the world that homosexuality is a natural behavior that is caused by genetics. I previously described a man who told me that he had a clear memory come back to him of being molested as a small child by his father. He remembered telling his father, "You're not supposed to be doing this," and his father said, "I suppose you're going to tell your mother and I'll never see you again." He promised his father that he would not tell anyone, then when he left the room he completely repressed the memory and forgot about it until twenty years later. During his childhood he felt that he was different somehow, and he believed he was a homosexual, and became involved in several homosexual relationships. After this memory surfaced, however, he concluded that this early incident was the reason for his attraction to other men, and he suddenly lost all interest in male sexual relationships.

He had some feelings of shame over this sexual abuse, which is very common in cases of sexual abuse, and I asked permission to pray for this man. He gave me permission, so I prayed and asked the Lord what He wanted this man to know about his belief that he was shameful and bad and that he should have told someone. I told him to listen quietly and tell me if any thoughts came to his mind. "I'm innocent; I'm not guilty; I have no need to be ashamed," he replied. I asked him if those thoughts felt true and he said that they did. Then I prayed again and asked the Lord if there was anything that He wanted this man to know about his belief that he should have told someone. "It was out of my hands," he responded. "I didn't have the ability to defend myself because I was a child. I was afraid to not see my father again and I immediately blocked this out of my mind."

"So, how do you feel now as you think about that sexual abuse?" I asked. "I see myself as guiltless and innocent. I didn't want it or ask for it" he replied. "What emotions do you feel now as you remember that incident?" I asked him. "I don't feel guilty anymore. I feel free. I feel a sense of freedom and lightheartedness. I feel free!" he laughed. We talked for a few minutes about how the Lord is able to set us free from all of our emotional bondage, then as he was leaving I asked him one final time how he was feeling emotionally. "I feel no anger, no resentment, and I don't hate myself," he said. He smiled as he was leaving and said, "It feels good that I don't have to hate myself anymore."

This man spontaneously relinquished his identity as a homosexual when he remembered being molested as a child and he concluded that this early-life experience had led him to believe he was different. But he still had feelings of guilt and shame for what happened to him as a child, and the Lord brought him truth to set him free from this shame. The truth is that this man was an innocent child, and he was not dirty or shameful because of what happened to him because it was his father's fault and not his. The truth is also that he had no genetic or biological predisposition to be a homosexual, but the Lord had to tell him this so that he could be set free from his feelings of shame. As each of us learns to pray about our feelings of shame, the truth will also set us free from the lies that hold us in bondage to sin.

OTHER OBSESSIVE OR COMPULSIVE BEHAVIORS

In addition to the classic forms of addictions just discussed, there are many other compulsive behaviors that believers struggle with for which they need help.

Gambling

In Chapter 6 we discussed a young woman who had an addiction to methamphetamines and had her children removed from her custody as a result. In our second session we prayed about her deep feelings of grief over the loss of her favorite aunt, and she found tremendous emotional relief from our prayer. When she returned the following week she still felt free of this grief, but she confessed that she also had an addiction to gambling and she had upset her husband by losing about $900 at a casino.

I asked this woman what had happened that led her to go gambling, and she said that she was mad at her brother who was being selfish and irritating, and she went to the casino to get away from him and to get her mind off her troubles. I asked her what made her angry at her brother, and we made a list of the things that upset her about him. I led her in a prayer and she gave her anger to the Lord and asked Him to carry it for her. Afterwards, she felt that her anger was gone.

The following week she reported that she had no more urges to gamble. We continued meeting for prayer sessions and she continued releasing her anger and grief, and began taking the initiative to pray on her own about her emotions. She reported on one other occasion that she had gone to a casino and spent $25, but she never again spent large amounts of money on gambling, and her husband was very relieved and impressed at the change in her.

Compulsive gamblers have many underlying feelings that lead them to gamble, and they need help in identifying these feelings and learning how to release them into the hands of the Lord. Most gamblers will not experience as quick relief as this woman did, but if they will persist in praying about the underlying emotions that lead them to have the urge to gamble, they can be set free from this compulsive behavior.

Obsessive-Compulsive Behaviors

A prayer partner and I had seen a young woman numerous times and she had received much healing through prayer. Thinking that we were about finished with her issues, I asked her if she wanted to meet again and she said she did. She said that she had some compulsive behaviors that she had dealt with for many years including touching things with both hands, doing everything eight times, counting her steps, and having a compulsive routine for almost everything she did. I had never noticed that she had these compulsions but we agreed to meet again to pray with her about them.

When we met with her I asked her how long she had been struggling with these compulsive behaviors and she said that around age 12 she began touching everything with both hands, and then she couldn't stop doing this and it gradually became worse as she developed more compulsions. It began after her grandmother made her sleep in a room by herself one night, and she was restless all night and couldn't sleep for fear that someone would break into their house. She felt that touching objects with both hands would somehow prevent something bad from happening. This fear was rooted in her younger years when her drug-abusing mother brought men home with her who would enter her room at night or who would vandalize their home. She was always fearful that she was going to be touched or hurt by these men, and she began engaging in this ritualistic behavior to protect herself.

I asked the young lady if I could pray for her, and I told her to visualize herself at age 5 lying in bed by herself and thinking that she was going to be hurt or touched by men at night. She closed her eyes and I prayed for her, and asked the Lord what He wanted her to know about her belief that something bad was going to happen to her. She said, "He said that even when I'm asleep His eyes are always open and He is watching over me to protect me." "How does that make you feel?" I asked. "Safe. He wants me to feel protected and safe and restful in Him." She said she was no longer scared nor felt alone in that early memory.

I encouraged her to think about age 12 when her grandmother made her sleep in her own room, and being afraid of sleeping alone. She closed her eyes, and I prayed and asked the Lord what He wanted her to know about her fear of sleeping alone. I asked her if she had any thoughts come to her mind. "I can be in a room alone and He's still watching me and protecting me. He wants me to know that He's my best friend and I can talk with Him at any time and know that He is with me." I asked her how that made her feel and she began crying. She said, “It shocks me that He cares that much about me and such little things in my life with all the billions of people there are in the world.” She said that her tears were tears of joy at seeing the goodness of the Lord and how much He loved her, and she said that she felt peaceful.

I asked this young woman what she thought would happen if she did not touch things with both hands and she said, “If I don’t touch things with both hands I am afraid that something bad will happen.” I prayed for her and asked the Lord what He wanted her to know about that belief. She said, “He said nothing I do is going to make something happen or not happen. He controls everything.” She said that thought made her feel “weightless and comforted” and took away her fears. I encouraged her to go to the door in my office and touch the handle with one hand and see how she felt and she did this and said she felt okay, with no anxiety. “He wants me to know that He is in control and He just wants me to follow him,” she said. I asked her if she had counted her steps on the way to the door and she said she had not and she felt calm. She didn’t even notice that she had not counted her steps.

We reviewed some of her other compulsions such as washing her hands eight times, walking back and forth from her car to the front door of her house eight times, avoiding stepping on cracks, eating each food item on her plate one at a time, and laying her clothes out in a specific order each day when getting dressed, and she was able to visualize engaging in each of these actions one time instead of eight times without feeling any anxiety. She said that she always touched pages of a book with both hands and using her right hand first and then her left hand to read each line, so my prayer partner gave her some reading material and we asked her to read it using just one hand and reading it just once. She was able to do this without any discomfort.

She also said that she was fearful of having a car accident and had a lot of compulsive behaviors connected to her driving. I prayed and asked the Lord what He wanted her to know about her belief that she needed to practice these compulsive behaviors or else she would have an accident. She smiled and said, "This is the best answer He has ever given me. He told me that I was using my routines when I had an accident at age 16. My routines didn't help me. The reason that I lived was because He kept me alive and protected me." She said that made her feel really good and she said, "I would never have thought of that!"

As we ended the session she was smiling and had tears of joy in her eyes. She said that she was happy to know that God loves her so much that He would speak to her like this and take away her fears. We prayed together and thanked Him for being so wonderful, and for healing her heart and taking away her fears and replacing them with His peace. Several hours later she texted me to tell me that she was free from her compulsive routines and felt peaceful and calm without engaging in them.

EATING DISORDER

Woman Loses Anger and Weight

A young woman came for help with her anger and stress, which she believed made it difficult for her to lose weight. She said that she had a short temper, and as we talked about her past I learned that she had had some trauma in her childhood and she was angry at her mother, at her first husband who abused her, and at her present husband. Over several months we prayed about her anger at these people and she gradually began feeling more cheerful and calm, and became more patient and less short-tempered.

After the New Year she came to see me and was very happy. She said that she had no more anger toward her mother, and she was even teaching her how to overcome her own anger and grief. She also said that she and her husband were fighting and yelling less because she felt a lot more calm than before, and when he got upset she stayed calm so their fights did not escalate. On New Year's Eve she decided to start getting up earlier and beginning her day by relaxing and reading the Bible. She felt so much more relaxed and calm that she began writing down what she was eating, began eating more healthy and began losing weight. She was thrilled and said, "I can tell this is going to stay because it feels different!"

She told me that she saw a picture of her former boss on Facebook and she felt a twinge of anger, but she said she did not want to stay angry. So, we talked about her former boss and how badly she had treated her. Her boss believed that she was in league with another employee who had quit and started up a competing business, so she began treating her badly. Her boss tried to provoke her to quit so that she would not have to pay any unemployment on her, but she refused to quit. The boss wrote her up for bogus things, gave her impossible tasks to complete, tried to get her to sign a blank disciplinary form, and made her work late hours that kept her from her family. When she finally found another job, her boss refused to answer her phone calls and texts, so she had to drive to her house to return her computer and notify her that she was quitting. Her boss had not spoken to her since that day. Just talking about her boss stirred up her anger, but after identifying 14 resentments she gave them to the Lord and asked Him to take them from her. Afterwards, I asked her how she felt. She said she felt neutral and she no longer had any anger toward her. She is determined to remain calm and full of peace.

Having released all her anger toward her husband and toward people who had wronged her in the past, she was able to eat in moderation and to stick with a reasonable diet. She left our last session feeling peaceful, smiling with joy, and eager to see her dietitian, because when she lost her anger and the emotional burdens she was carrying, she felt much lighter and was also able to lose weight!

CUTTING AND SELF-INJURY

Set Free from Depression and Cutting

A girl was brought to me after her parents learned that she had suicidal thoughts and had been cutting on herself. She was very pleasant and did not appear depressed, but admitted that she had suicidal thoughts. I gathered background information on her to identify the source of her depression, and she disclosed that she had had eleven significant losses in the last ten years. I explained to her and her parents that 87% of all depression is rooted in losses, and asked her which loss was the most troubling to her. She told me that the loss of her maternal grandmother a year before was the most painful to her.

I shared with this young lady and her parents how she could get rid of her grief by making a list of the things she missed about her grandmother, and then praying and asking God to take it from her and carry it for her. She believed in God and went to church, but was uncomfortable with the idea of praying with me, so I told her she could do this by herself at home. I set up an appointment to see her again the next day, due to her admission that she was having suicidal thoughts. When she came the next day I asked her how she was doing, and she said she had had a good evening and had no more urges to cut herself, and she was not depressed. I asked why she felt better and she said she did what I suggested and made a list of the things she missed about her grandmother. She pulled out the list and showed it to me and she had written out 23 things she missed. She said she had prayed to God and asked Him to take away her grief, and she immediately felt better, slept well, and felt no more sadness. She did all this on her own!

I asked her who else she missed a lot, and she told me she missed her maternal grandfather. She agreed to let me help her make a list of things she missed about him, and she identified twenty things. She told me how she missed fishing with him, camping with him, watching TV with him, and sitting on the porch watching nature with him. She also missed his love and affection for her, his big smile when she entered the room, his sense of humor, and sitting on his lap with her puppy while watching TV. I asked her if she would be willing to let me lead her in a prayer to give all her sadness to the Lord, and this time she gave me permission. She prayed and gave all her grief to Him, and then said she felt "a lot better." She told me that she actually felt happy! Since she was feeling so good, I set up a session for the following week.

When she returned the next week she said she still felt "a lot better" and had had no suicidal thoughts or urges to cut herself in the last week. Her parents were thrilled and amazed at how much her mood had changed. We prayed some more, this time about her anger toward her biological father and some grief over the loss of an aunt who had died. She received complete healing for these painful emotions, and when she told her parents how she had prayed about her father and felt no more anger or sadness they were even more excited. They were all amazed at the greatness of God to set her free from her destructive impulses!

Set Free from Compulsive Cutting

A young lady came to me who was deeply depressed and had been cutting on herself for several years. Her parents were both Christians who loved her and were concerned for her, but she felt a compulsive desire to harm herself which she could not control. The first time I saw her she had a lot of grief over the loss of her grandmother, and we prayed about this and she was relieved of this grief. When she came the second time, she looked better and was smiling more, but she still felt very depressed and had cut herself again. She told me that she was most depressed about the loss of her dog, and her concern about her boyfriend's health. We made a list of five things she missed about her dog which she had had as a companion her entire life, and she prayed about this grief and gave it to the Lord. She still felt some grief so she identified seven more things she missed about the dog and we prayed again. This time she said she felt better and was no longer sad about her dog.

She then began talking about her boyfriend, who had cancer and was expected to die. It made her sad that she would probably never get to marry him, he wouldn't be in her life anymore, she would miss his phone calls and texts and hearing his voice and words of comfort. She made a list of 18 things she would miss about her boyfriend's personality and things they did together, and then she prayed and gave her grief to the Lord. Afterwards she said that she felt better and was no longer so sad.

When she had first met her boyfriend, he told her that he had cancer, but she grew close to him. She said that she was angry at God for putting such a sick person in her life. She was also angry that he was not improving in spite of the hours that he prayed for healing, and she was angry that her father was also dying. She felt that God must hate her for taking away all the important men in her life, and she made a list of seven reasons for her anger toward God. After praying, she said that her anger was gone and she wanted to be baptized and get back with the Lord.

This girl also had strong feelings of shame about herself for things that she had done, and she made a list of four or five things that made her feel worthless, shameful, and bad. I led her in a prayer to confess these things, and then I prayed and asked the Lord what He wanted her to know about her belief that she was bad and shameful for all the things she had done. She said that the following thoughts came to her mind: "I'm not dirty, bad, and shameful. He forgives everything and sees me with love. He forgives me and I want to go back to church and turn away from my sins so I can get back with God."

When I saw her a week later she was smiling, cheerful, and was no longer depressed or cutting herself. She still had some more emotions to resolve, but she had been set free from the strong feelings of shame that had been afflicting her and making her want to harm herself. She began going to church and enjoyed it, and was so happy she was full of joy and peace. It was a joy to see what the Lord did in her life through a few simple prayers.

VERBAL AND EMOTIONAL ABUSE

A young man came to me for help with his anger, marriage, and anxiety. He said that he argued a lot with his wife and said mean things when arguing with her, but he was a Christian and did not like being this way. This is another good example of how many Christians struggle with behaviors that they want to change but cannot. He said that he thought that this was rooted in his relationship with his father because his father had an explosive temper and was abusive to his mother, and had yelled and said hateful things to him when he was growing up. It also made him very fearful and anxious when his father came home late, because he knew he was drinking, so he avoided going home. This anxiety led him to have panic attacks and to get sick at school. Although he said he got along well with his father as an adult, he still talked about and cursed his father in his sleep at times.

I shared with this young man how he could release his anger by making a list of the reasons for his anger toward his father, and then praying and asking the Lord to take his anger from him. He agreed to try this. When he returned the next time, he said that he wrote down some resentments toward his father and gave them to the Lord. He was less angry and was less mean to his wife, but still had some anger. So we talked more about his anger, and he shared how, as a child, he lived in constant fear of punishment, and fear of what could happen. He identified ten more things that made him angry at his father, and he prayed and gave his anger to the Lord. I asked the Lord if there was anything that He wanted his man to know. He just said, "It's not my fault" and that felt true to him. I asked this man how he felt and he said, "I kind of feel sorry for him." I asked why he felt sorry for his father, and he said that his father's dad was ten times worse. He said he felt no more anger, and he felt "lighter."

The next time I saw this man he said that he had come to peace with his father, but he had some anger toward his stepmother, who was very good to him but tolerated his father's anger and sometimes provoked him. We made a list of twelve reasons for his anger toward her, then he prayed and gave his anger to the Lord. I asked the Lord if there was anything that he wanted this man to know. He said, "Her dad was abusive to her mother and her. That's all she knew; she didn't know any better." He then said he felt a lot better, and felt no more anger toward her.

The next time I saw this young man he said he was doing "really good." He was being a lot more patient with his wife, and was much less angry. He also said he had been praying a lot more and feeling good, and his wife could tell a difference in him, and she thanked him for being patient with her. They began praying together, and he said he is praying every day about his worries and irritations. He even felt a lot less anxious, and was no longer having panic attacks. When I asked him what he attributed this change to, he replied that he thought it was due to the prayers about specific sources of his anger, and he was excited about sharing this with his family, friends, and church.

This case illustrates a very important lesson I have learned about couples. This man did not like being angry and mean to his wife, but he didn't know how to overcome it. Most of the time the anger that causes problems in a marriage is due to unresolved anger that the spouses have towards others in their past, and once they resolve this anger they get along well. This is why it is so important that couples pledge to "not let the sun go down on [their] anger" and begin by uprooting and releasing all anger they have towards those in their past. May God help each couple who reads this to make this pledge so that their marriage will be blessed.

The Importance of Discipleship

One of the fundamental needs of new believers is to be discipled by an older believer, who can help them learn the basics of the Christian life and learn how the Lord desires them to walk as a believer. When the new believer is a child, it is the parents of that child who should ideally disciple them and teach them the basics of the Christian life. In Chapter Six we discussed the importance of discipleship in equipping believers with the life skills they will need to deal with the challenges of life without crumbling. The Lord Jesus spent three years discipling His twelve disciples and preparing them for life without Him. The apostle Paul followed the same pattern by spending years with young believers like Timothy and Titus, who travelled with him to various cities on his missionary journeys, training them and teaching them how to live for Jesus.

Most believers grow up without the help of a discipler or the benefit of knowing how to pray effectively about their emotions, but once they learn these simple prayer principles they will become essential tools they will use throughout their lives. Every believer needs to learn these principles and learn how to be sanctified and to become progressively more like Jesus each day. Many Christians struggle with their emotions so much that they live defeated lives and give up, but when they learn how to live in freedom, they become excited about the Lord and want to serve Him and tell others about Him.

Our desire is that many Christians and churches will use this program to teach their members how to pray about their emotions, so that they can have strong spiritual lives, strong marriages, strong families, and strong churches. Some sins are simply the result of individuals not seeking to follow the Lord or trying to live life without a daily reliance upon Him. But many sins in the lives of genuine believers are the result of negative feelings they have from their past, which Satan uses to tempt them, and they need help to be set free from these feelings so they can overcome their sinful impulses. The apostle Paul stated this clearly in 1 Thessalonians 4:3-4 when he wrote, "This is the will of God, your sanctification, that is, that you abstain from sexual immorality; that each of you know how to possess his own vessel in sanctification and honor."

SECTION D:

Being a Disciple of Jesus

19

OVERCOMING MARITAL PROBLEMS

It has never been more important than it is today for the church to know how to cultivate strong marriages, because the institution of marriage has never come under such severe attack as now. With the legalization of homosexual marriages and the increase in the numbers of couples living together without being married, the Church must be able to help those couples that are struggling so they can maintain their marriage. Marriage counseling can be extremely difficult, but since I have learned this prayer ministry I have seen a lot of "impossible" marriages saved. The following is an example of one such marriage.

A Hopeless Marriage

A Christian couple came for help with their marriage. The husband admitted he had some anger issues but said that he had never been abusive with his wife. He was calm and rational and admitted that he was very close to divorce but he came hoping that somehow his marriage could be saved.

The wife was a very emotional person who had a history of abuse, and she had made some serious accusations of her husband that he strongly denied and which sounded delusional. Although she admitted that she had some problems, she insisted that she had already been "healed" and she didn't believe that she needed any help. She just wanted her husband to get healed, and she got upset and angrily vented non-stop for the entire first session. It looked pretty "hopeless" after this first session.

In the second session they met separately with different prayer counselors and both of them made a list of reasons for their anger and released them. We were hopeful but then the wife got upset at her husband for some things he had written down confidentially about his feelings and she refused to come anymore for counseling. I had no choice but to try to meet with the husband privately and help him deal with his underlying emotional issues, although he seemed to be the most stable and mature partner and his wife really seemed to need the most help.

In the next session with the husband I developed a prayer plan for him that included three losses, four sources of anger, and some feelings of shame he needed to resolve. We first discussed his grief over the loss of a former girlfriend and his father, so he made a list of what he missed about each of them and gave it to the Lord. His grief was immediately lifted and he felt much better.

In our next session he prayed about some anger that he had toward the former girlfriend and toward a man who had mistreated his father and hurt the family. We also prayed about some feelings of guilt and shame he had toward his father who died young. He felt extremely guilty for not helping his father financially when he could have, before he died an early, painful death. He admitted that he believed, "I'm bad and shameful and a failure because I did not help my dad."

I prayed and asked the Lord what he wanted this man to know about those beliefs, and the thoughts that came to his mind were, "I've always been with you and always will be." At this point he said he had a picture of Jesus come into his mind with His arm around this man, comforting him. He began sobbing and weeping heavily, and I asked the Lord if there was anything else He wanted this man to know. This time he said Jesus reminded him of His scars and said "It's finished!" He then visualized all his sins in a burning trash heap and said Jesus had cast them all into the fire. This was a very emotional experience for this husband, but afterwards he said he felt completely "at peace" and said "I'm forgiven."

Outcome of the Case

This husband received so much relief and healing from this last session that his anger left and he began responding differently to his wife. They began getting along well and were satisfied and no longer talked about divorce. For the next two years they continued to do very well even though the wife never got healing for her past abuse. This was a very difficult case that seemed hopeless at one point, but the Lord brought healing to the husband and saved this marriage even though the wife may have had worse problems than him.

Marital counseling is extremely difficult, but I have seen a lot of "impossible" marriages saved through this prayer ministry. During the years that I used secular approaches to marriage counseling I never saw any marriages saved, but since I began using this prayer ministry I have seen many difficult marriages saved. We have to remember that "With God, all things are possible" (Matthew 19:26).

Marriage and the Bible

Marriage is from God and is rooted in the Bible. In Genesis 2:18 the Lord said, "It is not good for the man to be alone; I will make him a helper suitable for him." In chapter two of Genesis the Bible says that the Lord cast the man Adam into a deep sleep and took one of his ribs and formed a woman from it, then brought her to him. The Bible then says, "For this reason a man shall leave his father and his mother, and be joined to his wife; and they shall become one flesh" (Genesis 2:24). God created women to be helpers for their husbands, and he made women different so that they could enjoy and complement each other.

God also created mankind male and female, so that it requires both to procreate and to reproduce children to perpetuate the human race. It was also part of his plan that they remain together to raise those children, because both the father and the mother provide unique benefits for the children. It is ideal for a man to be a hard worker so he can provide for the physical and financial needs of the family, while the wife bears children and nurtures and cares for them as they grow up. The Bible says, marriage is a good thing and "He who finds a wife, finds a good thing, and obtains favor from the Lord" (Proverbs 18:22).

Today, there are many children being raised by one parent, and sometimes this is unavoidable. Some single-parents do extremely well in raising children and working. But this is extremely stressful and difficult and limits the amount of individualized attention that children can receive from their single parent. Of course, most families today limit themselves to having 2 or 3 children, but in prior times in history there were much larger families and it would be very difficult for a single parent to work full-time to provide for five or six children, then take care of them alone when they were home. The emotional, physical, and social costs to our society of raising children in single-parent homes is enormous.

Marriage and Society

The Old Testament laid the foundation for marriage and the family, and the nation of Israel became a light to the world of God's design for marriage and the family. But this deteriorated over the years as the nation of Israel rebelled against the Lord and He allowed them to be overcome by surrounding nations.

When Jesus entered the world, He had a profound impact on marriages and families in the Roman empire. In the Roman empire there was rampant immorality and homosexuality, and women were considered property of their husbands. What Jesus taught about women and marriage was radically different than what was being practiced during His lifetime. Jesus taught that women were equal to men, marriage was permanent, and children were precious.

Marriage is the backbone of a society, and as marriage goes, the family goes, and the society goes. Our culture has changed dramatically in the last fifty years due to the disintegration of marriage and families, and it is the responsibility of the Church to teach and model God's plan for marriage and for families. Where Christianity is strong, marriages will be strong and families will be strong, but when marriages suffer, the children will suffer and crime and social problems will increase, as we see happening today.

Marriage Research

The Barna Research Group periodically conducts surveys across the United States to monitor the state of marriage in the country. In September of 2008 they found that most people desired marriage. "Among all adults 18 and older, three out of four (78%) have been married and half (51%) are currently married" (Barna, 2008).

They also found that, "Among those who have been married, more than one out of every three (35%) have also been divorced ... 18% of them divorced multiple times." They concluded that, "The likelihood of married adults getting divorced is identical among born again Christians and those who are not born again."

When they broke down the divorce statistics by denominations they found that the divorce rates of all protestant churches were 34%, non-denominational churches were 29%, Catholics were 28%, and Evangelicals and Conservatives were 26%. Interestingly, Asians had a divorce rate of 20% due to cultural differences, which is lower than that of most churches.

The Impact of Divorce

A national survey found the most frequently cited cause of emotional distress was relationship problems, including divorce, separation, and other marital strains. In a study of 800 employee assistance program clients, 65% rated family problems as "considerable" or "extreme." Thus, divorce and marital problems are a major source of stress for adults.

In *Genes, Environment, and Psychopathology*, by Kenneth Kendler and Carol Prescott (2006), researchers found that parental deaths in childhood led to depression, but the emotional impact of the death diminished over time. In contrast, parental divorce was found to be strongly related to the development of a wide range of problems, including anxiety, depression, anger, oppositional behavior, and substance abuse. In addition, the impact of parental divorce upon the child's tendency to abuse alcohol never decreased over time. Therefore, divorce has a strong negative impact upon children that lasts long into their adult years.

Marital Counseling Effectiveness

The negative impact of divorce upon children and adults underscores the importance of having effective marriage counselors available to assist couples in distress. However, it may surprise many people to discover that most counseling training programs do not provide training in marital counseling, or provide very minimal training so that counselors are very poorly equipped to help couples with their marital problems. Psychotherapy research has shown that "no specific modality of psychotherapy did better than any other for any disorder; psychologists, psychiatrists, and social workers did not differ in their effectiveness as treaters; and all did better than marriage counselors and long-term family doctoring" (Seligman, 1995, p. 965). Thus, most individuals who receive marriage counseling are less satisfied with the outcome than those who receive individual counseling.

When I completed my master's degree in psychology, I had a theory of counseling for individuals but had no theory for how to deal with couples. I read a book on Behavioral marital counseling called *Helping Couples Change,* by Richard Stuart (1980). This was an extension of the theoretical approach I was using for individuals, but I was unprepared for what I found with my first couple. I was prepared to identify the behavioral problems of the individuals and to teach them good communication skills, but counseling quickly deteriorated into an argument in my office. The husband began yelling at his wife and threatening her and I confronted him with a protective instinct. I knew immediately that I had made a mistake and that I had instantly lost my therapeutic rapport with the husband. I saw them several times and tried to coach them on how to listen to each other and problem-solve, but after three sessions they never returned. This first marriage counseling attempt was a miserable failure.

Psychodynamic-Behavioral Model

I tried to prepare myself for my next couple by reading a new book on marital counseling called, *Marital Therapy: A combined psychodynamic-behavioral approach* that offered a different approach to marital counseling (Segraves, 1982). It seemed like a sensible approach as I studied it, and it wasn't long before I had the opportunity to see another couple. A man that worked in the same facility that I did asked for marital counseling for himself and his wife. I did not know him well, but had occasional contact with him and he seemed to be a very calm, professional person.

I was surprised to hear his wife talk about his angry outbursts at home that had damaged their marriage. After listening to them share their marital problems I shared with them my theory of marital counseling (which I had just learned) and the husband was very receptive to it. His wife, however, knew it wouldn't help them because she knew how serious a problem he had with his anger that was not addressed in the counseling theory. After our first session the wife wisely refused to come back, because she had enough intuitive sense that the theory would not help her husband with his anger issues, which were central to their marriage problems.

Family Therapy Approach

After these unnerving first experiences in counseling couples, I decided to return to graduate school to study marriage and family therapy, so that I would be better equipped to help couples who were struggling in their marriages. I consulted with a number of professors and they all recommended using a family systems approach with couples so I went back to college to study marriage and family therapy. I studied the *Handbook of Family Therapy* by Gurman and Kniskern (1981) and learned the basic concepts of family systems theory.

I focused on the theoretical approach developed by Murray Bowen, who wrote, *Family Therapy in Clinical Practice (1978).* I began using Bowenian family systems therapy and drawing family genograms to connect their struggles to cross-generational issues. It was an interesting, new approach that was nonthreatening to families and they generally enjoyed the first several sessions when they talked about their individual families. It was also helpful in generating some insights and avoiding confrontations, but it led to little improvement in the marriages.

Marriage Damaged by Affair

I saw a Christian couple who were having marital problems as a result of the husband having an affair with a co-worker. He confessed his failure to his wife and asked for her forgiveness and appeared to be very sincere in his desire to save his marriage. He strongly affirmed his love for his wife and promised her that it would never happen again, but his wife was so deeply hurt and untrusting that she was obsessed with wanting to know everything that happened during the affair. I didn't know how to help her with these issues and I didn't know how to help the husband to identify the underlying emotional issues that led him into the affair.

After several counseling sessions, they ended the counseling after the wife eavesdropped on my private session with her husband to try to learn the details of his affair, and she got very upset at him. I had no idea how to help her overcome her feelings of hurt and her obsession with learning the details of her husband's infidelity. Once again I found marital counseling to be extremely difficult and unsuccessful, in spite of having completed another graduate degree in marriage and family therapy.

Difficulty of Marital Counseling

I continued attending seminars and conferences to learn more about marital counseling, and I eventually returned to college to get a Ph.D. in Counselor Education. I took classes in the family therapy school and sought advice on how to do marriage counseling. I even wrote a lengthy paper describing a number of different marital counseling theories in my effort to find something that could help me be more successful in counseling couples.

In spite of my tireless efforts to learn how to do effective marriage counseling I had no success in helping couples. I found marital counseling to be very difficult and ineffective and frustrating. I continued to attend workshops on marital counseling whenever possible. Over time I learned that other therapists also found it to be unpleasant and difficult, and they confirmed that marriage counseling requires a different approach than individual therapy. I also learned that very few counselors are provided training in their coursework to know how to help couples.

The First Successful Case

After I learned this prayer ministry I saw a couple in Nashville where the man was involved in an affair. This was identical to the last marriage counseling case I had, and this man's wife was also hurt deeply and was distrusting, but she sat and observed as I helped the husband pray through his emotional issues. He was repentant, and his wife understood the underlying emotional issues as I prayed with her husband about them. She also witnessed his emotional healing, and eventually she allowed me to pray with her about her feelings of anger and hurt. Using the simple principles of this prayer ministry, she was able to release her anger and to forgive her husband.

This couple remained together, and they began to minister to other couples who were struggling, and began referring other couples to me. I was amazed that after ten years of studying marriage counseling and trying various techniques, that praying with the spouses about their underlying emotional issues was far more effective than any secular or Christian counseling approach that I had ever tried. I had more opportunities to counsel couples, and found that I was able to help many of them using prayer ministry principles.

Basic Conflict Principle

I learned from these experiences that serious conflicts in marriages are the result of unresolved emotional issues from the past of the spouses that lead them to be angry and overreact. Couples in serious conflict overreact to one another and never resolve their feelings completely. I learned that any time individuals overreact to their partner it is ALWAYS due to unresolved feelings from their past that are reawakened by the current relationship.

When there are serious marital problems, both partners usually have some emotional issues that lead them to overreact to one another and lead to an escalation of conflicts. However, when the underlying emotional issues of the spouses are resolved, couples are then able to communicate well and resolve their own issues. This is the basic conflict principle that can guide the prayer minister to effectively minister to couples.

An "ideal" marital counseling approach would be to have both spouses come for counseling when both of them are motivated to get help with their issues and to save their marriage. Ideally, I would like to do a social history with both of them to identify their underlying emotional issues and to create a prayer plan for each of them. I would like to alternate between the spouses, first praying with one of them and then praying with the other so that they can begin getting along well and communicating to resolve their own issues.

If possible, I would also like to have a female prayer partner to pray with the woman about her issues while I am praying with the husband about his issues, to speed up the healing process. Although this is the ideal marriage counseling scenario, this "ideal" seldom works out, and I usually find myself working with only one of the spouses. Even when this happens, it often can result in a saved marriage when one of the partners receives healing.

Man Comes Alone for Marriage Counseling

A man came for counseling regarding his marriage. He told me that he and his wife had been married five years and they had two young children. One of their children had some serious, chronic health problems that required frequent hospitalization, and his wife had quit her job to care for him. This was very emotionally and financially stressful for them, but this man sincerely wanted help and wanted to save their marriage for the sake of his son.

He openly admitted that he "did wrong" to his wife and family and cheated on her for two years with a co-worker. He had ended the relationship a year and a half earlier and he was desperately trying to work things out, but she was understandably very hurt and bitter. He and his wife engaged in a lot of fighting and arguing, and he tried to stay calm and not get upset with her, but it led him to drink in order to calm himself. He told me, "I feel like I'm going out of my mind," and he said he wanted help to save his marriage.

This man said that he had used drugs when he was in his twenties and he went to prison twice, but he had been working steadily and trying to be a good father. He admitted that he drank excessively but he had been going to AA and NA and was trying hard to quit drinking. He stated that his wife had been married one time before and raised one child. He described her as moody, depressed, angry, and violent when angry. She often yelled at him and the kids, but was a good mom, though not affectionate to him; in fact, she wouldn't even let him touch her.

After listening to this man and gathering background information on him I explained the "Basic Conflict Principle" and shared with him some illustrations of how to release feelings of anger, grief, and shame. He indicated that he was okay with prayer to resolve his anger and grief, and I shared with him the following prayer plan goals. He gave verbal consent to use prayer to help him with these goals and we began meeting.

His prayer plan consisted of a list of the sources of his anger and the significant losses he had experienced. Sources of anger included his biological father who treated him like he didn't exist and disowned him, his mother who was overbearing, depressed all the time, and spoiled him, and his wife, whom he stated was very angry, screamed at him frequently, cussed at him, and expressed no appreciation for him. His losses included the loss of his girlfriend and his child after he impregnated his girlfriend at age 15, the loss of his maternal grandfather at age 18, the loss of his paternal grandmother at age 24, and the loss of his maternal grandmother at age 42. After making this pray plan we were ready to begin our prayer sessions.

Our next session was devoted to gathering background information, discussing treatment techniques, and agreeing on the prayer plan. In our second session he told me that he asked his wife for forgiveness, and he said he had been sober for two weeks and was getting along fairly well with her. She was starting to want him to touch her occasionally. We discussed the loss of his maternal grandfather at age 18, and he identified seventeen things he missed about him and was able to resolve this loss. We also discussed and prayed about the loss of his maternal grandmother and he identified twenty things he missed about her. He was able to completely resolve these two losses and felt much better afterwards.

In our third session he told me that he had gone to church, which he enjoyed. He admitted that he drank twice but he was doing better now. He was able to think about his maternal grandparents without any negative feelings. We discussed his anger toward his wife and he identified seventeen resentments he had towards her, and then he released this anger. Afterwards he said he felt much better and felt no anger toward her.

At our fourth session he said that his wife was "up and down" emotionally and had been upset a lot, but he was trying to stay calm with her. We talked about his anger toward his biological father who treated him like he didn't exist and disowned him. He identified ten resentments he had toward his father and released them. His wife was upset about their son and the agonizing medical treatments she had to witness. She hugged her husband and apologized to him for how she had been treating him.

In our fifth session this man told me that he had had a rough week with his wife, but she cried and said she didn't want to be like her mother. He said, "It just floors me how good she's been." He said that he wanted to pray with her about her anger but she wasn't willing yet. He told me, "I've been to treatment before, but this works!" We discussed his anger toward his mother who was always depressed and spoiled him. He listed six resentments he had towards her and he released his anger towards her.

In our sixth and last session, we discussed the loss of his paternal grandmother at age 24 and he identified twelve things he missed about her, and then he prayed and released this grief. He told me how grateful he was for the prayer session. He said that he felt no more anger toward his wife and that they were getting along much better. He admitted that he drank one beer but did not drink excessively or get drunk. We reviewed our previous sessions and he affirmed that he had no anger toward his father, mother, or wife. He had resolved his losses of his maternal grandparents and the loss of his paternal grandmother, and he only had good feelings and memories of them. All of his sadness and anger was gone. Regarding his marriage he said, "things are good." He was getting along well with his wife, his wife and mother were still spoiling their son, and he said his wife was touching him more. He was very encouraged and hopeful.

Individual vs. Couples Sessions

From my previous failures in marriage counseling you can probably understand why it is so exciting to me to share stories like this. It is very exciting to see marriages like this one saved. Even when only one partner will come for counseling, as in this case, this approach to marriage counseling can still profoundly improve the marriage.

It is still preferable to have both spouses come for marriage counseling for the maximum impact on the marriage. When counseling couples, it is best to see them together initially and then separate them if they cannot tolerate the interview without becoming volatile. Individual sessions are needed with volatile couples and when discussing "sensitive" issues, such as previous affairs or relationships they have had. Even though they may be seen separately for much of the time, it is helpful to bring them together periodically to see how they are doing. When they are seen together, it is very important to maintain confidentiality about matters discussed in the individual prayer sessions.

Marriage Counseling Goals

During the first counseling session with a couple there are four goals that I want to accomplish. First, I want to identify the major problems in the marriage, not to resolve them or to coach the couple in these problems. I ask how long they have been together and then ask what type of problems they are having. If they become accusing and argumentative, I explain that I am not immediately going to help resolve any conflicts but just want a general sense of what type of problems they are having. Second, I want to assess the motivation for counseling that each of them has. Third, I want to conduct a social history on at least one of the spouses, and possibly both of them, to identify and understand the underlying grief, anger, and shame issues of both spouses/individuals. This is difficult to accomplish in one hour, so typically I will get a partial history on one of them. Finally, I want to explain the "Basic Conflict Principle" and healing process and ask them "if you could get rid of those underlying emotions that make it difficult to communicate, would you like to?" Helping them understand this basic principle is important to giving them a desire to meet again. If they are both interested in meeting again, I set up another appointment to help them begin resolving the underlying issues. If only one spouse is willing to meet, I will set up an appointment to meet with him/her individually.

During my first couples counseling session there are a number of general relationship questions that I routinely ask to open up the conversation. I usually ask them what brought to seek counseling, how long they have been together, and what kind of problems they are having? After getting a general idea about their problems I usually ask each spouse what their concerns about their relationship. As a gauge of the seriousness of their problem I also ask them if they ever gotten violent with each other, if they have ever separated, and if either of have ever had any affairs. Many times couples will openly admit that they have had affairs and this has been a source of conflict, but if either of them has had a secret affair, they will usually choose to not disclose it at this time. Finally, after getting this background information I select the spouse who seems to be the one with the most anger or the most motivation to change, "Do you mind if I ask some background questions?" I then try to quickly gather enough background information on that spouse to get some idea about why he or she is experiencing marital conflicts, based upon past, unresolved emotional issues.

During my second session with a couple I try to meet with them together, if possible, to save time and to teach them both how they can be set free. If they are too volatile to tolerate being in the room together, then I will see them separately and try to help them with their individual issues. But if the couple can sit together without fighting I will select one of them to begin the prayer process. Often I will begin with the most motivated spouse or the one with the most prominent emotional issue that is interfering with the marriage. I will try to work on one spouse's underlying issues of anger or grief, to demonstrate how the prayer process can help resolve it and make the person immediately feel better. This gives them both hope and helps them to see how simple the prayer process is. Once the spouse experiences some significant emotional change, I like to discuss that with them and explain that this is how the Lord can change their feelings and enable them to get along better and feel better.

In subsequent sessions I usually ask them what has happened since the last session, to get a sense of whether they have had any serious conflicts or incidents. I also like to review the previous session and check to see if any healing from prior sessions is still lasting, in order to confirm the resolution of issues or to do additional praying about the issues. Then I try to identify any immediate crises that need to be addressed, and deal with any crisis issues that the couple identifies. If there have been no new crises, I will simply identify another underlying issue from the prayer plan and see if the spouse wants to resolve it. Again, as one partner begins to get healing, I want to see if the other one is ready to begin getting some healing.

Doing a Social History

In Chapter Six we talked about how to do a social history on a prayer client, and this same process is important for helping couples. This social history cannot usually be accomplished on both partners in an hour, so it may require two sessions, but with experience a prayer minister can do one spouse in the first session. This background information helps you understand both of the individuals and identify underlying issues that contribute to their marital conflicts. It also gives the spouses insight into each other and into their own reactions to one another. Specifically, it helps the prayer minister to identify any underlying grief, anger, or shame that is contributing to their marital problems. It also helps the spouses understand how their personal problems began, and how they continue to affect their relationship. Once the sources of their emotional issues are identified, it is very simple to create a prayer plan for each of them and to obtain their agreement to work on these issues.

When I first meet with a couple, I begin by asking some of the general relationship questions identified previously. After I learn about their conflicts I want to do a social history to understand what they have experienced previously that has contributed to their conflicts. I usually introduce this phase of the interview by asking "Do you mind if I ask you some information about your background so that I can understand you both better?" Once they give me permission, I begin asking questions to understand their anger, grief, shame and relationship problems.

The components of this social history have been previously discussed, but will be briefly summarized here. Parental influences are a significant factor in an individual's emotional life so it is important to learn about each spouse's parents and their relationship with them. It is also very important to understand their relationship with each sibling and individual raised with them. Then it is important to understand how they got along with their peers in school, if they were teased, bullied, or had plenty of friends. Romantic relationships are a frequent source of anger and grief so it is important to learn about all significant relationships in childhood. Adult romantic relationships are also very influential and lead to feelings of grief and anger, so these need to be discussed. Finally, it is important to learn about any traumas such as physical, verbal, or sexual abuse and it is also important to ask about any significant losses of life or relationships. Many people will neglect to mention losses because they consider these normal life experiences and do not realize the impact they have upon their emotions, so it is critical that the prayer minister ask specifically about these losses.

The primary goal of this social history is to identify anything that could be a source of feelings of grief, anger, or shame that may be affecting the individual emotionally and relationally. Once you complete this history on both spouses you should have a good idea of the origin of their emotional barriers. If you still cannot understand the reason for their problems, ask for their help, because there are always underlying emotional reasons for a person's anger, distrust, drinking, drug abuse or compulsive behavior that interferes with a marriage.

After gathering this information, it may be helpful to summarize your observations and explain to the couple that it is very difficult to communicate with each other due to these issues. Then you can ask them, "If you could get rid of these feelings of anger, grief, and shame would you like to?" If they consent to meet together again, you can begin to systematically work through their prayer plan to resolve the identified issues.

COMMON MARITAL ISSUES

The most common problems that lead to serious marital problems are poor communication, angry outbursts, and affairs. Communication skills training and conflict resolution training are not usually effective with couples, because the spouses are so emotional that they cannot communicate without fighting, and just telling them to stay calm and listen to their partner does not work when they are full of anger. The resolution of affairs cannot be resolved through apologies and reassurances when the anger and hurt is deep.

Other common problems found with couples are addiction problems, sexual problems, financial problems, and prior relationships. When one spouse has an addiction or sexual problem, they cannot resolve this through simple promises; they need to learn how to release their anger and resolve the underlying emotional reasons for the addiction or sexual problem. Financial problems are also frequently based upon underlying emotional factors that need to be identified and resolved, and former relationships need to be completely resolved. Each of these specific marital issues will be briefly discussed and illustrated.

Communication Problems

A woman described in Chapter 8 came for help with feelings of depression and anger toward her husband. She was angry at him for being gone so often and not spending time with her or talking with her. They had no emotional intimacy or communication between them. I shared with this woman how she could be set free from her anger through prayer and she was receptive, so I asked her if she would like to get rid of her anger toward her husband. She hesitated and then admitted that she was having an affair and was not ready to release her anger toward her husband. I talked with her about how she could be set free from all her negative feelings when she was ready.

This woman returned three weeks later and had a completely different attitude toward her husband. He had come to realize how he had damaged their relationship and asked for her forgiveness. He also began to shower her with compliments and began talking with her and listening to her. By the time she returned to see me she had forgiven him and their communication had improved dramatically. I asked her how her marriage was going and she said they were getting along "great" and she said that her husband was "an incredible man."

Most couples will not restore their emotional intimacy and communication so quickly. They need to learn how to release their anger first and then they can improve their communication. However, as long as their resentments remain, it will be very difficult to get them to speak to one another in a civil way and to have good communication. Once the spouses resolve their anger toward each other most couples are able to communicate just fine.

Anger Problems

Anger is a very common problem in troubled marriages. In fact, if every couple committed themselves to live by the principle of not letting the sun go down on their anger (Ephesians 4:26-27), there would be very few divorces. In a previous chapter I shared a story about a couple that was on the verge of divorce. They had frequent arguments during which the wife became enraged and violent, and even tore doors off their hinges. After we prayed about her anger toward her sister and mother during her childhood, she became very mellow and quit having angry outbursts. Their marriage immediately improved and was better than it had ever been.

Such stories are very common, because anger is the emotion that usually leads directly to conflict and divorce. Virtually every couple that is quarrelling has significant anger issues for which they need healing. Anger is the number one issue that damages and destroys marriages, and yet it can be easily resolved by identifying the sources of anger, identifying the specific reasons for their anger toward each "source," and then releasing the anger into God's hands through prayer.

A woman came to me who struggled with depression and anger. She talked about her husband and how badly he had treated her and torn her down emotionally throughout their marriage. When they were first married he asked if she had had any previous boyfriends, and when she told him about one prior relationship he became insanely jealous and obsessed about this former boyfriend. She said that he picked fights with her all the time, he put her down and called her names, he claimed that she never backed him up on anything, he would not forgive her and let go of the past, and he yelled at her all the time. She said she could never express herself for fear that he would get upset and begin yelling at her and intimidating her. We made a list of eleven resentments she had toward her husband.

I asked this woman if she would like to get rid of her anger and she laughed and said, "There are just two ways for me to get rid of this anger: divorce or death." I explained that there was a third alternative; to give it to the Lord and let Him carry it for her. She agreed that she would like to do this so I led her in a prayer and she told the Lord everything she resented about her husband and asked him to carry it for her. When she finished praying I asked her how she felt; she said, "I don't feel much; I feel okay." She told me that she no longer felt any anger; she just felt neutral toward him. She didn't believe it was possible to release her anger, but in just a few minutes she was able to release it completely, and she left smiling and feeling lighter. This did not resolve her husband's problems, but it did improve their communication. It also enabled her to remain calm when dealing with him so that she did not further damage their marriage, and it enabled her to hear from the Lord regarding what she should do about her husband's behavior.

A man came for help with his anger which was damaging his marriage. He had received some healing previously but came determined to eliminate all his anger, which he had carried all his life. He told me how his mother clothed him and fed him and never physically abused him, but she never showed him any love or affection, either. She never hugged him or told him that she loved him and as a young child she ignored him when he tugged on her dress and tearfully asked her how Jesus could take him to heaven. She never had a kind word for him and never gave him any praise or encouragement. After opening Christmas presents she wanted the kids to get out of the house and stay outside. Even after this man was grown she called him insulting names and treated him with contempt, and when his wife died she seldom offered to help him with his son.

We made a list of eight resentments he had toward his mother, and then we prayed. He told the Lord the reasons for his anger and asked Him to carry them for him. I asked the Lord what He wanted this man to know. He said, "Your mother sees and understands her mistakes. Forgive her, my son, as I forgave your mistakes." I asked him how he felt now and he said, "My knees and arms are relaxed. I don't feel any anger. I feel sorry for her; now she knows and understands her mistakes." His anger which he had carried for over 50 years and which was destroying his marriage was gone, and he just felt sorry for her! Eliminating this anger made him much more calm with his wife and prevented him from causing any more damage to his marriage.

Infidelity Problems

Extramarital affairs are a growing problem and a major cause of marital problems. The prayer minister must be prepared to help both spouses with their feelings of anger, grief, and hurt in order to bring healing to the marriage.

A woman said that she knew she needed to forgive her husband for his infidelity but that it was very difficult because of his attitude. She said that he treated her well and was very nice to her the first several years of their marriage, but then one day she saw him with a young woman in his car and she confronted him about it. He denied he was having an affair for three weeks until his wife suddenly developed an STD which she could not have gotten from any other source. Her husband finally admitted his infidelity, but it completely destroyed her trust in him and destroyed her desire for any affection or intimacy with him.

"I had my heart ripped out again" about five years later, she told me, when a church friend told her that her husband was having another affair with a woman who lived next door to this friend's sister. When she confronted her husband again, he denied it again, but when the evidence was presented to him he eventually confessed his infidelity with another town prostitute. She said she was so angry at him that she said she would have shot him if she'd had a gun. She told him to leave and they separated at that time but she was so depressed and angry that she was unable to hold down a job and every time she drove by the other woman's work site she said her gut wrenched.

This woman stated that she still spoke to her husband and he told her that he asked God to forgive him and she needs to also. However he picked at her faults, blamed everything on her, and told her that she was not acting like a Christian because she was still angry at him. He also bragged about his affair and laughed about it, but told her that she had sinned a lot more than him and that he had not caught up with her yet on his sinning. These comments just further enraged her but she knew that she needed to forgive him.

I asked this woman if she would like to get rid of her anger if she could, and she said "Yes." We made a list of twenty things she resented about her husband and then I led her in a prayer to tell the Lord why she was angry. She ended the prayer saying, "Lord, I'm tired of being angry so right now I choose to give it to you and ask you to take it from me and carry it for me." After this prayer I asked her how she felt and she said, "I feel better. I don't feel anything right now." I reminded her of the many things she said she resented about her husband then asked her again how she felt. She said, "I feel at ease; there's no anger." I asked her what she thought about this, and she said, "It's great! To me that's a miracle! People say it's a miracle when someone with cancer gets well, but this is a real miracle." With her anger gone she was able to listen to the Lord for guidance in how to respond to her husband's behavior.

Unfortunately, affairs do occur among Christian couples and this often destroys the marriage, but healing can occur when the individuals give the Lord their feelings of anger, grief, and shame that need to be released. The devil loves to destroy marriages, but the Lord loves to bring healing and to restore marriages to protect the family and bring glory to Himself. Affairs and divorces can be avoided when couples learn to give the Lord their anger and emotional burdens so that they have joy and peace.

Past Relationship Problems

Many times married couples today have been married two or three times previously, and their experiences from these unsuccessful marriages continue to affect them emotionally. This is especially true when there were children involved and the spouse lost custody of their children, or if they have to have continuing contact with their former spouse when exchanging care of the children. This is one reason why social histories are so important; so that you can identify any past relationship problems and identify any unresolved emotional issues related to them. Even serious relationships formed during middle school or high school can affect the individual's feelings toward other significant relationships.

After being hurt by previous significant relationships, some individuals are very angry, suspicious, or jealous of others. Each one of these prior relationships needs to be explored and resolved so that their anger, grief, and shame will not repeatedly bleed over into their present marriage. When talking about past relationships, it is usually best to do this without their spouse being present, because it can trigger off feelings of jealousy or distrust when they hear their partner talking about their former romantic relationships.

Alcohol and Drug Abuse Problems

Chapter 16 was devoted to a discussion of how to overcome addictions. Alcohol and drug abuse frequently lead to marriage problems when one of the spouses is addicted. When I encounter such couples I usually ask the addicted person how long they have been drinking or using drugs, and when they began drinking or using drugs regularly. Then I ask what happened prior to the onset of their regular use of alcohol or drugs, and try to identify any losses, anger, or shame that they had prior to their substance abuse. I explain that there are always underlying emotional issues that lead to substance abuse or regular substance usage.

I previously described a couple who came for counseling after the husband was ordered to receive counseling for domestic violence. He had badly abused his wife while drunk, and he promised her that he would never drink again if she would not leave him. This does not usually work, but his wife stayed with him and he quit drinking, but she was still afraid of him when he got angry, because he had a lot of unresolved grief and anger from childhood abuse, and from previous relationships. We systematically addressed each of the sources of his anger and grief until they were all resolved, and he never drank again. He resolved his grief, anger and shame, and this enabled him to stop having urges to drink. When I last saw this couple I asked his wife how he was doing and she said, "He is a sweetheart," and she couldn't remember the last time they had had a serious argument. They acted like a newly wedded couple, holding hands during the session and as they left my office.

Alcohol and drug problems must be addressed as separate issues when they cause marital problems, because people with addictions abuse drugs for multiple reasons, not just because of their bad marriage. Of course, sometimes addicts tell their partners that they drink because of them, but that is not true. There are always other factors contributing to their substance abuse, and these need to be addressed and resolved independently from their marital problems.

Gambling Addiction

Gambling is a very destructive addiction that can destroy marriages and families. I counseled a woman whose husband had had a gambling addiction for a long time, but it was aggravated by the death of his brother. After the death of this man's brother, his compulsive gambling increased because his gambling was driven by negative feelings, and he gambled to keep his mind off of troubling matters and to feel better.

This woman had been hiding her money and credit cards from her husband for a long time due to his gambling, but one day she discovered that her guns were missing. When she asked her husband about them he sheepishly admitted he had pawned them for gambling money. She was infuriated that he would do this and he also pawned off an item that she had bought him for his birthday. She was enraged to think that she might have to lock up all her valuables to prevent him from pawning off anything else of value. She was so angry that she wanted to hit him, so she told him to just leave the room.

Her anger was justified but she did not want to stay angry. She was angry because she could no longer trust him to buy anything for her, she had to watch him all the time, he was destroying their family, and he was choosing gambling over his marriage and family. She made up a list of six reasons for her anger and then said a prayer and gave it all to the Lord. After asking the Lord to take her anger from her and carry it for her, I prayed and asked the Lord what He wanted her to know. She reported the following thoughts: "You know what has to be done; you're not alone; you have to think about your daughter."

After praying I asked her how she felt. She told me that her anger was gone and she no longer felt like hitting him. In fact, she said, "He can't make me mad, now." She was calm but resolute in taking measures to protect herself and her daughter from his destructive gambling addiction without any destructive anger to interfere. The Lord took all her anger and gave her His peace, and I explained that when we are calm and free from anger the Lord can guide us and tell us what we need to do in every situation. This woman had a challenge ahead for her, but without her anger, and with God's guidance, she was equipped to handle it. She spoke calmly and firmly with her husband and told him that either she or his gambling had to go. He stopped gambling and they are still together.

People often mistakenly believe that they need to hold onto their anger because their anger will motivate other people to change, but that is not true. The apostle Paul was clear in Ephesians 4:26-27 that we should not hold onto our anger overnight and that when we do it gives the devil an opportunity in our lives. This woman's anger led her to act out in anger, and it was harmful to her child and led her to engage in several sinful behaviors. When she released her anger the Lord enabled her to calmly deal with her husband.

I counseled another couple in which the husband had a serious gambling problem, which he denied. However, his gambling was so compulsive that it was a serious problem in their marriage because he began spending the money his wife had set aside for their mortgage payment. He also found $500 that his son had saved and hidden, and he spent this money, which created a lot of ill feelings toward him. Eventually, his wife left him to protect herself and her children from her husband's compulsive gambling. She had to sell their home and move into a much smaller home due to her husband's gambling. The husband never admitted that he had a gambling problem or that he had negative feelings about his extremely abusive childhood that were leading him to gamble.

Those with gambling addictions have deep, underlying feelings of grief, anger, and shame, and they need help to be set free from those emotions in order to be free from their addiction. Being angry at an addict will not change them or motivate them to change; it may actually fuel their addiction. Those around the addict need to learn to rest in God's peace and look to Him for wisdom to know how to deal with their loved one.

Sexual Problems in Marriage

There are many types of sexual problems that can cause marital problems, including pornography, phone sex, prostitution, pedophilia, fetishes, voyeurism, and other forms of sexual deviancy. In Chapter 16, I described a case involving a Christian man who compulsively dressed in female clothes. Such behaviors are always driven by underlying emotional issues that need to be identified and resolved.

Pornography is a problem for many men that upsets their wives and damages their marriages. In Chapter 18, I shared a story about a Christian man who struggled with pornography and it upset his wife so much that she told their pastor. This man needed help in learning how to identify the underlying feelings of loneliness that led him to seek relief through pornography. He learned this behavior as a young man before he was saved, but after his salvation he continued to have the impulse to look at pornography when he felt lonely or felt bad. When he learned to identify the source of his feelings of loneliness and pray about them, he was able to gain victory over the pornography.

I have worked as the director of two sexual offender programs, and I learned that there were a wide range of deviant sexual behaviors and perversions that people practice. I also learned from this experience that all of these perversions and deviant practices were rooted in feelings of anger, grief, and shame from childhood experiences. Although all men struggle with their sexual thoughts and desires, most men do not struggle with these sexual perversions or deviant sexual behaviors.

Some couples struggle from a lack of normal sexual intimacy. This can occur in men, but it occurs more frequently in women who have been sexually abused, and who are repulsed by the thought of engaging in any sexual activity because it reminds them of their sexual abuse. Sometimes it is so extreme that the woman cannot stand to be touched by her husband. When this occurs, the sexually abused person can receive healing of their sexual trauma, and that should resolve their repulsion of normal sexual relationships in their marriage.

Financial Problems

Lack of financial discipline by a partner can lead to overspending and marriage conflicts. When this occurs, the prayer minister should look for the underlying emotional issues that lead to this pattern of impulsive spending. This can be done by asking the compulsive spender to give you an example of a recent time when he/she went on a spending spree, and ask him how he felt prior to the spending spree.

I prayed with a woman whose father had committed suicide when she was 18 years old, and she received healing of her anger, grief, and shame from this suicide. One surprising result of this emotional healing was that she quit having the impulse to go on spending sprees, which had created some marital problems for her. Whenever a spouse spends excessively there is always an underlying emotional reason for the spending, which needs to be identified so that they can resolve it through prayer.

Beyond Prayer Plans

Sometimes couples can pray through all the identified issues on their prayer plan and there are still marital problems. This may be caused by not completely resolving certain emotions and events previously discussed, or by not identifying all the sources. In such cases it is helpful to identify their feelings of anger, grief, or shame, and ask them when the first time was that they felt this way. This will usually take them back to the original source so they can pray again and try to completely resolve the memory.

There may also be some additional losses, anger sources, and shame issues that were not included in the original plan. For example, the person may disclose some other examples of sexual abuse or significant losses that were never mentioned previously. If there are continuing marital problems it is certain that something was missed, and this simply needs to be identified.

Failures to Save Marriages

Sometimes there are couples whose marriage cannot be saved due to the lack of cooperation by one of the spouses. A couple was seen with a husband who had been very violent, abused drugs, didn't work and went to prison. His wife was a very nice Christian woman who worked, went to church regularly, and kept trying to save their marriage. However, her husband took money from her to support his drug usage, so she was enabling him in his drug abuse. This husband was seen twice for counseling, talked with me about his history, and he even appeared to release some anger. But after the second session he said he had prayed on his own about his other sources of anger (which was very unlikely) and he refused to participate in any more counseling sessions.

The wife was much more cooperative and made a prayer plan. She prayed to release her anger toward her husband and her mother, and she released some grief for the loss of her father at age two. She gave her sadness and anger to the Lord. After releasing this anger and grief over the loss of her father I asked the Lord if there was anything that He wanted her to know. The thoughts that came to her mind were, "I've been your Father all along," "you are loved," and "one day you'll see Him." After these thoughts came to her she was very happy and said she felt "peaceful." In this peaceful state of mind, she made the decision to move away from her abusive husband who continued to manipulate and abuse her.

This marriage was not saved, because the husband was unwilling to discuss his anger or to release it. The Lord could have set him free if this man had been willing, but he was not. When individuals like this are unwilling to release their anger or to give their negative emotions to the Lord, they cannot be helped. The Lord can set anyone free, and the prayer principles of this ministry do work when applied correctly, but the person has to be willing to turn to the Lord for help. This is why Jesus asked the man at the pool of Bethesda "do you want to get well?" (John 5:6). We would be wise to follow His example and ask the same question to people we are trying to help.

Another reason for failure is that there may be some significant traumas or events that the prayer ministry client has not disclosed to the prayer minister. I saw a woman who was doing very well and was excited about this ministry because she had resolved so much trauma from her past, but she disclosed at our last session that she had been sexually abused by ten additional people. After sharing this she disappeared with a former boyfriend and drug user, and abandoned her child. Even though she had received much healing, she had a lot of other unresolved traumas that she had failed to disclose previously.

A third reason for failure is that some people have deeply repressed memories that they are afraid to disclose, so they simply avoid disclosing very important events from their past. A married woman requested help with her sexual difficulties with her husband. She had been married two years to a man she described as a "wonderful Christian man," and she had never consummated their marriage because she felt repulsed by him when he tried to touch her. She said that she wanted to be a missionary, and she thought she should resolve this issue before she went on the mission field. I prayed for the Lord to take her to the source and origin of her feelings of repulsion by touching, and she immediately began crying out saying, "No, no, that's not true!" She stopped the session and refused to go any further because she had a visual image of a man lying on top of her that looked like her father. This was too distressing to her, so she stopped the prayer session and never returned for more healing.

The Church and Marriage Counseling

Marriages are important to God because they are the foundation of society and are necessary for raising emotionally healthy children. Strong marriages lead to strong churches and a strong society, but when the biblical model of marriage and families is abandoned, many social problems result. The apostle Paul taught the early Christians, "Husbands love your wives, just as Christ also loved the church and gave Himself up for her...wives submit to your husbands" (Ephesians 5:25, 22). Peter also said to the wives, "Wives adorn yourselves with a gentle and quiet spirit so that your husbands, if they are disobedient, may be won without a word, as they observe your chaste and respectful behavior" (1 Peter 3:1-2). He went on to tell husbands, "Grant her honor as a fellow-heir of the grace of life, so that your prayers may not be hindered" (1 Peter 3:7). These scriptures underscore the importance of marriage to the Lord. When a biblical model of the family is taught by the Church and modeled by believers, the entire world and our society will benefit and experience the stability that comes from following the teaching of the Lord.

It is the responsibility of the Church to be the "salt of the earth" and to be the "light of the world" (Matthew 5:13-14). The Church needs to teach Biblical standards for marriage, and it also needs to demonstrate to the world how to forgive and to love their spouses. But the world has no solution for the marriage problems and violence in the world. These simple prayer principles being taught in this ministry are effective for setting people free of their anger and disabling emotions. The Church needs to teach these principles for how to release anger, resolve grief, and overcome shame, regularly from the pulpit and in classes, so that everyone in the Church knows these liberating truths and can practice them.

One of the primary components of this ministry is to teach believers to apply Ephesians 4:26-27 to their lives and "Do not let the sun go down on your anger and do not give the devil an opportunity." What an amazing transformation would occur if churches simply taught people how to live by this principle. It would be wonderful to see mature couples in every church taught this ministry so they can help other couples, and see the divorce rate drop dramatically in our churches.

Marriage counseling is not very effective because the world has no solution for anger, grief, or feelings of shame. But the Lord can set individuals free from the anger, grief, and shame that damages their marriage and harms their children. Even if only one spouse gets healing it can often save the marriage, and the Lord will be glorified as families are restored.

May God help each of us to do our part, beginning with our own marriages and spreading to our churches. As the Church demonstrates to the world how to have lasting marriages, full of peace and joy, the world will be drawn to the Church.

20

OVERCOMING THE IMPACT OF DIVORCE

Throughout this book we have given several examples of individuals who have received healing after experiencing a divorce. But there are so many people in our churches and society who have suffered from divorce that it is critical that our churches know how to minister to them so that they can be healed. Many believers in our churches are hindered in their spiritual and emotional lives from being all that the Lord wants them to be, as a result of a divorce.

Divorce is very destructive to the adults who experience it as well as to the children of the divorcing parents. In previous chapters, the findings of The Virginia Twin Study were cited, indicating that divorce has a more extensive and lasting emotional impact upon children than death of a parent. The death of a parent was found to lead to depression which lasts up to fifteen years, but divorce leads to anxiety, depression, and substance abuse, and its impact upon the tendency to abuse drugs never stops.

THE IMPACT OF DIVORCE UPON CHILDREN

Young Man Releases Anger about Divorce

I saw a young man who was very depressed and was having suicidal thoughts. Knowing that most depression is rooted in loss, I asked him when his depression began and he told me that it began after his father divorced his mother and left the family. The young man lost his grandfather at age 10, and when his father left him two years later he became very depressed and angry. I prayed with him first about the loss of his grandfather. We made a list of 12 things he missed about his grandfather and then gave it to the Lord in prayer, and asked the Lord to take it from him and carry it for him. After praying the young man said he felt no more sadness and felt "kind of happy." This is the first time he had ever prayed for God to take some feelings from him and carry them and he was pleasantly surprised to see how well it worked.

Then we talked about the loss of his father and his anger toward his father for leaving the family. He was angry that his father left them, he quit talking with the children, he hurt their mother, he screamed at her, and then he remarried and started a new family without any regard for his first family. We made a list of nine reasons for his anger and he prayed and gave his anger to the Lord and asked Him to take it from him.

After the prayer he said he still felt angry, so I asked him why he was still angry and he said that his father left them and didn't try to be a father. We prayed about this and gave it to the Lord but he said that he still felt angry. I've learned that when prayer does not give complete peace it usually means that we missed something, so I asked him, again, why he was still angry. He told me that he couldn't believe that any parent would do that to a child, his brother was deeply hurt by his father's abandonment and began using drugs, his sisters were so hurt that they became depressed, and he had become depressed also by his father's selfish actions. We then prayed a third time and gave these resentments to the Lord and asked Him to take them from him.

After this third prayer I asked the Lord if there was anything that He wanted this young man to know. "Everyone is okay now," he said. I asked him how he felt now and he said, "I don't feel angry. It helped us to learn to not grow up and make the same mistake with our children." He was surprised, again, to see how the Lord took his anger from him and gave him peace about his father. I asked him what emotion he felt and he said, "Calm." All of his anger had left him and he felt peaceful and calm while thinking about his father.

There are many children, like this young man, who are angry toward a parent and have become angry or depressed because of a divorce. It often leads to rebelliousness, depression, suicidal thoughts, or drug abuse but Jesus is able to take these feelings and set them free. It is wonderful to share this simple process with young people to show them how the Lord can set them free from the harmful impact of divorce and to teach them that Jesus is their best friend and He will heal their broken hearts.

Parents' Divorce Leads to 38 Years of Anger

A man said that his friends told him he had an anger problem. He stated that he was the oldest of five children and that his parents fought a lot, but they took him to church and remained together until he was 17 years old. When he was age 17 his mother admitted that she was having an affair and his parents divorced, which was devastating to this young man and his younger siblings. While his mother ran off with another man, his father struggled to raise the five children on his own. He could no longer afford their nice home so they had to move to a "dilapidated" home. His mother never expressed any remorse for how she had destroyed their family and she eventually had affairs with many other men, which was very embarrassing to this young man. He became so angry at his mother that he refused to see her or talk with her for 20 years. He had two sisters that lived with their mother who were deeply damaged by her as well.

We made a list of 12 resentments this man had for his mother. I asked him if he would like to get rid of his anger and he said that would, so I led him in a prayer, telling the Lord what he resented about his mother. He was so overwhelmed with emotion while praying that it was difficult for him to pray, but he eventually told the Lord everything he resented about his mother and asked the Lord to take it from him. I asked him afterwards how he felt about his mother and he said, "I feel sorry for her. She doesn't know what she has done. I feel no anger" (Reminiscent of the words of the Lord Jesus on the cross, "Father, forgive them; for they do not know what they are doing," from Luke 23:34).

A friend who came with this man was amazed at the power of God to set him free from his anger so quickly. On their way back home to another state, they stopped to see this man's sister whom he had not seen or talked to for 15 years. After releasing his anger toward his mother he was so full of peace and joy that he wanted to reconnect with other family members. What a miracle to see such emotional healing as people give their anger to the Lord.

THE IMPACT OF DIVORCE UPON ADULTS

Those who have experienced divorce often report that divorce is more difficult for them than the death of a spouse. The death of a spouse can be a significant trauma that leads to depression, but when the loss of the spouse is voluntary and ongoing as it is with divorce it has a much greater emotional impact upon the spouse. There are ministries and support groups available around the country for the divorced to help divorcees deal with their divorces. Since there are so many hurting individuals, these support groups are well attended. They provide divorced persons the opportunity to talk with others about their pain and struggles. However, these support groups do not teach how to overcome the emotional pain from their divorce, and so they last a long time and never bring complete resolution or peace to the divorced.

The Emotional Components of Divorce

Divorced people experience a range of different emotions from their divorce, depending upon the specific circumstances of their divorce. The most common emotions experienced from divorce are anger, grief, shame, and sadness. Each of these emotions can be resolved through the prayer principles presented in this book, and the goal of this program is to enable divorced people to find complete resolution of their negative emotions so that they experience peace. When divorced people resolve their negative feelings they are able to enjoy life again, make wise decisions, and provide the best parenting possible for their children.

Each emotion that the divorced person experiences from their divorce needs to be identified and resolved. In some cases this will be very simple because the main emotion they feel is anger, or grief, but in other cases it will require more extensive attention. In many cases these emotions can be resolved in a single session, and in most cases the emotions resulting from a divorce can be resolved completely in two or three prayer sessions so the individual can move on with their life and not be weighed down emotionally for a lengthy period.

Devastating Divorce Leads to Anger, Sadness and Shame

A woman came to me regarding her feelings of betrayal, anger, sadness and shame when her husband left her after 14 years of marriage. She invited a close friend of hers to live with her and her husband while she supported them with her job and her husband was studying for another career. They had a child together and then this woman learned that her husband and girlfriend were having an affair. He refused to break up with the other woman and they continued the affair in this woman's home.

When she filed for divorce the husband begged her to wait two years so he could complete his studies. She was understandably enraged and deeply hurt by his infidelity, his lies and deception, and his open relationship with this other woman in their home. We made a list of 13 reasons for her anger and she prayed and asked the Lord to take her anger from her and carry it for her. I asked the Lord if there was anything that He wanted her to know. The thoughts that came to her mind were, "I can do this... it's not the end... I have people who will help me." These thoughts felt true to her, she said.

She told me that she still felt annoyed at her husband because she wasted 14 years with him and she would never be able to trust him again. She prayed and gave these annoyances to the Lord, then

I asked the Lord, again, if there was anything that He wanted her to know. "Things will be fine... It will take her some time but your daughter will be okay." These thoughts felt true to her and she said she felt relieved. All her anger was gone and she said that she just felt pity for her husband that he had strayed and she said, "It's his loss."

I asked her if she had any other negative feelings and she said she felt shameful because she should have known better than to allow her husband to spend time with her friend. I prayed and asked the Lord what He wanted her to know about her belief that she was shameful and bad for letting this happen. The thoughts that came to her mind were, "It wasn't my fault...he is the one who made the choice." She told me that her shame had left her and she felt peaceful and calm. There was no more anger, sadness, or shame. The Lord lifted all her emotional pain from this difficult situation and gave her peace so that she can be the best mother possible to her daughter.

We ended by talking about how good the Lord is and how He spoke to her and gave her truths that set her free. She was not certain of her salvation so I shared the gospel with her and she left confident that she was going to heaven. Even in the midst of difficult circumstances the Lord wants us to have His peace and joy and this woman left smiling, and full of his joy and peace.

FINDING HEALING OF ANGER AND HATRED

Woman Regains Her "Warm and Fuzzy Voice"

A woman came to a Set Free meeting and asked for prayer for her anger toward her ex-husband. She said that her friends and family used to compliment her on her "warm and fuzzy voice" but she had become bitter and angry after her divorce 15 years earlier. While she was married, her husband was emotionally abusive and used the Bible as a weapon and told her to be submissive to him, then he had multiple affairs. After their divorce he spitefully told her that he never loved her or wanted to marry her. He was irresponsible and never provided financial support for her and their children so she had to raise the children alone for many years, which was a severe burden and stress. He treated their daughter terribly because she looked so much like her, and he even challenged her faith when he was with her, but he spoiled their son and treated him like a king so he became very egotistical. In spite of his financial neglect and emotional abuse of his children he acted like a doting father in public so everyone would think he was a good father. Fifteen years of this treatment had made this woman resentful instead of warm and cheerful as she had previously been.

I asked her if she would like to get rid of this anger and she said that she would. I explained that the first step was just to be honest and to identify all her resentments toward her husband, which we had just done. The second step was to tell the Lord her resentments and ask Him to take them from her and she was willing to do this. So, I led her in a prayer and told the Lord why she was so angry at her ex, then she asked the Lord to take her anger from her and carry it for her. Afterwards, I asked her how she felt and she said, "I'm free of this. I'm at peace." I asked her if she felt any anger and she said she had no more anger but she had some sadness that her ex was missing out on some amazing kids, that her kids don't get to see their little sister, and that they have started becoming angry. We prayed about this sadness and she gave it to the Lord. After that she said that she felt, "Neutral, calm, and relaxed."

Since then she has repeatedly affirmed that she is still peaceful and calm about her ex-husband and has no more anger toward him, and her "warm and fuzzy" voice has come back. She was set free from 15 years of anger in a single prayer session! It would be wonderful to see every divorced person in our churches set free from their anger like this and give glory to God for setting them free. Several months later she wrote and gave the following report.

Follow-up Report: It's Really Gone!

"I want you to know God is amazing and has truly taken away my anger toward my children's father. My anger has stayed gone. Sometimes, when something happens I might have a twinge of something, but in my next breath I remember God willingly took this anger from me and then it's gone. And!!! It's REALLY GONE! I can spend my energy on my voice, the tone and the words I choose, while the kids and I are discussing whatever it is that is upsetting them in regards to their dad. I actually find myself thinking of reasons why he would say or do what he is saying or doing. I am careful not to give excuses, I have never done that. Since I prayed to let this anger go, out of nowhere my ex sent my oldest girl (in college) $290.00 to repay her for what she paid on her spring tuition and the rest "just because." Unfortunately my oldest daughter is holding on to anger and pain and frustration toward her dad and is not interested in letting it go. I am praying for God to break down her barriers so she can be humbled to let it all go. I am praying she will soften and want to let go. Thank you again for being obedient to God and His call in your life to help others. I will keep praying my girl will have the "want" to let go and let God."

Surprised by Peace after Releasing Anger

A woman came to me for help with her anger. She had a history of traumas and mistreatments but was most angry at her ex-husband because he was unfaithful to her and refused to pay any child support to help her raise their son. She was also angry at him for not spending time with their son, for not working, for lying to her about his affairs, for wasting money on drugs, and for blaming her for her son not being able to see his father. This woman appeared to be a little skeptical about this prayer process but she was desperate to get help for her anger because she was afraid that she would lose her job if she didn't get help. I explained how she needed to be completely honest about her anger and then give it to God in prayer, so we made a list of ten things she resented about her ex. I then led her in a prayer and she told the Lord why she was so angry at her ex, and she asked Him to take her anger from her and carry it for her.

I prayed and asked the Lord if there was anything that He wanted her to know, and told her to be quiet and let me know if she had any thoughts come to her mind. She looked very surprised and then smiled slightly and said, "Everything will be okay." Those words reminded her of her grandfather who used to tell her that and they brought a tearful smile to her face. I prayed again and asked if there was anything else that He wanted her to know. She smiled again and said, "I can do it by myself [raise her son]," and she said that that made her feel good. I prayed again, "Lord, is there anything else?" and she said, "My son is a good son and he'll turn out okay." She appeared a little tearful but said that she felt relieved. Once more I asked, "Lord, is there anything else?" She said, "Everything is going to be okay."

This woman was very surprised how these thoughts came to her mind and the peace that they brought to her heart. She told me that she felt no more anger toward her ex and she laughed and said she felt blessed. I asked her if she felt any negative feelings toward her ex and she said, "No. I actually feel sad for him that he is missing out on our son. He's really a great kid; he's smart and hilarious." She told me how her son had recently seen a full rainbow and exclaimed to his mother, "Look mom! God is going to bless us!" She was so surprised to hear words of comfort from the Lord and to be relieved of her anger. She went from being very angry at her ex to feeling pity for him because he was missing out on raising their son, and she felt deeply grateful to the Lord for her son. The Lord set her free from her anger and gave her great peace and joy for being blessed with such a good son.

Man Releases Anger toward Ex-Wife

A man came for help with his drinking. He stated that he had begun drinking at about age 13 and he left home at age 15. I shared with him that people who become addicted do so because of underlying emotional issues like anger and grief which make them feel badly, and they look for something to make them feel good, then they become addicted. He told me that he had gone to AA meetings and had completed two inpatient treatment programs but he was a "chronic relapser." I explained that treatment programs are ineffective because they do not know how to help people get rid of their anger, grief, or feelings of shame, and I shared with him how he could get rid of these feelings through simple prayer. After I shared with him how to overcome feelings of anger or grief he said he believed in Jesus Christ and prayer and he was willing to try it.

He told me about his background and he admitted he had feelings of anger toward his abusive father and mother and his ex-wife, and he had eight significant losses that also troubled him. I asked him which of these troubled him the most and he said it was his divorce that bothered him the most. He had been married for 26 years and one year earlier his wife had an affair and left him, and she had refused to let him see his daughter in the last year. He said that his wife had four affairs, took everything he had, began living with another man, and blamed him for the divorce. She also got a restraining order against him, filed false criminal charges against him that led to the revocation of his professional licensure, and destroyed his credit. He identified 17 reasons for his anger toward her then I led him in a prayer and he told the Lord the reasons for his anger and asked the Lord to take his anger and carry it for him.

When we finished praying he prayed, "I give myself to you, Lord." I asked him how he felt and he said he felt better and felt no more anger toward his wife. The next time I saw him he told me that he wrote down some more resentments and regrets and gave them to the Lord and he felt no anger toward his ex-wife. He said, "It's working; my wife and I are talking civilly now. I go out every morning and sit and pray. I'm quite amazed at the situation with my ex-wife... all of a sudden she has completely changed!"

The Lord took away his anger and this led to a dramatic change in his attitude and heart which changed the way his wife responded to him. He also told me that his urges to drink had decreased and he was feeling good. He turned his anger over to God and doors began opening for him in his relationship with God and with his wife!

From Hatred to Feeling Sorry for Ex-Husband

A woman told me she had been married five times and felt a lot of hatred toward her last one. I asked her how she felt when she thought about her last husband and she said, with a calm look on her face, "I'd like to choke him until his very last breath and just before he went unconscious I'd let him go." She was a Christian woman and she said, "I know you're not supposed to hate but I do, because of all the things he did to me." I asked her if she would like to get rid of those feelings of anger and hatred and she said she would, so I asked her why she resented him so much.

She told me how he degraded her verbally by calling her names and insulting her, how he physically abused her and beat her, and how he treated her like a slave and made her wait on him. She said that he did these things in front of their children which scarred them, he lied to her all the time, was ungrateful for all that she did for him, and killed all her cats. He also complained about her cooking, treated her daughter badly, used racist words all the time, and made her pay their bills with her money so that he could buy whatever he wanted with his money. This woman made a list of 20 things she deeply resented about her ex-husband and then I led her in a prayer in which she told the Lord all these things she resented and she became tearful. Then she asked the Lord to take her anger and hatred from her and replace it with His peace.

When we were finished praying I asked her how she felt. She said, "I feel sorry for him because of all the things he missed out on." I asked her if she felt any anger toward him and she said she did not. Most Christians are not as honest as this woman in admitting that she hated her ex- and would like to choke him but she was honest with the Lord about it and then she gave her anger and hatred to Him and He took it and replaced it with His peace.

She Never Wanted a Divorce

A woman told me that when she married her first husband she had a deep desire to remain married forever. Her own mother and father divorced and then she was molested by her stepfather. This was so damaging to her that she was determined to make her marriage work. She met her husband in college and when they got married she got pregnant and had a daughter that died a few days after she was born. This was devastating to her and made her depressed and angry at the doctors. She wanted to leave the home that constantly reminded her of her daughter so her husband reluctantly agreed to move with her to Oklahoma to be near her family. They had a son together and both she and her husband worked to support their young family.

But her husband was unhappy being so far away from his mother and he resented her for it. He also had difficulty holding a job and he lost his job so she supported their family for six months while he looked for a job and played video games during his spare time. He never wanted to spend time with their son so this woman often had to ask him to stop playing his video games and spend time with their son. Then one day she found a pile of job applications he had filled out but had never turned in and she realized that he had not been applying for work at all. This upset her because she was supporting their family with her income while he was just staying home playing video games. They were struggling financially, their bills weren't being paid, and they had no money to buy their son a birthday present, and she found a receipt in his laundry for $60 that he had spent on a video game. She was enraged to realize that she was supporting their entire family while her husband was doing nothing but playing video games and wasting their money on video games when they couldn't pay their bills.

Although she didn't believe in divorce she felt she had no choice but to file for divorce so she could survive and her husband happily returned home to be with his mother. He found a job and began to send her child-support money but he continued to live with his mother. He bought his son a cell phone but rarely called him and as he grew older it hurt her son to see how little interest his father took in him. This woman remarried to a good, responsible man but it made her angry that she was the sole care-giver for their son and that her ex-husband cared more about video games than his family. It also made her angry that he was so irresponsible and immature and could not stand to be away from his mother, and she felt compelled to divorce him.

She identified twelve things she resented about her ex-husband and she prayed and gave these resentments to the Lord, but she still felt some anger. So, we made a list of four more resentments she had toward him: he was still not participating in their son's life, her son was hurt by his father's lack of interest in him, he was still very self-centered, and she couldn't explain to her son why they divorced. She gave these four resentments to the Lord and asked Him to take them from her. After praying this second time I asked her how she felt. She had a pleasant smile come over her face and said, "I have a peaceful feeling; I feel no more anger or frustration." She left feeling peaceful and calm and with no more anger toward her ex-husband.

Man Set Free from Grief over Divorce

At a seminar that I conducted, I asked for a volunteer who had some unresolved grief who would like to experience emotional healing. A man spoke with me during a break and told me that he had been through a divorce a year ago from his wife of 20 years. He wasn't sure if he had any unresolved issues but as we spoke it sounded like there was some grief over the loss of his wife and I asked him if he would be willing to pray in front of the group. He said that he was willing to do this but he was really unsure whether he had anything to pray about.

After lunch we gathered together again and I invited him to come to the front and I gave him a microphone. I asked him what he missed about his wife, and as he began talking he immediately burst into tears, saying how he missed calling her his "China doll." It was obvious that he deeply loved her and missed her, even though he thought he had no unresolved feelings. He slowly began to recall everything that he enjoyed about her such as her beautiful blonde hair, her eyes, her tiny fingers and feet, and her perfume. He talked about her personality characteristics that he missed such as her love for people, the way she loved their children, her cheerfulness, and her encouragement to him spiritually. He said he missed going to church with her, the awesome meals she fixed after church, the ministry they did together, and he enjoyed just sitting with her on the couch and combing her hair. He cried through each of these memories and the audience wept with him, until we had a list of 29 things he missed about his wife.

I then led him in a prayer and he cried through each item he named and then he gave his sadness and grief to the Lord. I prayed and asked the Lord what He wanted this man to know. "It will be okay," he said. I asked him how he felt and he said he felt peaceful and a lot lighter. I probed to see if there was any more grief or sadness and he said there was none; he just felt peaceful and calm! We discussed the session with the audience and answered some questions. The man's pastor was present and he tearfully asked forgiveness for not helping him with his grief. This brought more tears to the eyes of many people. Everyone was "amazed at the greatness of God" (Luke 9:43).

Set Free from Shame, Aloneness, and Hurt

A woman told me that her grown daughter was distancing herself from her and was not answering her texts so she felt unloved and unwanted by her daughter, except when she needed some help with babysitting. I asked her when was the first time she felt unwanted. She said she felt this way when her husband traveled a lot and did not want her to go with him. He became involved with other women and she blamed herself and believed she was not good enough and she felt alone. I prayed for her and asked the Lord what He wanted her to know and she had the thoughts come to her, "I didn't cause the divorce or create the problem. I had no control over my husband." She said she knew it wasn't her fault they got divorced but she still felt bad and felt that she was not good enough. I prayed and asked the Lord to take her to the source and origin of those feelings. She remembered feeling this way with her mother who worked two jobs and as the oldest of four children this woman had to take care of her younger siblings, do all the chores, and prepared dinner for them. Her mother fussed at her a lot and never thanked her for her work. She felt that she could never do enough to please her mom. I prayed and asked the Lord what He wanted her to know about that belief. She said, "Mom was overworked and stressed. I wasn't bad; I was a very good kid. I was good enough."

This eliminated her feeling that she was not good enough but then she said she felt angry at herself. She recognized that her ex-husband had a lot of problems and she felt the Lord had tried to warn her but she chose to ignore His warnings and this made her feel foolish and shameful. I prayed again, asking the Lord for truth about this and the following thoughts came to her mind: "He loves me and wants me to be happy. I'm not foolish or shameful and I'm not alone; my sister, mother, brother, children, and grandchildren all love me." She felt better but remembered feeling very alone and repulsive because her husband treated her so badly that when he came home late at night she often drove to a local store parking lot and slept in the car, then went back home in the morning to awaken and feed her children and go to work. She felt so alone and repulsive as she thought about this so I prayed again and asked the Lord what He wanted her to know. "I allowed my husband to make me feel alone and repulsive, but I wasn't and I'm not. God loved me so much; He gave me the strength to go to school and teach. He was with me; this was my husband's problem, not mine."

After these thoughts she told me that she had no more anger or feelings of shame or repulsiveness. She smiled and said she was very blessed. The Lord took all her feelings of aloneness, shame, and rejection and replaced them with truth and this led her to experience the "peace of God that surpasses comprehension" (Philippians 4:7).

Set Free from 38 Years of Grief after Divorce

I prayed with a man about the loss of his wife through divorce, and the loss of a very close friend. He first talked about his wife and what he missed about her. He said that he missed being with her, talking with her, fishing with her, raising their kids together, and spending the holidays together. He missed her "golden smile," her big brown eyes and beautiful hair, and her love and affection. He identified 15 things he missed about her, then he prayed and asked the Lord to take his grief and sadness from him. After this prayer I asked him how he felt and he said, "I feel happy and thankful to have had her in my life." He also said that he felt calm.

We then talked about a close friend of his who died over 30 years earlier, and we made a list of twelve things he missed about this friend. He prayed and told the Lord what he missed about him, then he asked the Lord to take his grief from him and carry it for him. When I asked him how he felt, afterwards, he said he felt "happiness" and had no more grief or sadness. He even chuckled at the memory of the funny laughter of his friend.

A week later I saw this man again and asked him how he felt now about the loss of his ex-wife and his friend. He said, "That's pretty amazing! Normally I spent my whole day just thinking about her but now I don't. I feel okay." He said that when he previously talked about his other friend he became very tearful and he could barely talk about him, but he said, "Now, I'm not choked up from talking about him!" This man was amazed at how quickly he was able to resolve his grief and how it changed his life so that he was no longer so emotional about these losses.

Set Free from Resentments toward Ex-Wife

I counseled a man whose wife left him unexpectedly after 13 years of marriage and took their daughter from him. He always tried his hardest to be a good husband and father and it broke his heart when she left him with no explanation and tried to keep him from seeing his daughter. He had to pay over $700 per month for child support even when he lost his job due to health problems. In addition to the anger and grief that he felt from this divorce, it was more painful to him that she received primary custody of their daughter and he had so little control over her life. His ex-wife was a poor example to her daughter, allowing boyfriends to stay overnight with her and drinking in front of her. When his daughter received some inappropriate texts from a boy, this man had little power to intervene due to her mother's lack of concern. It was upsetting to him that she always had the last word to say about their daughter.

As we discussed these concerns it became clear that he had a lot of justified anger toward her. I asked him if he would like to get rid of those resentments if he could and he said he would. We made a list of his resentments toward his ex-wife. He said he resented her manipulations and control, her leaving him when he was giving 100% effort in their marriage, her taking their daughter from him and trying to keep him from seeing her, her laziness and making him do the cooking, cleaning, and laundry when they were married, and her show of favoritism to her other two children. We made a list of 18 resentments and then I asked him if he would be willing to tell God these resentments and ask Him to take them from him. He was willing so we prayed and named each resentment and asked the Lord to take them from him. Then, I asked the Lord if there was anything that He wanted this man to know.

"I remember asking God to be there when I couldn't. I have to trust God to be there. God has the last say," he said. "How does that make you feel?" I asked. "No anger. God will take care of it; God won't fail me." I asked him again how he felt and he said, "Peace. I can trust Him and He has already begun to restore my relationship with my children since I've begun releasing my anger and resentments."

Woman Set Free from Hatred of Ex-Husband

I prayed several times with a woman about her anger and disappointment in her son who abused drugs and was repeatedly incarcerated. Each time we prayed she felt more peaceful but a few days later her anger came back when she spoke to him again. I suspected that her anger was rooted in some earlier source so we reviewed her history and identified ten people toward whom she had some unresolved anger. The one that stirred up the most anger was an ex-husband whom she said she hated.

I asked her what she hated about this man so much. She talked about his drug abuse and lying and cheating. He never held a job but he drained her and her mother's bank account, he taught her son to use and sell drugs, and he abused her mentally and physically before she finally left him after ten years together. It especially made her angry that he wasted ten years of her life, he ruined her son's life, and he cheated on her. We made a list of 20 resentments she held toward this man and then I asked her if she would like to get rid of her anger. With some hesitation she said she would and she agreed to let me lead her in a prayer.

She prayed with tears and anger and told the Lord each thing she resented about this man, then she asked the Lord to take her anger and carry it for her. When we were done I asked the Lord if there was anything He wanted her to know. The thoughts that came to her mind were, "I am carrying them for you" and "You are forgiven." Then I asked her what feelings she had while thinking about her ex and she said, "Nothing. No anger or hate. I just feel relieved and calm." I probed several times and reminded her of his infidelity and negative influence on her son to see if there was any anger and there was no sign of any anger. She remained calm and smiled. Five minutes earlier she was very angry and vehemently saying how much she hated this man, but after giving her anger to the Lord her anger was gone.

This was a miracle to see her strong anger leave so quickly. She said that her son reminded her a lot of this man because he had such a negative influence on her son; releasing this anger helped her to respond more calmly to her son's behavior in the future and helped her to be a better mother to him. It is wonderful to see captives set free from anger through the power of prayer and through the Lord when nothing the world offers can do this. Anger management does not work and medications don't set people free from anger.

"I Hate Divorce"

Divorce can be very devastating, and from the stories shared in this chapter it is easy to see that it can lead to anger, hatred, parenting problems, substance abuse, vocational problems, and even criminal behavior. At the very least it can lead to unhappiness and spiritual dullness. As devastating as divorce can be, however, it does not have to cause all these problems. The Lord understands how devastating divorce is to everyone involved, which is why He said in Malachi 2:16 "I hate divorce." He wants to take all of the pain from your divorce and set you free to serve Him.

This does not need to take a long time in therapy or require a commitment to a year of support groups. The Lord can quickly set you free from each negative emotion that you have from a divorce, as you learn to talk with Him about your emotions. From attending a Set Free meeting or reading Set Free literature you can find freedom and peace after your divorce, no matter what happened or no matter how badly your partner treated you. The Lord Jesus said, "Take heart; I have overcome the world" (John 16:33).

It is our hope and prayer that this truth will spread to churches everywhere so that those who are suffering can find help. The secular world cannot help you overcome your grief, shame, or anger, but the Lord can. One of these days it is our hope that you can go to any church to learn how to pray effectively about your emotions and find freedom in Jesus, the "Wonderful Counselor…[and] Prince of Peace" (Isaiah 9:6).

21

DISCIPLESHIP AND PRAYER

In the mental health profession I am accustomed to individuals coming to me for help with their emotional difficulties. People who are going through a divorce, who have had a significant loss, or who are struggling with depression, anxiety, or substance abuse are referred to me by a doctor or their pastor for counseling and I help them identify their feelings and teach them how to overcome their emotional struggles so that they feel better. It is also my goal to teach them how to turn to the Lord for help each time they encounter future problems, because I want them to learn how to directly go to Him for comfort rather than call me each time they need help.

Pastors are the same way; they expect to be called upon in times of struggles but they want their congregational members to learn how to go directly to the Lord for help. No pastor wants his members to call him each time they need prayer; he wants them to learn to have a close relationship with the Lord so that they find their constant comfort in Him. Therefore, he teaches them how to pray, just as the Lord taught his disciples how to pray.

This prayer ministry involves two simple prayer principles that every believer should learn so that they can go directly to the Lord for help rather than go to a professional counselor every time they struggle with their emotions. The goal of a prayer minister in this ministry is to teach others how to pray about their emotions, so that they experience joy and peace, and so that they will develop a close relationship with the Lord. Some clients never try to pray on their own; they simply want to talk to a counselor whenever they are upset and have the counselor solve their problems. My goal is not to be a counselor who solves an individual's emotional problems, but to teach them to turn to the Wonderful Counselor and Prince of Peace whenever they are distressed

GOD'S PURPOSE FOR HEALING

Luke tells the story, in his gospel, of ten lepers who encountered Jesus as He was traveling to Jerusalem. They stood at a distance and cried out to Him to have mercy on them and heal them of their leprosy (Luke 17:11-19). He instructed them to go show themselves to the priest, so they headed to the priest, but on the way there they suddenly found that they were cleansed of their leprosy. One of the ten turned back and went to Jesus and began glorifying God with a loud voice and "he fell on his face at His feet, giving thanks to Him. And he was a Samaritan" (Luke 17:16). Jesus said to him, "Were there not ten cleansed? But the nine—where are they? Was no one found who turned back to give glory to God, except this foreigner?" (Luke 17:17-18).

Jesus was full of compassion and gladly healed many people, but His desire was that the healing would lead the person into a closer, loving relationship with Him. Jesus was not just a miracle worker and His healing was not an end in itself, but He did miracles to lead those who are healed to worship Him and to love Him. The same is true for those who experience emotional healing through prayer. God's desire is that such healing will bring men and women into a close relationship with Him.

The same principle is found in John 6 where Jesus had fed five thousand people with just five loaves and two fish. This great miracle should have led every one of them to believe in Him, but they did not. Some of these people wanted to "take Him by force, to make Him king" (John 6:15), but He withdrew to a mountain to spend some time alone. Then the next day the multitude heard that Jesus had gone to Capernaum and they followed Him there, but their motive was not to follow Him or worship Him. He said, "Truly, truly, I say to you, you seek Me, not because you saw signs, but because you ate of the loaves, and were filled" (John 6:26). His miracles did not lead them to become His disciples; they simply enjoyed seeing miracles and getting a free meal.

The Lord will do miracles in our lives as we pray and cast our cares upon Him, but He does not simply desire to relieve us of our burdens. He wants us to become His fearless followers and live bold, victorious Christian lives that are full of joy and peace. He wants us to learn to "pray without ceasing" (1 Thessalonians 5:17) and to cast all our cares upon Him (1 Peter 5:7) so that He becomes a friend who is closer than a brother (Proverbs 18:24).

The Impact of Answered Prayers

A young man was described in a previous chapter, who said that he didn't believe in God because he considered himself to be a scientific person. I challenged him to do an experiment and try to give his anger to God and ask Him to take it, and see if it happened. The first week he returned and said that it worked because he was no longer angry at his grandfather. The following week I challenged him to give his anger and grief over the loss of his former girlfriend to the Lord and let Him take it. When he returned the following week he said that his anger and grief were gone and he had not thought any more about her. When I asked him what he thought about this, he said that when he saw how quickly his anger and grief left him, this was the physical evidence he needed to know there was a God, and he asked Jesus to forgive him and come into his heart.

People who are skeptical about God or about prayer are impacted when they experience such a dramatic emotional change in their lives, especially when they have held these feelings for a long time or have tried other techniques, such as psychiatric drugs. This young man not only became a believer as a result of answered prayer, but he also said, “Everyone needs to know about this,” and he began volunteering to help promote Set Free Prayer Ministry.

Ready to Go Door-to-Door

Another young man came to me because he was addicted to synthetic marijuana known as K2. His substance abuse began two years earlier after his parents divorced and his grandfather, who was his only good father-figure, died. He also had some feelings of anger and hurt at his rejection by his biological father and his stepfather. I spoke with him about how addictions are caused by unresolved negative emotions such as anger and grief, and I shared with him how to be set free through prayer. Due to lack of time I was unable to actually lead him through a prayer, so I gave him a copy of the grief booklet and encouraged him to pray on his own about the loss of his grandfather.

When I saw him the following week he immediately said that he was doing “a lot better.” He told me that he had made a list of what he missed about his grandfather, and he prayed about it and gave it to God. He said that it felt like God was standing beside him, and he said, “It was weird but it worked.” This young man admitted that he still had some urges to use drugs, so I asked what other negative feelings he needed to work to resolve. He told me that he felt most badly about his biological father, so we talked about him and made a list of what he resented about him.

Together we made a list of nine reasons for his anger and he then told the Lord about this and asked the Lord to carry his anger for him. After this prayer he said he felt unwanted and unloved (feelings of hurt) and he told me that he felt that it was his fault that his parents had separated (feelings of shame). So, I prayed and asked the Lord what He wanted this young man to know. “My mom wants me and loves me,” he said. Then he added, “I know God loves me, too.” I asked him if it still felt true that he was unwanted and unloved and he said, "No, because I still have my mom and stepdad." I asked him what he thought about that and he said, "It's weird. It's kind of funny." He stated that he had no more negative feelings about his biological father. He told me that his mother sometimes told him that he was going to grow up to be like his father and that made him feel bad, so I prayed and asked the Lord what He wanted this young man to know about that. "That's not true," he said. "I know God is helping me." I asked him if it still felt true that it was his fault that his parents separated and he said, "No. I was only six months old. It was the drug's fault."

We then talked about his feelings toward his stepfather whom he said favored his sister and who never spent any time with him. He felt neglected and believed he was not good enough. We made a list of six resentments he had toward the stepfather and prayed about them and gave them to the Lord. I prayed and asked the Lord if there was anything that he wanted this man to know. "No. I heard the word 'No' and I saw the word 'NO' in big white letters," he said. "I'm loved, I'm good enough, I'm okay. I forgive him for that. He was a good guy who took care of us but he just didn't spend time with me. He was not the father-figure that I wanted." I asked him how he felt toward his stepfather and he said that he felt good about him. Then he said, "It's crazy how I feel different every time I pray. It's really weird!"

The following week when he came back he excitedly proclaimed that he was doing "a lot better," had gone to church with a friend, and had not used any more K2. He said that he felt good and calm and he had not had any fights with his mother in a long time because she was no longer "pushing my buttons." He even said that he gave an anger booklet to a friend and that it helped him. He admitted having some anger toward his mother who used to take out her anger on him and had verbally abused him because he resembled his biological father. We prayed about this anger and gave it to the Lord and then I asked him how he felt. "Good; no negative feelings at all. I can see her shaking me (as a child) but I don't feel angry anymore. It feels so weird; I can't wait for Mom to feel this!" I asked him what he thought about this and he said, "It's awesome; I'm spreading the word! You don't need meds; all you need is this little booklet! I feel great!" He asked for some more anger booklets and said "I'll go door-to-door and spread the word!"

He was so excited to see how the Lord had set him free from his anger and given him peace that he became excited about sharing this with others. When people receive emotional healing from the Lord they often become excited about His goodness and His healing and want to spread this to other people.

"You've Got Me Praying Every Morning"

I saw a woman who said she was a preacher's kid but she had not prayed or gone to church for a long time. She was very angry at her husband who had died years earlier, and when I prayed with her about her anger, she released it and felt peaceful and calm. When she came to her next session she told me, "I've been in a different state of mind. I've been so positive. I'm at peace. It feels nice." She told me that every morning she had been closing her eyes and saying a little prayer and that God listens to her. This was a new experience for her in her Christian walk.

As she talked she began to realize that she still had some anger toward her mother. She said that she never felt loved by her, and she stayed at her neighbor's house most of the time to avoid her mother, who was critical of her and who was very dominant over her father. Her mother was always mad at her and this woman felt like she could never please her. Although her mother was elderly, she had never admitted that she mistreated her daughter, and her daughter never felt that her mother loved her. Her mother's doctor told her that she should be forced to walk and not stay in her wheelchair, but when she took away the wheelchair, her mother called Adult Protective Services on her, and this made the woman mad.

She identified nine resentments she had toward her mother, and when I asked her if she wanted to get rid of her anger she tearfully said, "I'm tired of carrying it." She prayed and asked the Lord to take her anger from her and carry it for her, then I prayed and asked the Lord if there was anything that He wanted her to know. She had no thoughts but said, "I love her. I loved her laughter, when she got so tickled. She had some good qualities; she loved my children. I can remember the happy times now." This woman began recalling other good times she had with her mother and said she felt no more anger toward her. She said, "I can see the positive, now." Her peace and smile returned to her and she talked about how excited she was about learning how to pray about her emotions. She said to me, "You've got me praying every morning!"

That's what happens when people learn how to give their bad feelings to the Lord and they begin to hear His voice of comfort, through the Holy Spirit. It gives them peace and joy, and revives their prayer life and their relationship with the Lord. This preacher's kid was angry at her parents and had virtually forsaken her faith but it was revived as she learned to pray about her feelings and discovered that God is truly good.

GOD'S PURPOSES FOR MIRACLES

The Lord performed miracles for a variety of reasons, but there were times that He did no miracles. For example, Matthew tells about the experience of the Lord in his hometown. Matthew 13:58 says, "He did not do many miracles there because of their unbelief." Since the purpose of most miracles was for people to believe in Jesus, when He encountered people who disbelieved He did not do miracles for them. There are other purposes for miracles that also have to do with our response to Jesus.

Getting Us Excited About Him

A woman wrote the following e-mail message to me:

> "I wanted to share my recent Facebook message. This past Monday week my closest dearest friend passed

away. She learned she had terminal cancer in May and was given a prognosis of 6 to 9 months to live. I walked by her side on this journey. We were never sad, but looked at it all as a new adventure. She and I loved each moment of life together. We believed the Lord could heal her at any moment if He chose. We went to a healing service in July as well as many other memorable precious moments together. I've had waves of disappointment, sadness, loss, and even feelings of false beliefs that I let her down. I'll be writing more about the details of each 'wave' that hit me from Monday to Thursday...and there were many."

"My prayer for myself this past week was for Him to give me the clarity of what exact emotion I was having inside the 'wave' so that I could take it straight to Him so He could carry it for me. I'm a walking testimony that grief does not have to take time. It's so amazing and I have such a Peace that is unheard of and not possible from the world's perspective this quickly after such a loss. I'm so on fire about His Power! I've looked death in the face and all the feelings that come after and the Lord has carried them ALL! With Him, ALL things are truly possible! Praise His Mighty Name!"

Bringing Sincere Skeptics to the Lord

I met a woman and her husband who came for help with their marriage and her depression. Her mother had been verbally and physically abusive with her and she had experienced some significant losses. She told me that she used to believe in God but was pretty much an atheist now. I cautiously shared with her that I had found a way to help people get rid of anger, grief, and shame and gave her an example of how a young man was set free from his grief through prayer. I told her that I did not want to offend her or make her uncomfortable since she did not believe in God, but she assured me that she was willing to try prayer if it would help her.

For several sessions we met and prayed about her feelings of anger, grief, and shame, and each time she felt her negative emotions lift from her and she smiled with surprise. Her husband was amazed as he observed this process work for her week after week. When I prayed with her about her anger toward her mother, her husband was even more angry at his mother-in-law than she was, and he got rid of his anger at the same time by praying along with his wife. After several sessions she told me that she was doing really well and her husband agreed that she was doing well. But she was worried about a trip she and her husband had planned, because they were taking her brother-in-law, whom she disliked, and who was critical of her. She said she would like to get rid of her anger toward him, so we made a list of what irritated her about him. She told me that he was jealous of their marriage, he provokes them to get into fights, he loves to argue, and he treats her like she is stupid. She also complained that her brother-in-law interferes with their personal business, tries to tell her what to do, disciplines her dog roughly, and gets "snippy" with her. After identifying eight resentments she had, this woman prayed and told the Lord these resentments and asked Him to take her anger.

After her prayer, I asked her how she felt. She said, "A lot less annoyed with him; he thinks he's helping people. He's a good guy. He came to visit me in the hospital." I asked her if she still felt some anger and she said she felt no more anger or irritation toward him, and she smiled a big smile. I reminded her of how she told me initially that she was an atheist and asked her if this praying had changed her thinking. She told me, "I have completely renewed my faith! If I'm having a problem now, we pray together."

It's wonderful to see how the Lord graciously answers prayers and carries the burdens of unbelievers, and then they begin to believe in God and become strong prayer warriors. Jesus said, "He causes His sun to shine on the evil and the good, and sends rain on the righteous and the unrighteous" (Matt. 5:45). When people see the power of prayer and the goodness of God in setting them free, they begin to seek Him and love Him. Emotional Healing Prayer is a wonderful evangelistic tool because those who experience healing and peace are struck at the goodness of God and often turn to Him afterwards. This is what Paul meant when he said in Romans 2:4 that "the kindness of God leads...to repentance."

Skeptic Becomes Giddy with Joy

A young lady was referred to me for help with her depression. She was reluctant to pray about her issues with me and admitted that she was very skeptical, even though she believed in prayer, because she considered herself a "scientific" person. As we talked about her anxiety she told me about how her father used to yell at her and abused her sister, and this stirred up feelings of anger in her and she became very tearful. I asked her more about her father and she told me that he pushed her when she was pregnant, and how upsetting it was when he abused her sister. He quit a good-paying job and wouldn't work, then he spent all their money on himself so that she had poor clothes and the kids at school teased her about her clothes. When she began working to earn money he began stealing money from her. In addition, he screamed at her, cussed at her, and said hateful things to her every day and mistreated his mother, who was taking care of her. While talking about these things she became very tearful and upset, but I listened calmly and encouraged her to keep talking.

After identifying twenty-two resentments she had, I asked her if she would like to get rid of her anger and she said that she would. So I led her in a prayer, and she tearfully told the Lord how angry she was at her father, then she asked Him to take her anger from her and carry it for her. I prayed and asked the Lord what He wanted her to know. She sat quietly for a while and wiped away her tears, and I asked her if any thoughts came into her mind. She said,

"I'm loved by my teachers, my grandparents, my sisters, and by the church members." I asked her how she felt and she said, "A sense of peace; I can talk now; I'm not choked up." I asked her to think about her father and tell me how she felt toward him and she said that she had no more anger toward her father. She said, "I feel bad for him now. He probably went through the same things I did; it doesn't excuse what he did, but I feel sorry for him."

"What do you think about that?" I asked. "I was skeptical," she replied, "because I'm a scientific person, but I'm calm now and I have this giddiness inside me," she laughed. "I can breathe easily, now. I feel looser and happier." She talked for a while and all her tears and sadness were gone, and she was still beaming with joy when she left my office. The Lord took her justified anger toward her father and replaced it with peace!

Skeptic Astounded by Healing

A large, burly man came to me who was referred by the courts for anger management and domestic violence classes. I gathered background information from him and learned that he came from an abusive home where he was emotionally and physically abused by his father, mother, and brother, and he was bullied by his peers in grade school. Then when he was eleven years old his favorite uncle, who loved him and spoiled him, died, and at age 16 a close cousin died. As he grew larger and older his anger increased and he began to bully the bullies in middle school and high school. At age 19 his best friend died, and this further traumatized him and led to more emotional pain and anger. He lost four other close relatives and friends and with each loss his rage increased.

During the first session I did not have time to share with this man how he could be set free, so when he returned the following week with his wife I began to share with him how he could find release from his anger and grief through prayer. I assured them that if they were uncomfortable with praying I would not mention it again. His wife immediately said she was comfortable with it, but this man was not sure. He told me that he had been baptized at age 18, but when his best friend died at age 19 he turned away from God and he considered himself an agnostic now. I asked him, if I could show him how to get rid of his anger or grief through prayer would he consider that there might be a God, and he immediately said, "Yes."

We talked about his grief over the loss of his favorite uncle at age 11 and made a list of 12 things he missed about him. He didn't show much emotion while talking about his uncle so I asked him how he felt. He told me that he felt like crying. I then led him in a prayer and he told the Lord how he missed spending time with his uncle, being spoiled by him, laughing and having fun with him, playing cards with him, and just being with him. We prayed and asked the Lord to take those feelings of sadness and grief from him, and I asked the Lord if there was anything he wanted him to know. He sat silently for a minute then said, "It'll be alright." I asked him if that felt true and he said it did. "How do you feel now?" I asked. "A big burden's been lifted. He wouldn't want me to be sad. I feel at peace about it now. I feel happy!"

I instructed this man to think about his uncle and try to stir up any negative feelings, and as he did so he said that he felt a little sad because he still missed his uncle's smile and laughter. I prayed with him again about these two things and asked the Lord to take his sadness from him. Afterwards, I asked him again how he felt and he said, "I don't feel any sadness; it's gone." He was astounded, and his wife said it was like "magic." I told them that I believed it was truly a miracle and this man, who was an acknowledged skeptic and agnostic a few minutes earlier, agreed that it was a miracle. I asked him if he was comfortable with this prayer process and he told me adamantly that he was; he was eager to return for more healing. The following week when I met with him, he told me that he had prayed about three more losses on his own and had been set free!

What a privilege we have to use prayer to bring healing and hope to people like this. When you try everything the world has to offer and nothing helps and then the Lord sets you free, you get excited about the Lord! You have to share it with other people. What a tool this is for emotional healing, evangelism, and discipleship to lead people to the Lord or to bring them closer to Him through prayer!

Muslim Man says "It works!"

I met a young Arabic man at an athletic club and asked him if he was a Muslim. He said that he was but that he was going to a Christian church to learn about Christianity, and he was involved in a Bible study at work with some of his employees. I had studied Islam, so I asked if he knew the two major differences between Christianity and Islam. I explained that the two biggest differences were that Christians believe God loves everyone, and that it is possible to be 100% sure of their salvation. Islam is very legalistic and has many rules to follow, so no one can know for sure that they are going to heaven, and the god of Islam does not love the infidels.

Several weeks later he told me about a co-worker who had lost his father and was grieving, and I asked him if he had ever lost anyone close to him. He said that he had lost his wife three months earlier; he admitted that he missed her and tried to stay busy so he would not think about her. I told him that I could show him how to get rid of his grief and sadness through prayer. He was very interested but not ready, yet. Then one day we went to play racquetball and the courts were closed so I suggested that we go to McDonald's and talk about Islam or pray about his wife. He said that he didn't want to talk about her but when we sat down he began talking about his wife and his father and his anger at both of them.

He told me that his wife had a seizure disorder and deliberately neglected her health because she could not give him children. She was very jealous of him, she was more loyal to her parents than to him, and he felt suffocated and embarrassed by her. He identified 22 things he resented about her and I wrote these on a napkin, then I led him in a prayer and he gave his anger to the Lord. Afterwards he said he felt at peace. Then we talked about his father and he identified 15 things that he resented about him, and I led him in a prayer and he gave this anger to the Lord. Afterwards, he said he felt grateful for his father and he felt good and had no anger. He exclaimed, "This works! I'm not angry. I feel cool." The following morning at 6:30 am he texted me and said, "Sir, the thing works! I woke up happy!"

This man moved away before I had a chance to lead him to the Lord but He was more receptive to the Lord after experiencing healing of his anger and grief. I trust the Lord to continue to work in his heart and life through other believers, to draw this man to Him by showing His continuing kindness and grace to him.

Learning that He is Always with Us and is our Best Friend

A woman came for help with her depression which she had had for over twenty years. She was not close to her mother, but was very close to her grandfather until he had died seven years earlier. He was a good Christian man and a leader in his church, and she missed spending time with him, going to church with him, and seeing him up front in the church singing in the choir. I explained to this woman that most depression is caused by grief, and I explained how she could be set free from her grief by being completely honest about her grief and giving it to the Lord. When I asked her what she missed about her grandpa, she said she missed his wisdom and getting advice from him, and talking with him about the Bible. She said that she missed hearing him tell her that he loved her, sitting with him on his porch and talking, helping him feed the cattle, and riding to town with him in his truck. She also missed seeing his smile, hearing him joking around and kidding her, and seeing his gray hair, his Dicky pants, and the long-sleeved shirts he always wore.

After she identified twenty things she missed about him, I asked her if she would be willing to say a short prayer and tell the Lord these things, then ask the Lord to take her grief from her. She said that she would so I led her in a prayer and she gave her grief to

Him. After the prayer I asked her how she felt as she thought about her grandpa. She told me that she only had happy memories and no longer felt any sadness, but she said, "I wish I had someone to talk to for direction." I prayed for her and asked the Lord what He wanted her to know. She smiled and said, "I can go to God and talk to Him. He can be my best friend. God loves me." I didn't have to say a word. These thoughts filled her with joy and comfort.

She not only got rid of her grief and sadness but also came to realize the truth that Jesus was now her new best friend and she could always talk to Him and get her advice from Him. The classic hymn, "What a friend we have in Jesus" describes this sentiment well. Jesus was called "the friend of sinners" (Matthew 11:19). The Lord desires each of us to learn to talk to Him at all times and to learn to talk with Him about our feelings. One result of developing such an intimate relationship with the Lord is that we learn to "pray without ceasing," which the apostle Paul instructed the believers in Thessalonica 5:17.

SANCTIFICATION AND PRAYER

Being Saved and Set Free

In Chapter 18 we discussed the concept and doctrine of sanctification, which is the doctrine pertaining to how a believer can progressively become more like Jesus and less controlled by sin. It is important for every believer to understand the difference between being saved and being set free. Many people are genuinely saved; they have sincerely confessed their sins and asked the Lord to forgive them and enable them to live for Him. But they continue to sin, because the Bible tells us that we still have a sinful nature within us that leads us to be selfish and to do things that harm ourselves or others.

Some sin is the result of simple selfishness and self-centeredness, but many sinful behaviors and compulsions are the result of negative feelings that lead individuals to do things that make them feel better. Simply praying about these feelings in a generic way or studying the Bible and memorizing it does not make these feelings stop. But the Lord can set us free from those troubling emotions as we learn to pray about our feelings and give them to the Lord, or receive truth that sets us free from them.

I suggested in that chapter that there are four critical components to the sanctification process. First, the individual needs to maintain a close walk with the Lord through reading the Word, prayer, and fellowship with other believers. Second, believers need to learn to pray effectively about their emotions and to cast all their cares upon Him. Third, believers must learn to "walk in the Spirit" and pray for truth to enable them to experience the peace of God in their daily lives. As they do this, the Lord promises to bring them truth to set them free of their negative emotions. Fourth, as believers learn to do these three things habitually and daily, they will manifest the fruits of the Spirit, first by experiencing the emotions of love, joy, and peace, and then by developing the character qualities of patience, kindness, gentleness, goodness, faithfulness, and self-control.

Through the process of praying about our emotions and learning to walk in the Spirit, we come to enjoy God's peace and we develop a desire to share the good news with unbelievers. As we learn to "abide in Him" and "walk in the Spirit" we will enjoy more and more of the fruits of the Spirit, and we will be set free from bondage to those compulsive sins that disturb us as believers.

Struggling with Sin: "I Thought I Had Changed"

In Chapter 18 I shared about a man who came for counseling shortly after being released from prison where he said he had given his life to Jesus. He studied the Bible, took Bible correspondence courses, and took every class available in his effort to break free from his past, but the first day that he was free he fell into sin, and was devastated because he thought he had changed. He told me very candidly about his past, how he had been molested several times as a child, and had been beaten violently by his father and hurt by women, and in spite of his sincere desire to follow Jesus he was struggling with feelings of anxiety, guilt, anger, and shame. He told me that it was causing him to doubt his faith, and he pleaded for help.

Many people, like this man, struggle with sinful urges and are overwhelmed with their emotions, even after they have genuinely received Jesus as their Savior and dedicated their lives to following Him. We talked about his anger toward his abusive father, and he was able to release it and then he felt love for his father.

He began to smile as he talked about his freedom from his anger toward his father. He commented about how simple it was, and he was filled with hope that he could be set free from his past and his emotional bondage through Jesus and prayer.

Many believers struggle with sin, like this man, and turn to the church and to their spiritual leaders but find no help from them, and they begin having doubts about their own salvation. Sometimes they are referred to mental health professionals who tell them that they have a brain disorder or chemical imbalance and they need to be on psychiatric medications. But the Lord is the Wonderful Counselor, and He heals broken hearts and sets the captives free as they learn to cast all their cares upon Him and turn to Him for truth to set them free. The apostle Paul said, "Who will set me free from the body of this death? Thanks be to God through Jesus Christ our Lord!" (Romans 7:24, 25).

The Bible is God's Word and is given to believers so that "the man of God may be adequate, equipped for every good work" (2 Timothy 3:16). We must study the Bible diligently and know it thoroughly so that the Lord can guide us through it, but this does not mean that we can neglect prayer or the ministry of the Holy Spirit. The Bible teaches us about the importance of prayer, telling us to "pray without ceasing" (1 Thessalonians 5:17) and "devote yourselves to prayer" (Colossians 4:2) so believers must learn to pray, in addition to studying their Bible. Likewise, the Bible teaches us that we must learn to "walk by the Spirit" because the apostle Paul instructed us in God's Word, "walk by the Spirit, and you will not fulfill the desires of the flesh" (Galatians 5:16).

Just as prayer is essential to discipleship and sanctification, so too, walking by the Spirit and hearing from the Holy Spirit are essential components of discipleship. Many believers believe in the importance of the Bible in the growth and walk of the believer, but they ignore the role of the Holy Spirit and deny that the Holy Spirit can guide us into the truth in any way other than through reading the Bible. For many believers the Trinity consists of God the Father, God the Son, and God the Holy Bible. Although they profess to believe in the Holy Spirit they do not allow the Holy Spirit to teach them, other than through reading the Word. Prayer and guidance by the Holy Spirit, as taught in this ministry, are also essential tools that the Lord has provided the believer for gaining victory over sin in their lives.

As believers learn to pray about their emotions, give their fact-based emotions to the Lord and pray for truth about the underlying lies they believe that cause their belief-based emotions, they will experience peace and joy in their lives. And as believers experience joy and peace in their lives they will have more love for others, and the other six fruits of the Spirit will progressively grow and become manifested in their lives.

"I Want to be Happy Again"

A woman told me, "I'm a Christian... I'm a disciple of Jesus Christ" but she said she had been depressed and taking antidepressants for over 30 years. She said, "I used to think you won't get depressed if you're a Christian" and "I didn't believe in mental illness until I got depressed." I asked questions about her background and how her depression began and learned that her mother-in-law had died when she was 29 years old, and then a baby niece died a year later when she was pregnant with her daughter, and this is when her depression began. She told me that her doctor said she had post-partem depression, but I explained that 87% of all depression is rooted in losses, and that her depression was probably connected to these losses. Then I explained how she could resolve her losses and she became hopeful and said, "I want to be normal and enjoy things I used to enjoy. I want to be happy again."

She said that her greatest sadness at this time was about her mother who had died three years before. She told me that her mother was her closest friend and she missed talking with her all the time, taking care of her, and visiting her in the nursing home. She also missed her sound advice, her encouragement, her positive attitude, her laughter and joking with her at the kitchen table, and her sense of humor. We made a list of fifteen things she missed about her mother, and then we prayed, and she told the Lord what she missed about her, then asked Him to take her grief and carry it for her. I prayed again and asked the Lord if there was anything that He wanted her to know, and the only thought that came to her mind was, "She doesn't have to struggle to breathe anymore." "So, how do you feel now as you think about your mother," I asked. She said, "I do feel peaceful." I encouraged her to try to stir up her sadness and grief and she tried but said again, "I do feel better." She said she had no sadness or grief.

I asked her what she thought about this and she said, "It's so simple; it's amazing to know the Bible teaches us to give everything to Him. I really am hopeful." This woman had felt hopeless about her depression for 30 years and never thought she would feel good or be happy again, but after experiencing peace about the loss of her mother she felt hopeful and happy again. As she continued to pray about her other losses her depression went away and she was able to feel normal again. It's sad that so many Christians live with depression like this woman and have believed the lies of the enemy that there is no hope because, like her, they were told by their doctors that they had a chemical imbalance.

What this woman experienced is the natural response to having a life-changing encounter with the Lord. We can see that same response from the woman that Jesus met at the well in John 4:39-42.

After her encounter with the Lord she was excited and ran back to town to tell everyone about Him. John 4: 39 says, "From that city many of the Samaritans believed in Him because of the word of the woman." In Luke 8:38-39 the demoniac whom Jesus delivered from bondage begged Jesus to accompany Him but Jesus sent him away saying, "'Return to your house and describe what great things God has done for you.' And he went away, proclaiming throughout the whole city what great things Jesus had done for him."

THE THEOLOGY OF EMOTIONS AND DISCIPLESHIP

The Discipleship of Jesus

When Jesus chose the twelve disciples, He taught them for three years to prepare them for their mission of spreading the gospel throughout the world after His departure. He repeatedly instructed them to follow His example and to be like Him, and He warned them to expect persecution. In His final hours before His crucifixion, He taught them many important things, such as their need to love one another, to take up their cross and follow Him, and to pray at all times.

A critical part of the discipleship training that Jesus provided His disciples was teaching them how to pray about their emotions and to cast their cares upon Him. Consider the following statements that He made to them. "Come to Me, all who are weary and heavy-laden, and I will give you rest...for My yoke is easy and My burden is light" (Matthew 11:28-29). In this Scripture He taught them to cast all their burdens upon Him so they could experience His peace. He illustrated this same lesson in Mark 4:39 (KJV) when He calmed the storm by commanding the winds, "Peace, be still." In the Sermon on the Mount He taught them not to be anxious but to trust in God. He said, "Do not be anxious, then, saying 'What shall we eat?'" (Matthew 6:31).

John 14-17 records the intimate conversations that He had with His disciples in the hours just prior to His arrest and crucifixion. In John 14:27 He said, "Peace I leave with you; My peace I give to you; not as the world gives do I give to you. Let not your heart be troubled, nor let it be fearful." He was teaching His disciples that it was His desire for them to experience God's peace and not to be agitated or fearful. In John 15:11 He told them that He desired them to have joy in their heart, when He said, "These things I have spoken to you, that My joy may be in you, and that your joy may be made full." Taking these two Scriptures together Jesus taught His disciples that they could have peace and joy, regardless of their circumstances. Again, in John 16:22 Jesus said, "You too now have sorrow; but I will see you again, and your heart will rejoice, and no one takes your joy away from you."

Jesus comforted His disciples in John 16:33 by saying, "These things I have spoken to you, that in Me you may have peace. In the world you have tribulation, but take courage; I have overcome the world." He gave His disciples no rosy picture of the life that would be theirs as His followers; He told them that they would experience tribulation, but He assures them that they can overcome it just as He did. When Jesus prayed to the Heavenly Father in John 17:13 He once again told them that in spite of the persecution and tribulation they would have, they could have His joy. He said, "These things I speak in the world, that they may have My joy made full in themselves."

Teachings about the Comforter Holy Spirit

Not only did Jesus promise His disciples that they could have joy and peace, but He indicated repeatedly that this would occur as a result of the work of the Holy Spirit in their lives. In John 14:16-18 He said, "I will ask the Father, and He will give you another Helper, that He may be with you forever; that is the Spirit of truth… I will not leave you as orphans." The Holy Spirit, He indicated would be our "Helper" and this word is translated as "Comforter" in the King James Version, which gives a slightly different emphasis to the role of the Holy Spirit in our lives.

In addition, Jesus said that the Holy Spirit would teach us all things that we need to know: "But the Helper, the Holy Spirit, whom the Father will send in My name, He will teach you all things, and bring to your remembrance all that I said to you." (John 14:26). He further affirmed this ministry of the Holy Spirit in John 16:13, where He said, "But when He, the Spirit of truth, comes, He will guide you into all the truth, for He will not speak on His own initiative, but whatever He hears, He will speak; and He will disclose to you what is to come." The Spirit, we are told, will guide us into all the truth, which presumably is one way that He gives us comfort in times of tribulations.

This teaching about the Holy Spirit is so vital to the believer that Jesus told the apostles, "Because I have said these things to you, sorrow has filled your heart. But I tell you the truth, it is to your advantage that I go away; for if I do not go away, the Helper shall not come to you; but if I go, I will send Him to you." (John 16:4-7). It was probably inconceivable to the disciples that it was actually beneficial for the Lord to leave them, because they enjoyed His physical presence to teach them, to demonstrate how to respond to their enemies and their difficulties, and to comfort them. Little did they realize that the same comfort would be available to them through the Holy Spirit after Jesus ascended to glory.

Teachings about Discipleship

Jesus taught many things about discipleship. In John 15:5 and 8 Jesus said, "He who abides in Me, and I in him, he bears much fruit; for apart from Me you can do nothing... By this is My Father glorified, that you bear much fruit, and so prove to be My disciples." He indicated by these words that His desire for His disciples is for them to be productive, to lead others to become His disciples. He spoke in Luke chapter 8 and Matthew chapter 13 of the good seeds that "Produced a crop a hundred times as great" (Luke 8:8). These are believers who are fruitful and who bring many others into the kingdom of God.

In the "parable of the sower" Jesus spoke of a sower who went out to sow some seed. He said that some of the seeds fell beside the road and were "trampled underfoot, and the birds of the air ate it up (Luke 8:5). He explained that these seeds represent those who hear the word of God but "then the devil comes and takes away the word from their heart, so that they may not believe and be saved." (Luke 8:12). These seeds represent individuals who were never saved. Second, Jesus said that some seeds fell on "rocky soil" and they "grew up" but withered away because they "had no moisture" (Luke 8:6). Jesus explained that these seeds represent individuals who "receive the word with joy… but "have no firm root; they believe for a while, and in time of temptation fall away" (Luke 8:13). The commentary of Jesus found in Matthew 13:21 says that " this is the man who hears the word, and immediately receives it with joy; yet he has no firm root in himself, but is only temporary, and when affliction or persecution arises because of the word, immediately he falls away." This seed represents those who fall away and are unproductive due to trials, afflictions, and persecution.

Then, there were seeds that fell among thorns "and the thorns grew up with it, and choked it out" (Luke 8:7). Jesus explained in Luke 8:14 that "these are the ones who have heard, and as they go on their way they are choked with worries and riches and pleasures of this life, and bring no fruit to maturity." These believers become distracted with pleasures and riches and never produce any fruit for the Lord. Finally, there were seeds that fell in the good soil (verse 8), and these are the ones who have heard the word in an honest and good heart, and hold it fast, and bear fruit with perseverance" (Luke 8:15). Jesus describes them as seeds that "produced a crop a hundred times as great" (Luke 8:8). This is His desire for His disciples, that they become fruitful and reproduce themselves spiritually and lead many others into His kingdom, producing "a crop a hundred times as great."

There are many other important principles that Jesus taught His disciples that we should teach disciples today. For example in Luke 6:27-28 Jesus taught us how to respond to our enemies: "Love your enemies; do good to those who hate you, bless those who hurt you, and pray for those who mistreat you." He taught in Matthew 6:14 that we should forgive others who offend us. He said, "If you forgive men for their transgressions, your heavenly Father will also forgive you."

The apostle Paul taught his disciples the same principles. In Ephesians 4:26-27 he wrote, "Be angry, and yet do not sin; do not let the sun go down on your anger, and do not give the devil an opportunity." This is a vital principle that must be taught all believers to enable them to live productive, fruitful lives. He wrote to Timothy, a young man who traveled with him on his missionary journeys, 2 Tim. 2:2, "The things which you have heard from me in the presence of many witnesses, these entrust to faithful men, who will be able to teach others also." In other words, Paul is teaching him to pass on his teachings to those whom they are discipling in the Lord.

Praying without Ceasing

In this program we emphasize the need for three critical pledges. Chapter 6 discussed the importance of making the pledge to "not let the sun go down on your anger" (Ephesians 4:26). This is the first and most important pledge for a believer, because anger is the greatest hindrance to spiritual maturity. This pledge is probably the greatest single factor in producing emotional and spiritual health and in having good relationships. The second pledge, discussed in Chapter 7 was to "not grieve as the rest who have no hope" (1 Thessalonians 4:13). Grief is another very significant hindrance to spiritual health and those who have had significant losses often turn from the Lord and become depressed and unproductive in their lives. In Chapter 12 a third pledge was presented, namely to "not let your heart be agitated" (John 14:1). The importance of this pledge lies in the fact that shame and fear are forms of "agitation" that destroy many lives. Believers must know how to identify and resolve their shame, and fear to prevent the enemy from destroying them.

This chapter has focused on the critical need of the believer learning to "pray without ceasing." Believers need to study the Word of God diligently, but they also need to learn to pray intimately with the Lord and learn to pray about their emotions. Believers are urged to make a commitment to learn to "pray without ceasing" by making it their constant practice to talk with the Lord throughout the day, sharing their thoughts and feelings with Him, as they would a close friend. This practice is also critical for the spiritual growth of the believer and for spiritual fruitfulness in their lives.

Prayer makes the difference between intellectual Christianity and passionate Christianity. The Lord wants us to be passionate about Him and this cannot happen until we learn how to talk with Him as we would our closest friend. This commitment is necessary for believers to be able to experience this type of closeness to the Lord and this type of excitement about Him.

Conclusions

Learning to have joy and peace is a critical part of discipleship, because when we do not have joy and peace, we are weak and it gives the devil an opportunity in our lives. As believers encounter trials and afflictions they can "wither away" by the scorching heat of the sun and be unfruitful. Jesus taught us to cast our cares upon Him and to give Him our emotional burdens so He can carry them for us.

He also taught us to receive comfort from the Holy Spirit as He speaks truth to us to give us His peace. There is no other effective way to resolve belief-based emotions like fear and shame, and these emotions can destroy us. As we learn to identify the source of our fear or shame, identify the underlying lies we believe, and then pray for truth, the Holy Spirit will guide us into truth and set us free from our fear and shame.

We must have peace in our hearts in order to be disciples of Jesus. If we do not teach disciples how to pray about their emotions, they will experience defeat and be unfruitful, because the worries, cares, and trials of life will choke out their spiritual life. On the other hand, as we learn to trade our emotional pain for peace, we will be full of joy and love and be fruitful in our lives, leading many others to salvation.

22

SPREADING THE GOOD NEWS

Several years ago I bought a new laptop computer at Best Buy and when I got it home I found that it had some problems, so I returned to the store and exchanged it for another one. While I was standing at the Geek Squad counter I was wearing my jade "Set Free" shirt and I decided this was a divinely arranged opportunity to speak with the computer tech who was waiting on me. He was a large man with several body piercings, which I have found are often indicative of feelings of anger or shame, and I asked him if he knew anyone who had any anger or grief.

He looked at me and I explained that I had learned a way to help people with grief and anger, and I offered him booklets entitled "Overcoming Anger" and "Overcoming Grief." I told him that I had been a mental health counselor for 25 years and had never found anything that helped people with anger or grief until I learned a simple prayer process for healing them. He looked interested and then told me that his mother-in-law was a psychologist and he admitted that he did have anger issues. He said he would read the booklets and try them.

When I got home with the second computer I found that it also had some problems and was not working properly so I returned it. I saw the same tech as before and asked him if he had read the anger booklet. He said, "Yes, I did, and it worked. I have had anger for a long time and this really worked. Everyone needs to learn about this." I decided to upgrade to a better computer and he helped me with the transaction.

I had several more occasions to return to Best Buy due to computer problems and spoke with this man each time. He told me that he had made copies of the anger and grief booklets to give to his neighbors, so I provided him a supply of the booklets to share with others. He was so excited to get healing that he wanted to share it with others, and I get excited too each time I see someone get set free, so that I keep sharing it with people. Now I look for these "divine encounters" each day to share about the Lord with other and to share how they can find healing for their emotions.

Sharing the Good News

Growing up I witnessed my father sharing the gospel with people everywhere he went. He became a Christian as a young adult and was so excited about the message of salvation by faith that he began sharing his faith immediately, like the apostle Paul did after his conversion. My father did not consider evangelism to be a chore or obligation but a privilege. His life was radically transformed and he was excited about salvation by faith, so it was very easy for him to share it. To him it was like giving away candy to people. He carried gospel tracts with him everywhere he went and he never passed up an opportunity to share the gospel. I accompanied him on some occasions when he did some street evangelism and I helped pass out tracts, but I was embarrassed and self-conscious. When I became a believer at age 8, I knew that I should share the gospel with others but I was extremely shy and found it frightening. My life had not been radically transformed at age 8, so I only occasionally made awkward attempts to share the gospel with my friends.

As an adult I overcame my shyness and began sharing the gospel with confidence and peace. But I did not share it with the passion of my father and others like him who had an evangelistic heart. That passion which was seen in the apostle Paul and drove him to evangelize the entire Middle Eastern area, usually comes from radical life transformations. My sheltered life from growing up in a Christian home did not create in me the excitement that comes from a radical transformation.

Since I began using the prayer principles of this ministry, however, I have become very excited about sharing with people how they can have peace in their heart. Having studied psychology and counseling for nine years, and having worked for twenty-five years as a professional counselor seeing very meager results, I became excited as I saw how simply people could be helped with their emotional issues through prayer. Now that I see so many people set free so quickly through the use of simple prayer principles, and I see people who have learned this ministry also helping individuals with serious emotional problems, I get excited about sharing these simple, life-transforming principles. I have also had many encounters with people in public places and been able to share with them how to pray about their emotions.

Everywhere I go I realize that there are people who struggle with depression, grief, anger, divorce and other emotional issues, and I enjoy talking with people and sharing this with them. Getting people to pray and to receive emotional healing is a wonderful step toward talking with them about the Lord, or toward renewing their faith. It is my prayer and hope that through this ministry many others will become excited about their faith and begin sharing it on a daily basis with those they encounter at work, in their families, in their churches, in their neighborhoods, and in their daily, random encounters.

Overcoming Doubts about Salvation

Set Free Prayer Ministry is an evangelistic ministry as well as a prayer and discipleship ministry. We believe in the doctrine of salvation by faith alone, apart from works, as proclaimed throughout the New Testament through the words of Jesus (John 3:16) and through the writings of the apostle Paul who proclaimed, "By grace are ye saved, through faith, and that not of yourselves; it is the gift of God; not of works, lest any man should boast" (Ephesians 2:8-9 KJV). We participate in jail and prison ministry, homeless ministries, substance abuse ministry, and we partner with other organizations reaching out to needy individuals. Our goals are to help people come to salvation, and learn how to be set free from their emotional bondage so that they will become productive, fruitful believers who will spread the gospel to others.

One of the tools that we use in Set Free Prayer Ministry to share the gospel is a small booklet called "Overcoming Doubts about Salvation." This booklet is basically designed after the "Four Spiritual Laws" of Campus Crusade for Christ, but leads off with the question, "Are you 100% sure that you are going to heaven when you die?" We like to lead off with this question because so many individuals claim to be Christians who are depending upon their works to get them to heaven, and because many believers are insecure about their salvation due to their lack of a victorious life.

Using this booklet we begin the conversation with others by asking, "Are you 100% sure that you are going to heaven when you die?" If the person says he/she is, then we will ask them what makes them so certain, and see if he/she is basing their hope upon their good works or upon their faith. If he/she is not confident of salvation or is basing their hopes upon their works, then we ask, "Would you like to be 100% sure that you are going to heaven?" If they say they would then we share the following four principles with them.

The first principle is that God loves them and wants them to go to heaven when they die, because He says in the Bible that "He is not willing that any should perish but that all should come to repentance" (2 Peter 3:9) and "He desires all men to be saved and to come to a knowledge of the truth" (1 Timothy 2:4). The second principle we share is that every man is sinful and condemned to judgment in hell, based upon Romans 3:23 that says "all have sinned and fallen short of the glory of God." The third principle is that Jesus died for our sins so that we can be forgiven for our sins and go to heaven. John 3:16 says "For God so loved the world that He gave His only begotten Son, that whoever believes in Him shall not perish, but have everlasting life." Then, finally, we share the fourth principle that there is only one thing they have to do to have eternal life; receive Him by faith as payment of sins, confess their sins to Him and ask for forgiveness. Whoever believes in Him is forgiven for their sins and given eternal life "by grace through faith, apart from any works" (Ephesians 2:8-9) and will never face condemnation.

Our goal is not to simply bring miraculous healing of emotional struggles in people, but to see them drawn to the Lord and to a life of continual dependence upon Him, and love for Him. We have seen that as people get healing they are persuaded that prayer works and that they need the Lord. If they are unbelievers who have struggled with anger, grief, shame, or any other emotional struggle, they are often drawn to prayer, return to church, and come to salvation after receiving relief from some emotion that they have struggled with for a long time. The person may not be receptive to the gospel immediately after their first emotional healing, but usually it leads them to begin praying and later they receive the Lord for salvation. This is our goal with Set Free Prayer Ministry, and to help believers get excited about the Lord, grow strong in their faith, and lose their fear of sharing their faith.

DIVINE ENCOUNTERS

Set Free at McDonald's

There are hurting people everywhere we go, so I look for opportunities to share the Set Free message wherever I go. I was invited to Mississippi to meet with some Choctaw Indians who were making a new, modern translation of the Bible into Choctaw. They were interested in hearing how this prayer ministry might help their people overcome emotional traumas. The hotel where I stayed did not have a very good breakfast, but I tried to be friendly to one of the hotel staff members who asked if I was there on business or pleasure. I explained that I was in town to meet with a group to talk with them about the Set Free Prayer Ministry and to teach them how to be set free from anger and grief and shame. This woman was very interested in this and I gave her an Anger booklet and gave a brief explanation of how to get rid of anger. She said that she would read it and make copies of it for her staff also. I gave her some additional copies of the Anger and Grief booklets for her staff and we had several more brief discussions later that morning. I was excited to have already ministered to someone by 7:00 am.

Then I went to a nearby McDonald's to eat and to read my Bible. While reading I wondered if we were still in the same time zone that I came from, so when a gentleman sitting nearby got up I asked him for the time. He told me the time then said, "I noticed you are reading the Bible." He told me that he reads the Bible also and we began talking. I explained that I was there to meet with some people and tell them about Set Free Prayer Ministry and he was very interested in hearing about it. He told me that he lost his wife, his job, his house, his land and his dog three years ago and the Lord had told him that He wanted to use him to help others. I offered to pray with him about his wife if he wanted help and he said he would like that, so we moved to a private area of the restaurant.

I asked what he missed about his wife and he told me that he missed her companionship, her laughter, her cooking, her love and affection, doing things with her, hearing her voice, her encouragement, and just sitting with her and talking. He listed 19 things he missed about her, then we prayed and named each of these things and he asked the Lord to take his grief from him. When I asked him how he felt afterwards, he said he felt sad. This is very common for people once they release their grief, to find that they also have some sadness, so I asked him what made him feel sad. He told me that he believed someone killed her by a blow to her head and he knew the person who probably did it, who later died, also. He was also sad because she died so young, at age 49, and her children treated her badly, and she would never get to see them get married.

We then prayed about this sadness and gave it to the Lord. I asked him again how he felt and he said, "I'm happy where she is; she's in heaven." He said that he felt no more sadness or grief; he just felt "peaceful and calm." Then he added, "I feel like a burden's been taken off."

He began smiling and thanked me for praying with him and said, "This was not just an accident that we met here. The Lord arranged this." He said that he attended a Baptist church and he felt the Lord wanted to use him to minister to others, perhaps to share this prayer ministry with others in the area. I left excited that I had ministered to two people before 7:30 am and hadn't even met my Choctaw group yet. It's exciting to be used by the Lord and to see His hand working and opening doors to the ministry. There are hurting people everywhere to minister to as we open our eyes to see them and take advantage of the divine encounters the Lord provides for us.

Set Free at Airport Shop

I wandered around an airport, early one morning, while waiting for my flight to take off. It was very early and there were very few people in the airport at that time of day so I went to several shops in the airport, just window shopping. A young lady in one shop asked me if she could help me and I told her that I was just browsing. Then it occurred to me that this might be a divine encounter since there were no other customers in the store to distract her, so I took a grief booklet out of my pocket and asked her if she knew anyone that was struggling with grief or depression. She said that she lost a sister when she was younger and she said that was very difficult for her. I shared with her that she could get rid of her grief by making a list of things she missed about her sister and asking the Lord to take it from her. I gave her an illustration of how this works and I volunteered to pray with her if she wanted to get rid of her grief, and she agreed.

I asked her what some of the main things were that she missed about her sister, and she briefly told me about her sister and how close they were, and we made a list of about nine things she missed about her. I then led her in a prayer, which she repeated, and she told the Lord what she missed about her sister, and then she asked the Lord to take her grief and carry it for her. Afterwards, I asked her how she felt while thinking about her sister. She cried and then smiled and said that she felt much better. She thanked me and was relieved and smiling when I left her in the shop. I felt good also because the Lord had allowed me to minister to someone while waiting in the airport.

Set Free at Haiti Airport

After a short-term mission trip to Haiti I checked in my bags at the small Cap Haitien airport and went to the waiting area to wait for my flight. It was a very small waiting room so I had only a few seating options, but I sat by a young man who was obviously a visitor and not a Haitian. We exchanged a few courtesies as I settled into my chair and made myself comfortable. The young man was very friendly and began talking with me. I was surprised at how clear his English was when he spoke so I asked him where he was going. He told me that he was from the Philippines and he was going home. Still curious I asked him what brought him to Haiti and he said that he was with the United Nations security forces, but that he was going home because his father had died a week earlier.

I gave him my condolences and asked him how he was doing. He said that he was fine, but I recognized that this was another divine encounter. I shared with him that I was a mental health counselor and that I helped people with grief, and I had learned a way to help people release their grief. I asked him how he was doing emotionally about the loss of his father. Although he said that he was doing okay, I followed up with another question and asked him if he felt some sadness or grief, and he admitted that he did. I shared with this young man how I had tried other methods of dealing with grief and they did not work, but then I learned that when people made a list of things they missed about someone and gave it to God in prayer, that their grief lifted. I asked him if he would like to try this and he consented, saying that he was a Catholic and believed in prayer.

I asked him what he missed about his father and he shared with me a number of things he missed about him. Then I led him in a prayer and he told the Lord what he missed about his father, and asked the Lord to take his grief and sadness from him. When we finished the prayer, I asked him how he felt about his father while thinking about him. He told me that he felt peaceful and calm and was confident that he would see him again. I felt privileged to be able to help this random stranger find some peace and experience the goodness of God.

Set Free at Burger King

One day I went to a Burger King for lunch and I was wearing a shirt with the Set Free logo. The store manager who was waiting on me looked at my shirt and asked what "Set Free" was. I explained that it is a ministry that helps people overcome feelings of anger and grief, and overcome addictions. He told me that when he got saved four years earlier God took away his addiction to meth, but he continued to have problems with his anger. I told him that I would be glad to show him how to get rid of his anger during his break, and he agreed to call me when he was on break.

I went shopping and in about an hour the manager called me to say that he was going on break, so I returned to the store and sat down with him in the restaurant. I asked him if there was anyone he was angry toward, and he told me that he got along well with his father and could not think of anyone he was angry toward. I asked him when he began using drugs and he said it was about age 15 after his father died. We talked about his grief over the loss of his father and made a list of the things he missed about him. Then I led him in a prayer and asked the Lord to take his grief and carry it for him. I asked him how he felt afterwards, and he told me he felt peaceful and calm.

This man was able to think about his father without feeling any grief or anger. He was amazed at how quickly his grief left him and how calm he felt. Each time I returned to that store I checked on this man, and each time he assured me that he had no more grief over his father, and his anger had improved. This was one more divine encounter I had that gave me the opportunity to minister to a stranger and talk with him about the Lord. He told me that he was already a Christian and had been delivered from drug abuse, but he was still struggling with his anger.

Set Free in Private Church School

A children's minister who attended Set Free meetings saw a nine-year-old girl sitting in the hallway of his church crying. He asked her why she was crying and she said, "I miss my daddy." He asked her where her daddy was and she said, "he died a year ago and I miss him so much." A staff member of the church school saw them talking and said, "Susie, you need to go to your class! This girl is always crying about missing her dad and we've told her that she just needs to get over it." The children's minister told the staff member that he would take her there in a few minutes.

He asked the little girl what she missed about her daddy. She told him how much she missed playing with him and going with him to visit a good friend of her father's. She shared eight things that she really missed about her father. Then the minister asked her if she would like to pray and give her sadness to God, and she said "yes." He led her in a prayer and she told the Lord what she missed about her father, then she asked Him to take her sadness and carry it for her. The minister asked her how strong her sadness was on a 10-point scale, with 10 being the highest and she said it was a 2. They bowed their heads and the minister prayed for her again and asked God if He had anything He wanted her to know about her father. She said, "God wants me to know that my daddy was with Him and doing fine; I will be okay; and my daddy knows I'm okay."

She was smiling and was no longer sad so the minister took her to her classroom. Three weeks later he asked her how she was doing and she said that she was no longer so sad about her father and she was happy about talking to God. She had a big smile on her face and was getting along well with the other children and doing well in class, because this children's minister knew how to pray with her about her grief and sadness.

Most adults don't know how to help children with their grief and get frustrated with them. Many children in our public schools have anger and grief issues due to family problems, losses, and divorces, and then they act up in class or are inattentive. These children are often sent to a school counselor who diagnoses them as having ADD or ADHD, and they are placed on medications, rather than dealing with the underlying emotional issues they are facing. Thank God that there is a way to help them resolve their emotional pain through prayer rather than by giving them dangerous drugs that do not solve their problems. Jesus does love the little children and He wants us to teach them how to be set free from their grief, anger, and sadness through prayer.

Set Free in Jail
"Better than Methamphetamines!"

I saw an inmate who prayed about her grief over the loss of her 18-month-old child eleven years before. She wept as she prayed about this loss, but when she was done she was peaceful and calm and said that this felt better than meth ever did. It is amazing to see the things that God does as people cast all their cares upon Him and listen to the Holy Spirit to bring comfort to them, and they feel this incredible peace, which is better than any drugs.

I saw another young woman who had gone eight days without using meth but was struggling with strong urges to use. She was still working, but was afraid that she would lose her children and her job if she couldn't get off her meth, and she was desperate for help. I shared with her how she could be set free by letting the Lord take away her emotional pain through prayer, and she said she was willing to try anything.

She tearfully talked about her past and the many losses she had experienced, but the most painful loss was at age 14 when her maternal grandfather died and she began using drugs to ease her pain. She was very close to her grandfather and spent a lot of time with him. She missed his soft voice, his calm temperament, his affection, and his unconditional love and acceptance. She also missed his laughter and smile, spending time talking with him and going for walks with him, and many other things. We made a list of 31 things she missed about her grandfather, and we then prayed and told the Lord about each thing she missed. She sobbed as she fought her way through the list, barely able to speak the words. But when she finished her prayer and asked the Lord to take her grief from her she calmed down and quit crying. I asked her how she felt and she said she felt calm and neutral and said, "I don't feel like crying."

What an amazing thing this is to witness over and over, even with people who are doubters. As this woman continued to come for healing I knew that she would be set free from her urges to use drugs.

Angry at God

At the local jail I spoke with some female inmates about how to get rid of anger. One of them came up afterwards and asked for prayer. She said that she was angry at two former husbands and at God. She was very tearful and said that it was hard to admit that she was angry at God but she wanted to be honest and wanted help in getting rid of it. I asked her why she was angry at God and she burst into tears and began sobbing so heavily that I could barely understand her. She said that her mother abandoned her, she was adopted by her grandmother who died when she was 12 years old, her first husband physically abused her, her second husband died from cancer, and her third husband emotionally abused her and took her children from her. She was angry at her former husbands but also was angry at God for allowing these tragic things to happen to her.

I asked this woman if she would like to get rid of her anger and she said that she would, so I led her in a prayer and she told the Lord why she was angry at Him. Even as she prayed she sobbed so heavily that I could barely understand her, but then she told the Lord that she was tired of carrying these feelings and she asked the Lord to carry them for her. She suddenly quit crying and wiped away the tears. She became calm and said that she was no longer angry at God. We then prayed about her anger toward her two former husbands, and when we were finished she just smiled and said that she felt lighter. What a joy it is to see people like this woman, who was so broken, give their burdens to the Lord and be lifted by Him to set them free.

Inmate Saved but not Set Free

I spoke to a group of inmates in the local county jail about how to be set free from anger and grief. I asked one of the young men if he had any grief or loss and he said that he had lost his father three years before, and his eyes reddened and he became tearful. I asked him if he would like to get rid of his pain and sadness about his father, and he said he would; he was even willing to allow three other inmates to observe our prayer session so they could learn how to do this.

I explained that there were two steps to resolving his grief. First, he needed to be honest about his loss and make a list of what he missed about his father. Second, he needed to pray and ask the Lord to carry his grief and sadness for him. He said that he got saved at age 13, but then his father got sick, and he prayed and asked the Lord to keep him alive until he was 18 years old. He took care of his father for five years, but he carried a lot of sadness during those years. His father did live until this young man was 18 years old, but on New Year's Eve when his father asked him to sit with him for the evening, he went out with some friends and smoked some weed. While he was out with his friends, his father died on New Year's Eve, and this led him to abuse drugs badly, which led him to be locked up in jail.

This young man told me that his father was his best friend, and he missed talking with him, taking care of him, and watching TV and movies with him. He also missed his jokes, his sense of humor, his smile, his praise and encouragement, and his love and affection. He said he even missed his cooking and hearing him call him his "candy man." We made a list of 15 things he missed about his father, then we prayed and asked the Lord to take his grief and sadness and carry it for him. As he prayed he shed tears, and his friends gave him toilet tissue and patted him on the back to encourage him. When he finished his prayer I asked the Lord if there was anything that He wanted this young man to know. He said, "My dad loves me and wouldn't want me to be crying for him; he's in a better place. I can't go to him for advice but God is there for me. They both love me."

I asked him how he felt and he said, "Happier. My heart doesn't hurt anymore. I feel a sense of peace." He told me that he regretted that he did not spend more time with him, and he felt bad and shameful for not being with him when he died. I prayed about his feelings of shame and asked the Lord what he wanted this young man to know about his belief that he was bad and shameful. He said, "He knows how much I loved him. We all do things we regret, but we learn from it." I asked him, again, how he felt and he said "My heart doesn't hurt now." His feelings of grief and shame were both gone and he sat there smiling. We talked about what a miracle it is to see the Lord lift these feelings so quickly, and how the Lord wants us to learn to cast all our cares upon Him and let Him carry our emotional burdens for us.

This young man said he was saved at age 13, but he had feelings of sadness that led him to abuse drugs; now he is set free from these negative emotions so that he can enjoy God's peace and joy and follow the Lord.

Set Free in Youth Shelter School

A teacher had just gone through some training for Set Free Prayer Ministry and she emailed me the following story: "Just wanted to let you know that I am doing well and I had an opportunity to use this technique on a youth at the shelter last week. A 13-year-old boy was struggling with anger issues and defiance towards authority, mainly teachers, and did not want to go to school (a behavior program within his school). I took him to school one morning and he was argumentative with the teacher and department head and they decided to send him back to the shelter since he was obviously not going to cooperate."

"On the way back I pulled the car over in a church parking lot and asked him if he wanted to get rid of his anger. He said 'yes' and I asked him if he trusted me. He said he did (we had had a previous conversation the day before about his faith and how important faith was to his mother) and I asked him to tell me about everything he was angry about and people he was mad at. He talked for several minutes and I kept asking him what else, who else? He kept talking until he had tears in his eyes and I asked him if he wanted to tell God about his anger. He did that by laying each thing onto a perceived platter and then raised it up to God, asking Him to take it from him. I asked him how he felt and he said he felt good. Then I asked him on a scale of 1 - 10 how he felt and he said 6. I asked him if there was anything else he was mad at or about."

"He told me he was mad at God for his life so far. Then we repeated the process and gave his anger to God, and he rated himself at 3. I asked him what else he was angry about and he said he didn't know, so I prayed and asked God to show him. A few minutes later he said that he knew what it was. He told me that he was angry with himself for his behavior and bad choices. He then placed those things on the platter and asked God to take them from him, then he prayed for forgiveness. Later he rated himself at 0 and said he felt 'great.' He was peaceful and calm, and I asked him what he wanted to do now, and he said he wanted to go back to school!"

"I took him back to school and called an hour later to see how he was doing. The department head that I had spoken to earlier that morning told me that she was just about to call me to report on this boy and how amazed she was at his very recent choice to come to her for advice about something that had triggered him in the classroom. She said they talked about it and she praised him for using very effective coping skills. He continued to do well and the staff were amazed at his change of attitude."

Set Free in Grade School

A school teacher who had been trained in Set Free Prayer Ministry noticed that a little girl in her class was crying. She gave the children an assignment to work on and then went to the little girl and asked her what was wrong. The girl told her that she missed her grandmother who had died. The teacher sympathized with her and comforted her, then asked her to write out what she missed about her grandmother. The little girl went to work and began writing. Soon the class was dismissed and the teacher went to the girl and asked to see her list. She had made a nice list of about 13 things she missed about her grandmother.

The teacher asked her if she would like to get rid of her sadness and the girl nodded and said she would. The teacher explained that if she would pray and tell the Lord what she missed about her grandmother and ask God to take her sadness, He would take it. She asked the girl if she would like for her to lead her in a prayer about her grandmother and the girl said she would, so the teacher led her in a prayer telling the Lord what she missed about her grandmother and then giving it to God. When she was done, the teacher asked the Lord what He wanted her to know. The little girl smiled and said, "She is okay. She is happy." Her grief and sadness were suddenly lifted and the little girl was smiling.

The point of these stories is that we have opportunities to share this message with people everywhere we go, because there are hurting people everywhere who need to know these prayer principles.

Once you experience peace and relief through prayer about your feelings, you will find many opportunities to share it with others.

Other Encounters

Encounters on a Cruise

My wife and I went on a cruise and I had many opportunities to pray with people and to share this ministry with them. The first night on the cruise I was sitting in the dining room late at night and got into a conversation with one of the crew members working there. Her name was Olivia and she was from Indonesia, and as we talked I told her how she could get rid of any anger through prayer. She told me that she was angry at her father for being unfaithful to her mother, he was a neglectful father, and he had other children toward whom he showed more love and caring. We made a list of 11 things she resented about her father, then she asked God to take her anger from her and carry it for her. Afterwards, I asked her how she felt and she told me that she just loved him and she felt like giving him a hug. Since he was not there on the ship she asked if she could give me a hug! Each day I saw her she said she had no more anger toward her father.

There were two couples sitting nearby who overheard some of our conversation, and when Olivia left, one of the women was curious about our conversation. I shared with these two couples what I did for a living. I explained how I help people be set free from feelings of grief, anger, and shame through prayer. I asked if any of them had any grief that they would like to get rid of. One of the women said that she had a close friend who had committed suicide two months before and she still thought about it about 11 times each day. She told me that it makes her angry that her friend never reached out to her or anyone before she ended her life, and she left behind four children, 3 grandchildren, and a new husband. Her suicide hurt all of these children and many friends, and it made this woman angry that she was so selfish. It also made her mad that the woman was a nurse and she stole some medication and injected it into herself, so it was a systematic, planned suicide, and yet no one knew she was depressed or suicidal. All of this made her very angry at her friend's selfishness.

We prayed about her anger and she told the Lord why she was angry; then she asked the Lord to take her anger and carry it for her. I prayed and asked the Lord if there was anything that He wanted her to know; she said, "I feel peace, and It's not my fault." I asked her if she felt any anger toward her friend and she said "No." Her anger was gone, her feelings of guilt were gone, and she just smiled and said she felt peaceful.

The following evening I was sitting in the same spot in the dining room, reading my Bible. A young man came up to me and said, "Something told me to talk to you." He asked what I was reading and I told him the Bible. He was not a Christian or Bible reader so I explained that I enjoy reading the Bible so much because I see how God is able to take our anger and grief from us and give us peace. I asked him if he had lost anyone close to him and he said he had not, but when I asked him if he had lost any girlfriends he said he had recently broken up with his girlfriend. He said that she was still hung up on a former boyfriend named John, and she even called him by the former boyfriend's name at one point. He was angry at her for lying to him, and he lost his trust in her. We made a list of 8 reasons for his anger, then he prayed and gave it to the Lord and asked Him to take it from him. Afterwards, he said that he felt love for her and had no more anger. His eyes were tearful at the sudden change and I asked him if he was 100% sure that he was going to heaven. He was not but he said he would like to be, so I shared the gospel with him using the booklet, "How to Overcome Doubts," and he received the Lord as his Savior!

I also shared with him how to be set free from his obsession with his girlfriend if she is untrustworthy, by giving his grief to God and asking Him to take his sadness from him. This young man left smiling, with a lighter heart and a joyful heart, knowing that he is going to heaven when he dies. This prayer ministry is a wonderful tool to use to reach others for the Lord, because once they experience God's power to set them free from their emotional burdens their heart opens up to Him. What a privilege and joy it is to share God's goodness with others!

A Miracle Family Encounter!

A friend called me excitedly to tell me what had just happened. He and his wife had assisted me in some prayer ministry sessions and observed how to help people release their anger, but neither of them had ever done it themselves. One evening the husband's 16 year-old daughter was upset and crying after having a conversation with her biological mother over the telephone. Her stepmother asked her what was wrong and the girl told her that she was upset about the way her mother treated her. The stepmom asked her, "Would you like to get rid of that pain?" She said, "Yes" and her stepmom then spoke to her father and said, "Here. Show her how to do that."

My friend was taken aback and felt unprepared to do this on his own. After some stammering and hesitation he did just what he had observed me doing in prayer sessions. "Let's make a list of what you are angry about" he told his daughter. She began talking and her father made a list of her resentments as she talked. After making a short list she ran out of ideas so her father prayed, "Lord, is there anything else she needs to add to her list?" She began thinking of other resentments toward her mother, and soon they had a long list of reasons for her anger. By this time she was crying and shaking with emotion.

Her father led her in a prayer, telling the Lord why she was angry, and then led her to pray, "Lord, I'm tired of feeling this anger so right now I choose to give it to You and I ask You to carry it for me. In Jesus' name I pray. Amen." As soon as they finished praying the daughter suddenly quit shaking and crying and sat there calmly. It was like turning off a faucet of water! She said she felt good and was no longer angry. Her father prayed for her again and said, "Lord, is there anything that you want her to know?"

"It isn't my fault that my mother treats me like this." Her father was astounded to hear her say this, not ever suspecting that she blamed herself for her mother's behavior and profoundly relieved that the Lord healed these feelings of shame she had been carrying. "Does that feel true?" he asked her. She said that it did; she was assured that it was her mother's problem, not hers. She said she no longer felt anger; she just felt sorry for her mother, and they prayed together for her mother. The father was thankful that the Lord healed these feelings his daughter had so that she would not have to carry them into her adult life and allow them to lead her to make poor decisions in her life.

"It was a miracle!" he told me. Both he and his wife are still rejoicing in the miracle they observed as they prayed for his daughter and saw her healed instantly of her anger and of the feelings of shame she was carrying which they did not know were present. "What an awesome God we have!" he said.

Ethical and Legal Issues

For those like the school teacher who prayed with the young girl in school about her grief over the loss of her grandmother, there are legal issues related to using this ministry on the job. Of course, there is the growing condemnation by liberals in the country who condemn any form of public communication about God or any public use of prayer, and we reject this as a distortion of the United States Constitution which nowhere states that there must be a separation between church and state. The Constitution states that the government shall not infringe our religious rights, and the Declaration of Independence stated that, "all men are created equal, and are endowed by their Creator with certain unalienable rights." However, in the current liberal environment in the United States we have to be aware of how the interpretation of the Constitution has been corrupted, and how believers must be discrete and cautious in sharing spiritual matters and praying with others.

I work for an organization that has the motto, "Faith, Family, and Culture," and that begins all of their meetings with prayer, but it is still a secular organization and not a Christian organization, so I have learned how to discretely pray with people. When I initially began working for this organization, I was cautioned several times about sharing my faith or praying with clients, so I adopted several practices that have kept me out of trouble. First, I listen very carefully to my clients to identify any indications that they have Christian values or a personal faith. Second, after listening to their presenting problems and gathering background information to understand it, I share with them how I attempted previously to help people who had problems with anger, grief, shame, or fear and found that my techniques were ineffective. Third, I share with them a story that illustrates how I have seen people overcome grief, anger, shame, or fear through a simple prayer process used in this ministry. Fourth, I clearly state to each client that I realize this is a faith-based technique and I assure them that I am not trying to push any spiritual or faith-based techniques upon them. I tell them that if they are uncomfortable with this I will not bring it up again, but if they are okay with it I would be glad to teach them how to do it. Fifth, I do my best to help them using cognitive therapy if they are not receptive to anything faith-based, even though I know it will probably not help them much.

My primary job, as a mental health professional, is to help people who are in emotional distress to find relief and overcome their health, relational, vocational, and marital problems that brought them to the counseling agency. If I use techniques that I know will not help clients, like grief counseling, anger management, or behavioral marital counseling, then I am being an unethical counselor. Ethically, counselors must be honest and realistic with their clients in their efforts to help them. One experienced therapist who conducted a workshop on counseling ethics that I attended for continuing education credits, stated that when trying to help clients with trauma we must be honest with them and tell them that they are not going to feel better as a result of treatment. Our job, she said, was to help them adjust and learn some coping skills for their trauma-based fears. This woman was correct in stating that counselors should be honest with their clients and not lead them to false expectations of therapy.

Using this criterion, ethical counselors should not use anger management or grief counseling with clients without informing them that they will not feel better afterwards. I cannot ethically use such techniques since I am aware of their ineffectiveness, but I realize that I cannot force my values and faith-based techniques on clients. I simply explain to them in a simple, matter-of-fact way and ask for the client's consent before trying to pray with them for emotional healing. Informed consent is an ethical requirement for mental health counselors, and I always obtain informed consent before praying with clients or encouraging them to use prayer. Set Free Prayer ministers are encouraged to do the same, and as they learn to do this it will keep them out of trouble. Since I began using these five principles I have had no problems with my employer.

Evangelism and Set Free Prayer Ministry

The Apostle Paul was witnessing to Sergius Paulus, the proconsul of Cyprus, and when Elymas the magician opposed him he struck him with blindness in the name of Lord. When the proconsul witnessed this miracle he believed in the Lord and was saved. "Then the proconsul believed when he saw what had happened, being amazed" (Acts 13:12). The Lord often saves people after they witness the power of God to set people free supernaturally.

I prayed with a woman in the local jail who had lost her brother just three weeks earlier as the result of a tractor accident. This woman requested prayer because her grief was so painful and raw. She stated that she was very close to her brother, who was the only person she could talk with openly, and she missed his kindness, his caring, and his love and affection. She also missed his presence, his sense of humor, and his ability to listen well without judgment. She said she missed doing things with him like going fishing, swimming, and canoeing, as well as camping with him, listening to country music, and barbecuing with him. We made a list of 13 things she missed about him, then she prayed and told the Lord what she missed about him and asked Him to carry her grief for her. After giving her grief to the Lord I prayed and asked the Lord if there was anything He wanted her to know. The thought that came to her mind was, "He's in a better place and he is not hurting anymore." She said that she felt peaceful and felt no more grief or sadness.

I asked her what she thought about how the Lord took her grief from her so quickly, and she said she was amazed. Then I asked her if she was 100% sure that she would go to heaven when she died and she said she was not. I used the booklet "How to Overcome Doubts" and shared the gospel with her. She had never prayed to receive Christ before and she said that she wanted to so I led her in a prayer and she received the Lord as her Savior!

This ministry is a wonderful evangelistic tool, because once people are healed of their anger or grief their heart is suddenly softened to the Lord. The Lord wants people to be saved, and He will heal them, if necessary, to show them how much He loves them and how much they need Him. This young lady needs more healing in her life. It's wonderful that she got saved, but she then needed to be discipled and taught how to pray to be set free. Just one healing prayer session will not usually heal clients of their legal problems and emotional issues.

Making the Church Relevant

The early New Testament Church was full of excitement because they were witnessing miracles, and because radical transformations were occurring in the lives of people like the apostle Paul, and like the persecuted believers in Acts 13:52 who were not fearful or intimidated by the government or Jewish religious leaders. The church was "filled with joy and with the Holy Spirit," so their faith was relevant to their life experiences and enabled them to live with joy in the midst of persecution.

Although the New Testament does not clearly state that the believers were praying as we do in Set Free Prayer Ministry, it does give strong hints that they were praying powerfully and effectively for one another, and this was the key to their victory. They were taught to "confess your faults to one another, and pray for one another, so that ye may be healed" (James 5:16, KJV) and "Be anxious for nothing, but in everything by prayer and supplication with thanksgiving let your requests be made known to God. And the peace of God, which surpasses all comprehension, will guard your hearts and your minds in Christ Jesus" (Philippians 4:6-7). The apostle Paul also taught the churches to "pray without ceasing" (1 Thessalonians 5:17) and "devote yourselves to prayer" (Colossians 4:2).

Today the Church is weak on prayer; you can hardly find churches that still have prayer meetings weekly. Most of those that have "prayer meetings" actually have a Bible study in which they collect prayer requests at the beginning of the meeting and then have one person pray collectively for the group. In order for the Church to be relevant to the emotional needs of its members, it must return to the practice of the early Church and be devoted to pray for one another and to confess their faults to one another. As individuals learn to pray about their emotions, and pray for one another, the Church will grow strong. Churches today do not know how to help those who are struggling over divorces, marital problems, anger, grief, depression, or anxiety. They simply refer their hurting members to a "professional" who refers them to a doctor for medications. There is no biblical precedent for this; rather the Bible states that we can experience love, joy and peace, as a by-product of "walking by the Spirit" and learning to cast all our cares upon Him.

A young woman came to me for a court-ordered evaluation of her substance abuse. I delved into her background, identifying the experiences in her life that led her to begin abusing drugs. She had been abused and was angry at many people, she had several relationship break-ups that hurt her, and she had some significant losses that led her into depression. However, she stated that she was clean and sober and was no longer angry, grieving, or depressed. When I asked her how she resolved these issues she told me that she got saved and began going to church and praying. When I probed more specifically, knowing that most churches do not know how to help individuals with such issues, she told me how she had prayed about her anger and given it to the Lord and He took it. I asked about her past abuse and how she overcame it, and she told me how she had prayed about it and the Holy Spirit told her she was "clean" and it wasn't her fault. She said that she prayed a long time about her past and her feelings and she said, "I had a Holy Spirit counseling session" that set her free from her negative feelings.

I was very amazed but pleased to learn how this young woman had, on her own, been able to pray about all her emotional issues that had led her to abuse drugs. She convinced me that she had resolved her underlying emotional issues without my help, but through simple prayer to the Lord about her negative emotions. This leads me to believe that the early Church engaged in such prayer because they were "continually devoting themselves to prayer" (Acts 1:14). They did not turn to the doctors or professional counselors of their day for help. The Lord wants to do the same for the Church today. He is able to heal our broken hearts, and set the captives free as we devote ourselves to prayer and praying "without ceasing."

Going Into all the World

There are very few pastors who actively share the gospel with people on a regular basis, and there are even fewer Christians who do so. One Baptist Director of Missions shared with me that he had questioned the pastors in the churches belonging to his association and asked how many of them had shared the gospel with someone in the last month, and none of them had. One of the primary reasons for this is that so many of the pastors struggle emotionally that they are not excited about the Lord and what He can do for them.

Pastors who try to get volunteers to go door-to-door to share the gospel have great difficulty getting any volunteers, because most of them are frightened and lukewarm about their faith.

The great commission was fulfilled in the early Christian Church because there were many believers who had been radically transformed by the gospel. They were excited, bold, and fearless, because they were full of the Spirit and walking by the Spirit. The Spirit does set us free when we learn to talk to the Lord and listen to him so that we find freedom from grief, anger, shame, and fear, and become "unencumbered" by our emotions. When believers experience this freedom they will get excited about the Lord and go into all the world to preach the gospel to everyone. And as they preach the gospel they will make disciples and teach them to observe all that the Lord commanded them (Matthew 28:19-20), including how to pray for freedom and to walk in the joy and comfort of the Lord. This is the desire of Set Free Prayer Ministry, to see many people get saved and set free to serve Him.

23

MORE ABOUT MEDICATIONS: THE WORLD'S WAY VS. GOD'S WAY

A report by Medco Health Solutions, Inc. (2011), *America's State of Mind.* estimated that 20% of all adults in the United States were taking at least one psychiatric drug in 2010. Since the U.S. Census Bureau estimated that there were nearly 309 million people in the United States in 2010 and 76% were adults, this means that there were around 47 million adults taking psychiatric drugs then, and surely more now.

Because of the widespread use of psychiatric drugs and the number of Christians who are taking these drugs, it is important that believers have some knowledge of the other types of psychiatric medications that are affecting the lives of so many in our society. Previously we have addressed the use of antidepressants and antianxiety medications, but in this chapter I want to discuss the dangers and limitations of other types of psychiatric medications. Of course, as Christians begin to oppose such a profitable industry as the pharmaceutical industry, we can expect some fierce resistance from them, and from those in the medical profession who have embraced their usage.

Opposition to Prayer Ministry

When the apostle Paul began his missionary journeys and began spreading the gospel, he was opposed by the Jewish leaders due to their jealousy. But when he arrived in the city of Philippi in Acts 16, he cast out an evil spirit in a young girl who was bringing much profit to her master by fortune-telling (Acts 16:16). Paul and Silas were then seized by her masters, who dragged them to the market place before the city authorities, and they were beaten and incarcerated without a proper Roman trial. They were supernaturally released when God sent an earthquake to free them, and the Philippian jailer was converted. Paul's persecution was intensified as the gospel set people free and this interfered with the financial profit of some merchants in Philippi.

Acts 19 tells about the experiences of the apostle Paul when he was establishing the church in Ephesus. After being in the city for over two years, many people had believed in Jesus as Paul preached and taught that idols were false gods but that Jesus was the one true God. A silversmith by the name of Demetrius made his living by making silver shrines of Artemis, and his business began to suffer as a result of Paul's ministry. Demetrius spoke with other craftsmen who were also losing business because of Paul's teaching, and they were filled with rage at Paul and his traveling companions.

A large crowd gathered together and shouted angrily at them and almost started a riot, until the town clerk spoke to them and calmed them down and dispersed them. The city of Ephesus endured Paul's teaching until it began to affect some of them financially, and then the opposition to his teaching grew strong. Paul left Ephesus soon after that and went to Philippi, where he was opposed by the Jews, and everywhere he went after this he was followed and opposed for a variety of reasons. Even though he was preaching the good news of salvation by grace through faith, he was rejected and persecuted for religious, personal, and financial reasons.

When I began to teach this prayer ministry I expected other Christians to welcome it and get excited about it as I had, but this did not happen. I have found similar opposition to the teaching of this ministry, by unbelievers and by believers. Some Christians and pastors do accept it immediately, but many are skeptical and slow to embrace it for a variety of reasons. Some believers say that it is "too easy" and they won't even give it a chance, but continue using the same ineffective techniques they have used for years with other believers. Other Christians reject it because they already believe in prayer and their prayers have not set them free, so they are resistant to trying something so similar. Many Christians and pastors reject it because they, or someone in their family, are already taking psychiatric drugs, and have been convinced by their doctor that they have a chemical imbalance or a brain disorder. They continue taking ineffective medications, and become hostile if you suggest to them that medications are not as effective as God's solutions. When pastors reject this ministry, they close the doors to the healing of believers in their church, and prevent them from experiencing peace and victory in their lives.

In addition to these reasons for rejecting this ministry, there are pastors and professional Christian counselors who reject it because they have spent six years of their lives going to college to learn how to help others, and they don't want to dismiss their training as worthless. They take pride in their education and being able to feel they are uniquely qualified to help those suffering from emotional struggles. They delude themselves into thinking that they have special wisdom and the ability to help others with their problems. If they were convinced that their treatments were ineffective, they might be forced to receive new training that might not be accepted by other professionals in their field, or even to consider taking up a new career.

Of course, psychiatrists are in an even more difficult position, because if they conceded that their medications were ineffective, they would have no income at all, unless they could start another type of medical practice or specialize in helping clients withdraw from their psychiatric medications. It is understandable, therefore, that psychiatric professionals would be very threatened by the claims of this ministry. Pharmaceutical representatives are in a similar position; they would have to change careers if they concluded that their medications were ineffective and possibly harming others. For all of these reasons and more, many people are quick to reject the teachings of this ministry, and similar ministries that provide effective, biblical alternatives to traditional counseling and psychiatric treatments.

Pharmaceutical Industry

The pharmaceutical industry is a multi-billion dollar industry that spends an enormous amount of money and effort advertising their medications. Dr. Breggin tells the story in his book, *Medication Madness* (p. 246-260), of the harrowing experiences he had in 1994 in dealing with a lawsuit against Eli Lilly and company, who knowingly marketed the antidepressant, Prozac, which they knew caused mania in people and led to high rates of agitation and suicide attempts. He was hired as a consultant and expert witness to represent the plaintiffs in a lawsuit against Eli Lilly. During his investigation, Dr. Breggin had access to personal company records from the early marketing and development of Prozac, and he found that the researchers knew that clients were reporting drug-induced violence and suicidality, but this fact was ignored and buried by the company.

Dr. Breggin was prepared to present his findings in court, but as a result of their powerful monetary influence, the company was able to influence the lead attorney for the plaintiffs to prevent him from presenting his findings. As a result of legal manipulations, a sham trial was held in which the jury decided in favor of Eli Lilly, but the judge overruled the case because he recognized that it had been rigged and he changed the verdict to being settled with prejudice by Eli Lilly. Most lawyers regarded the trial to have been won by Eli Lilly. As a result of this trial, Dr. Breggin was regarded as a serious threat to Eli Lilly, and most of his subsequent cases against Lilly have been settled satisfactorily out of court, for the plaintiffs, without any admission of fault by the company, and none of them has gone to trial.

These companies make billions of dollars each year selling psychiatric medications. The antipsychotic medications bring in the most revenue of all psychiatric medications, with antidepressant medications next. In 2010, antidepressants were the second-most frequently prescribed medications in the United States (Breggin, 2013, p. 57). The pharmaceutical companies have invested large amounts of money in out-of-court settlements to prevent the adverse side effects of their drugs from being exposed. They continue to market psychiatric medications with serious adverse side effects such as violence and suicide, because they make such heavy profits from them. Since they make billions of dollars on these medications, they have the legal resources to compensate those who have been harmed and who can afford to take them to court, thus preventing any challenges to their unethical practices.

Medication took away All Her Feelings

A Christian woman came for help with her grief and anger. She told me that she had been depressed for over 35 years since her grandparents had died, and she had taken Prozac for a while, which took away her depression and all her other feelings. She said, "You could have cut off my arm and I would have looked at it and said 'You cut off my arm,' without any emotion. It not only took away my depression but all my good feelings, too." She discontinued all her medications on her own, and she wanted help in overcoming her anger and depression. She had been molested five times as a child, and had been married and divorced five times, and had at least ten significant losses, and she admitted that she had a lot of hatred.

I explained to this woman how to overcome her grief by being completely honest about the things she missed about her grandparents, then praying and asking God to take her grief from her. She said she was a Christian and believed in prayer and was very willing to try this. We made a list of what she missed about her grandfather, and then she prayed and gave her grief and sadness to the Lord. Afterwards she said she felt peaceful and calm about the loss of her grandfather. I saw her several weeks later and she said, "I feel a lot better." She stated that she prayed on her own about the loss of her grandmother, her mother, her stepfather, and her son-in-law, and she felt complete peace about each of these losses. I asked her to rate her depression on a 10-point scale and she rated it as a zero and said she felt no depression. She said, "I know you're not supposed to hate, but I do."

We talked about the five men who molested her as a child and her five former husbands, many of whom abused her physically. She said the one she had the most anger toward was her second husband who abused her emotionally, verbally, sexually, and physically. She stated that he cheated on her, he was angry and controlling, he left her for another woman, and he held a gun to her head and threatened to kill her. He also blamed her for everything, believed women were inferior, and made her feel worthless, and he made her feel like it was her fault that he abused her. We made a list of twelve things that she resented about him, then she prayed and told the Lord these things and asked Him to take all her anger from her. I asked the Lord what He wanted her to know and she said, "He had his own problems; it wasn't my fault that he abused me." She said she felt peaceful and had no more anger or feelings of shame. She said, "I'm excited, because once I get rid of my hatred I can lose weight!"

This woman had a lot more anger and grief to resolve but after one session and praying on her own about four more losses, her depression left. Since she was willing to pray on her own she was able to release the rest of her anger quickly and feel even better, and be completely set free from her destructive past and able to serve the Lord with joy. What a joy it is to see the Lord set this woman free from her depression which she had for over 35 years, with no healing from psychiatric medications.

Psychiatrist Baffled

A woman came from out of state for some prayer ministry. She was struggling with feelings of depression and anxiety that were so strong that she took a leave of absence from her work and visited a psychiatrist, who placed her on several medications. After beginning these medications her symptoms increased, and she began having suicidal thoughts, and began pacing, hyperventilating, and having racing thoughts. A close friend of hers drove her to Oklahoma to see me.

When we first met I did a background history in order to identify any past traumas that might have contributed to her emotional struggles. She had a close family and no traumas prior to age 19 when her father died. This loss was traumatic for her, but then she lost her brother and experienced the loss of three grandparents around age 21, the loss of a close uncle at age 25, and the loss of her best friend at age 26. We prayed about the loss of her father and she reported having no more sadness or grief when thinking about him after we prayed. She reported that she had strong feelings of grief, sadness, anger and loss when talking about her brother, so we focused on this loss and began praying through it. First, we prayed about the loss of her brother and we made a list of 16 things she missed about him. After that we prayed about some feelings of anger and sadness she felt toward her brother and she was able to release them. Then, we prayed about some feelings of shame and blame that she felt toward her brother, and as we prayed, the truth came to her mind to set her free from these feelings of shame.

She stated that she felt a great deal of relief after dealing with the loss of her brother, and she felt peaceful when thinking about him. We talked about the prayer process and how the Lord is able to set us free from our negative feelings, but we did no more praying that day. The following morning we met again and she reported that she was still feeling very well. Then she asked me why she was so compulsive about her work and worked such long hours. I asked her to imagine that it was closing time and to visualize a client walking to the clinic door and wanting her assistance; I asked her how that made her feel. She told me that she felt guilty and bad if she turned the client away, so I asked her to try to remember any previous time in her life when she felt that same feeling. She could not remember any prior time so I prayed and asked the Lord to take her to the source and origin of these feelings. She then recalled a time when she had worked at a clinic with patients who were dying from cancer, and an alcoholic woman was dying from cirrhosis of the liver.

As this woman was dying her 16 year-old son was standing by watching and cried out, "Do something! Can't you see my mom is dying?" This woman said that she felt "I should have done more." I prayed for her and asked the Lord what He wanted her to know about that belief and the thoughts that came to her mind immediately were, "There's nothing I could have done. The son was desperate and dealing with his own grief." After a few more insights came to her mind she reported that she felt very peaceful and calm, with no more feelings of guilt or shame.

This woman stated that she felt a tremendous relief from that prayer, and she said she no longer felt any anxiety or depression. Later that day these two women drove back home and periodically texted me to tell me that this woman was still feeling peaceful and calm. When they arrived at their home they texted me to say that she was feeling great. The following day the friend texted me "'Susie' is doing great this morning." That night she texted me again and told me that her friend went back for an appointment with her psychiatrist and she sent me the following messages: "Just talked with 'Susie'. Her psychiatrist is really scratching her head about how Susie could be so quickly healed. Said she was really wondering about her diagnosis. Susie described a little about prayer ministry and told her it was a miracle. The doctor agreed but seemed to want to take credit for it at which Susie said no and that she didn't need the meds and wanted her help to get off them. The psychiatrist agreed that she probably didn't need them! Woohoo!"

The secular world has no solution for feelings of grief, anger, or shame. All they can do is prescribe medications to numb our feelings, but the Lord is able to take away the pain and replace it with His peace. We have an awesome God who sets the captives free!" "Oh, sing to the Lord a new song, for He has done wonderful things!" (Psalms 98:1).

The Mental Health Profession

The mental health profession was historically resistant to the psychoanalytic theory of Sigmund Freud, and Behavior Therapy was one of the alternatives developed in opposition to psychoanalytic therapy. Behavior Therapy was a very scientific approach to dealing with human behavioral problems, focusing upon the modification of observable and measurable behavior changes, rather than vague internal concepts like id, ego, and superego that could not be measured, and this attracted me to it in my early years of training. I enjoyed learning and using behavior modification principles, and this branch of therapy had a strong influence in the educational field, as teachers were trained in how to create behavior modification programs for controlling classroom behaviors of their students. It was wonderful to have these behavioral principles to use with children, and even to use them with adults in marriage counseling and in dealing with anxieties and other clinical problems. Even today I use these principles with children and teach them to parents who have difficulty controlling their children's behavior. It is an effective way to modify the behavior of the parents in order to modify the behavior of their children.

However, when I became involved in working with alcoholics and drug addicts, I began to expand my thinking about behavior therapy because of the need to account for cognitive factors involved in substance abuse. Around that time, in the 1970s, Cognitive Behavior Therapy began to emerge, and I began to conceptualize human behaviors and emotions to be influenced by the individual's beliefs. Cognitive Therapy taught that negative emotions were the result of distorted or irrational thinking, and that the task of the therapist or counselor was to identify the underlying distorted thinking and to challenge it. This was much more sensible to me than the psychoanalytic concepts advocated by Freud, and there were many scriptures that supported the basic principle of cognitive therapy.

Dr. Breggin documents in *Toxic Psychiatry*, that in the early 1970s the American Psychiatric Association was in a financial crisis, and they made a pact with the drug companies to promote their drugs. With only one ethical dissenter to this pact, the board of directors of the association voted to start accepting large sums of money from the drug companies in order to avoid bankruptcy, and in exchange the association agreed to defend the drug companies against attacks against their drugs (Breggin, 2008b, p. 52). Unaware of this pact, I experienced a sudden switch in the clinical field when my co-workers quit trying to help individuals with depression and simply began referring them to psychiatrists for medications.

In the 1980s there was also a sudden shift among mental health professionals as psychiatrists began increasingly to exert their influence and to treat all human emotional and behavioral problems as "brain disorders" and "chemical imbalances." The pharmaceutical industry had a great influence in this transition, because psychiatrists were having difficulty making a living and were convinced by the pharmaceutical companies that they could make more money by advocating medications than by attempting to do therapy with clients. The pharmaceutical companies invented the "chemical imbalance" theory as a way to market their pills, and the psychiatrists joined with them in promoting this belief, even after it was invalidated by researchers and rejected by leaders in the psychiatric field.

The role of the mental health professionals changed from being a counselor/therapist to providing "medication-management" counseling for clients, to encourage them to do what their doctor said and to be compliant in taking their medications. "Compliance" became the key word when mental health counselors spoke with their clients about their medications. Shortly after this, in the new century there was a strong push in the mental health field to train mental health professionals to deal with what were called "co-occurring disorders," referring to their supposed medical needs first and then to encourage clients to continue with their other treatments.

Churches and Christians were historically distrustful of mental health professionals, and were hesitant to refer church members to secular counselors due to the disparate values and beliefs of most therapists from that of their Christian clients. In the 1990s Christian colleges and seminaries began providing mental health counseling programs in their schools, and Christian counselors began to multiply. Many larger churches began hiring professional counselors to provide counseling for their church members.

Unfortunately, the counseling programs in the Christian colleges and seminaries trained their students in secular techniques that varied little from their secular counterparts, other than by using Scriptures, prayer, and biblical values. Their techniques, however, were the same as their secular counterparts, because the Christian counseling and psychology departments had no effective techniques of their own. As the mental health field began to embrace the philosophy of biologic psychiatry, and the belief that individuals with emotional and behavior problems had brain disorders or chemical imbalances, the Christians colleges began teaching the same. Today, most Christian colleges and seminaries have counseling programs that have fully embraced the belief that most human behavioral and emotional problems are rooted in genetic and chemical problems that can only be corrected by trained medical professionals. Many Christian colleges follow the example of their secular counterparts so that they will be regarded as legitimate and be respected, and so their credentialing programs will meet state licensing requirements.

One exception to this, are the fundamental Christian schools that have totally rejected secular approaches to counseling and have gone instead to so-called "Biblical Counseling" approaches. While these programs offer some useful insights and approaches and do teach some useful biblical principles, they narrowly interpret scripture passages and reject other biblical principles that could be integrated into their model. Most importantly, they also fail to offer biblical alternatives that are actually effective with their Christian clients. None of them known to this author is able to help individuals overcome feelings of grief, serious anger problems, or feelings of shame from sexual abuse. They quickly and globally reject any approach that they believe accepts any secular principles, even when the principles can be well documented within the pages of the scriptures.

One of the clearest examples of this is the teaching of the apostle Paul about anger in Ephesians 4:26-27. This passage clearly states that anger is not sin because it says, "Be angry, and yet do not sin." This passage also clearly indicates that anger is not wrong but can lead to sin if an individual lets "the sun go down" on their anger. Such anger can also "give the devil an opportunity," which means that unresolved anger can lead to sin in the future, and it also means that the past can profoundly affect an individual's future. This sounds to some like a Freudian belief in the importance of past experiences, but it was clearly stated in the scriptures 2000 years before Freud. So-called "Biblical Counselors" generally refuse to talk about past issues or accept the principle that the past affects us, and they do not believe that unresolved traumas and problems from our past can still affect us today.

Other Types of Psychiatric Medications

In Chapter 5 we discussed some of the serious limitations and adverse side effects of all five major types of psychiatric medications: antidepressants, antianxiety medications, antipsychotic medications, mood stabilizers, and stimulants. In later chapters we also discussed depression and anxiety, but have said little about psychoses, attention-deficit disorders, or mood disorders or the use of psychiatric medications for "treating" these disorders. In the following section of this chapter we will briefly discuss these three classifications of mental disorders to help the reader have a better understanding of these conditions and their treatment with medications.

Antipsychotic Medications

First of all, what is the truth about schizophrenia and antipsychotic medications? How can we help those who experience thought disorders with delusions, hallucinations, and extreme feelings of paranoia without resorting to medications? When I initially entered the mental health professional system, I was a behaviorist and was very skeptical of the reality of schizophrenia. Soon I met sincere Christians who were diagnosed as schizophrenic and I was convinced that there were individuals with thought disorders, delusions, and hallucinations. But I did not know how to treat such individuals without the use of psychiatric medications, because training in the treatment of schizophrenia is not provided in most graduate schools. Psychiatric institutions used only medications for treating schizophrenia.

To begin this discussion of schizophrenia it is helpful to bear in mind two very significant facts. First, over the past 35 years, treatment outcomes for people in the United States with schizophrenia have worsened, so that they are now no better than they were at the beginning of the twentieth century when the treatment of choice was wrapping the insane in wet sheets (Whitaker, 2002, p. xiii). Second, the World Health Organization has found through repeated studies that the treatment outcomes for schizophrenia in the United States and other developed countries are much worse than those found in the poorer countries of the world. Those who suffer a psychotic break in poor countries like Nigeria or India have a good chance of recovering within a couple of years, but those who suffer a psychotic break in the United States or other developed countries are likely to become chronically psychotic (Whitaker, 2002, p. xiv).

The reason for this may be revealed in the results of a 20-year follow-up study conducted by psychologist Martin Harrow from the University of Chicago, who has been conducting a study on the long-range effect of antipsychotic medications on schizophrenics. He and his colleagues provided a 20-year follow-up report in

Psychological Medicine (Harrow, Jobe, and Faull, 2016, p.2). These researchers found that antipsychotic medications led to chronic psychosis, and that schizophrenics who never took antipsychotic medications had significantly fewer psychotic activities than those who took these medications. This means that although these medications can quickly subdue the inappropriate behaviors of these individuals, in the long term, they prevent the individuals from improving. Thus, the fundamental claim of psychiatrists that these medications are essential for the treatment of schizophrenics is simply false. The truth is that these medications lead to chronic psychotic disorders, and interfere with the ability of these individuals to heal over time.

What exactly is schizophrenia, and what causes it? Most psychiatrists believe it is a brain disorder that leads individuals to have a break with reality and to become seriously delusional and paranoid, and to hallucinate. Schizophrenia is a thought disorder and a form of psychosis. Dr. Breggin says, "Psychosis is a devastating loss of confidence and trust in other human beings. When social relationships become unendurably terrifying, and other people become objects of terror, the individual becomes lost in the nightmarish state called psychosis. People going through what psychiatrists diagnose as schizophrenia are enduring a horrific loss of relationship to other people, usually accompanied by overwhelming feelings of distrust, humiliation, and powerlessness" (Breggin, 2008b, p. 236). He believes that schizophrenia is not a brain disorder, and he states that "a caring, reality-oriented relationship with an experienced therapist can often quickly reverse the downward spiral" (Breggin, 2008b, p. 236). This "caring" relationship is impossible with modern psychiatrists, who force such patients into hospitals against their will, and then force them to submit to drugs and electroshock that destroy their trust and their ability to think clearly.

Psychologist Bert Karon, professor at Michigan State University, is author of the textbook, *Psychotherapy of Schizophrenia* (1981). In this book he describes a successful form of treatment that was developed around the beginning of the 1800s, called the "Moral Treatment." This treatment was created by the Quakers as a successful treatment approach in England and was reproduced in the United States a few years later. Award-winning medical journalist, Robert Whitaker, describes this treatment for schizophrenia in his book *Mad in America* (2003, p. 24-36), where the Quakers believed in the treatment of schizophrenics with compassion and dignity. They believed in keeping these patients constructively occupied with walks, gardening, reading, writing, education, and games like chess. They didn't even try to talk the patients out of their irrational thinking, but they turned their minds to other concerns. Over the first fifteen years of this "Moral Treatment Model" not a single attendant was seriously injured by a violent patient, and 70% of those who had been ill for less than a year recovered and never relapsed (Whitaker, 2002, p.24).

This same "Moral Treatment" was provided in the United States in the early 1800s with similar results. Up to eighty percent of those treated in the United States with "Moral Treatment" recovered from their madness and returned to their families (Whitaker, 2002, p. 27). This successful treatment model was eventually discarded, however, due to the placement of these programs under the supervision of doctors and due to the overcrowding of these institutions. These early treatment programs were replaced, unfortunately, with various forms of physical treatments that were punitive and dehumanizing. However, the success of the Moral Treatment model demonstrates that schizophrenia is not a brain disorder or disease, but can be treated successfully without medications.

Dr. Karon is a reputable psychologist who has had extensive personal experience in the treatment of schizophrenics and believes, like Dr. Breggin, that schizophrenia is the result of traumatic experiences in a person's background that make them terrified of relationships and abandonment. He writes in his textbook, "I learned that fifteen years of terrible, chronic disability could be remedied by psychotherapy" (Karon, 1981, p. 1). He states that "Patients are frightened, confused, usually lonely, and often angry human beings" (Karon, 1981, p. 3), and "all of the symptoms of schizophrenia may be understood... as attempts to deal with terror (anxiety seems too mild a term) of a chronic kind" (Karon, 1981, p. 42).

In contrast, most psychiatrists believe that schizophrenia is a brain disorder and do nothing to treat schizophrenics other than to place them on medication, in spite of the fact that treatment programs around the world have shown that acutely psychotic patients have better outcomes when treated without antipsychotic drugs (Breggin, 2013, p. 55). Dr. Karon writes in his textbook, "Genetic and physiologic theories are usually generated by investigators who have never talked or listened to any schizophrenic individual for any length of time. In a few cases, they have attempted therapy under difficult circumstances hampered by critically inaccurate theories. They have concluded that because they were unsuccessful, the patient must be untreatable" (Karon, 1981, p. 40).

Interestingly, guidelines given by the American Psychiatric Association for the use of antipsychotic medications include use of them for only 2-3 years (Harrow, M. Jobe, TH and Faull, RN, 2016, p. 1) but there were never any studies conducted to assess the usefulness of these medications beyond the first three years, until the study completed by Dr. Harrow and his colleagues. The results of Harrow's study and the findings of the World Health Organization are not likely to impact the practices of psychiatrists, due to the amount of revenue brought into the pharmaceutical companies and psychiatrists by psychiatric medications. According to Dr. Breggin, "As of April 2011, three atypical antipsychotic drugs were in the top 20 of all U.S. pharmaceutical products in regard to their total revenues... No other type of psychiatric drug, even the antidepressant class, was close in generating revenues, mostly because the antipsychotic drugs are so much more expensive" (Breggin, 2013, p. 40). In spite of their ineffectiveness, it would be very difficult to get psychiatrists and pharmaceutical companies to acknowledge these results and decrease their use of them, because they bring so much profit to these two professional groups.

In addition to their poor long-range results and their failure to bring recovery to schizophrenics, there are many other drawbacks and problems with antipsychotic medication. According to Dr. Breggin, "All antipsychotic drugs clog the brain and mind by performing a chemical disruption of frontal lobe function, the equivalent of a pharmacological lobotomy" (Breggin, 2008b, p. 225). They operate basically by disabling the brain, just as with a lobotomy. In addition, there are serious adverse side effects from these medications, including severe apathy and indifference, heat intolerance that can cause death by heat stroke, and mental impairment (Breggin, 2008a, p. 302). From 40% to 50% of patients taking antipsychotics also experience tardive dyskinesia, (Breggin, 2013, p. 42), "a persistent and usually irreversible disorder that causes disfiguring grimaces and tics and potentially disabling abnormal movement of arms, hands, legs, and neck, as well as the muscles of speaking, swallowing, and breathing" (Breggin, 2008a, p. 134).

In addition, from 20 to 75% of schizophrenic patients experience akathisia, "an experience of inner torture with a compulsion to move" which can "produce suicidal and violent behavior" (Breggin, 2008b, p. 236). When individuals experience these serious adverse effects and they want to withdraw from their medications, they discover that "withdrawing from antipsychotic drugs can be extremely difficult and sometimes impossible ... children or adults who have taken these drugs for months or years often become more psychotic than ever when they try to withdraw" (Breggin, 2008b, p 302).

In summary, antipsychotic medications are ineffective in reducing long-term psychotic episodes, lead to serious adverse side effects that are the result of brain damage, and are extremely difficult to withdraw from by those who experience the serious side effects. It would be far more beneficial for those interested in helping individuals with thought disorders such as schizophrenia to look to the successful treatment programs of the past and to learn from those like Dr. Karon and Dr. Breggin who have successfully treated schizophrenics without medications, by providing a caring environment for them while helping them to be productive members of society as they receive help resolving their underlying emotional issues.

Dr. Harrow provides valuable information in his report on the 20-year follow-up study of schizophrenic patients treated with, or without antipsychotics. He states in his report that 34% of schizophrenics recover from their psychotic behavior and are able to maintain employment, without the use of any medications. When these individuals are given antipsychotic medications their rate of recovery is only 6%. Given such outcome research, those responsible for helping family members and friends with serious thought disorders ought to avoid the long-term use of antipsychotic medications and look for compassionate, treatment alternatives for them. Treatment programs around the world have shown that acutely psychotic patients have better outcomes when treated without antipsychotic drugs (Breggin, 2013, p. 55). Since these individuals are often angry, terrified, lonely individuals due to experiences in their past, they can be helped with these feelings through the use of this prayer ministry as they learn to trust their caregivers and begin discussing their feelings.

Stimulants

Now, let's consider children with hyperactivity problems who are diagnosed with attention-deficit disorders (ADD) who primarily have difficulty focusing on tasks, or attention-deficit hyperactivity disorders (ADHD) in which the child is both inattentive and hyperactive. What would happen to these children if the stimulants used for hyperactive children were unavailable? A recent study found that 10% of all children are taking methylphenidate or similar stimulants to control their so-called attention-deficit disorders. In 2009 12.3% of boys and 5.5% of girls aged 5-17 were diagnosed with ADHD according to the CDC (Breggin, 2013, p. 73).

There is no doubt that some children are very hyperactive and unable to focus on school work, but that does not mean that it is due to a chemical imbalance or brain disorder that is a valid medical syndrome (Breggin, 2013, p. 83-84). Hyperactivity and inability to focus are often due to poor parenting, family problems such as fighting and divorce, and due to emotional issues that cannot be corrected by medications, such as grief from losses. The use of ADHD medications may temporarily improve a child's focus, but there are no long-term benefits beyond the first eight weeks. The FDA stated, "Long term effects of Ritalin in children have not been well established" (Breggin, 2008, p. 285) but "within an hour after taking a single dose of a stimulant drug, any child tends to become more obedient, narrower in focus, and more willing to concentrate on humdrum tasks and instructions" (Breggin, 2008, p. 303). However, a U.S. Department of Education review reported that "Long-term beneficial effects have not been verified by research" and concluded, "Teachers and parents should not expect long-term improvement in academic achievement or reduced antisocial behavior" (Breggin, 2008b, 198).

In addition, there are several other reasons why parents should be very hesitant to place their children on these medications. First, parents are seldom told that methylphenidate (Ritalin) is "speed" (Breggin, 2008a, p. 300). Parents who knowingly allow their children to use illegal street drugs are guilty of child abuse, but they allow their children to be given methylphenidate, which is chemically very similar to cocaine. Second, research has shown that stimulant drugs used for ADHD are extremely addictive and make children exposed to them much more likely to abuse cocaine in early adulthood (Breggin, 2013, p. 77-78). Third, a 36-month study funded by the National Institute of Mental Health concluded that there were no long-term positive effects from stimulant drugs, and that stimulant drugs stunt growth (Breggin, 2008b, 198). Fourth, "Stimulant medications... cause potentially irreversible tics, insomnia, depression and suicidality, OCD, apathy, overstimulated behavior, cardiovascular risks, and mania and psychosis" (Breggin, 2013, p. 84). Given these serious factors and the lack of long-term benefit received from these medications, parents should seek help from competent counselors for their hyperactive children (there are competent counselors who can help parents learn some basic parenting and disciplinary skills without knowing how to do this prayer ministry). Of course, some hyperactivity or inability to focus is due to poor teaching, and teachers who have difficulty holding the attention of their students should be provided some training to improve their skills.

Educating children is a very important and challenging task, and it is greatly complicated by the presence of children who are unable to focus on their work, or who are so hyperactive that they are distracting to other children in the classroom. Who can blame teachers for wanting to help these children sit still and listen? Of course, there is a behavioral difference between boys and girls, because many girls are more cognitively mature than boys their age and are better prepared to sit quietly and engage in classroom behavior. Boys, on the other hand, have difficulty sitting in a classroom for hours at a time to learn things that are difficult for them, and most of them would rather be outdoors playing sports or engaging in physical activities. It is interesting that 12.3 % of boys are diagnosed with ADHD and only 5.5% of girls are diagnosed with ADHD. This suggests that the prescription of these medication to boys is an attempt to get them to behave more like little girls than like boys. Understanding these differences between boys and girls ought to motivate educators to have shorter classes, and provide more breaks from boring classroom activities for those who complete their work quickly and accurately.

Not only is hyperactivity more common with boys, it is often evidence of emotional difficulties in the child's home, and of poor disciplinary practices by the parents. Children who witness violence at home, or marital conflicts between their parents, or loss of parents due to separations or divorces, are frequently preoccupied at school and unable to focus on their school work, because they are worrying about losing their parents and family. Taking a stimulant like Ritalin will not resolve these problems at home. Sometimes, children display behavior at school that is disruptive, because they have not been taught at home how to behave. Their parents may complain about their behavior, and may be very frustrated at them and scream at them, but they do not know how to effectively and calmly discipline them. When these children are medicated in order to calm them, the underlying family and disciplinary problems go untreated, and the child comes to believe that he or she is bad.

As a mental health counselor I have found that when families who receive help for the marital problems in the home, and parents are taught effective disciplinary principles that the behavior of the child improves at home and at school. However, when the child is simply given some medications for their hyperactivity, these basic causes of the hyperactivity go untreated. Good family interventions that use the prayer principles of this ministry to help the parents with their emotional struggles, and then provide the parents with some training in effective disciplinary procedures, will resolve most of the hyperactivity and inability to focus on school work.

Mood Stabilizers

What about those with so-called bipolar disorders? How should we help them? First, it should be understood that bipolar disorders are greatly over-diagnosed, and that the diagnosis of bipolar disorders has increased dramatically during the last decade. Even young children who have temper tantrums are increasingly diagnosed as having bipolar disorders and medicated. "Between 1994 and 2003, there was a 40-fold increase in diagnosing bipolar disorder in children, and the trend has been escalating since then" (Breggin, 2008a, p. 23). Much of this, according to Dr. Breggin, is probably the result of individuals taking antidepressants for years, which is known to cause mania.

Mood stabilizers like Lithium and Depakote cannot be used like antipsychotic drugs to quickly subdue an individual, but they are used for the long-term control of so-called bipolar disorder. Dr. Breggin states that, "Nowadays they are given to many children and adults who have but the faintest signs of a manic-like problem, such as irritability and mild mood swings in adults or temper tantrums in children" (Breggin, 2008b, p. 232).

One of the original medications used for treating bipolar disorders was lithium, which was "originally promoted to the public and to the mental health profession as the ultimate example of a specific biochemical treatment for a specific psychiatric disorder" (Breggin, 2008a, p. 193). "It was discovered when it was accidentally found that injections of lithium into guinea pigs immediately made them inactive and even flaccid. Numerous studies of normal volunteers have confirmed that lithium knocks people out of touch with their feelings, puts a dark glass between them and other people, and reduces their motivation to do anything. In the process it leaves many people with memory dysfunction and other cognitive deficits" (Breggin, 2008b, p 232). The truth is that anyone who takes lithium will find that it constricts their thinking and emotions severely, which may be seen as an improvement by some parties. Lithium has a "generalized brain-disabling, deactivating effect. This effect may at times reduce the occurrence of manic episodes, but it does so by reducing overall brain function. Even in regard to reducing the frequency of manic episodes, its efficacy is doubtful and it causes manic withdrawal reactions" (Breggin, 2008a, p. 200).

Numerous problems have been found with the use of lithium for individuals. First, "Several studies have shown cognitive impairment in short-term memory, long-term memory and psychomotor speed in bipolar patients taking lithium" (Breggin, 2008a, p. 204). Second, "Mood stabilizers, when prescribed for months and years, can cause chronic brain impairment" (Breggin, 2013, p. 107). Third, researchers at the University of Wisconsin "found that many patients became demented or otherwise deteriorate severely when abruptly withdrawn from lithium" (Breggin, 2008a, p. 212). According to Dr. Breggin, patients who stop taking the "mood stabilizer" lithium will be exposed to a much higher risk of having a manic episode than they were before taking the drug. In other words, they are suffering from withdrawal mania. Instead of admitting that a patient is suffering from withdrawal mana, the doctor is likely to say, "See, I told you that you need to take lithium for the rest of your life" (Breggin, 2008b, p. 238).

Dr. Breggin states that "The FDA has also approved a group of antiepileptic drugs specifically to treat 'bipolar' disorder, especially the long-term suppression of mania…. These drugs were originally approved and used as anti-seizure drugs. They tend to suppress the electrical activity of the brain" (Breggin, 2008b, p. 232). All mood stabilizers have a global impact on the individual's cognitive functioning rather than a specific impact upon the so-called mood disorder for which they are supposedly being prescribed. "Mood stabilizers… act by suppressing overall emotional responsiveness. Individuals become less able to feel and less able to identify and express their feelings" (Breggin, 2013, p. 107). Dr. Breggin states, "By interfering with the overall electrical processes in the brain, lithium gums up the brain and, hence, the mind" (Breggin, 2008b, p. 233).

In 1995, researchers conducted a study of patients treated with lithium for bipolar disorder who were carefully monitored for compliance, and "despite this, 73% of the patients relapsed into mania or depression within 5 years" (Breggin, 2008a, p. 211). Thus, the use of lithium for bipolar disorders is not very effective.

How can individuals who are diagnosed as "Bipolar" be helped? If they are taking drugs or medications that are making them manic, these drugs need to be gradually withdrawn under the supervision of experienced medical providers. Dr. Breggin's book *Medication Withdrawal* is a valuable and essential book for medical providers who want to learn how to assist clients in the withdrawal process. Individuals diagnosed with "bipolar" disorders usually have many unresolved feelings of grief that lead to episodes of depression, and they also have strong, unresolved feelings of anger for which they need assistance. I have found that as I have prayed with such persons about their anger and grief that their mood swings improve very rapidly. The following is one such example.

Set Free from "Bipolar Disorder"

I have seen many people who were diagnosed with a "bipolar disorder" who have responded very well, and quickly, to prayer ministry. Many times these people feel doomed to a life-long dependence upon psychiatric medications that destroy their cognitive abilities, dull their emotions, prevent them from experiencing joy, and make them feel physically fatigued. When they are informed that they can overcome their anger and grief and stop their extreme mood swings, they are often excited and are filled with hope.

A young woman was referred for counseling by her grandmother due to her extreme moodiness and anxiety attacks. She said she was diagnosed with a "bipolar disorder" three years earlier when she began arguing frequently with her parents and screaming at them. She stated that her parents fought a lot and yelled and screamed at each other, especially after her father had an affair and her mother would not let it go. She felt that their fighting was her fault, and she became angry at her mother for telling her that she was an accident. Because of all the fighting and chaos in her family she began using drugs and drinking in middle school. Then in high school, she cheated on her boyfriend and felt guilty and shameful, and he broke up with her. She also lost a grandparent and a great-grandparent which made her sad. After high school she had another boyfriend and he cheated on her, and this added to her anger and depression.

As she shared these experiences it was obvious why she was so depressed and angry, but she had been told she was "bipolar" and was medicated. She decided to get away from her angry home atmosphere and to live with her grandmother. She took herself off her medications because they weren't helping her, but her anger and depression continued. I shared with her how she could be set free from her anger through prayer but she was reluctant to pray with me and my prayer partner. She did, however, agree to try to pray about her anger toward her parents on her own.

When she returned three weeks later, she said that she had prayed about her anger toward her parents and she was not angry at them anymore. She had made a list of everything she resented about both of them, and then asked the Lord to please take her anger. After that she realized that her parents' fighting was not her fault, and she said that she began getting along better with them. Now her mother wants to be "best friends" with her. She also prayed on her own about her most recent boyfriend who had cheated on her, and she was no longer angry at him or grieving over him. She realized that he is an alcoholic and she was better off without him. He talked with her about his new girlfriend and it didn't even bother her now. All of this amazing emotional change came about by her making her own lists and praying on her own.

I asked this young woman about her high school boyfriend and she admitted that she missed him and felt guilt and shame for cheating on him. She said she dealt with her guilt by going outdoors and relaxing and then forgetting about it. I explained how she could get rid of her guilt and not just suppress it, and she said she would like to do that. Then I asked her if she would like to be 100% sure that she is forgiven and going to heaven and she said she would, so I used the booklet entitled "How to Overcome Doubts" to explain the gospel to her. She prayed to the Lord and confessed her sins and invited Him into her life.

After this she said she felt no more shame about her high school boyfriend, but she still missed him. She talked about things she missed about him, including his friendship, caring, affection, his eyes, and the fun times they had together. She identified 18 things she missed about him, then prayed and asked the Lord to take all this and carry it for her. When I asked her how she felt afterwards, she chuckled and said she felt "relieved" and "happy." She rated her depression as a 1, on a 10-point scale, and left the session smiling.

The Lord is so good that He answers the prayers of the unbelieving when they seek His help with their emotions. All of the anger she had released on her own happened before she even knew the Lord, but it softened up her heart to Him and to prayer. This young woman found relief from her mood swings by her own prayers, and from one prayer session with two prayer ministers. What a joy it was to see such profound change in this woman's life so quickly, and to see her come to faith in Jesus after just two prayer sessions.

Societal Violence and Psychiatric Medications

In the discussion of anti-depressants in Chapter 10 and the other psychiatric medications in Chapter 11, it was mentioned that many of these medications can cause aggression and violence. But how serious is this risk, and do the benefits of the medications out-weigh the possible risks of them, as most doctors will report? Physicians usually minimize the risks involved, and do not really believe that anyone commits murder or suicide as a result of the medications that they prescribe. What does research tell us about this risk?

Since it is estimated that 20% of all adults in the United States were taking at least one psychiatric drug in 2010, there are around 47 million adults taking psychiatric drugs. If the risk of violence from these drugs was only .1% (a very low estimate) this would still mean that over a year's time there would be more than 128 acts of violence each day, by adults on psychiatric drugs, and not including violence by children on these drugs. The advocates of psychiatric drugs claim that the "benefits" from these drugs outweighs any risks of violent behavior, but the destruction to these individuals whose lives are destroyed through violence is immeasurable.

Readers are again encouraged to read Dr. Breggin's book, *Medication Madness*, to grasp the reality of this threat. A used copy can be purchased for about $10 on Amazon.com for the interested reader. In this book Dr. Breggin describes fifty cases which he personally investigated involving individuals who committed acts of violence, murder, and suicide as a result of taking psychiatric medications. There are numerous cases similar to these that are reported to the FDA, so there is no doubt that these medications can lead to suicide and murder. However, the frequency with which this occurs is unknown, and it is complicated by the refusal of agencies to release medical records of individuals involved in such actions.

In a 2010 scientific review of all reports of violence and homicidal ideation made to the FDA over a 69 month period, 31 out of 454 prescription drugs had a disproportional rate of reported violence or homicidal threats, and two-thirds of drugs had no reports of violence. Twenty-six of the 31 drugs were psychiatric drugs and the drugs that caused the most violence were Chantix (a smoking cessation aid), 11 antidepressant medications, 3 drugs for ADHD, and 5 sleep aids and tranquilizers. Breggin concluded, “This study should end the controversy. Psychiatric drugs do cause violence” (Breggin, Jan. 13, 2013, blog on naturalnews.com).

Dr. Breggin obtained the drug company’s official report to the FDA on May, 14, 1999 regarding the Columbine shooting in Colorado, and found that one of the shooters, Eric Harris, was taking the antidepressant Luvox at the time that the shootings occurred.

James Holmes, the Aurora, Colorado movie shooter was in treatment with psychiatrist Lynne Fenton in the months before he assaulted people in the movie theater on July 20, 2012. He had no known criminal record prior to the killing of 12 people in the theater. A court hearing revealed that four prescription bottles had been removed from his home, but the identity of these medications has been withheld from the public (Breggin, 2015).

Likewise, the Newtown murderer, Adam Lanza, was taking psychiatric drugs when he killed 20 children at the Sandy Hook Elementary School on December 14, 2012. A former neighbor in

Newtown, Connecticut described him as "A really rambunctious kid" and stated that he was on medication, but no information has been released concerning his medication use.

The Navy Yard mass murderer, Aaron Alexis, was taking the antidepressant trazodone when he committed the violent assaults on September 16, 2013. The FDA-approved label for trazodone lists the following side effects: "anxiety, agitation, panic attacks, insomnia, irritability, hostility, aggressiveness, impulsivity, akathisia [psychomotor restlessness], hypomania and mania" (Breggin Blog, September 18, 2013, breggin.com).

Chris Harper Mercer, the Oregon college shooter, was taking psychiatric medications, including sleeping aids, but the specific type of medications he was taking have never been disclosed to the public (Breggin blog, October, 2015, madinamerica.com).

Virtually all of the mass murders that have occurred in our country over the last twenty years and have had wide publicity, have one thing in common. They were all committed by individuals known to be taking, or suspected of taking, psychiatric medications at the time that they committed their acts of violence. Since it is already known that these medications are capable of causing violence in individuals with no violent history, they are strongly implicated in these public acts of mass violence. After all, they are known as "mind-altering" drugs because they do indeed alter the state of mind, but not necessarily in the way that they are intended or advertised. And yet the media and pharmaceutical companies prevent disclosure of the medication link due to concerns that it might decerease their drug sales.

Recommendations on Psychiatric Medications

The evidence that is now available regarding the harmfulness of psychiatric medications and their effectiveness should lead individuals to seriously question their use when doctors recommend them. Christians in general, and Christian leaders and pastors in particular, need to become educated about these fact, and be very skeptical about those who strongly advocate psychiatric medications and have no alternatives to recommend.

The advertising and propaganda by the pharmaceutical companies has been extremely effective, and it is very difficult to persuade most Christians that these medications are both ineffective and harmful, because of the almost universal acceptance of them by Christian doctors and pastors. It is so complicated to sort through the medical facts regarding these matters, and it is so effectively blocked by pharmaceutical companies and doctors, that it is overwhelming for the average person to try to understand these issues on their own. However, there are so many people whose lives have been destroyed by these medications and have gone for years and years following the advice of their doctor, only to find that they have wasted their entire lives trusting them and are no better off, but have actually grown worse. It is very sad to hear the testimonies of people who have listened to the advice of their doctors, psychiatrists, and pastors and whose lives have been destroyed. The readers are strongly encouraged to read *Anatomy of an Epidemic* by Robert Whitaker who provides a clear summary of the research on psychiatric medications that has been established by psychiatric researchers themselves, but is not known by most physicians.

Dr. Breggin and a growing number of other doctors and researcher provide us with strong evidence from scientific studies of the harmfulness of psychiatric medications, and their ineffectiveness in healing the emotional needs of the individuals. He recommends that individuals not take these medications but seek help from a competent, caring, empathic therapist who will listen to them. He has written in his books that over 40 years of psychiatric practice he has never prescribed psychiatric medications for individuals with emotional problems, except when he is helping them slowly withdraw from the medications. We should be very thankful for men like Dr. Breggin, who has been described as "the conscience of psychiatry," who has devoted his life to educating those who are willing to listen, and to teaching them about the ineffectiveness of psychiatric medications and their serious, adverse side effects.

In addition, those who are spiritually-minded and receptive to learning to use prayer for resolving their emotional struggles will find that the principles described in this book are very effective in setting people free. You will find, as I have, that the Lord is able to do what no psychiatrist, psychologist, counselor or medication can do. He can carry your emotional problems for you and give you His perfect peace. May each reader seek to find this peace in his/her life through the Lord Jesus, the "Wonderful Counselor, Mighty God, Eternal Father, and Prince of Peace" (Isaiah 9:6).

WARNING: Most psychiatric drugs can cause withdrawal reactions, sometimes including life-threatening emotional and physical withdrawal problems. In short, it is not only dangerous to start taking psychiatric drugs, it can also be dangerous to stop them. Withdrawal from psychiatric drugs should be done carefully under experienced clinical supervision.

24

THE ULTIMATE GOAL: TURNING THE WORLD UPSIDE DOWN

As I begin this last chapter, I am shocked by another recent mass killing and the state of affairs in our country. On June 12, 2016 a shooter by the name of Omar Mateen, killed 49 people in Orlando, Florida in a "gay" bar. Initially, it was thought that he was simply a radical anti-homosexual, but it was quickly learned that he was a Muslim whose parents immigrated from Pakistan. Suddenly, attention was brought on the violent attitudes of Muslims toward homosexuals, which has been ignored for the last 15 years since the attacks on the World Trade Center.

The State of our Country Today

Our President simply downplayed the obvious religious nature of the attack and once again ignored the violence of Muslims and blamed it on weapons. One month ago the President unilaterally announced that all schools and colleges must provide open bathrooms, dressing rooms, and locker rooms to those who are sexually confused, to allow any person to use them who feels they are actually a member of the opposite sex, in spite of their biological organs. As the second term of this President draws to a close, an all-out assault on Christian values is occurring. This same President who is supporting Muslim causes and ignoring the attacks on our country by Muslims, has led the attack on traditional marriages and celebrated the decision by the Supreme Court to prevent states from prohibiting homosexual marriage by lighting up the White House in rainbow colors.

The two terms of this President's administration have also been marked by repeated acts of mass violence around the country. Each time an act of mass violence has occurred he has preached against the evils of weapons and blamed the weapons, and the lack of mental health treatment, for the violence in our country. In the decades prior to the Muslim attack on the World Trade Center, our country had already pulled away from its Christian foundations by banning prayer from public schools, and rejecting Christian marriage in favor of open sex and relationships outside of marriage, so that more and more children were raised in homes without fathers, or in a single-parent home. In the 1970s, abortion was legalized by the Supreme Court, and it came to be used as a birth-control method, bringing strong feelings of anger, grief and shame to many young people. This placed a great deal of stress on families where the children grew up with angry and stressed parents, so it was no surprise that the children were also angry and depressed and resorted to drug abuse and violence in our country. It is also no surprise that crime and violence continue to increase in the country, as the country has rejected Christianity and the foundational moral principles upon which it was established.

Then, in the 1990s there was a big push to accept homosexuality as simply an "alternative life style," in spite of the AIDs epidemic that it started. Homosexuality was celebrated as an unavoidable biological deviation that had to be accepted by everyone. President Clinton advocated the acceptance of homosexuality in the military when he was elected as president. Then the attack on the World Trade Center led to the refusal to acknowledge the true enemy, Islam, and President Bush led the initial war against "Terrorism" while refusing to address the evil of Islam. President Obama vowed to fundamentally change America, and spent the eight years of his administration working to destroy every Christian value he could, and attacking Christians at every opportunity, while embracing the religion of Islam that declared war on our country.

With the destruction of the family in our country, the disintegration of marriages, the increase of immorality and sexual perversion, and the celebration of homosexual marriages, our country is in a state of disarray. Islam is on the attack, and has vowed to destroy our country and take over the world, with their violence, their hatred of Christians and Jews, their oppression of women, and their endorsement of pedophilia. Very soon we are likely to see the promotion of child marriages, polygamy, and pedophilia, and the condemnation of all Christians as hatemongers, bigots, and homophobes. Although this country was founded upon Christian principles, Christianity is now under attack from both the outside and the inside of our country.

Transforming the World

What can Christians do today to stop this attack and prevent further deterioration? The Bible has a lot to say about how to transform a society and the world in a positive way for Christianity, because the world was in a similar position before the coming of Jesus into the world. In his book *How Christianity Changed the World*, sociology professor Alvin J. Schmidt (Schmidt, 2004) documented how Christianity radically changed the world by influencing laws, art, literature, philosophy, education, and moral standards. It improved the status of women and children, abolished slavery in most countries, promoted religious freedoms, strengthened families and marriages, and created societies that valued freedom, families, and equality. This did not happen in a matter of years, but over a period of centuries as His apostles and followers lived according to His teachings.

When Jesus entered the world, He taught by word and example the importance of women and children, and He taught moral principles that have profoundly changed the world for good. He taught us to love one another, and He went beyond the basic morality of the Ten Commandments to interpret the spirit of the Law. Not only did He teach that murder was a sin, but that whoever was angry with his brother or neighbor was committing murder in his heart. He taught us by word and example to "love your neighbor as yourself," and applied this to helping those who were despised in the world, like the Good Samaritan did. He taught that it was not only sinful to commit adultery, but that "everyone who looks at a woman with lust for her has already committed adultery with her in his heart" (Matthew 5:28).

After Jesus was crucified, His disciples continued spreading His teachings and His example, and began to spread them throughout the world. They were persecuted, and every one of the apostles, except John, was executed eventually, but the Church continued through the centuries to preach the same message of love, forgiveness, and kindness to our fellow men and women. It was the teachings and values of the Church that led to the establishment of the United States as "one nation, under God," and to the belief expressed in the Declaration of Independence that "all men are created equal and are endowed by their Creator with the inalienable rights of life, liberty, and the pursuit of happiness." These liberties are now under attack as the radical Left, who hate Jesus, are attacking our freedoms of speech and religion.

However, we have the same God and Holy Spirit Who radically transformed the world from the times of the Roman Empire when Christians were persecuted, up to the present. The same Holy Spirit Who changed the world at that time, can radically transform our society and world today as believers submit to His leading and example, and as churches spread the life-transforming principles of the Bible.

Radical Transformations

In the early Church, as recorded in the book of Acts, the Christian Church was established by the apostles and followers of Jesus, in the midst of much persecution. But the persecution did not stop the advance of the Church; rather, it contributed to it, and facilitated the explosion of the church into existence. The Holy Spirit guided the apostles as they spread the gospel and as they performed many miracles in the name of Jesus. The result was that "Everyone kept feeling a sense of awe; and many wonders and signs were taking place through the apostles" (Acts 2:43).

In Acts 3 the writer describes the miraculous healing of a lame man when Peter and John were entering the temple to pray. This crippled man was lying at the door of the temple seeking alms from Peter and John, when Peter spoke to him and said, "Silver and gold have I none; but such as I have give I thee: In the name of Jesus Christ of Nazareth rise up and walk" (Acts 3:6, KJV). The man stood up and became so excited about his healing that he began leaping and praising God in a loud voice so that everyone became aware of the miracle that had just happened. This caused such a stir among the people that the religious leaders heard about it and came to see what was happening.

Not only was this a physical miracle of healing, but it was an emotional miracle as well, because these timid, uneducated men began boldly proclaiming the gospel and responding calmly to the threats and intimidation of the authorities. Peter and John were placed in jail and the next day were placed in the center of the elders and scribes and priests and questioned viciously, but Peter was "filled with the Holy Spirit" and calmly and boldly proclaimed the gospel of Jesus to them. Acts 4:13 says, "Now as they observed the confidence of Peter and John and understood that they were uneducated and untrained men, they were amazed, and began to recognize them as having been with Jesus." It was a miracle to see these uneducated fishermen with so much confidence and wisdom.

More such miracles happened regularly during the beginnings of the New Testament Church. Paul was radically transformed after his supernatural encounter with the Lord on the road to Damascus, from being a violent persecutor of the Lord to being a radical evangelist.

He soon went into the streets of Jerusalem and proclaimed Jesus as Lord, and became the staunchest defender of Christianity and the greatest proponent and missionary for the church.

In Acts 13, when Paul and Barnabas proclaimed the gospel in the city of Pisidian Antioch, the Jews were filled with jealousy (Acts 13:45) and "instigated a persecution against Paul and Barnabas, and drove them out of their district. But they shook off the dust of their feet in protest against them and went to Iconium." The Scriptures tell us that the disciples were "continually filled with joy and with the Holy Spirit" (Acts 13:50-52) in spite of the persecution. Believers were walking in the Spirit and their lives were being radically transformed. They were able to endure persecution and to be full of joy and peace, through the power of the Holy Spirit.

Today the Holy Spirit is present in the life of each true believer, and wants to empower us and fill us with His joy and peace. But Christians today must learn how to allow the Holy Spirit to set them free from their emotional bondage so that they, too, will become excited about Jesus and not be intimidated by the world. When believers are radically transformed emotionally and are set free from their anger, grief, shame and fear they will want to spread the gospel and share the goodness of God with others. This is the goal of this ministry; to teach believers how to find freedom and joy and peace from the Lord, so that they will transform the world through God's power.

Turning the World Upside Down

When Paul and Silas went to Thessalonica, they went to the synagogue and reasoned with the Jews from the Scriptures to show that Jesus was the Messiah. And many of the Jews believed on Jesus, but the Jewish leaders became jealous of them (Acts 17:5) and formed a mob and set the city in an uproar, telling the city authorities "These that have turned the world upside down" had come there also (Acts 17:6, KJV). They stirred up the crowd and city authorities so much that the believers in Thessalonica sent Paul and Silas away by night to Berea to protect them.

It is interesting that they were described as those "who have turned the world upside down," and this was intended as a criticism, but it was actually a great compliment. The gospel of Jesus was having such an impact on the world that the Jews were complaining that the Christians were turning the world "upside down."

What the world needs now is the same as what was needed then; it needs to be transformed and turned upside down morally, religiously, and socially. All of the moral and legal changes that have occurred in our country in the last fifty years need to be overturned so that our society once again has a biblical foundation and our country reflects the Lord. This change will only occur as believers release their anger and are transformed. Once the Church of America is transformed, then our society will be transformed as well.

Dancing for Joy

A man came to me after wrecking his car while driving under the influence of alcohol. He barely escaped death, and as a result of his accident he received his second DUI and admitted that he had a drinking problem and needed help. I took time to collect some background information from him, and learned that he had lost his father at an early age, which led to some depression and anger, and then in his teenage years he began drinking excessively. Other losses and traumas led to more negative feelings and intensified his drinking problems.

After gaining this background information I explained the dynamics of addiction to him, telling him that many people experiment with alcohol or drugs at some time in their lives but most people do not like feeling high or drunk and they never develop an addiction. However, when an individual does like being high or drunk, it is always due to some underlying painful emotions that they want to numb, which makes the high or numb feeling feel really good. This man understood this principle, and nodded in agreement that he had some strong emotional pain that led him to begin abusing alcohol, and agreed that it is very difficult to stop abusing it when he still has unresolved emotional pain from his past. I explained to him how the Lord can take away his emotional pain through prayer, and he became excited and stated that he was raised in a Baptist church, and he was excited to learn that the Lord could set him free from his grief and anger.

The next day I met with him and we talked about his father, whom he lost at age 12. I asked him what he missed about his father, and we made a list of about 16 things he missed. I then led him in a prayer to give these losses to the Lord, and asked the Lord to take his grief and sadness from him and carry it for him. After we prayed, I asked him to think about his father and tell me how he felt. He told me he felt nothing, so I instructed him to think about his father again and try to stir up any negative feelings. He tried, but said he felt nothing but calmness.

I asked him what he thought about his sudden change in feelings. He immediately became animated and smiled and said, "This would be a great ministry to get involved in. I feel like getting up and dancing," he said with a big smile. I shared with him about the Set Free meetings we hold every week in his town. His reaction reminded me of the lame man whom Peter healed in Acts 3:8 who began "walking and leaping and praising God" after he was healed. When you experience the Lord's healing after being in bondage for so many years, you can't help but get excited about Jesus.

Holy Spirit Counseling Sessions

I previously related that I saw a young woman who was referred to me for a substance abuse evaluation and counseling. She admitted that she had used drugs extensively in the past, but claimed that she was no longer using drugs and was going to church. I have met many people who quit using drugs temporarily and began attending church, and I knew that this was not usually the end of their drug abuse. I talked with her about her past to learn what types of losses she had, and to learn about the sources of her anger that led her to begin using drugs.

She admitted that she used to be very angry, so I asked this young woman what had happened to her anger. She told me that she had prayed about her anger to each person and confessed it to the Lord and asked Him to take it, and it had left her, one person after another. I inquired about her grief over some of her losses, and she informed me that she had prayed about each source of her grief and had been set free from her grief. She told me that when she got out of jail she had prayed extensively and had a prolonged prayer session in which she prayed about a lot of emotional issues from her past. She described this as a "Holy Spirit Counseling Session," and she attributed her freedom to this. I was convinced that she had, indeed, been set free through her prayers and through the Holy Spirit, not simply through her salvation.

Around the same time period I saw a young man who had had his child removed from him and his girlfriend due to their drug abuse. He and his girlfriend were separated, and he began living with his parents, going to church with them, and getting his life straightened out. One day when his girlfriend brought the child to him, his mother found drugs inside the baby's diaper bag and she reported this to the state Department of Human Services. The child was removed from both parents, who both admitted having used drugs formerly, and both parents were required to submit to a drug abuse assessment.

When I met privately with this young man, I inquired about his background to understand why he had previously abused drugs. He sounded like he was indeed drug free, but I wanted to know if he was truly healed or just temporarily abstaining from his drug abuse. I learned about some former relationships he had had and his resentments toward these previous women, and he told me how he had forgiven them. I asked how he was able to release his anger toward his parents that he previously admitted having, and he said that he did a lot of praying in his church.

This man also said that when he got saved, he released a lot of anger because he knew that if he was going to give his life to

Jesus he could not hold onto any anger. After our conversation, I was convinced that he had truly released the anger and grief from his past that had led him to begin abusing drugs. He, too, had a life-changing encounter with Jesus and a "Holy Spirit Counseling Session" that set him free from the emotional bondage that led him to abuse drugs. It wasn't simply the salvation experience that set him free, but his salvation paired with his continuing prayers to release all of his anger that gave him freedom.

The New Testament does not specifically present the prayer principles in the same fashion as presented in this book, but there is much evidence that Christians in the early New Testament Church engaged in "Holy Spirit Counseling Sessions" like those described above. The scriptures do instruct us to "pray in the Spirit" (Ephesians 6:18, Jude 1:20) and to "walk by the Spirit" (Galatians 5:16), and there are many examples of the Holy Spirit guiding believers into truth in the book of Acts (See John 16:13). Paul was warned by the Spirit to not speak the word in Asia (Acts 16:6) and when he traveled to Jerusalem by ship he was warned by the Spirit that everyone should remain in the ship (Acts 27:23-31) for them to be safe.

The Church today needs to learn to "walk by the Spirit" and "pray in the Spirit" as the believers did in the New Testament Church. This requires honesty with the Lord about our feelings, and learning to cast all our cares upon Him, and letting Him guide us into all truth. As the Church today begins to confess their faults to one another and pray for one another, the Holy Spirit can bring healing and truth to the believers so that they will experience freedom like that described above.

The Impact of Heroic Grace

Chapter 2 made reference to the shooting deaths of 9 innocent black Christians on June 17, 2015 by Dylan Roof, during a Bible study. He sat with these Christians in a Bible study at the Emmanuel African Methodist Episcopal Church in Charleston, South Carolina, then left and returned with weapons and killed nine innocent people. He stated that he wanted to start a racial war, but he failed in his efforts because those who survived from the church told him the next day at a court hearing that they forgave him and were praying for him to repent and come to know Jesus. Their response totally diffused the anger of those in their community who were ready to riot and react with violence.

A reporter by the name of Rich Lowry wrote, "Emmanuel African Methodist Episcopal Church in Charleston, S.C., has taken an unspeakable crime and made it the occasion for an astonishing Christian witness. In an unforgettable scene at the bond hearing last week for Dylan Roof, tearful family members of the victims told Roof that they forgive him and that he should repent. They were voices of LOVE responding to hate, of unbelievable mercy and forbearance in the face of cruelty and murderous provocation, of an almost miraculous faith" (Lowry, 2015). Lowry also reported that members of the media wondered how the family members were capable of such "heroic grace."

Another reporter by the name of Jonah Goldberg wrote, "Not being a Christian, I can only marvel at the dignity and courage of the victims' relatives who forgave the shooter. If I could ever manage such a thing, it would probably take me decades. It took them little more than a day" (Goldberg, 2015).

These people were able to love Dylan Roof because they had the love of God within them, and they forgave like Jesus taught and literally forgave this troubled young man before the sun could go down on their anger. As remarkable as their response was, they were simply following the example of Jesus and the teaching of the apostle Paul. What is sad is that such behavior is so uncommon for Christians, that it surprises people when they witness such a reaction. Christians are much more likely to carry anger indefinitely over petty matters and to quarrel among themselves in their churches. If there were many other churches like this remarkable one in South Carolina, our society would undoubtedly change for the good.

Making the pledge ne to never let the sun go down on their anger would have a profound impact upon individuals. These individuals would be happy, get along well with friends, family members, fellow employees, and neighbors. Their calm attitudes would help de-escalate tensions wherever they worked, and they would be peacemakers among their friends and colleagues.

This pledge would also have a dramatic impact on marriages. Those who live by this pledge would have disagreements with their spouses, but would not overact or explode with anger or violence toward them. Couples who made the pledge along with their marriage vows would experience very few divorces, because they would not be prone to affairs or other divisive behaviors if they had no anger, and they would be able to communicate effectively about their marital conflicts. In addition, the children of these individuals would grow up in more stable home environments and feel more loved and accepted since their parents were free of anger.

If this principle was taught regularly by pastors and practiced and taught by them, so that everyone in their church began to live by this principle it would revolutionize that church. The Church would enjoy a great degree of harmony and unity and demonstrate love in a remarkable way. Instead of fighting and splitting, like so many churches do, these churches would resolve their problems and demonstrate love for one another so that they would be known, as Jesus said, by their love for one another (John 13:35).

Once the churches began practicing this principle, many people would be drawn to them for help with their marriages and their anger, instead of turning to mental health counselors or to psychiatric medications. It would bring such emotional healing that many of those with substance abuse problems would be set free, those with other criminal behaviors and social problems would cease to engage in their problematic behaviors. Anger is what drives most antisocial behaviors, so in the absence of pervasive anger in a society, there would be much less crime.

Anger is a major contributing factor in many types of mental disorders, including substance abuse problems, physical abuse, sexual abuse, marital problems, anxiety, PTSD, and depression. As individuals learn how to overcome their anger, many of these mental disorders will decrease drastically in our society. There is an increasing number of mass murders occurring in our society and the secular world does not know how to deal with this, including mental health providers. As churches begin to teach how to overcome anger and as more and more individuals find freedom from anger through the Church, fewer individuals will turn to mental health professionals and medications to solve their problems. They will begin to refer friends and family members to church, instead of to their local mental health professionals, to find true help for their emotional and mental problems.

In addition to teaching individuals how to overcome anger, churches could easily teach them how to overcome grief and depression through prayer, since it utilizes the same principle. Grief is the number one cause of depression, with 87% of all depression occurring as the result of some type of loss. Grief is also at the root for most other forms of mental illness. The world has no solution for grief or depression, so as the Church begins to step up and bring healing to individuals through prayer, it will bring much healing and bring glory to God and draw more people back to the Church.

Resistance to the Message

In spite of how simple the principle is for resolving anger and grief, the world will scoff at such practices. Most medical professionals will reject it because it would reduce the number of people turning to medical providers for help with their emotional struggles, and it would lead to the loss of revenue from prescription sales. Some will probably attempt to charge Christians who pray with others about their anger with practicing medicine without a license, if they begin to lose patients and income.

The resistance to this ministry also comes from other Christians and from churches and pastors. It is a remarkable and puzzling discovery to learn how many pastors are indifferent to, or actually opposed to trying this ministry. It seems to threaten some pastors who like to believe they have special insights into God's Word that enable them to help those who struggle emotionally. Many of them are already taking psychiatric medications, or their family members are taking psychiatric drugs, and they resist the inference that they are failing.

Perhaps it should not surprise us to see such skepticism and opposition, because the enemy is always opposing those things that will bring the most glory to God. He is not fearful of seeing believers go to doctors and counselors for help, because they will never experience true victory or freedom through pills and secular approaches. But when believers claim to help others through Spirit-based praying, he is quick to raise questions in the minds of believers and unbelievers, because he does not want to lose control of them.

The Lord Jesus was even surprised when he revealed Himself repeatedly to His disciples after His resurrection and they were slow to believe that He was truly resurrected. Mark 16:14 says that Jesus "reproached them for their unbelief and hardness of heart, because they had not believed those who had seen Him after He had risen." He reproached them because he was astonished at their stubborn unbelief. Likewise, it should not surprise us to find that many believers are slow to believe the Lord when He tells us to cast all our cares upon Him, so that He can carry our burdens for us.

Pastoral Grief Counseling Fails

A woman came for help with her depression. She had been taking antidepressants for three years since her father had died, but they were not helping; she was still very depressed. I asked her if she had ever had any counseling, and she said that she received some grief counseling from a pastor she had been referred to by the same organization where this prayer ministry had been presented repeatedly. She told me that the grief counseling of this pastor did not help her.

According to research, nothing helps resolve grief, and subsequent studies have failed to provide any significant hope in the field of grief counseling. I tried for over five years to share this with pastors and Christians in my county, and some Christians learned how to do it very effectively. What amazes me is that all pastors do not jump at this opportunity and teach it in their churches to help church members deal with their grief. I have been doing seminars for five years, and writing stories each month in a local monthly Baptist newsletter, but very few pastors attend the seminars or teach this powerful prayer process to their congregations.

This woman said she first became depressed three years before when her father died. She had never had any depression previously, and she had no other mental health issues previously. She grew up in a Christian home with a mother who was loving and affectionate and was actively involved in her church. Her father was an alcoholic and was unkind to her mother when drunk, but he never mistreated this woman. She never used drugs or alcohol, and she remained married to the same man for 34 years. When her father died she became depressed, then a year later her brother died, and the following year her mother developed serious health problems, and she lost contact with her grandson. These four significant losses in the last four years led to her depression, so I began praying with her about each of these losses.

I shared with this woman how she could overcome her grief by two simple steps: First, she needed to be honest about her grief and make a list of what she missed about the person. Second, she needed to tell the Lord what she missed about each person and ask Him to take her grief from her. We first talked about her father, and she identified 17 things she missed about him, then prayed and asked the Lord to take her grief and sadness from her. After we prayed, I asked her how she felt, and she smiled and said she missed him but the sadness and grief were gone. Taking medications for three years and getting grief counseling did not help her with this grief, but a few minutes of prayer did. It doesn't take a mental health professional to do this; in fact, secular counselors cannot show clients how to overcome grief and do not believe it is even possible.

We met again and talked about this woman's loss of contact with her 3-year-old grandson, and she identified 16 things she missed about her grandson and 5 reasons for her sadness. She prayed and gave this grief and sadness to the Lord, and she felt much better. We then prayed about the loss of her brother, and she identified 15 things she missed about him, prayed, and gave her grief to the Lord. When we finished praying about her losses, this woman was at complete peace. Her depression was gone, and she was smiling and full of joy and peace. The Lord set this woman free through prayer, using this simple prayer ministry. This ministry had been offered for over five years to pastors and churches in her area, and yet her pastor had no knowledge of this ministry, and no idea how to help people overcome grief.

God's Desire for the Church

The Bible states that the Church is the "pillar and support of the truth" (1 Timothy 3:15), so it is the main instrument that God has provided for bringing change into the world. Jesus told His disciples that they were the "light of the world" and the "salt of the earth" (Matthew 5:13-14), and both of these titles and metaphors indicate that the believers, who comprise the Church, are intended to have a leading role in changing the world.

The Lord desires for the Church to be a lighthouse to the world, and it is through the Christian Church that He wants to bring people into His kingdom and to give them victory and peace in their lives. In the book of Ephesians the apostle Paul describes God's plan for the church. In Ephesians 1:23 Paul says that the Church is "the body of Christ," and in chapter 2:19-22 Paul says,

> *So then you are no longer strangers and aliens, but you are fellow citizens with the saints, and are of God's household, having been built on the foundation of the apostles and prophets, Christ Jesus Himself being the corner stone, in whom the whole building, being fitted together, is growing into a holy temple in the Lord, in whom you also are being built together into a dwelling of God in the Spirit.*

According to this verse the Church is God's household, building, and temple and is the "dwelling of God in the Spirit."

In Ephesians 3:10-11 Paul wrote, "that the manifold wisdom of God might now be made known through the church to the rulers and the authorities in the heavenly *places. This was* in accordance with the eternal purpose which He carried out in Christ Jesus our Lord." This passage states that it was God's eternal plan that the Church would fulfill God's purposes to the heavenly rulers and authorities. In other words, God has an eternal plan that He is fulfilling through the Church; it is the major instrument of God to fulfill his purposes in the world of spreading His good news to all the world. In Ephesians 5:25 Paul says "Christ also loved the church and gave Himself up for it."

When Jesus ascended to heaven after His resurrection He told the apostles and believers to remain in Jerusalem until the Holy Spirit came upon them. Once the Holy Spirit came, the Church was born and empowered to take His message throughout the world. The book of Acts chronicles the spread of the gospel and the Church throughout the world, by the power of God. Christ loves the Church and it is "the body of Christ." It is His desire that the Church spread and be the visible representation of Himself on earth, and that genuine believers be His arms and legs for showing His love and power to the world.

It is the Church that must lead this charge and demonstrate God's power to change the world. The Church is the "pillar and support of truth" (1 Timothy 3:15) and must teach believers how to "walk in the Spirit" (Galatians 5:16) and be set free from grief, anger, shame, addiction, and depression. As the Church leads and teaches believers to turn to the Lord for counseling, rather than to secular counselors or secular-trained Christian counselors, the Lord will be glorified and His people will discover that He is the "Wonderful Counselor."

Time for a Showdown on Mount Carmel: 1 Kings 18

In 1Kings 18 the Lord directed the prophet Elijah to go to Mount Carmel to meet with King Ahab. The Lord had brought three and a half years of famine to the country for their idolatry and rejection of Him, and He was ready to end the drought. He instructed Elijah to send a message to King Ahab to meet with him on Mount Carmel, so Elijah sent the message and met him at the appointed time. Ahab showed up with 450 false prophets of Baal and other false prophets.

The king had been searching for Elijah in order to kill him because of his opposition to Ahab's evil rule of Judah, and when he saw Elijah he called him a "trouble maker." Elijah replied to him saying that Ahab was the "trouble maker," and he challenged him to a contest to determine which of them was following the one true God. He told Baal's prophets to build an altar and place a sacrifice upon it, then to call upon their god to bring fire down from heaven to ignite the sacrifice. Then he said that he would do the same and whichever god sent fire from heaven was the true God. So Baal's prophets prepared their sacrifice.

The scriptures tell us that the false prophets of Baal cried out to their god all day long, and leaped around their altar, and cut themselves but nothing happened. Elijah taunted them and told them to cry out louder because their god may have gone on a journey or may be sleeping, and they continued interceding and crying out to their gods all day, but nothing happened.

Then at the end of the day, Elijah built an altar and placed a sacrifice upon it. He had the men of Judah dig a trench around it and then instructed them to pour 12 large jugs of water on it so that it was thoroughly drenched with water. Then he raised his eyes to heaven and prayed to the Lord:

> *O Lord, the God of Abraham, Isaac and Israel, today let it be known that You are God in Israel and that I am Your servant and I have done all these things at Your word. Answer me, O Lord, answer me that this people may know that You, O Lord, are God, and that You have turned their heart back again.*
>
> *Then the fire of the Lord fell and consumed the burnt offering and the wood and the stones and the dust, and licked up the water that was in the trench.*
>
> *When all the people saw it, they fell on their faces; and they said, "The Lord, He is God; the Lord, He is God."*
>
> *(1 Kings 18:36-39)*

This supernatural display of the power of God through the prayer of Elijah, demonstrated to all Judah that the Lord is the only truc God. But James tell us in James 5:16 and 17 that "Elijah was a man with a nature like ours" and instructs us "confess your faults to one another, and pray for one another, so that ye may be healed."

The Lord used the prayers of Elijah to demonstrate His power, and He wants to use our prayers to demonstrate His power today. People are being delivered supernaturally through the prayers of believers as they follow the simple prayer principles of this ministry, and as believers use this, the power of God will be revealed so that it will be known that He alone can set men and women free from emotional bondage. In the same way that Elijah prayed openly and boldly for the Lord to ignite the offering with fire, we can pray boldly and confidently for Him to heal people of their grief and anger.

The mental health system and the psychiatric profession are failing miserably to help those with emotional and mental struggles. Each new act of mass violence in our country demonstrates this, because most of those committing these acts are already taking psychiatric medications and have already been through the mental health system. It is time for another showdown between the gods of this world and the one true God. It is time for the Church to step up and demonstrate to the world how the Lord is the Wonderful Counselor, and He can set men and women free from their emotional bondage through prayer.

Transforming the Church: Sunday Morning Christianity

The Lord wants to transform each of us and to transform the world through the Church, but the Church is failing badly. Not only is the Church not teaching how individuals can find freedom and peace, but they are attempting to provide all of the teaching necessary for their church in a weekly 60-minute service. Most churches today do not have a weekly prayer meeting, other than a Bible study that is preceded by one person praying through a church prayer list for those who are sick.

The early New Testament Church met day-by-day and spent time confessing their faults to one another and praying for one another for healing. They "devoted" themselves to prayer for one another, and throughout the book of Acts believers gathered together for prayer. This is not happening in churches today, and the Church cannot be adequately nourished when believers gather for a 1-hour meeting on Sunday morning to sing a few songs and hear a 30 minute message.

The Sunday-morning Christianity that we see today is inadequate to meet the needs of those in the Church. In order for us to get back to the New Testament pattern, churches are going to need to spend significantly more time together, teaching, encouraging, and praying for one another. The Church must become relevant to the emotional needs of its members by providing regular teaching on how to pray effectively about emotions, so that believers will find freedom in their lives and experience the fruit of the Spirit.

This program provides tools for churches to teach believers how to pray effectively about their emotions. There are two primary components of this program. The first component is the teaching component which involves studying this book together over a 24-week period. There are 24 chapters that can be taught over a 24-week period in a typical Sunday School class setting. Each chapter has a 30-minute DVD to go along with it that can be shown to a class, and this can be followed by a discussion by the class leader who has a copy of this book to use as the Teacher's Manual. During 24 weeks believers can learn how to pray about their emotions.

The second component of the program is a prayer-group component. Just reading this book and learning how to pray about emotions will not change lives. Changed lives will occur only as individuals begin praying about their emotions and begin to experience the freedom that comes from prayer. There are four workbooks that have six chapters each, and these chapters are coordinated with the chapters in this book. These workbooks are designed for use with small groups of men and women who can meet together to study the workbook together and to pray for one another. It is in these small groups that men can meet with other men and share their personal emotional struggles, and learn how to resolve these problems through prayer. In the same way, small groups of women can meet with other women and share their personal struggles, and learn how to pray about their emotional struggles and find freedom.

This type of sharing will be threatening and uncomfortable to many Christians who are accustomed to hiding their struggles from others, and who pretend to be happy, but it is essential for believers to humble themselves and to confess their faults to one another in order to experience freedom. But there are eternal rewards that come with such humility and corporate prayer. The scriptures tell us that as we confess our faults to one another and pray for one another, we will be healed (James 5:16). May God use this book and the workbooks to equip churches to help those in their church to find healing, victory, joy, and peace.

> ***"May the Lord of peace Himself continually grant you peace in every circumstance" (2 Thessalonians 3:16).***

BIBLIOGRAPHY

Alcoholics Anonymous: 3rd Edition (1976). New York: Alcoholics Anonymous World Services.

Allen, John (2010). *The Global War on Christians*, Random House.

American Psychiatric Association, *Diagnostic and Statistical Manual of Mental Disorders-IV (2004).*

American Psychiatric Association, *Diagnostic and Statistical Manual of Mental Disorders-V (2013).*

American Psychiatric Association (2003). *The Textbook of Clinical Psychiatry,* American Psychiatric Publishing Company, Washington, D.C.

Barna Research Group (2008). "New Marriage and Divorce Statistics Released," Barna.org, March 31, 2008.

Breggin, Peter (1991). *Toxic Psychiatry: Why Therapy, Empathy and Love Must Replace the Drugs, Electroshock, and biochemical Theories of the "New Psychiatry".* New York: St. Martin's Griffin.

Breggin, Peter (2000). *Reclaiming Our Children* (Perseus Books, Cambridge, Mass..

Breggin, Peter (2008a). *Brain-Disabling Treatments in Psychiatry,* New York: Springer Publishing Company.

Breggin, Peter (2008b). *Medication Madness.* New York: St. Martin's Griffin.

Breggin, Peter (2012). "Xanax Facts and Whitney Houston." Breggin.com, posted 2/22/12.

Breggin, Peter (2013). *Psychiatric Drug Withdrawal: A Guide for Prescribers, Therapists, Patients, and Their Families.* New York: Springer Publishing Company.

Breggin, Peter (2015, October 15). *madinamerica.com.* Blog Retrieved July 7, 2016.

British Medical Journal Open (2012). (British Medical Journal Open 2012:e000850 doi:10.1136/bmjopen-20120000850).

Carey, Benedict. "Anger Management May Not Help at Al*l.*" *NYTimes.com.* November 24, 2004. http.//www.NYTimes.com (accessed April 3, 2014).

Dieter, Melvin E. and Hoekema, Anthony A. (1987). *Five Views on Sanctification,* Zondervan.

Felitti, Vincent J. (2002). "The Relationship of Adverse Childhood Experiences to Adult Health: Turning gold into lead, VJFMDSDCA@msn.com."

Felitti, Vincent J. (2004). "The Origins of Addiction: Evidence from the Adverse Childhood Experiences Study", Department of Preventive Medicine, Kaiser Permanente Medical Care Program, 2/16/2004.

Fischer, Bryan (2010). "But is Franklin Graham right?" Renewamerica.com, April 23, 2010 blog.

Genevro, Janice I., Marshall, Tracy, and Miller, Tess (2003). *Report on Bereavement and Grief Research.* Scientific Advisory Group, Center for the Advancement of Health.

Glenmullen, Joseph (2000). *Prozac Backlash,* Simon & Schuster, New York.

Goldberg, Jonah (2015). "The Dignity of Charleston Flies in the Face of the Left's Uninformed, Anti-South Bigotry," *National Review,* June 24, 2015.

Gotzsche, Peter (2013). *Deadly Medicines and Organised Crime: How Big Pharma Has Corrupted Healthcare,* **Radcliffe Publishing, London/NewYork.**

Gurman, Alan S. and Kniskern, David P. (1981). *Handbook of Family Therapy,* New York: Brunner/Mazel.

Harrow, M, Jobe, T.H., & Faull, R.N (2014). Does Treatment of Shicophrenia with Antipsychotic Medications Eliminate or Reduce Psychosis? A 20-year Multi-follow-up Study. *Psychological Medicine,* page 1-10.

Hoekema, Anthony A. (1962). "The Struggle Between Old and New Natures in the Converted Man," *Bulletin of the Evangelical Theological Society* 5, no. 2 (Spring 1962).

Jennings, Ann (1994). *The Journal of Mental health Administration* 21(4): 374-387)

Karon, Bertram P. and Vandenbos, Gary R. (1981). *Psychotherapy of Schizophrenia: Treatment of Choice,* Jason Aronson, Inc.

Kendler, Kenneth S., John Myers, and Sidney Zisook (2008). "Does Bereavement-Related Major Depression Differ From Major Depression Associated With Other Stressful LIfe Events?" *American Journal of Psychiatry,* (Guilford Press) 1449-1455.

Psychopathology: Understanding the Causes of Psychiatric and Substance Use Disorders. New York: Guilford Press.

Lowry, Rich (2015). "The Majesty of the Black Church," *National Review,* June 23, 2015.

Medco (2011). America's State of Mind. *Medico health solutions.* Retrieved from http;//medco.mediaroom.com/

Moncrieff, Joanna (2009). *The Myth of the Chemical Cure: A Critique of Psychiatric Drug Treatment,* New York: Palgrave Macmillan.

National Academy of Sciences (2008). "Treatment of Posttraumatic Stress Disorder," The National Academies Press.

Neimeyer, Robert and Currier, Joseph (2009). *Current Directions in Psychological Science,* Vol. 18, No. 6, p. 352-365.

Pies, Ronald (2011). "Psychiatry's new brain-mind and the legend of the 'chemical imbalance'," *Psychiatric Times,* blog.

Rottenberg, Jonathan (2010). "The Road to Depression Runs Through Grief," *Psychology Today,* Dec. 2010.

Schmidt, Alvin J. (2004). *How Christianity Changed the World.* Zondervan.

Segraves, R. Taylor (1982). *Marital Therapy: A Combined Psychodynamic-Behavioral Approach,* New York: Plenum.

Seligman, Martin, E.P. (1995). "The Effectiveness of Psychotherapy." *American Psychologist,* Dec. 1995, p. 965-974.

Shear, Katherine, Ellen Frank, Patricia R. Houck, and Charles F. Reynolds. (2005). "Treatment of Complicated Grief: A Randomized Controlled Trial." *Journal of American Medical Association,* 2601-2608.Smith, Edward M. (1996). Beyond Tolerable Recovery. Alathia Publishing.

Stuart, Richard B (1980). *Helping Couples Change,* Guilford Press.

Vine, W.E. (1940). *Expository Dictionary of New Testament Words,* Nelson Publishers.

Weis, Rick (2005). "U.S. Leads in Mental Illness, Lags in Treatment," Washington Post, June 7, 2005.

Whitaker, Robert (2002). *Mad in America: Bad Science, Bad Medicine, and the Enduring Mistreatment of the Mentally Ill,* New York: Basic Books.

Whitaker, Robert (2010). *Anatomy of an Epidemic: Magic Bullets, Psychiatric Drugs, and the Astonishing Rise of Mental Illness in America,* Broadway Books.

Whitaker, Robert (2016). "Psychiatric Drugs and Better Approaches: What Have We Learned?" Empathic Therapy Conference, March 4, 2016.

XANAX XR© CIV. (2011). "Complete prescribing information," Retrieved from http://labeling.pfizer.com/ShowLabeling.aspx/id-543.

Proof

63746274R00284

Made in the USA
Charleston, SC
09 November 2016